Mateo Martínez and Julia Soto, Alfonso's parents, taken about 1935. Courtesy of Dr. Raul Aguero.

MASTERS OF ANIMALS

LIBRARY OF ANTHROPOLOGY

Editors: *Anthony L. LaRuffa, Joel S. Savishinsky*

Editorial Assistant: *Phyllis Rafti*

Advisory Board: *Richard Blot, Mary Ann Castle, Robert DiBennardo, May Ebihara, Paul Grebinger, Mario D. Zamora*

MASTERS OF ANIMALS
Oral Traditions of the Tolupan Indians
Honduras

ANNE CHAPMAN

Centre National de la Recherche Scientifique,
Paris, France

GORDON AND BREACH

Switzerland USA Japan UK France Germany Netherlands
Russia Singapore Malaysia Australia

Gordon and Breach Science Publishers

5301 Tacony Street, Drawer 330
Philadelphia, Pennsylvania 19137
United States of America

3-14-9, Okubo
Shinjuku-ku, Tokyo 169
Japan

Post Office Box 90
Reading, Berkshire RG1 8JL
United Kingdom

Private Bag 8
Camberwell, Victoria 3124
Australia

58, rue Lhomond
75005 Paris
France

Glinkastrasse 13-15
O-1086 Berlin
Germany

Y-Parc
Chemin de la Sallaz
CH-1400, Yverdon, Switzerland

Emmaplein 5
1075 AW Amsterdam
Netherlands

Originally published in the French in 1978 as *Les enfants de la mort: univers mythique des indiens tolupan (jicaque) du Honduras* by the Centre d'Etudes Mexicaines et Centraméricaines, Mexico City.

© 1978 by the Centre d'Etudes Mexicaines et Centraméricaines, Mexico City.

Cover photo: Alfonso with his blowgun, 1959.

Library of Congress Cataloging-in-Publication Data

Chapman, Anne McKaye, 1922–
    [Enfants de la mort. English]
    Masters of animals : oral traditions of the Tolupan Indians,
Honduras / Anne Chapman.
      p.   cm. -- (Library of anthropology, ISSN 0141-1012)
    Includes bibliographical references.
    ISBN 2-88124-560-9. -- ISBN 2-88124-565-X (pbk.)
    1. Jicaque Indians--Legends.   2. Jicaque Indians--Religion and
mythology.   I. Title.   II. Series.
F1505.2.X5C4813 1992
398.2'089975--dc20   92-11055
                                           CIP

In memory of
Alfonso Martínez and Todivia Soto
and for the youth of Honduras

CONTENTS

Introduction to the Series xiii
Preface xv
Acknowledgements xix
Fieldwork 1

CHAPTER I   Tolupans: Past and Present 11

CHAPTER II Alfonso Martínez, Himself 59
   Childhood 59
   Courting 66
   Marriage 70
   Neighbors 75
   Dreams 77
   Children 79
   The Cacique's Advice 80
   Mateo's Advice 81
   Other Advice 81
   A Passport for Sulaco 82
   Cedros of the Compadre 83
   A Permit in Yoro 84
   The Parties 86
   Insults in Comayagüela 87
   Fevers in Talanga 88
   San Marcos for Maize 89
   Generous Tegucigalpa 91
   La Gringita 93
   There Are a Lot of Ways to Kill 94
   I Am Confident 95
   Lempira (Author) 95
   Lempira (Alfonso) 95

CHAPTER III Origins 99
   Myth 1. The Creation of Human Beings 99
   Myth 2. The First Nation 104
   Myth 3. The Death of the Indians 105

Myth 4. Our Lord Encounters the First Monkeys 109

Myth 5. Our Lord in Love 111

Myth 6. Our Lord Quarrels with the *Ladinos* 112

Myth 7. The Death of the *Ladinos* 113

Narration 1. Alfonso Comments 117

Myth 8. A Rich Man Arrives in Glory 118

Myth 9. The Origin of Maize 120

Narration 2. A Family without Children 121

Myth 10. The Origin of Beans 121

Myth 11. The Child Who Created Plants 122

Myth 12. The Origin of Frost 125

Myth 13. The Origin of the Rivers 128

Myth 14. The Little Old Man Defends the Earth 131

Myth 15. How the First Fire Was Stolen 132

Myth 16. Opossum and the First Fire 134

Myth 17. The World Almost Fell Down 135

CHAPTER IV The Heavens **137**

The Tomams (Author) 137

Myth 18. Tomam Makes Thunder 140

Myth 19. The Little Ear of Corn Complains to
                His Master 140

Myth 20. The Little Old Man Visits Heaven 141

Narration 3. Alfonso Wanted to Marry One of
                Tomam's Daughters 142

Myth 21. Tomam the Younger Causes a Flood 143

Narration 4. The Jívaros Watch Over the Mortals 145

Grandfather Thunder (Author) 146

Myth 22. Grandfather Thunder, Master of the Wasps ... 146

Narration 5. Wasps Have Lots of Enemies 147

Narration 6. Grandfather Thunder's Axes 147

Narration 7. Grandfather Thunder Brings the
                Lightning 147

The Master of the Wind (Author) 148

Myth 23. The Impertinent Wind 148

Earthquakes and Mourning (Author) 149

The Master of the Clouds (Author) 150

Myth 24. How the Clouds Work 150

The Master of the Frost (Author) 151

Myth 25. A Cloud Gets Upset 151

Narration 8. Alfonso Advises the Frost 152

Myth 26. The Stars Are "Monkeys of the Night" 152

Narration 9. The Sun Wears Glasses 153
Myth 27. The Five Suns 154
Narration 10. An Eclipse of the Sun 155
Myth 28. An Eclipse of the Moon 156
Myth 29. The Death of a Young and an Old Nen 157
Myth 30. Nen Takes Revenge and So Does the
     Little Old Man 157
Tata Dios (Author) 158
Myth 31. Tata Dios Is the Master of the Dogs 158
Myth 32. Tata Dios and the Master of the Snakes 159
Narration 11. "Let the Lazy Indians Work" 159
Noventa (Author) 160
Narration 12. Noventa Advises the Wildcat 160
Myth 33. Noventa Scolds a Hen 160

CHAPTER V Mother Earth and the Masters of Animals **163**
Mother Earth (Author) 163
Myth 34. Mother Earth Is Thirsty 164
Myth 35. Mother Earth Complains to Tomam 164
Narration 13. Mother Earth, the Great Provider 166
Narration 14. "I Am Afraid of the Earth" 166
Narration 15. "But I Joke with Her" 167
Narration 16. The Earth Does Not Like to Be
     Dug Into 168
The Masters of the Animals (Author) 168
Bones of the Game Tied to Posts in the Huts (Author) .. 169
The Master of the White-Lipped Peccary (Author) 170
Narration 17. Alfonso and the Master of the Peccary 170
Myth 36. The Master of the Peccary and the
     Baptized Indian 171
The Majordomo of the Peccary (Author) 172
The Master of the Deer (Author and Alfonso) 172
The Deer's Magic Stones (Author) 173
Myth 37. The Master of the Deer Scolds a Hunter 174
Narration 18. The Deer Hunt and Dreams 176
Narration 19. Alfonso Meets the Master of the Deer 176
The Majordomo of the Deer (Author) 177
Myth 38. The Master of the Deer Scolds His
     Majordomo 177
Myth 39. The Majordomo of the Deer Kills a Hunter 178
Narration 20. Alfonso and the Majordomo of
     the Deer 179

The Master of the White-Collared Peccary, the Coati,
    Monkeys and Various Birds (Author) 179
Narration 21. "The White-Collared Peccaries Are
                    a Nuisance" 180
Narration 22. "Last Year I Killed Three Coatis" 181
Myth 40. The Coati Complains to His Master 181
Myth 41. The Harpy Eagle of the High Cliff 182
The Master of the Mice (Author and Alfonso) 182
Myth 42. Four Big Animals Wager 183
The Master of the Tapirs, Bees and Doves (Author) 184
Myth 43. The Master Protects His Bees 185
Narration 23. You Must Ask Permission to Extract
                    Honey from a Hive 187
Narration 24. The Master of the Bees Punishes
                    Alfonso 187
The Master of the Snakes, Armadillos, Opossums
    and Pacas (Author and Alfonso) 189
Myth 44. The Master of the Snake and the Little
                    Old Man 189
Narration 25. Alfonso Bitten by a Snake 195
Narration 26. Old Antonio Bitten by a Snake 197
Myth 45. The Opossum and the Armadillo
                    Encounter the Tiger 197
Narration 27. "I Do Harm the Armadillo" 199
The Master of the Raccoons (Author) 200
Narration 28. Alfonso and the Raccoons 200
The Master of the Agouti (Author) 200
Narration 29. Leonor and the Agouti 201
The Master of the Snails (Author) 201
The Master of Fish (Author) 201
Myth 46. The Master Complains of Poisoning
                    His Fish 201
Narration 30. Alfonso and the Master of the Fish 202
Narration 31. Alfonso Scolds the Master of the Fish 203
The Masters of Certain Birds (Author) 203
The Master of the Cockroaches (Author) 204
Myth 47. The Master of the Cockroaches Is Generous ... 204
Myth 48. The Master of the Cockroaches Is Deceiving .. 204
Narration 32. The Earth Is the Master of the Beetle 205
Myth 49. The Master of the Lice Is Insidious 205
Narration 33. The Devils Are Masters of the Mines 206
The Master of Sickness (Author) 207

Narration 34. Sickness for Sale 207
Rabbit the Great Trickster (Author) 208
Myth 50. Rabbit and "Tiger-with-a-Broken-Molar" 208
Myth 51. Rabbit Drowns Tiger 208
Myth 52. Tiger Hunts Monkey and Coati Kills Tiger 209
Myth 53. Rabbit Ties-up Tiger and Peccary Kills Him ... 210
Myth 54. Rabbit and "Coyote-with-a-Burnt-Backside" ... 212
Myth 55. Rabbit Goes to Glory 212
Chichinite (Author) 214
Myth 56. Chichinite Fights with the *Ladinos* 214
Myth 57. Chichinite Finds a Wife 216

CHAPTER VI Death and Afterlife 221
The Devils (Author) 221
Narration 35. Seductive Devils 222
Myth 58. The Devil Ground-up a Dead Mortal 223
Narration 36. The Error of Terrencio 224
Narration 37. The Death of Felipe 224
Narration 38. Matías Is Seduced by a Female Devil 225
Narration 39. The Last Days of José 227
Narration 40. Leonita Liked *Ladino* Men 228
Narration 41. Fabían Tries to Take His Wife to the
                         Other World 230
Narration 42. The Death of Alfonso's Father 230
Narration 43. The Death of His Grandfather 233
The Guatecasts (Author) 233
Questions and Answers (Author and Alfonso) 234
   1. What Is the World of the Dead Like? 234
   2. Up There, How Do They Know When Someone
      Is About to Die? 235
   3. Why Are the Dead Buried? 235
   4. Why Do You Put a Jar on Top of the Grave? 235
   5. Why Does the Jar Have a Hole in It? 235
   6. Does the Spirit Go Directly to the Other World? 235
   7. How Does One Get to the Other World? 235
   8. And the River That One Has to Pass? 237
   9. What Happens When Someone Arrives There? 237
  10. Why Does One Have to Return to Get a Strand
      of Hair? 237
  11. What Else Occurs When a Dead Mortal Lies? 239
  12. Why Do Children Die? 240
  13. And Women Giving Birth? 240
  14. And the Youth? 240

15. Why Do Some Hide in Caves? 241
16. How Do You Feel About Death? 241
17. Those Who Kill Themselves, Do They, Too, Go to
the Other World? 241
18. Are the Dead Ever Born Again? 242
19. Can a Live Mortal Visit the Other World? 242
Narration 44. Cleto Returned Twice from the Other
World 242
Myth 59. The Man Who Followed His Wife to the
Other World 244

CHAPTER VII Shamanism and Divination 249
The *Punakpan* (Shaman) (Alfonso and Author) 249
Narration 45. Alfonso Wanted to Be a *Punakpan* 251
Narration 46. The Bad *Punakpan* 251
Narration 47. Journey to the Other World 252
Narration 48. Traveling through the Air 255
Myth 60. The *Punakpanes* and the Winged Snake 255
A *Brujo* Named "Gruperas" (Author) 256
Narration 49. Gruperas Married One of Tomam's
Daughters 257
Divination (Author) 259
Involuntary Corporal Movements Considered
Omens in America (Author) 260
Narration 50. The "Proof of the Knee" 261
The "Proof of the Cords or Strings" (Author) 262
String Magic in America (Author) 262
Alfonso Performs the "Proof of the Cord" (Author) 265
A *Ladino* Speaks of the *Prueba de la Cabuya* (Author
and Jesús López) 270

CHAPTER VIII Analyses 273
Historical Process: Mythology and Culture 273
Myth and Reality 275
Problems Which the Mythological Thought
Proposes 276
Mythology as a Classificatory System 277
The Classification Structured on the Notion
of Duality 277
The Classification Based on the Concept of Masters 279
The Masters of the Animals in the World 282
Final Comment 284
Bibliography 287
Index 301

INTRODUCTION TO THE SERIES

One of the notable objectives of the Library of Anthropology is to provide a vehicle for the expression in print of new, controversial and seemingly "unorthodox" theoretical, methodological and philosophical approaches to anthropological data. Another objective follows from the multidimensional or holistic approach in anthropology which is the discipline's unique contribution toward understanding human behavior. The books in this series will deal with such fields as archaeology, physical anthropology, linguistics, ethnology and social anthropology. Since no restrictions will be placed on the types of cultures included, a New York or New Delhi setting will be considered as relevant to anthropological theory and methods as the highlands of New Guinea.

The series is designed for a wide audience and, whenever possible, technical terminology will be kept to a minimum. In some instances, however, a book may be unavoidably esoteric and consequently will appeal only to a small sector of the reading population — advanced undergraduate students in addition to professional social scientists.

Our hopes for the readers are twofold: first, that they will enjoy learning about people; second, and perhaps most important, that they will come to experience a feeling of oneness with humankind.

Anthony L. LaRuffa
Joel S. Savishinsky

PREFACE

Among all the Indians of the Montaña de la Flor, Alfonso Martínez was the only one I knew who took pleasure in conversing with me at length. He related myths and legends and talked about his family and his life, sometimes on Don Jesús' ranch but more often in his home in the mountains, where his wife, Todivia Soto, always made me feel welcome. He had learned a great deal from his father and elders, long since deceased, and seemed pleased that I was an attentive listener. A great majority of the chapters presented here were narrated by him, so it is fitting that his photograph appear on the cover of this book. I met Alfonso in 1955 and we remained close friends until his sudden death in September 1969 from an epidemic, which also claimed the lives of Todivia and their youngest child, Maria. I was notified of his death soon thereafter, but was unable to return to his homeland until 1971.

Alfonso had an inquiring mind and a vivid sense of humor. Although curious and often amused by the ways of his *ladino* (mestizo) neighbors and city people, he expressed no desire to emulate them. His manner was simple and direct, and he was unequivocal about his feelings and sentiments, lucid in his comprehension of the real world. He rendered feasible all that he spoke about, no matter how imaginary; he was passionately involved in his own culture. He talked for hours at a time with evident enjoyment, illustrating his tales with gestures and pantomime. He would leap from his chair to imitate the jerking pace of an old man or a wounded deer, lift his face to the heavens conversing with the gods, or lie on the ground as perfectly still as the corpse he was telling about. Although he spoke to me in Spanish, occasionally he reverted to his own language, as if unaware, then look at me and continue in Spanish. As I recorded many of the interviews, I encouraged him to speak in Tolupan.

He rarely started a story at its beginning and often mixed the themes without losing the thread of the narration. It was as if the entire oral tradition formed a single opus that could be told in a

great variety of ways as best pleased the narrator at the moment
and in almost any sequence. However, to render the oral tradition
readable, I have given titles to the different themes, presenting them
as "myths" and "narrations" (see end of chapter 1 for an explanation
of this labeling), and I eliminated many repetitions.

In contrast to most of his companions who would not speak
freely to outsiders, Alfonso had very few inhibitions and responded
to situations in personal rather than in purely cultural terms. His
lucidity and easy manner were in part influenced by his father,
Mateo Martínez. Mateo was the son of Juan Martínez, one of the
"founding fathers" of the Tolupan settlement, and was remembered
as an extraordinary person. According to Alfonso, his father told
him not to fear the *ladinos* and other outsiders but to treat them as
equals.

Alfonso, a hard worker in the field and devoted husband and
father, was always ready to fulfill a request, offer or accept a gift, or
proffer advice, an opinion or a comment. He was an attentive listener, respectful of others and never seemed impelled either to im-
pose or restrain himself. He seemed at ease in a well-defined reality
of feeling, experience and imagination.

Alfonso was about sixty years old when he died. He was of
average height for a Tolupan, about 5'5", and his skin color was
lighter than the others. Like all Tolupans, he had a full crop of black
hair which was worn in a bob. Sometimes he would grow a mustache or a straggly beard. He always donned the typical *balandrán*
— a long poncho made of denim — occasionally tying it between
his legs (giving a kind of diaper effect) to allow greater freedom
while walking. He owned a pair of sandals but usually wore only
one to brace himself on the muddy paths. He always carried a
pouch made of animal skin, a machete, sometimes a blowgun and
was accompanied by his faithful dog.

He was highly respected in his community because of his per-
sonality, intelligence and age. He and his family lived high in the
mountains, close to the huts where his mother and other kin lived,
five to six kilometers from the east entrance to the settlement. In the
latter years, when I knew him, he lived there with Todivia, Maria
and their eldest daughter, Celedonia, her husband, Domingo, and
their baby. A third daughter, Felipa, who was also married, would
sometimes visit them while I was there. Like him, Todivia was very
hospitable, though of a quiet nature; while Alfonso was talking, she
would often glance at me with an amused smile. Their hut over-
looked a wide expanse of forested land to the north. The other five

huts in the cluster were all located within a short distance of each
other, hidden among the trees. His mother, Julia, lived with her
youngest son, Guillermo, and his family. Another brother and
several cousins also lived close by. At the base of the mountain was
a stream where the women went to collect water in large earthen
jugs, wash clothes and bathe. Alfonso's coffee grove was nearby,
and though the location of his maize field varied every two years or
so, it was usually within walking distance from his home.

Although Alfonso was extraordinary in many ways, he was in
every respect representative of his culture. His relation to others
and to nature was founded on an explicit realization of the mutual
dependency of all living forms. This mutual dependence was
premised on the expectation of reciprocity not only with the members of the community but with all natural phenomena: the animals
of the forest, the trees and plants of the fields, the winds, the clouds,
the rain, and especially the sun, the moon and "Mother Earth."
Mutual dependency was, however, contingent on the notion of the
necessity of a certain hierarchy: the community of human beings
with their chiefs, animals with their supernatural masters, and all
that pertains to the realm of nature, including man, subject to the
dictates of a supreme deity, Tomam the Father — Lord of the
Universe.

His culture lived in him and was expressed through him in the
ways of the ancient Tolupans and those of their ever-changing
world. His decision to remain Indian signed his name to this tes-
timony, inspired by the vitality and beauty of the Tolupan tradition.

In the years since his death, I've come to realize more than ever
how exceptional Alfonso was as a human being — a most admired
and always-to-be-remembered friend. The joy of having known him
will, I hope, somehow be conveyed to those who accompany us
through these pages.

ACKNOWLEDGEMENTS

The initial field season, 1955–56, in the Montaña de la Flor was financed by the Buenos Aires Convention Pact Fellowship, with funds from the Honduran and United States governments. Many Hondurans aided me in this first endeavor, particularly Don Jesús Aguilar Paz and Dr. Raul Aguero.

After 1956, I returned for periods of three to four months each year until 1960, working mainly with Alfonso Martínez, who became my principal authority and great friend. During these years of intensive fieldwork, several ministries of the Honduran government, especially those in public health and education, were very cooperative.* The Instituto Hondureño de Antropología e Historia has always supported my research in every way possible.

In 1957, I obtained a grant from Columbia University. I wish to thank Dr. Vera Rubin, through whom I obtained funds from the Research Institute for the Study of Man, New York City, in 1958, and the Paul Radin Foundation in 1959.

In 1960, I moved to Paris and the following year became a member of the National Center of Scientific Research (CNRS). Through all the years that followed, this institution has supported my research and work in Honduras. Members of the French Embassy in Tegucigalpa have always been very helpful. To all, I express my deep gratitude and thanks.

Fieldwork in 1971 was funded by CNRS, the Programme Biologique International and the Honduran government. Dr. A. Jacquard, then director of the Institute National de Demographie, Paris, agreed readily to cooperate with the Honduran government by facilitating medical aid to the Montaña de la Flor.

The following season of 1972 was also financed by CNRS, as well as the Institute National de Demographie. I wish to mention my late sister, Elizabeth C. Halperin, who always encouraged me to continue my work in Honduras, often writing to me in the field and sending me vitamins.

With reference to the French and Spanish editions, which appeared under different titles,[1] this book has been revised and material added, especially the introductory fieldwork section. Material has also been added to chapters 1 and 2, and myths and narrations have been added throughout the text. Without the aid of the Research Institute for the Study of Man, its director, Dr. Lambros Comitas, and the executive secretary, Ms. June Anderson, it would have been very difficult indeed for me to prepare this work. Ms. Anderson reviewed the manuscript and gave me many pertinent suggestions. I thank Dowling College, Oakdale, New York, especially the Computer Center, for their extremely helpful collaboration. I also wish to thank Professor Anthony LaRuffa. I am very grateful to my dear friend and colleague, Dr. Lucie W. Saunders, whose enthusiastic encouragement has been decisive in the realization of this book.

NOTES

* Each season, the Ministry of Public Health supplied me with medicines (aspirins, antidiarrhea pills, vitamins and the like) to distribute among the Indians.

[1] Chapman 1978b and 1982.

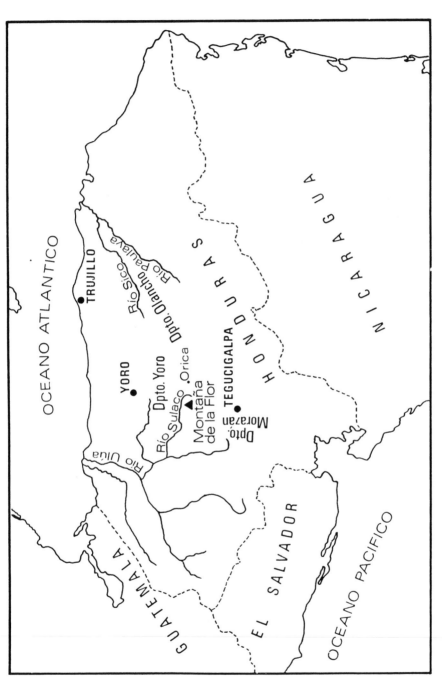

Location of the Tolupan-Jicaques in Honduras

FIELDWORK

La Montaña de la Flor (the Mountain of the Flower), located in the mountains of central Honduras, is the only existing community where the Tolupan Indians still speak their native language and preserve their ethnic identity. I began my study there in 1955. It is a dispersed, clustered settlement of mostly thatched-roof huts; a few of the dwellings now have tiled roofs and adobe walls. Neither a town nor a hamlet, it has no commercial center, civic center, or church. Now in 1991, however, there is a large, cement-floored adobe structure in the east section used as a school and meeting place. In 1965, a dirt road led to the settlement and could be traveled in the dry season by a double-traction vehicle. Today, the Montaña de la Flor can be reached from the capital of Honduras, Tegucigalpa, in about four hours. In 1972, the population was about 410: nearly one-third of whom were *ladinos* (mestizos) and *mezclados* (those born in the settlement of *ladino* and Indian parents). Today, there are approximately 600 inhabitants including the *ladinos* and *mezclados*.

The majority of the Tolupans live to the north, in the Department of Yoro, and call themselves "Jicaques," but they are very assimilated to the mode of the local *campesinos* (farmers). Many Jicaques are mestizos married to *ladinos*, although a few older people may still speak the ancestral language. A number of the settlements or hamlets in Yoro are identified as "tribus jicaques," although this is a misnomer. There is a certain ambiguity concerning what is Indian and what is *ladino*, and it is difficult to determine who or what is "really" Indian. But this confusion does not exist in Montaña de la Flor.

1

In the anthropological literature of the 1950s, there was only one short, though excellent, monograph on the Montaña de la Flor community by W. Von Hagen. It was quite evident to me from reading this study that a great deal more might be learned about this culture. One of my professors at Columbia University, William Duncan Strong, was the first person to encourage me to begin work there; he had done pioneer archaeological research in Honduras and knew about the "Jicaques." In Central America, the majority of field studies were being carried out in Guatemala and I was aware that very little ethnography was being done in Honduras with the Indians. This situation also motivated me to attempt the study, as I was tired of being a student. I wanted to do an original work and take my own risks.

The first year, 1955–56, Doris Stone, who had visited the Montaña de la Flor and written a brief account of her stay, kindly referred me to a school teacher, Professor Marcial Flores, in the nearest village, Orica, who was to become a very loyal and helpful friend throughout the years. He accompanied me on horseback to the settlement in September 1955 and introduced me to the neighboring *ladino* family of Don Jesús López, with whom I was to live during all the years of my work. They presented me to the two chiefs of the Montaña de la Flor.

That first season I came with two pack horses carrying a cot, sleeping bag, blankets, a kerosene lamp, several gallons of kerosene, a small stove, easily administered medicines, personal belongings, field equipment, canned food, rice, and coffee. After a day's ride with Don Marcial and a guide, a rather old man from Orica, also on horseback, who encouraged the pack horses to keep up the pace, we arrived at Don Jesús' ranch and were warmly welcomed. The López family, besides Don Jesús, a widower, consisted of the families of his only daughter, Doña Teodora, and his eldest son, Don Genaro, and first wife Doña Nieve Montés. The children were of various ages, the oldest being Teodoro Montés in his early twenties. They were as honest and friendly as they were poor, that is extremely honest and friendly in every way. They were poor, like many of the *ladino campesinos* in Honduras, simply because their work as subsistence farmers barely produced enough to cover the basic necessities. In order to wrench a living from the scarce good land, both men and women worked all day. Their unique respite from work was Sunday, when the women cooked, as usual, while the men mostly sat around chatting among themselves or playing with the children. There was no radio, no place to go and very few visitors happened by.

The first few days, I slept on my cot in the adobe house with Doña Nieve and the children. I soon understood that I had best accept Don Jesus' proposal to occupy the small hut nearby, which he offered to arrange for me. I realized that Doña Nieve's house was too small for me and all my equipment; that steadying myself on the edge of the cot while trying to type could be remedied; and the incessant curiosity of the children could be minimized. The mouse that occasionally fell or jumped on my cot from the rafters was a novelty which made us all laugh, as if it, too, were getting acquainted with the new visitor. Soon, I was well-installed in my private hut with a table and chair beside the cot, and still close to the others. Soon, too, the food I had brought was consumed, though my hosts had to be encouraged to share it with me. From then on, my diet was the same as theirs, except for the extra coffee. It consisted of beans three times a day, tortillas, usually soup with a small piece of chicken or a vegetable, fruit in season, especially bananas, and occasionally bread purchased from a *ladina* neighbor.

Doña Teodora prepared my meals which were served in the kitchen, a large hut almost in ruins. I usually ate alone, about noon and in the evening, chatting with Teodora while tossing tidbits to a little black dog who never failed to keep me company. When it rained, we had to move my small table around to the driest place in the kitchen, while Teodora, stepping over the puddles, somehow managed to keep the food dry. I sometimes asked one of the men why he didn't repair the roof. As I recall, it was repaired later.

I was especially fond of Teodora, then in her mid-forties. She was the only daughter of a family of nine sons. All through her childhood, and until her brothers left home, she and her mother had to grind maize and prepare the meals everyday for the ten males of the family. I have rarely met anyone so overworked, so pleasant and uncomplaining. Finally, she married a sullen, lazy man who used to stand around the kitchen staring at us, his arms folded over his chest, his large straw hat almost hiding his eyes. But she had two beautiful sons. Years later, the tragedy of her life was the death of her eldest son, then 27 years old. Her other son, Onofry, however, was very supportive of her until her death in 1985, when she had become almost completely blind. I saw her through all these years and never failed to think about the hardships that such poverty produces, especially for the women.

The other mother who lived on the ranch was Doña Nieve, as I always called her. She was older than Teodora, small, thin always impeccably clean no matter what the condition of her dress or apron. She, too, had two loving sons, but, again, the same tragedy. Her youngest son, Francisco Montés, whose nickname was Chico, was assassinated by a drunken cousin in 1959. She never recovered from this loss. She always seemed to be grinding tortillas for her family and the two orphaned children who lived with her. But she agreed readily to sit on the bench with me and liked to comment on who I had seen that day "with the Indians." Her other son, Teodoro, as Onofry, are now, in 1991, heads of families on the ranch, and greet me with their wives and growing children as if I had just departed a day or so before.

Genaro, whose first wife was Doña Nieve, was my unfailing companion during these years. He married a second time and lived about an hour's walk up the mountain with his wife, Doña Inés, and ten children. He refused to ride horseback or wear shoes. He liked to boast that he had never taken a bath in the river or anyplace else, and this was one reason why he did not get as sick as others did. He looked perfectly alright, rather Mexican in his wide-brimmed straw hat and handlebar mustache.

My most problematic routine was bathing in the stream, down a hill quite near the ranch, where the women went to fetch the household water. The area was very exposed all around. Manipulating limb by limb, half dressed while bathing did not bother me as much as the swarming insects … insects which also attacked me, though not my guides, in the mountains while visiting the Indians. This was virtually the only physical discomfort I had to endure. I was almost always covered with rashes; when the bites became seriously infected, either I went to the clinic, about a four-hour ride from the López' ranch, or took the long way back to Tegucigalpa.

I realized quite soon that being a woman and coming alone, that is without a colleague or companion, had more advantages than one might imagine at the outset. Being of the "weaker sex" and moreover not especially gifted for the practical things — such as saddling a horse, or tightening the cinch of the horse or mule under its belly when its load begins to slip — I relied on my friends for such tasks. Apparently they were pleased to help, partly, at least, because I thereby established a dependence relationship with them. The same was true among the Tolupans of the Montaña. The chiefs of the east section, especially Doroteo and later Cipriano, whom I knew best, obviously felt responsible for my safety. Several times while visiting there, I was taken into one of the huts, and told to hide because some *ladino* armed bandits from the north, the Department of Olancho, had descended upon them on horseback and were making trouble, looking for something to rob. Also, being alone I spent all my leisure time on the ranch, especially in the afternoons. When I tired of typing my notes, I chatted with the members of the families about anything which occurred to us, although not much about myself; not having children — children being the inexhaustible subject — and my life in the United States and later in France was too remote to make intelligible to them. Being alone I had no one to confide in and was brought into the family circle much more than I would have been had I formed part of a group of two or more strangers.

Then, and for a number of years afterwards, two days on horseback were required to reach the Montaña de la Flor, starting from a cattle ranch combined with a sawmill called San Diego located on the Juticalpa highway, a day's ride from Tegucigalpa. I stayed overnight in the sawmill thanks to the hospitality of the owners, who also lent me two or three horses and a guide. The ride to the Montaña was slow and tedious because of the pace; we were always overloaded and had at least one pack horse. The trip required two ten-hour days, spending the night in Orica. But it was partly thanks to this isolation that the Tolupans of the Montaña had conserved their traditions.

Though this first year (1955–56) I spent most of my time in the Montaña trying to establish contact with the Indians, I also made a survey, on horseback, throughout the neighboring Department of Yoro. The rest of the year was dedicated to research in the national archive of Tegucigalpa and the Archivo General de Guatemala in Guatemala City.

Several months passed before I was able to make real contact with the Indians, although the chiefs of the two sections of the community were friendly and permitted me to visit a few families nearby. Almost every weekday Don Genaro or his son, Teodoro, would patiently fetch a horse from the pasture, saddle it, and appear at my door about 8:00 a.m. Then we would make our way to the settlement, my guide on foot, about a thirty-minute slow ride. Once in awhile, I protested that I would just as soon walk but Genaro would hear nothing of it. Perhaps he imagined it was less tiring for me to ride, or perhaps he thought it more becoming that I be astride while passing the few local farmers on the trail or when we arrived at our destination.

The chiefs lived in huts behind the fences which demarcated the limits of the community. Although I came frequently, I could not simply drop in. Before leaving the settlement I would request another appointment with the chief I was visiting or send word to the other chief who would either agree at the moment or send me his reply to the ranch where I was living. Such protocol was required to be received by either chief and also to visit the families in their respective sections. When occasionally I was allowed to visit a certain family living father back in the mountains, the chief in question assigned one of his sons or another male kin to accompany me and my guide, usually Genaro. The chief had previously sent word to the male head of the family who had agreed to receive me. He had agreed for himself but not for his wife and children, who invariably were absent. When upon arrival I would ask about them, my host would glance at me sadly replying, "They are all dead." I had been told that they were hiding nearby and, trusting that someday I would meet them, I tried to avoid playing this game. I would only briefly comment that I was sorry.

I did not feel rejected by the chiefs or the heads of family for this reluctance to comply with my wishes. Having read Von Hagen, I had anticipated such delays. I knew from my experiences as a student in Chiapas, Mexico, that fieldwork might be a lifelong endeavor, though the Mayans were more accessible, perhaps because more sophisticated, and above all more acculturated than the Tolupans.

It was not until I met Alfonso Martínez in December 1955 that my luck changed. I first saw him at a funeral, the only one I ever attended. As I made it a matter of policy to initiate a greeting or, hopefully, a conversation with anyone who looked as if she or he would respond, I was amazed when Alfonso began talking to me. Moreover, he looked pleased. Through the years, he remained the only person in the group who conversed with me at length about the oral tradition. I did obtain data from the other Indians, but usually they would turn into interrogators. They asked if I were married, if not why not, and if so how many children. They inquired as to how long it took walking to get to my country, why I had come so far, and so forth. After dealing with their questions, sometimes replying *¿Quien sabe?* (Who knows?), I would attempt to persuade them to tell me about "the tradition": stories their parents or grandparents may have told them, anecdotes, anything. The typical answer to my inquiries was *¿Quien sabe?*.

The few women I met, during these first years, were as hospitable as they were shy, perhaps because they spoke little Spanish. They invariably invited me into their homes and sometimes offered me a cup of coffee, which they noticed I liked, with a tamale. But soon I learned, or sensed, that they thought me strange, because I wore pants and did not show them photographs of my children, not that I claimed to have any. My ignorance of their language was a handicap, but fortunately not an impediment.

Every season I would bring along things I thought they might need or desire. The rule of reciprocity prevailed. I never gave anything to anyone without the receiver returning some sort of gift: a few cobs of corn, tamales, beans or the like. Besides paying the López family for my room, board, rental of the horse, and so on, I paid Alfonso for the interviews. He would never accept more than what corresponded to a day's wage in the area and he, too, would often bring me beans or tamales and once in awhile a basket.

From 1957 to 1960, I went to the Montaña every year for three or four months and, again, late in 1964, always working principally with Alfonso. He would sometimes accompany Genaro and me when we visited families in the mountains. In January 1965, I saw Alfonso for the last time. When I learned of his death in 1969, I was deeply saddened and remain so.

In 1967, when I was a member of the Laboratoire d'Anthropologie Social at the Collège de France, in Paris, I made contact with the late Dr. Jean Sutter, one of the founders of population genetics in France and director of the Institute National d'Etudes Démographiques. He became keenly interested in the genealogies I had recorded of the families of the Montaña de la Flor. He considered the community to be an unusual "isolate," given its extreme endogamy. The entire population, except of course the *ladinos* who had married in, were descendants of the original eight founders of the settlement, c. 1866. Dr. Sutter suggested that a field study be carried out there with members of his Institute and that more work be done on the genealogies. Other obligations, in Tierra del Fuego, Argentina, made it impossible for me to accept his proposal at the time and, unfortunately, he died in 1970.

Later that year Albert Jacquard, a Swiss scientist who was carrying on the work of Dr. Stutter, had been appointed the new director of the National Institute of Demographic Studies, and had decided to organize the field study. A team was made up of a French doctor, Jean-Claude Quilici, a chemist, Jean Constans, and myself. The three of us worked there in early 1971. My two companions took blood and urine samples of the majority of the Indians in the east section and treated them for various illnesses.

I made sure that there were sufficient funds to repay the Indians for their cooperation, over and above being treated for ailments by Dr. Quilici. We purchased some fifty machetes and cloth for dresses in Tegucigalpa. Each person who agreed to be examined, and gave a small quantity of his or her blood and urine, was rewarded with either a machete or a piece of cloth. But the chief of the west section refused to cooperate. This did not surprise me, as I had been unsuccessful in contacting him. He was the son of the former chief, Leonor, whom I had known in years' past, and was even more reluctant to meet strangers than his father had been. Some of the results of this study were eventually published in French[1] and Dr. Jacquard used them in his doctoral thesis.[2]

That season I took care of a 10-year-old Tolupan girl, "Lupita" Martínez. We had rushed her to a hospital in Tegucigalpa because she suffered an intestinal collapse. A few weeks later when she was about to be released, the doctors advised that she not return immediately to the Montaña, for fear that she might have contracted measles, recently discovered in the hospital. Having completed the study, I arranged to stay with her in a hotel in the city for several weeks, until it would be considered safe for her to return. I grew very fond of her, taking care of her as if I were her big sister or favorite aunt;[3] she had not been infected and during the waiting period in Tegucigalpa we became fine friends.

I returned the following year, this time alone, to complete a survey of the Jicaque communities in Yoro; check certain genealogical data of the Tolupans of the Montaña; and to see Lupita. Since 1976, I have frequently visited friends in the community and the neighboring *ladinos*, especially the López family, until as recently as September 1991.

Through the years I worked there and during the later visits as well, I stayed on the ranch of the López family, mentioned earlier, who were very kind and helpful. During my first years there Don Jesús conversed with me a great deal. I last saw him in 1960, the year he passed away. He was born in the region and had maintained friendly relations with the Indians through many decades. Another *ladino* who gave me important data was Don Francisco Mejia who died at the age 90 in 1957. He also had known the Indians all his life and had successfully pleaded in their favor with the federal government in 1929, when he was mayor of the *municipio* (county) of Orica where Montaña de la Flor is located, to grant them the land they occupied as an *ejido*, a communal holding. Until 1988, I maintained friendly relations with his son, Professor Marcial Flores, a grade school teacher who later became director of his school. Thanks to him I kept in contact with the Tolupans during my absences, as no one in the Montaña or at the López ranch was literate. I was saddened to learn of his death in 1991; I thought this had occurred, because I had not received any reply to my letters.

The method of fieldwork I employed was based principally on the ethnographic diary, typing interviews, daily experiences, and commentaries. I recorded some of the myths told to me by Alfonso, but only when he came to the ranch; the recorder was too cumbersome to take on horseback to the settlement. By the end of my study, I had a diary of well over 1,000 single-spaced pages. I also worked a great deal on annotating genealogies, beginning with the eight adults who founded the community c. 1866. Most of the population even today is descended from these four couples (see diagram, chapter I), despite some marriages with *ladinos* and the one Jicaque woman from Yoro who married a man in the Montaña de la Flor and settled there.

One of the main problems in making up the genealogies was identifying the biological fathers; this was often a cause for disagreement among my informants. Besides the usual problem of children being conceived by "extramarital affairs," the high mortality rate of the adults resulted in many serial marriages. Though I obtained more cooperation for the genealogies than I had managed for other inquires, Alfonso remained my most reliable source. By 1972 I had annotated over 1,100 individuals, representing five generations.[4] The endogamy was such that several pairs of cousins were found to be more related genetically than some siblings. The genealogies also revealed an extraordinarily high percentage of deaf-mutes, as will be explained near the end of chapter I.

To conclude these comments on fieldwork, I might add that the photography was very important. I would have liked to have at least one photograph of every individual in the community, but this was impossible. When I wanted to take several shots of one person the usual reply was, "You have already taken one, why do you want another?" Frequently they refused to be photographed at all. Although I always made it a point to offer the person his or her photograph, often it was refused or accepted with little or no interest. This contrasted to the *ladinos*, who time and again requested that I photograph them and were pleased to receive the pictures. When I became aware of their dislike of being photographed, I would not even take my camera along when I went to visit. As far as I know, there was no idea of loss or damage to one's soul or spirit by being photographed and no one ever asked to be paid for posing, as often happens in Guatemala. They seemed to think that taking their photographs was an imposition and somehow threatening. Only Alfonso did not object to being photographed, though he did not seem to have a particular desire to be given the pictures.

NOTES

1. Chapman and Jacquard 1971; Jacquard 1971, 1974; Pison and Vu Tien 1974; Quilici 1975; Quilici and Constans 1971; Von Hagen 1972. See an important recent publication by Sauvain-Dugerdil which refers to the Tolupan.
2. Jacquard 1973.
3. See Chapman 1975, for an article written about my experience with Lupita.
4. In the genealogies of the 1,100 individuals, a total of 873 were "pure" Indians, 55 were *ladinos* and the remaining 210 were *mezclados* (Tolupan-*ladino* parents). In 1972, I annotated 269 "pure" Indians, 15 *ladinos* and 125 *mezclados*, a total of 409 persons. Those who had left the community were: 9 "pure" Indians, 30 *ladinos* and 27 *mezclados*.

CHAPTER I

TOLUPANS: PAST AND PRESENT

The only existing Tolupan/Jicaque community, La Montaña de la Flor (The Mountain of the Flower), was founded about 1866, and for many decades it remained in virtual isolation deep in the "raw" mountains of central Honduras. Most of the people who compose the community — approximately 600 in 1991 — are descendants of the eight adults who found refuge from persecution in these mountains.

In the nineteenth century there were some 8,000 Tolupans/Jicaques north of the Montaña de la Flor, in the Department of Yoro.[1] Beginning about 1863 many were forced to collect and transport sarsaparilla from the mountains where they lived to ports on the Atlantic coast, and soon afterwards those who survived were deprived of their best land, became laborers on coffee and banana plantations and intermarried with equally poor mestizos. Although certain communities in Yoro still identify themselves as Jicaques, none of them retain the tradition and native language comparable to those of the Montaña de la Flor.

It is essential to bear in mind that this community was founded by a few families, that for now well over a hundred years it has been separated from its group of origin in Yoro, that it is surrounded by mestizos, that it has a very high mortality rate and that about one-third of the population is mestizo or *ladino*. If we think of it as a cultural entity, we are struck by what is lacking. There are few magical practices, and now virtually no rituals, celebrations or fiestas of any sort. There are few old people. Except for the newlyweds, most of the households are formed of broken families: couples, whose first or second spouses have died, offspring of former marriages, adopted children, single or widowed uncles and aunts, and so forth. Polygamy seems to follow no set rule and the term lends itself to misinterpretations. For example, in the late 1950s, one chief, Doroteo, had four "wives," that is these women lived together in his hut (three were widows, two of whom were not necessarily his sexual partners). His wife, Anita, was the mother of his oldest children and he had a baby with one of the other women. The other chief, Leonor Soto, had just one wife, Teresa.

The Tolupans of the Montaña have few prohibitions other than committing incest, drinking alcoholic beverages and having sexual relations while recovering from a snakebite. They neither sing nor dance nor play music, except a few young men who strum the guitar and pick up tunes they hear on their radios. Religious and magical practices are few; animal bones may still be tied to the posts of a few huts; an occasional wooden cross set on a roof, in a patio or in the fields; ashes scattered on maize plants to protect them against frost; "favors" given to the moon during an eclipse; divination performed and certain proscriptions observed during the period of mourning. These are about all the symbolic actions I observed or heard about. Historical documents of the eighteenth and nineteenth centuries suggest that their culture was more complex. Since the Montaña de la Flor was founded about 1866, it retained much of the nineteenth-century tradition until the introduction of coffee cultivation in the 1930s. This innovation generated profound changes which will be referred to presently.

What is surprising is that a vibrant oral tradition survived in the Montaña de la Flor, at least in the minds of some of the older Indians, among them Alfonso Martínez, that the ancestral language is still spoken and that even today, in 1991, this unique ethnic group still exists, despite the high mortality, increased poverty and its consequences, intermarriage with neighboring mestizos, encroachments upon their land, internal conflicts and so on.

The main thrust of this book is the mythology. Why? For several reasons: because this aspect of the surviving culture was virtually unknown to the outside world and a challenge to discover if more might be learned. I was aware that much of interest could also be learned about the forms of labor, the techniques of planting, the variety of crops, the impact of trade on the subsistence economy, the social organization, most especially the breakdown of the ancient patterns and the adoption of new forms of relating. While I did study these and other aspects of the culture, I chose to concentrate on the mythology also because my principal informant was very knowledgeable in this area and well disposed to communicate it to me. I had the impression that although some of the other older people were equally well versed in the oral tradition, as the years passed it was losing its vitality; it would be less significant to the following generations as the conditions of living were changing and in a certain sense becoming modernized.

The term "Jicaque" will refer to the historical Tolupans as well as to those of Yoro where it is most widely employed. "Tolupan" (sometimes spelled Torrupan) will be reserved for the Jicaques of the Montaña de la Flor because they use this name and undoubtedly it is the authentic one.

The denomination of "Jicaque" has a history of its own. As far back as the late sixteenth century, "Xicaque," as the word is usually written in the historical documents, was synonymous with barbarian, pagan, infidel, savage and the like. It applied to almost any semi-sedentary group in Honduras and Nicaragua who were part-time cultivators relying heavily on hunting and fishing. They were mobile and fearless people. The term referred to the ancestors of the Tolupans, Payas, Matagalpas, Sumus, Mísquitos, and others in eastern Honduras and neighboring Nicaragua. The term "Xicaque" is apparently derived from the Nahua word *chicahuacquê*, chicacquê or chicátic which signifies "an old person," "a robust or strong thing," "the strong ones" or simply "valiant." According to the Mexican scholar, Professor W. Jiménez Moreno,[2] the ancient Pipiles — the sophisticated Nahuas who departed from Teotihuacan (central Mexico) about 650 A.D., some of whom finally settled in Honduras — called these natives by this term.

That these semi-sedentary people were viewed as infidel savages by the Spaniards and colonists is not surprising, as they resolutely opposed the conquest and occupation of their land. They harassed, attacked and assassinated soldiers, missionaries, merchants and colonists, when and wherever they could. They pillaged plantations, stole livestock, did all the harm they dared. To thwart "the" enemy, they made alliances with other invaders: English, French, Dutch; pirates, filibusters, and the like. Even today the term "Xicaque" has not lost its derogatory connotation. In the Honduran countryside, the expression "you behave like a Xicaque" means that you are behaving in an uncouth manner.

Although at times the Xicaques reacted violently to the Spanish conquistadores and followers, their usual defense was not attack but rather retreat into the backlands, the almost inaccessible terrain of densely forested mountains and valleys where the Spaniards and early colonists rarely ventured.

In prehispanic times the Jicaque (Tolupan) culture was similar to that of the other semi-sedentary "Xicaque" tribes mentioned above. Among them the culture of the Mísquitos became radically transformed during the seventeenth and eighteenth centuries, mainly due to association with English pirates and filibusters and the later influx of Africans from the Caribbean who had escaped from slavery.[3] Before the Spanish Conquest the cultures of these groups resembled those of the tropical forest of South America far more than those of nearby Mesoamerica; however, the Jicaques undoubtedly had contact with their Mayan neighbors, some of whom were traders from Yucatan, especially at the headwaters of the Ulua River where they had established a port of trade. The Tolupans also probably mingled with the colonies of the ancient Pipiles, mentioned above, who settled in central Honduras during the seventh and eighth centuries A.D., as well as the more recent arrivals from central Mexico. Shortly before the Spanish Conquest, Aztec long-distant traders, the Pochteca, had come to Honduras all the way from Tlatelolco, sister city of the magnificent Tenochtitlan, capital of the Aztec Empire. Like the Yucatecan merchants, the Pochteca also had a port of trade farther down the Atlantic coast in Trujillo in Jicaque territory.[4] And by 1525 there were other "Mexican" communities, sometimes called "enclaves," in Honduras founded by Aztec warriors, auxiliaries of the Spanish conquistadores, namely Hernán Cortés and Bernal Diaz del Castillo, during their famous expedition to "Hibueras." The ancient neighbors of the Jicaques — the Lencas, the Payas and the more distant Sumus, Mísquitos and Matagalpas — apparently all spoke languages of the Chibchan stock whose center of dispersion may have been Colombia in the remote past.

The classification of the Jicaque language has been subject to some debate, although the Hokan hypothesis seems now to be generally accepted. Several reputable linguists, mainly Maurice Swadesh, Joseph Greenberg and William Bright, placed it in the Hokan family whose center of dispersion is considered to be the western United States.[5] David Oltrogge concluded in 1975 that the Jicaque language of Montaña de la Flor is related to Tequislateca or Chontal and more specifically to Subtiaba of Nicaragua. He considers these languages to be Otomangue and possibly affiliated with Hokan.[6] Another linguist, Lyle Campbell, also partially supports the Hokan hypothesis.[7] Comparative analysis of Jicaque with certain known Hokan languages suggests that the remote ancestors of the Jicaques arrived in Central America from North America some 5,000 years ago, long before the first glimmerings of the Mayan civilization.[8]

My analyses of the historical documents indicate that just prior to the Conquest and into the sixteenth century, the Jicaque (Tolupan) territory was limited on the west by the Ulua River, Gulf of Honduras, where the Jicaques were neighbors of different Mayan groups, including traders from Yucatan mentioned above. Their territory extended east along the Atlantic coast to the present town of Trujillo, site of the Pochteca port of trade, and inland to the Aguan River and the limits of the Department of Olancho, which was Paya territory. To the south the Jicaques reached the Sulaco River. In this area and in the upper Ulua Valley they were neighbors of the Lencas.[9]

In 1582 the Franciscan missionaries constructed a monastery in Trujillo on the Gulf of Honduras. But theirs was an arduous and frustrating endeavor. By about 1643, Trujillo was abandoned by the missionaries and colonists for 155 years, a victim not of the Indians, but rather of insistent attacks and plundering by the pirates and other adventurers, usually English, though sometimes French and Dutch.[10]

At the beginning of the eighteenth century, other Franciscan missionaries of the Order Propaganda Fide firmly established themselves in Jicaque territory inland from Trujillo, in a place named Luquigue, in the Department of Yoro. Today its colonial church and the ruins of its equally ancient monastery overpower the small town of Luquigue and bear witness to the determination of the Franciscans to christianize the elusive Jicaques.

In 1804 the governor of the province, Ramón de Anguiano, commented on the evangelization of the Jicaques in these terms:

> ... the Padres of the Fide Propaganda arrived and began penetrating this terrain with mulattos from Yoro, seizing several Indians by force of arms, as those of Guata, San Miguel, and various places in the area, who were civilized with the ladinos. This was the manner in which they initiated their Mission. With these captives they formed some towns with a church which, given this bad method, only the town of Luquigue has remained. Now there is no hope of forming another nor the means of continuing this good work because the Padres have gained total abhorrence [of the Indians] as stated above, and for this reason [the Indians] since a long time ago, live in the high mountains with complete mistrust, always fearing the persecution of the Padres but desiring to have dealings and communication with us.[11]

Nine years later, in 1813, a Franciscan inspector wrote as follows about the Jicaques of Yoro.

> And finally, very few of these Xicaques allow the missionaries to enter through their palisades. Usually they come outside to a cleared space to receive the gifts which are brought for them and they converse a little (*platican poquito*, which is the expression they use). Only when they feel

great trust in the Padres will they allow their women and children to come out. But those who live further inland do not come out at all nor do they allow anyone to approach their land. If one attempts to do so the Indians who guard the limits [of their territory] will take vengeance. They are not only inaccessible, they are in love with the brutal and idle life they lead. They hate civility and above all what mostly hinders the progress of their conversion are the pernicious advice and bad example given to them by the ladinos who trade with them for the sarsaparilla which abounds in their mountains. Nevertheless hardly a year passes without some families being converted to our Holy Faith. There are now two Padres PP [of the Propaganda Fide Order] in those reductions.[12]

According to the above manuscript, the Jicaque women dressed in a skirt and poncho of tree-bark fiber made pliable by strenuous beating. The men used a large poncho, called *balandrán*, which reached their knees, also made of tree-bark or of cotton cloth obtained from *ladino* merchants. Even as late as the early twentieth century, some Jicaque men in Yoro dressed in bark cloth which by then had been largely replaced by cotton cloth.[13] The women had adopted the peasant mode, consisting of a long skirt and a long-sleeved blouse also of cotton. That the Tolupan of the Montaña de la Flor traditionally do not consume alcoholic beverages is surprising and merits a special study. As early as 1813, according to the above document, the Jicaques of Yoro had "...the kindness not to get drunk, as they do not use fermented liquor."

By the early nineteenth century, when the above two reports were written, the raids along the Atlantic coast and inland had ceased. In Yoro, mestizos were living peacefully in hamlets on the plains and in the valleys. They cultivated land the Jicaques had occupied, obtained by force or purchase thus obliging the Jicaques to retreat to virgin forests high in the mountains of the Departments of Yoro and neighboring Olancho. There they formed small communities protected by *palenques* [palisades] and subsisted by cultivating, hunting, fishing and gathering wild products. They were still only partially sedentary, since they had to move as the soil became exhausted and the game scarce. But by then they were accustomed to exchanging products with itinerant merchants and had occasional encounters with missionaries.

The history of the Jicaques and knowledge of their culture during the nineteenth century can be partially reconstructed thanks to certain manuscripts, historical documents[14] and information I obtained from the older Indians in Montaña de la Flor and Yoro, which I visited in 1956 and again in 1972, as well as the *ladinos* mentioned here in "Fieldwork."

At that time the Jicaques in Yoro planted maize, squash and many species of edible tubers, for instance yucca (sweet manioc), potatoes, sweet potatoes and *malanga* (*Xanthrosoma sep.*) in large communal fields. Building fences, cutting down underbrush, burning and clearing the fields, planting, weeding and harvesting were all accomplished with such rudimentary tools as a wooden-tipped digging stick, a simple hoe, axe, and machete. None of the Indians, then and now, employ a plow drawn by oxen though they have seen the *ladinos* use them. The principal hunting weapons were the bow and arrow, without poison, a one-piece blowgun with small clay pellets as ammunition and traps of large wooden planks. They fished in the rivers, building dikes with branches across the narrowest sections, sometimes using vegetable poison to benumb the fish. They gathered wild fruits, edible roots and snails. Honey was also much sought after.

They lived in small groups, possibly from 200 to 500 hundred persons disseminated throughout the area. The entrances to the sites were safeguarded by palisades: high wooden fences having a gate which could be opened only from the inside. The traditional habitat was a large, multi-family thatched-roof hut. The division of each community into two patrilineal sections, "halves" or moieties, is undoubtedly prehispanic.[15] The basis for this hypothesis will become clear as the institution and realm of the celestial abodes of the two brothers Tomams are described.[16] The moieties still exist in the Montaña de la Flor, although they have lost many of their attributes.

Although the moiety chiefs worked in the fields along with the other men, they were given the first products of the communal harvests and a token of the game killed in a hunt. They represented their section to the outside world and would agree or refuse to meet strangers or itinerant merchants who came by. Bartering was invariably transacted through the chiefs.

Since early contact with the colonists, the Jicaques had bartered with merchants to obtain such items as salt, machetes and cotton cloth. The chiefs were also the contact agents for missionaries, government officials and sundry visiting dignitaries. They presided over marriages and were judges and executants of the penalties which they alone imposed on any accused found guilty. The offender was sometimes confined to a small hut, called a *cabildo*, used as a jail, located near each chief's house.

The main functions of the shaman, called *punakpan* in Tolupan and *zahorín* in Spanish, were to heal the sick and foretell the future. He accomplished the latter mainly by manipulating and decoding four knotted cords or strings, a magical operation called *la prueba de la cabuya* by which means he established contact with the supernatural powers, the controllers of destinies. (chapter VII)

By the middle of the nineteenth century this traditional way of life began to change, with the arrival of a Spanish Catholic prelate, Monsignor José

Manuel Subirana, who dedicated the last years of his life (1856–1864) to the Jicaques of Yoro. Like the previous missionaries, he aimed to persuade the Indians to abandon their ancestral customs, settle in hamlets, build chapels and behave like civilized Christians. But unlike his predecessors, Subirana visited numerous remote palisade settlements on horseback and persuaded many Jicaques to become completely sedentary. He provided twenty-one hamlets with what was considered a legal document, in the form of titles to the land they occupied. Thus, he hoped that they would open their hearts and arms to visiting priests and missionaries. He assigned a *ladino* agent (*curador*) to each hamlet to prevent usurpation of the land by outsiders and at the same time to dissuade the Indians from returning to a semi-nomadic mode of living.[17]

In 1956, a hundred years later, I encountered a *campesino* in Yoro who spoke of Subirana as "the Padre who conquered the Jicaques," and as the "Santa Misión." He sang the following refrain:

> The Santa Misión conquered the Jicaques.
> Baptized them with affection and love.
> The Santa Misión conquered the Jicaques.
> And the gates of heaven open widely to welcome him.
> The Santa Misión conquered the Jicaques.
> In less than ten years, he succeeded.
> The Santa Misión conquered the Jicaques.
> And shortly afterwards God called him to paradise.[18]

In March 1956 I was in the town of Yoro, capital of the Department of the same name in north-central Honduras, where I had come hoping to find some documents on Subirana. I was received in the parish house by a Canadian Jesuit Father who had been assigned to work in this region. We chatted briefly the first time I met him and the second day I inquired about whether or not Father Subirana might be declared a saint, as many of the *campesinos* already considered him to be. The Jesuit Father first spoke very highly of Subirana's labor among the Jicaques then he added:

> But you see, the fact that Father Subirana had not been canonized makes a great deal of difference. He may still be. Often it does not happen until a hundred years later. We need two first-class miracles for him. A miracle is first-class only when there is not the slightest doubt that it be the work of God. It is not easily come by. The classic example, of course, is Lazarus. If there be the slightest doubt — if there is any other, even plausible explanation — then the miracle is not considered first class. In cases of rapid recovery from consumption, for example, when the doctors are baffled,

when there is absolutely no worldly explanation for the recovery, only then do we recognize it as a first-class miracle. If the doctors say that perhaps the recovery was due to some unknown drug administered with the medicines, to some freak reaction of the patient to the medicines, to some psychological factor or anything of this sort; if there be the slightest suspicion that there may have been some such cause for the recovery, then it is not a first-class miracle, but second- or even third-class.

The Father suddenly stopped speaking and nodded "not yet" to a man servant waiting, broom in hand, at the entrance to the room. Again he rested his eyes on me. Hands lightly clasped in his lap, he continued:

For Father Subirana we need two first-class miracles, as I said. The fact that his body did not begin to decompose during the four days following his death, when he was carried by the Indians from Santa Cruz for burial here, is encouraging, but it is not a first-class miracle. When we begin to get some second- and third-class miracles coming in, it will be a good sign, as they usually precede the first-class miracles. But so far we haven't received any.

He continued talking while he glanced at his watch and then back at me.

About twenty years ago his grave was exhumed by Father E. who was then pushing his cause. But he became very discouraged when he found the body completely decayed. Only the bones remained. Father E. lost interest. He had hoped to find the body intact, the flesh almost as living. This would have been a very good sign.

People often come from Tegucigalpa and other places to visit Subirana's tomb here in our church. You have probably seen it already. Then, then you know that it is not very well kept up. We get a lot of complaints. But I can tell you quite frankly that we don't pay more attention to it because we are not pushing Father Subirana right now. When we begin to get some second- or third-class miracles, then it will begin to look encouraging. Then we will begin to take more interest in his shrine. In the meanwhile we are playing it down.

The priest assured me that they had no documents on Subirana or any others of historical interest besides the lists of baptisms and marriages he had already shown me. When I had come to see him the day before, he had inquired then if I were Catholic. When I replied that I wasn't, he simply nodded. Now, as I was leaving, he stood at the door of the parish house, tall and serene in his long black frock, and shook my hand, saying, "God bless you." I was sorry to leave that quiet seclusion. I closed the gate behind me, walked across the empty plaza in the heat of noon, turned up a dirt road and returned to the restaurant where I was the invited, though paying, guest.

Andrés, who lived near the Montaña de la Flor, recalled that his grandmother had told him that the Santa Misión played the guitar and sang to the Indians with a beautiful voice and taught the women to chant prayers. Later, I heard from Don Jesús López that many years ago the then very old chief in the Montaña, Pedro Soto, had told him about the visit of a missionary who had claimed to be Subirana, although the latter had been dead for a long time. To add insult to injury, he insisted on baptizing and marrying the Indians then and there. The chief became very irritated and replied:

> You do not look like Subirana. He had a delicate, pretty little face. You are ugly. His face was clean. You have a big beard. He had bright little eyes. You eyes are like *chiles*, pigs' eyes. Prove to me, if you are Subirana, then sing ... [he sang] ... Ay! you sing like a donkey. No. Get out of here. I was married by Subirana. I won't let you marry me again. Get out.

However, the memory of Padre Subirana was not venerated by all. One Tolupan/Jicaque surprised me by saying:

> Manuel Subirana behaved very badly with the Indians and this is why he died so soon from dysentery. God [Tomam] did not approve and this is why he sent him to the sickness. The Indians should be respected. We too are children of God.

In the early 1860s, the Jicaques became involved in events which proved to have dire consequences for them. The international market was offering high prices for the sarsaparilla root which had gained great popularity for beverages in the United States and Europe. Aware of the abundance of this root in the mountains of his jurisdiction, the governor of the Department of Yoro, Jesús Queróz, seized upon the opportunity. He ordered his soldiers to round up the Jicaques, escort them on foot to the mountains where the roots were plentiful and force them to collect the roots, even in rainy seasons when such labor was tedious in the extreme. The Indians were then lead like prisoners, by the same military guards on horseback, obliged to transport the roots in large bundles on their backs to the distant ports on the Atlantic coast, especially Trujillo and Tela, from where the product was exported.[19]

Unfortunately, some of the agents appointed by Subirana to protect the Indians turned against them and cooperated with the governor, by organizing the forced labor. In the decades that followed, many Jicaques fled from their newly founded hamlets, often pursued by the governor's soldiers, and returned to the "raw" mountains, which had always served as a refuge.

In 1956 my guide, "Tino," from Orica, the son of my friend Professor Marcial Flores, and I continued on horseback from the town of Yoro to Santa Marta, one of the hamlets Subirana had founded. The houses there were whitewashed, had tile roofs and were set up along the ridge of a mountain surrounded by the deep verdure of the groves and hemmed in by the forest covering. Coffee beans were being sunned in the patios of the houses.

From the few people we passed along the dirt road and the type of houses, I thought that probably there were no Indians living there and I wondered when they might have left. My curiosity was relieved by Doña Felicita with whom I took room and board. She was a large handsome woman who wore a black dress and a big white apron. Her father was the first *ladino* to settle there, some sixty years before. When he first came, so she told me, the Indians still wore bark clothes and hunted with blowguns and bows and arrows. Their cultivated fields looked like tangled mazes of vegetation; burnt stumps of trees protruded through the plants of maize and beans. They planted only "a few little sticks" of coffee, she added. The roofs of the huts were made of palm leaves and extended to the ground, as the huts had no walls at all. Her father, like other *ladinos* who came later, periodically brought mules loaded with merchandise — salt, machetes, and cloth — to sell to the Indians. He came with the intention of eventually acquiring land to plant coffee. Doña Felicita took me to visit the small unfinished chapel to show me a wooden image. It consisted of three figures: a central one about eighteen inches high and two small ones on either side about four inches high. The central figure, in a long black frock, represented Subirana, while the two small figures, I was told, were the Jicaques. They were in a kneeling position, their arms crossed over their chests, nude except for a loincloth. One clasped a blowgun, while the other was chained to the priest. She showed me this image with obvious affection. Carefully removing it from its glass case in a sideboard of the altar, while she commented, "Even though the Padres in Yoro say he is not a saint, we believe in him."

The second day in Santa Marta I visited an Indian family accompanied by a local *ladino* and Tino. An hour-and-a-half horseback ride brought us to two solitary adobe huts in the center of a patio which was covered with straw mats on which coffee beans were drying. Don Nestor, the proprietor, was at the door in front of children peering at us from around him. A handsome man somewhat over fifty, tall and lithe, he spoke with deliberation, greeting us in a stiff manner and offering chairs near a small table just outside the door. He told us that his parents were Jicaques but he had been orphaned at an early age and grew up among the *ladinos*. He had worked for a living since early childhood but had managed to learn to read and write. He spoke of the time when his people had been "in slavery," had been used like mules to transport sarsaparilla to the port of Tela, a week's journey over mountain trails. They had also been forced to work on the construction of government buildings in the town of Yoro.

These conditions had lasted well into this century. He said the Indians in the vicinity have no chief but he keeps the title of Santa Marta which Subirana left them. He added that the *ladinos* now occupy most of the land; the Indians had given it away in exchange for a little cloth, a few machetes, anything at all, but mostly for *guaro* — an alcoholic drink made of sugarcane, the poor man's whiskey. He explained that some did not realize what they were doing, while others thought they could easily find more land. He said there were still about ninety Indians in the vicinity, although the *ladinos* always say there are only a very few. He spoke of his plan to go to Tegucigalpa to inform the President of the plight of the Indians, most of whom are impoverished and deprived of any possibility of bettering their lot. Without my inquiring, he said that he was a "good Catholic," that he had given Doña Felicita 150 *lempiras* ($75) to finish the chapel, adding, "I am an honest man, may God or anyone be witness."

Next, my guide, Tino, and I visited the small town of Luquigue, which had been the center of an intensive missionary endeavor in the eighteenth century, as mentioned above. Here, as elsewhere, the *ladinos* had taken over the land of the Jicaques and then only a few christianized Indians lived near the town. Although they dressed like the other *campesinos*, they were easily identified by their physical type and a certain timidity in their behavior. The few we encountered knew some words of Jicaque and told us about their grandparents and stories they had heard from their parents.

The town is completely dominated by the imposing church and the ruins of the monastery. It was Easter Sunday, and the heavy door of the ancient church was wide open, letting sunlight penetrate the somber interior where shrouded women in black sang in dreary disharmony, kneeling or sitting on pine needles which covered the damp stone floor. Now and then a bat fluttered in the high rafters. Each woman held a candle and some a bouquet of wild flowers. The men stood stiffly, straw hat in hand, head bowed, while the priest whispered in Latin to the crucifixion. The candles on the altars illuminated the suffering images of Christ and the Virgin dressed as bizarre mannequins.

A few hours after leaving Luquigue, we reached level ground on the crest of the sierra and what seemed to me to be nature's cathedral. The sublime silence of the virgin forest of immense liquidambars and pine trees, devoid of underbrush, was pierced by streaks of sunlight, and distant songs of birds which echoed through the trees. Tino rode ahead and occasionally pulled up his reins to wait for me saying, "Do you hear that call? That's a *willowie*," or "That's a blue *sinkak*."

Some hours later we entered the first coffee groves of our destination, the hamlet of La Laguna Seca. The descent was steep and slippery. I wanted to continue on foot but Tino insisted that it was preferable for me to fall on the horse than vice versa and admonished me to hold tight. Upon arriving at the cluster of huts, we went directly to the home of a certain Lupe, whom my guide knew. A rather sturdy woman about forty years old with hair cropped short, she greeted us cheerfully. She was wearing a bright royal blue knee-length, sleeveless dress and shoes. Energetic, almost boisterous, she was nothing like any Indian woman I had ever met. Spanish was her native tongue and she knew a few words in Jicaque. She teasingly remarked, *Somos puros inditos aquí.* ("We are pure little Indians here.") Later she told me that she had been married to a *ladino*, the son of a merchant from a nearby hamlet. He had "disappeared" six years previously, probably, she thought, to the north coast to work for the banana company, "*la United*," that is, The United Fruit Company. During our two-day stay she kept me constant company and seemed quite intrigued with me, calling me "Anitilla." She was fond of exclaiming, "How lovely the streets of Mexico must be." She had once seen a postcard from Mexico City and it had greatly impressed her.

Lupe's mother was a small, delicate woman about seventy years old, dressed in the usual Indian fashion: a long skirt and long-sleeved, high-necked blouse of a once-colorful cotton print. She kept constantly busy feeding the chickens, serving meals, fetching wood for the fire. At times she would sit by the fire, smoke a cigarette with me or play with the puppies. She told me that the "old people" had come here from the hamlet called Subirana because the guardian there treated them very badly. Her parents had been married by Subirana, la Santa Misión. They had told her about his death and the "beautiful crowd of people" who had carried his body to Yoro for burial. While she was talking her daughter sang:

> The Santa Misión conquered the Jicaques.
> And all within ten years.
> With kindness and love he baptized them.
> And shortly afterwards God took him away.

Lupe's father had been prosperous. His parents were Indian and he spoke Jicaque as fluently as Spanish. He dressed as a *ladino* and, unlike most of the Indians, had made a small fortune by selling merchandise and the other Indians' coffee harvests as well as his own. But during the two years since his death, the family's prosperity had waned. I was there during the harvest, when the coffee beans were going out on muleback and *guaro* coming in also on muleback. It had already begun to rain and a few months later, when the trails would become impassable, the doors of the huts would close. In the nearby groves, the source for money to buy food and liquor would slowly ripen. I had been told by other Indians that people in this hamlet drank a great deal. I thought that I probably would too, if I stayed there.

I spent the next month visiting other hamlets, including one named Subirana where Lupe's grandparents had lived. It consisted of several adobe houses, whitewashed with red-tile roofs. All were inhabited by *ladinos*. Although they cultivated some of the land, the Standard Fruit Company, a branch of the United Fruit Company, the well-known North American banana trust, had occupied most of it for grazing cattle and for coffee groves — activities associated with the banana business. The landscape near Subirana, where some of the remaining Indians lived, is a rolling plain of short grass, dotted by patches of cultivated fields, enclosed by wooden fences. Their huts were located inside the fields. In this case, the original inhabitants were not elbowed out of the best land but rather squeezed in until it seemed that they might have to dig holes in the ground to survive.

I visited the hut of an elderly Indian man who lived with his wife and married daughter. He was bedridden and hardly spoke but the two women talked freely, mostly about their troubles and the hardships of the past, as they sat in a squatting position on the earth floor near the fire. There were about 400 Indians in the area, they said, but no cacique. The daughter remarked:

> My grandparents told me how they had to carry sarsaparilla on their backs to [the town of] Yoro, the women as well as the men. Many became hunchbacked. Many more got large sores on their backs. Those were terrible days. Some escaped, fled into the mountains but others killed themselves. Those who refused to work were thrown in jail.

And her mother added:

> My father was buried in the town of Yoro. He died there one day after he had taken a load of sarsaparilla. Many others

died along the trails. Those were terrible days. Now things
are not that bad, even though we are very poor.

In this same hamlet I was told that when an Indian died along the way, the
soldiers stopped only long enough to redistribute the dead man's load but
not long enough to bury him. Others succumbed to tropical diseases in the
ports on the Atlantic coast where the roots were taken for exportation. It is
difficult to determine how many perished during those decades of
"slavery."

Toward the end of the last century, the market for sarsaparilla declined
and exportation from Yoro almost ceased. Of those Indians who abandoned
their homes and hamlets to escape the exploiters, none found a more
secure refuge than those who fled to the Montaña de la Flor.

But for the Jicaques of Yoro, one calamity followed another. By the turn
of the century, the land on mountain slopes where they had retreated had
acquired a high premium for coffee cultivation. Until this time the *ladino*
farmers had preferred level lands for their crops of maize, beans and rice
and had left the mountainous lands to the Indians. But as the coffee groves
require a temperate climate the Indians were gradually pushed out of the
most fertile land in the hills and mountains onto the less productive lands
where most of them remain today. A concomitant to their increasing poverty was the need to supplement their meager harvest by working for pay on
the *fincas* (coffee plantations). This in turn accelerated the disintegration of
their communities and drew them into the towns to spend their wages on
food and other necessities — also on liquor.

The requirements to make a profit from coffee were very different from
those of sarsaparilla. Sarsaparilla exploitation attracted a manipulator
anxious to operate at a fast pace, unconcerned with the workers' well being
and determined to make a "hauling." The cultivation of coffee in Yoro was
undertaken for the most part by local farmers, many of whom were also
storekeepers and itinerant merchants who, as the market beckoned, tried
their hand at coffee to supplement their income. But they could not an-
ticipate a quick profit. They had to invest money and labor to tend the
groves while the trees grew and when they began to yield, hire a work
force for several months to harvest and process the coffee. In this sense,
sarsaparilla exploitation resembled plunder and the labor force "slaves,"
while coffee was productive and the labor force consisted of workers on
wages.

The cultivation of coffee has modified the structure of the peasant
economy and created a sector of landless Jicaque and *ladino campesinos*
living in conditions of uncertainty and poverty. The more fortunate have
access to parcels of land, either in communal or private holdings, dedicated

to subsistence crops and a few have sufficient terrain to plant coffee for sale on the market. Some of these communities rent portions of their best forest holdings to lumber companies which for many years have been exploiting the forests. The immediate benefits may be attractive, but the destruction of the forests in Yoro is having its well-known dire effects. The poverty of most of the descendants of the Jicaques in these hamlets was extreme in 1956 when I visited them for the first time and their condition had not improved when I returned in 1972. Several important recent studies of the problems faced by these *campesinos* are now available.[20]

Here we pick up the story of the adventures of the founders of the Montaña de la Flor, who about 1864 escaped from the "sarsaparilla slavery." The small party, three families, led by men later called Juan Martínez, Francisco Martínez, Pedro Soto, León Soto, and a few others, fled from Santa Marta to a neighboring department beyond the jurisdiction of the hated governor of Yoro, the "sarsaparilla baron" Jesús Quiróz. They feared persecution of one of their men who had apparently killed a soldier of the governor's troops. Inadvertently, by crossing over the mountain and entering the neighboring department, these few families isolated themselves not only from their own people but also from the ensuing economic transformations described above. This played a determining role in the assimilation and cultural loss of the Yoro Jicaques. The question arises, can a culture survive in the minds and hearts of very few protagonists? The story of these refugee families and their descendants offers an answer to this question.

Fleeing Santa Marta to the southeast, they remained for a few years in the mountain hamlet of La Laguna Seca, recently settled by other Jicaques who had fled from the hamlet of Subirana referred to above. In La Laguna Seca the families became acquainted with a certain Laureano Montés, a *ladino* storekeeper from El Tablero, a neighboring town. He told them about the uninhabited and unclaimed mountains farther to the south, located in the neighboring department of what is now Francisco Morazán, where the governor would never be able to trace them. He offered to lead them there and lend them machetes and seeds if they would promise to sell him maize once they were settled. The Indians agreed. The little group walked for two days, laden with their belongings, to what was to become their new home. A very high mountain had to be scaled and, since very few people had ever entered the region, there were no paths or trails.

The Indians had just settled when a militia did catch up with them. The governor was obviously determined to track them down. The militia, the "commission," succeeded in capturing a few of the men, bound them by the wrists and took them to Yoro where they were never heard of again.

The others hid, all except Juan Martínez, one of the chiefs, who shouted at the soldiers from afar:

> Hey, old goats! Commission of bandits! You'll not tie me up. Try and see. I'm fleeing by the order of God. You won't get your hands on me. Not in twenty years.

The commander of the militia shouted back, "Hey, old goat! You're as good as dead. We'll get you yet." And Juan Martínez replied, "It's for nothing that you call me an old goat. I'm fleeing for God. God is hiding me." Alfonso, the grandson of Juan Martínez who told me this, remarked:

> How could they catch Juan! He was a little *zahorín* (shaman). God [Tomam] sent Jívaro to warn him that the guards were coming after him. (chapter IV) Other Indians were caught but Juan didn't let himself be caught.

Some years later a commission came again. It ran into a neighbor, a *ladino* named Andaresio. The commander of the commission asked him, "Hey, you — Andaresio — have any Indians shown up here?" Andaresio replied:

> What do mean? What Indians? They all died eight years ago. Without working, how could they eat? They were so busy fleeing, how could they work? Don't be bothering here anymore. There are only *ladinos* around here. Don't you all hang around here anymore or we'll report you to Tegucigalpa. Only the Department of Yoro is your territory, not here.

Inadvertently, by settling in the Montaña the refugees severed their ties with their people, although through the following decades a few Yoro Jicaques visited them occasionally, notably two *punakpanes* [shamans] and a Jicaque woman married a Tolupan and settled there. In the 1920s, if not before, the *punakpanes* who came to the Montaña de la Flor were highly esteemed for their curing power, the advice they proffered and their ability to predict the future. (chapter VII) But the refugees had isolated themselves from the economic changes in Yoro which were shattering the tradition and converting the Yoro Jicaques into poor *campesinos*.

The name "Montaña de la Flor" applies to the cluster of mountains where the descendants of the Tolupan refugees live but originally it referred only to one mountain on the western fringe of the community. The topography is typical of western and central Honduras, in that it is part of an enclosure of mountains which surround a plain. The mountains reach an altitude of some 5,000 feet. Oak, pine and a palm called *suyate* are the most common trees; others such as liquidambar, cedar, *ceiba* (silk cotton tree) and mahogany are also plentiful. Two important rivers have their sources in this region: the Sulaco River to the west of the settlement, which encircles the mountains to the south, flows westward into the Comayagua River which joins the Ulua River and empties into the Gulf of Honduras; the other river, the Guayape, which at its headwater is called Guarabuqui, veers eastward and joins the Paulaya River in the Department of Olancho, reaching the Atlantic coast as part of the Negro River. On the southern limit of the plain, thirty-two kilometers from the Montaña, is the municipal seat of Orica, one of the oldest colonial towns in Honduras. When Juan, Pedro and their families first settled in the Montaña, it took eight days on horseback to reach Tegucigalpa, the nation's capital. However, they probably never had occasion to make the trip, nor did they ride horseback. They went to Orica only rarely, if at all. Nevertheless, the orientation of their community was to the south, as mentioned above; economically, geographically and politically they were separated from the Yoro Jicaques.

Juan Martínez, Pedro Soto and the others had accepted Laureano Montés' offer, knowing from long experience that the "raw mountains" (*montañas crudas*) held many advantages for them. Equipped with machetes, they could easily avail themselves of the abundance of wood, vines and palms for building houses, storage bins and fences; they could clear the land with machetes and fire, and plant seeds with their digging sticks. The region was healthy because of its sparse population, temperate climate and abundant water. The year is divided into a dry season, which usually begins in November, and a rainy season, which starts in April or May. The latter is interrupted by the relatively dry month of July and part of August, thus making it possible to plant maize and other crops twice a year in the valleys where the climate is warmer than in the mountains.

Equipped with bows and arrows, blowguns, machetes — later with shotguns and rifles — and dogs, the settlers had a wide choice of edible game: deer, monkeys, tapirs, raccoons, coatis, pacas, rabbits, agoutis, opossums, armadillos, two species of peccaries, squirrels, rodents and a variety of large fowls and fish. They would also find numerous snakes, sometimes eaten, skunks and coyotes. Many pumas, jaguars (called tigers), ocelots and smaller felines were killed for their skins by the Indians and later by the *ladinos*, who considered them a threat to their cattle. Now the larger felines are extinct in this area, as are the tapirs, monkeys and white-lipped peccaries. Among the most sought-after insects were the large ants (*zompopos*) which were eaten roasted and a great variety of wasps whose grub was, and is, highly appreciated. Honey was, and is, of course a great favorite and often collected in the forest. A species of stingless bee was even persuaded to make its hive in hollowed-out tree trunks about four feet long and supported by forked branches which the Tolupans judiciously placed alongside their huts.

Clearing and planting were organized by the two chiefs, Juan and Pedro, who determined when the work was to be done and how many men were needed for each task. The crops consisted mainly of maize — eleven varieties noted by the author — beans — sixteen varieties — squash, at least six different species of tubers including potatoes and sweet manioc (yucca), sugarcane and tobacco, as well as a vine called *patastillo* (also known as *chayote*) which produces a very nourishing fruit. Tobacco was a coveted crop and was, and probably still is, grown by almost everyone. The men smoked incessantly, now less, either with small pipes made from bullet cartridges and wood or simply rolling the leaf. They do not cure the tobacco as do the neighboring *ladinos*. Small quantities of onions, garlic, peanuts, chile and cotton were planted, as well as banana, orange, mango, plum and other such trees.[21] The fruits of these were consumed or given away. *Calabash* trees and gourd vines were highly prized for their heavily skinned fruits which were, and are, used as receptacles for eating, drinking and storing food and water. Snails, berries and other fruits, especially honey, were obtained in the forest.

Before the introduction of coffee cultivation in the 1930s, the two chiefs directed the labor in the communal fields of their respective sections and distributed the products of the harvest among the families. At this period, until the 1930s, there were one or more communal maize fields, milpas, in each moiety. In Pedro's section one of the first communal milpas was said to have been very large and to have yielded a great quantity of shelled maize. Only squash were planted with maize; the beans (*frijoles*) were added later in the individual milpas. The produce was distributed by each chief among the heads of families and the surplus traded with the *ladinos*. As in the past the chiefs worked in the fields and were given presents of food and game by members of their sections. Latter-day chiefs told me that those who refused to work, stole, fought or drank were put in "jail" — a small hut near the chief's house — or obliged to work several days or even weeks for the community, usually repairing the road that leads to the settlement. A "stock" had been employed in the Montaña. A man found guilty of some misdemeanor might be locked into the stock for days on end, until his legs and ankles were huge from swelling. This practice was abolished many decades ago and today serious offenses and crimes are reported to the judge at the municipal seat in the town of Orica.

Almost every family probably had, then as now, two or three skinny dogs which are coveted when proven good hunters. They do not seem to be treated as pets except when they are puppies. They are the same generalized short-haired mongrels kept by the *ladinos* in the vicinity. Cats are, and undoubtedly were then, also kept at near-starvation to incite them to hunt the mice and rats, as among the *ladinos*. Chickens, turkeys, ducks and pigs were much more abundant then. Pedro and Juan, the two chiefs, had a few head of cattle destined to be eaten. The cows were not milked, as the Tolupans were unaccustomed to dairy products, and did not take a fancy to either milk or cheese. When a cow or bull was slaughtered, its meat was divided among the members of the extended family. The hides were used as sleeping mats, as were deer skins. As the cattle grazed freely, probably then, as today, only when one was wanted for slaughter or sale did the Indians locate them, and often after weeks of searching they were found dead from a fall, disease or being poisoned by snakes. During the late 1950s, I saw a few monkeys, doves and parakeets in and near the huts. One family had two monkeys which they kept tied. They were brought into the hut to sleep at night and treated like pets.

Fishing was also frequently practiced by poisoning the water, "spearing" the fish with a machete, or simply crushing them with rocks — more recently with the aid of hook and line.

When the refugee families arrived in the "raw" mountains, they organized the terrain and themselves into two sections. This dual or moiety organization, as it is known in the anthropological literature, is found among a great number of groups at different levels of economic development the world over. Hoping to avoid recognition by their persecutors, the refugees adopted the surnames Martínez and Soto; these became the names of the families of the east moiety and the west moiety, respectively. From this very beginning, the east section has consistently had more "members" than its counterpart. The dividing line between the sections was a stream, now called the Quebrada de Beltrán, a tributary of the Guarabuqui River. Juan Martínez became the chief, or cacique, of the east section, and Pedro Soto of the west section. Of the other adults who came on the trek, Francisco Martínez and his wife, Caciana, chose to live in Juan's moiety and León Soto, a young man unrelated to the others, married the eldest daughter of Pedro Soto and settled in his section or moiety. The entrances to the sections were both located at the beginning of the trail leading to the south out of the mountains onto the plain. They were demarcated by palisades through which the *ladinos* were not allowed without permission of the chiefs. Behind the palisades, each chief constructed a multifamily thatched-roof hut, as did the other two families farther back in the mountains. And so began a new chapter in the saga of these families and their descendants, who were to become the last guardians of their ancient tradition. Although the majority of the present-day 600 inhabitants of the Montaña de la Flor are descendants of these original four families, the number of *ladinos* and *mezclados* has steadily increased.

The first settlers in the Montaña de la Flor established a sort of symbiotic relationship with their neighbors which enabled them to maintain a

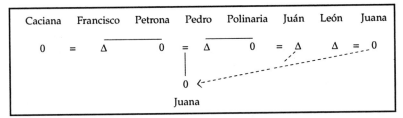

Diagram 1. Kin relations of the eight founders of the Montaña de la Flor.

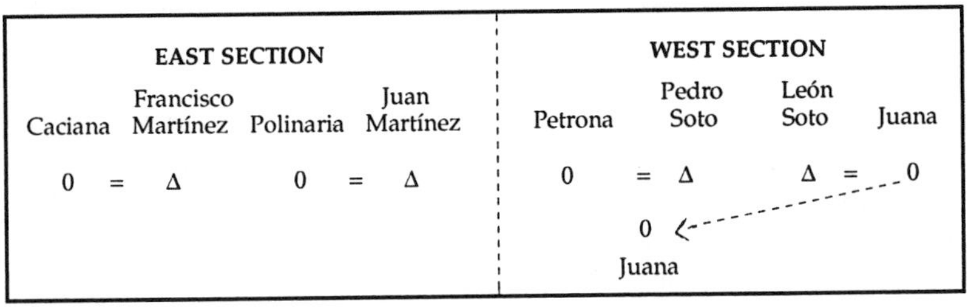

Diagram 2. The division of the four founding families into two sections.

certain cultural identity while carrying on commercial dealings with the *ladinos*, who came with mules loaded with merchandise they knew the Indians needed or desired. Since the Tolupans lived in the highlands facing a plain to the south where cattle ranches and bean cultivation predominated, they offered the *ladinos* mostly maize, sometimes tobacco, baskets, large cedar boards hewed by machete — used as doors, deer skins, chickens or turkeys. These items were exchanged for salt, unrefined sugar and manufactured goods brought from Tegucigalpa, such as machetes, axes, cotton cloth, needles, occasionally pocket knives, tin cups, glass-bead necklaces, cigarettes, aspirins and other store remedies. Also popular were small pieces of steel (*eslabón*) used with flint to make fire — later entirely replaced by matches and cigarette lighters — shotguns or rifles, gun powder used in hunting, and more recently radios, flashlights, batteries and nails. During this early period the men rarely, if ever, went to the nearby towns to trade in the stores.

The transactions with *ladino* merchants took place with the moiety chief through the gate of the palisade of each moiety. In the late 1950s, the entrance to the west section of the Montaña de la Flor still had such a palisade, while at the entrance to the other section there was only a low fence. In front of each entrance the Indians built a structure, called a *nacional*, which consisted of a thatched roof supported by four poles used as temporary shelter for itinerant merchants, their mules, horses and goods. Until about 1930, merchants were not allowed into the settlement and then, as later, they had to get one to the chiefs to agree to a day for trading, called *plaza*, a week or two in advance. Sunday became the favorite day for *plaza* and the reason why the Indians do not work this day. Before the missionaries changed the habits of those who lived in the cluster of the east moiety, of chief Cipriano, if there was no *plaza*, Sunday was undistinguishable from other days; while among the neighboring *ladinos*, Sunday was and is a day of rest. At this early time, the transactions usually took the form of barter, as the Indians were still not accustomed to trading with money. Barter tended to favor the merchant. He acquired the goods, maize and other foods and later coffee, at equivalents which he himself determined, in view of his clients' need or desire for the merchandise he offered.

The most active merchants were and are store owners in the nearby villages or towns. Since around 1965, when a road was opened from the main highway via Orica all the way to the settlement, the merchants bring their wares by truck in the dry season at least, usually just prior to and during the two or three months of the coffee harvest. They trade to considerable advantage by advancing merchandise against a promise of payment in product. Many of the Indians still do not trust the merchants, who were often accused of cheating on weights and measures, of offering inferior goods and generally acting miserly. However, the Tolupans maintain friendly or at least businesslike relations with most of the *ladino* merchants. The *ladinos*, *mezclados* (children of "mixed" parents) and acculturated Indians living in the community, now mostly the youths, take the coffee beans to the villages or larger towns where they sell at a higher price and buy at lower prices in the stores. Occasionally, some of the traditional Indians will do so. The main reason they gave for not going frequently was fear of catching colds or fevers. (chapter II)

According to all reports the first two generations of chiefs assiduously avoided physical contact with the *ladino* merchants, the only outsiders with whom they maintained routine relations. This caution was based on century-old experiences: the Indians were aware of the dangers of contagious diseases such as the common cold, measles and tuberculosis which frequently caused many deaths. They refused to accept any object directly from the hands of the *ladinos*. The chief would extend his hand shielded by a large leaf upon which the *ladino* would deposit small goods or even coins, never bills. Subsequently, these objects would be wrapped in a corn husk and hung over the fire to be purified by the smoke. The larger items, such as machetes and cloth, would be set on the ground inside the gate of the palisade where the chief would pick them up once the merchant had departed. When I arrived in 1955 there was still one person, Fausto Soto, the brother of west moiety chief Leonor, who refused to accept anything from the hands of an outsider. When he was offered money from a sale or a cigarette, he would break off a leaf and place it on his outstretched hand to receive the object and this always through the boards of the palisade, without allowing the stranger to come through the gate. Later, however, I noticed that he did shake hands with certain *ladinos* and I, too, was able to chat with him inside the palisade.

Pedro's multifamily thatched-roof hut was some forty feet square, very large by present-day standards. According to his grandson, chief Leonor Soto, "A huge family lived there, everyone — Pedro and all his sons, Ulofia, Raimundo, Macario, Constantino, Beltrán, all together, and all worked together." Inside, each family had its separate hearth, eating and sleeping quarters. When the community was founded the first four residences, two in each moiety, were of this type. Near each dwelling there were several large storage bins, wooden structures some twenty-two feet square, set on poles about four feet high. In 1955, when I first came to the Montaña, there was still one multifamily hut occupied by seven families, each with its separate living space. When it deteriorated a few years later, small one- or two-family huts replaced it. It was the last communal habitation in the Montaña de la Flor and probably in the entire Jicaque area of Yoro.

A sexual division of labor prevailed in all activities except harvesting the garden products and gathering edible food, which both men and women performed. The women also sometimes helped the men harvest the maize — and later coffee, fish, and collect firewood. This description refers especially to the early period in the Montaña but is still largely valid today among the most traditional families. Virtually all the men farmed, hunted, constructed their houses and furniture and kept the trails open by cutting down the overgrowth of vegetation. Only a few were proficient at weaving the sturdy baskets and small hammocks, used sometimes as cradles but mostly for storage in the huts, and fiber bags in which they transported crops on their backs from the milpas to their homes. Some men made pouches of animal skins in which they carried personal items such as the small pipes mentioned above. Some also knew how to fashion large planks of cedar, sometimes eight feet by four feet, which were used to form their platform beds and doors. These were occasionally sold to the *ladinos*. Those who manufactured the single-tube blowguns and bows and arrows were well known.

At this early time, the first generation, most of the men probably still made their tunics (*balandranes*) from bark cloth. They still make strips of bark. First they are soaked in water, then pounded with a specially made wooden mallet on a grooved log and dried in the sun.[22] The women made dresses and some mens' and boys' tunics from the cotton cloths obtained from the merchants. The Tolupans or Jicaques in general have never been known to weave cloth but the women spun coarse thread with wooden spindles and a calabash used as a whorl with their home-grown cotton. For adornment they made necklaces from seeds called *lágrimas de San Pedro* (tears of Saint Peter), to which they tied feathers and tiny pieces of fur. Both sexes wore these necklaces until quite recently. It is hard to say just when a few Tolupan women learned to make utilitarian pottery from the *ladino* women — the jars and large plates (*comales*) used in cooking — but most preferred to purchase pottery from these same neighbors. Gourds and *calabashes* served as receptacles for water and food, as they still do.

The women made the traditional cakes of yucca which are no longer prepared. Then, as now, the most time-consuming female task was the preparation of meals. Maize was boiled, ground on a stone (*piedra*, called *metate* in Guatemala and Mexico) and made into tortillas, tamales, a maize beverage called pozol and *pinol*.[23] Beans (*frijoles*) were boiled and inserted in the tamales or eaten separately. Grinding corn on the stone is very tedious; and these chores are still performed in the Montaña as they are by many of the *ladinas*. However, the women have increasingly acquired mechanical hand grinders, though they still revert to the "stone" for the finer grinding required for tortillas. The tubers are either boiled or roasted, as are other foods, especially meat. The Tolupan women have learned to make the soft salty cheese called *cuajada* and most of the Indians, especially the children, have developed a taste for bread which they purchase from the *ladino* women.

On the subject of meals, I might add here that, unlike the *ladinos*, the Tolupans do not sit at a table for meals, nor do most use forks, knives or plates. Pocket knives or machetes are employed to peal fruit and cut or slice other foods. If the consistency of the food is somewhat liquid, they use the tortilla as a plate and break off pieces to scoop up the food. Hot vegetables and meat are served in a gourd. A large leaf was often used as a cup; now tin cups are very common. The inedible parts of food are tossed out the door, although usually several hungry dogs and cats will not let anything go to waste. Visitors are almost invariably offered food and one or another of the hosts will usually join them no matter what the time of day. The women serve from the fire and offer food to the men first. While eating they all sit or stoop almost anywhere in the hut, although usually near the fire. To return to final comments on the division of labor — caring for the children and yard animals, daily transportation of water in jars from the rivers and washing clothes were then, as they are now, women's responsibilities. As with the poorer *ladino* women, all this work occupied, and often still occupies, the entire day, from daybreak to nightfall.

Three types of labor may be quite clearly delineated. I will label them "communal," "reciprocal" and "individual." The first two are traditional and involved those who, in this early period in the Montaña, cohabited one big house. The communal labor was practiced mainly by an entire extended family in the large maize fields, the construction of houses, granaries, fences, and so on. This form of labor survives today when the men of a section, upon the request of their chief, cooperate to accomplish a given task, usually to repair the road leading to the settlement and, more recently, to build a schoolhouse. It also still prevails in the house clusters. This observation is based on data from three such clusters, where time and again the men commented, "We all work together," in the groves and milpas. When I asked the names of those who worked together, I was invariably given those of all, or most, of the adult males in the cluster. Although sometimes a man from an isolated house might join, there did not appear to be much random interchange of workers.

The second type of labor, reciprocal labor, called *mano vuelta* (turning the hand), a term taken from the neighboring *ladinos*, was probably the pattern extant among the different families which cohabited the large houses for tasks such as tending the family gardens and domestic work. Now, long after the abandonment of the communal patterns, it consists of a relationship between two or more men for tending the crops, building fences, huts, granaries and the like. The "host," who first proposes the work, provides his partner(s) with a noonday meal and if the work lasts more than one day, the host usually offers the evening meal and shelter. His partner(s) reciprocate in a like manner. This type of labor is not tied in with kinship; it is simply a temporary agreement between or among men who are on friendly terms and a means of avoiding hiring "hands." The men have a number of preferred friends with whom they reciprocate when a need arises. Alfonso commented, "When I help him for a week, he helps me for a week."

Finally, the third type of labor, which I call "individual labor," is largely an innovation adapted as a result of the breakdown of the communal patterns. Most of the domestic labor as well as transporting water from the stream or river to the hut, washing clothes and feeding the chickens, as performed by the women, is now done individually, although the women in a household may share the tasks. The same applies to collecting firewood, which is usually done by the men. All the craft work is of this type and men sometimes work alone in the fields and hunt alone with the blowgun.

When Juan and Pedro were still alive, until about 1910, the men and boys continued to dress in the long tunic or poncho, the *balandrán*. Then, it was usually made of bark cloth, later of cotton cloth, as today. It was secured at the waist by narrow strips of bark, now, more likely, by a leather belt. When the temperature drops, the men wear two or three superimposed *balandranes*. Some wore homemade sandals, while the majority were barefoot, as were the women. The women wore long cotton skirts and long-sleeved high-necked blouses. These styles lasted into the 1950s, when some of the men began wearing pants, shirts and straw hats. The younger women prefer shorter or short skirts, usually one-piece dresses, which they either buy or make themselves. The *ladinos* and acculturated Indians took more care of their clothes than those bound by tradition. The latter did not usually wash their clothes very frequently and often slept in them. But hygiene seems to be a personal affair. Some of the Tolupans, as the local *ladinos*, are always neat, while others give little attention to their appearance. Those who rarely bathe acquire a certain tinge of burnt wood from the pine which is most commonly used for the domestic fires. As they spend a good deal of time close to the fire in the huts, this odor permeates their clothes and bodies.

During the early period, when communal labor and reciprocal norms were still the rule, no money circulated within the colony and belongings were shared and loaned freely — especially firearms and axes. There was no special pattern of gift exchange, except for the marriage arrangements.

There seems to be no rule determining the choice of a spouse, except to avoid incestuous unions by marrying outside the immediate family and if possible to the exclusion of first cousins. The young people even at this early time were not obliged to choose a spouse from the opposite moiety, though this was, and is, sometimes recommended because the families were "more distant." Judging also from the genealogies, the moiety affiliation did not determine the choice of spouses. The moiety is localized, meaning that the territory is divided in two and that the place of birth determines the affiliation. A person may change his/her section simply by obtaining the agreement of the two chiefs, moving there and hence having the right to cultivate certain terrain. However, by and large, the Martínez families continued to inhabit the land pertaining to the east moiety and the Soto families that of the west moiety. Marriages did and do occur between members of the moieties. In this case, the bride would usually establish residence in the groom's section, Nevertheless she would remain nominally under the authority of her moiety chief, could appeal to him in case of necessity — as the desire to separate from her husband and return to live in her moiety — and she would be buried on the side of the cemetery pertaining to her moiety. Communal work, as well as visiting, was and is more frequent among the members of a moiety than across moieties or at random. Very seldom will the adults of the entire settlement take part in any activity or reunion.

Allegiance to the moieties is most clearly expressed in the relationship of the individual to his or her chief (cacique). The office is normally inherited through the patrilineal line, an old cacique making known which of his sons he deems most apt to fulfil this position. Outstanding among the attributes of the first chiefs, and still partially applicable, were:

- until about 1940, each chief presided over marriages which took place in the chief's house — of the groom's section, if the bride was from the other moiety. There, the young couple were given such gifts as food and domestic wares by both sets of kin; the groom, however, was obliged to work for his father-in-law. The chief acted as referee in competitive sports which were performed during the celebration; (chapter II)
- the supervision of work in the communal milpas, repairing the fences at the entrances, clearing the trails, and so on. After the communal milpas were abandoned, the chiefs assigned, or agreed to, the plots of land on which each head of a family planted his milpa and later coffee grove;
- barter or sale of products of the communal fields to the *ladino* merchants and distribution of the goods received to the heads of families — no longer an attribute of the chiefs;
- verifying that a person who had recently died be appropriately buried in the cemetery;
- exercising of authority over their sections: judgment of disputes among the members, designation and execution of punishments — such as extra work clearing the trails or road leading to the settlement, acceptance or rejection of requests from members to change residence to the other section;
- receiving official visits and representing their respective "tribes" in all matters dealing with the municipal authorities and the national government — the chiefs have retained this function.

Each chief is assisted by an auxiliary, usually a youth chosen by the cacique and obliged or persuaded to serve at least two years without pay. He acts as a messenger to inform members of the section, many of whom live several hours' walk from the chief's house, of the orders or requests of his chief. Also, he usually accompanies his superior when the latter is summoned on official matters to Orica or Tegucigalpa.

There is no memory of any native music or dancing. In remote times they probably played reed flutes and tambours, as did their neighbors to the southeast. At present, a few young men own guitars and have learned tunes from the *ladinos* or listening to the radio. I never heard or heard of anyone there singing.

No ceremonies were or are practiced upon the birth of a child, except the gesture of burying the umbilical cord. It is usually buried in the floor of the hut to avoid, so I was told, its' being eaten by an animal. None are known for puberty. The mourning and burial practices, such as have survived, relate to their fears of earthquakes and contagion by *vaho* (fetid vapor). (chapters IV and VI)

Soon after Alfonso's eldest sister, Margarita, died in 1958, I went to visit him accompanied, as usual, by Don Genaro. He suggested we take the footpath up to Alfonso's hut instead of the usual mule trail, thinking that we might meet the pallbearers on their way to the cemetery. And so it was. About half an hour's ride into the settlement, we sighted four men in the distance trotting rather slowly through the thickly shaded forest, two of whom were carrying Margarita's corpse on a stretcher on their shoulders. As we approached, we slowed down. I soon recognized Guillermo, Alfonso's brother, but not the other three men, none of whom I had ever met. They were Margarita's sons. Her corpse lay tightly wrapped in a guinea sack and tied with freshly cut palm (*suyate*) strips. One encircled the neck, another the chest, the third the lower part of the body, securing her arms and hands which were placed flat against the body and the last strip held her ankles together. All this gave the effect of a mummy.

I was distressed when I saw them, as I had known Margarita, though slightly. When they came to a stop, Guillermo was puffing and sweating. Genaro found something to say which was, "¿Como estan?" ("How are you?") To which Guillermo answered curtly, "Mal, como llevo mi tia." ("Badly, as I am carrying my aunt.") I thought he might begin to cry. As usual when excited or embarrassed he stuttered. I told him I was sorry and that I didn't even know she had been sick until I learned of her death. As we rode on, I glanced back and saw that they had rested one end of the stretcher on the ground and were changing bearers.[24]

Women are not permitted, or do not wish, to accompany the deceased to the cemetery, mainly, as I was told, to prevent being infected with the "fetid vapor" of the corpse.

Juan and Pedro died of old age around 1910 and were buried in the community cemetery which I visited in 1955. It is located in the east moiety about a kilometer from the chief's household. At that time, its oval shape was enclosed by a rock wall, four feet high and about three hundred feet in circumference. At the eastern and western extremities there were two gates consisting of horizontal ten-foot long poles. The deceased of the Martínez moiety were carried into the cemetery through the east gate and those of the Soto moiety through the west gate. The more recent graves were covered with branches of pine and a cross made of two twigs, two or three feet high, stood where the head of the corpse lay. Large pieces of broken pottery jars had been placed in front of the crosses. The older graves were only discernible by the mounds of soil covered over by weeds.

Fallen crosses and pieces of jars were scattered about. I was told that the graves were not placed in any order, except that children were buried with their heads toward the west and adults with theirs toward the east. (chapter VI, answer 9) None of the Indians who accompanied me there could locate the graves of Juan or Pedro. They pointed to an overgrown area, saying that they were probably there. Only the graves of those who had died in the last few years were identified.

Before the first chiefs died, each appointed a favorite son to succeed him. Juan chose his son, Domingo, and Pedro, a son by the name of Beltrán.

By the 1920s, it became evident that the soil which was being cultivated, within walking distance of the few groups of nucleated dwellings, was becoming exhausted. The demands of shifting, slash-and-burn agriculture could no longer be met. The community could not resume the semi-sedentary mode of existence of their forefathers because they were surrounded by poor mestizo farmers who not only limited their expansion but began encroaching upon the territory. Their population had grown; the first generation had lived long lives and borne many healthy children. The new chiefs realized that something had to be done. In 1929, with the mayor of the Municipality of Orica, Francisco Mejía, acting as their advisor and legal representative, part of the terrain they occupied was measured and in accordance with the agrarian laws of the nation, 3,200 *hectarias* (7,907 acres) were granted to them by the federal government as an *ejido*, a communal holding. But only part of the land which the Tolupans have been cultivating or letting lie fallow has been officially measured and included in the *ejido*. The grant specified that the "Jicaques" may not sell or rent any part of the communal land and that it be occupied and cultivated exclusively by the two "tribes" — each moiety was termed a "tribe."[25]

One day when Don Jesús accompanied me on a visit, he explained to the Indians in the most vivid manner the beauty of working with plow and oxen. He got down on his hands and knees and with a twig scraped about ten straight rows on the bare ground and, placing some maize kernels along the rows, he described how the plow digs the furrow between the two oxen while the man at the plow keeps a steady eye on the rows and a firm hand on the plow, knowing that behind him his son follows, sowing the maize. This method is called *regado*. Having completed his explanation, one of the Indians stooped to the ground, picked up the kernels, smoothed over the soil and proceeded to carefully place three kernels — or even six he said could be planted in one hole — an equal distance apart. This method is called *mateado*. The *ladinos* also use it when the soil is unusually fertile and planting is done on time, while if the soil is inferior and planting delayed, the plow and oxen are preferred. Other factors also determine the use of one or the other method by the *ladinos*. For instance, if the terrain is on a steep incline, the planting must be done by hand with the machete and digging stick. However, by and large, the *regado*, the agricultural technique, is preferred by the *ladinos*, while the *mateado*, the horticultural method, is the only one employed by the Indians.

The Tolupans use a digging stick made entirely of wood, while the *ladinos* insert an iron point on their stick. Each employs it in a different fashion: the Indians grip the stick with both hands near the top, digging the hole with an up-and-down movement, while the *ladinos* use the stick as a shovel, holding it at an angle. This difference in gestures is related to, or a function of, the differences in the sticks themselves, as noted above. Tolupans plant the yucca by inserting a small twig of the plant in the ground at about a 45-degree angle, while the *ladinos* lay two twigs across each other at right angles. Chief Leonor, who demonstrated the latter two methods of planting, assured me that theirs is superior and commented, "It produces a great abundance, from 10 to 15 yuccas for each plant."

Most fields are planted for one year only, and rarely more than two in succession. The rotation period is said to be at least five years. The first task is burning and clearing the field, done in March or April at the latest. Large tree trunks are left in the field where they fall. However, usually the land has been cultivated before, so it is only a matter of burning the four or more years' growth of vegetation. Afterwards the fences are built. These are the same kind as those constructed by the *ladinos*: three or four rows of horizontal rather thin trunks or branches from ten to fifteen feet long, tied to posts four to six feet high. No nails are used. Planting is done after the first rains in April or May. Maize is planted first, then beans and later the tubers. The earliest maize is harvested within two and one-half months, in July or August, while the "maize of the mountains" takes five to six months to ripen. Beans require from two and one-half to seven months, depending on the variety. The *chinapopo* (a lima bean) is a favorite of the Indians because the vine produces three or four years in succession. The *ladinos* normally do not cultivate this, as they consider it to be an inferior food. The Indians plant a far greater variety of maize and beans than the *ladinos*. Most of the Tolupans plant a second crop of maize and beans in October. However, this harvest is seldom as plentiful as the first.

They plant two species of squash: the *ayote*, which can be harvested within four months of planting, and the larger *chivero*, which takes twice as long. The *chayote* vine requires four to five months for its fruit to ripen. Most of the tubers ripen in six months to a year; however, a small type of potato planted by the Tolupans matures in two or three months. The tubers are harvested as they are needed because the soil keeps them from spoiling for some months after they ripen. Tubers are the staff of life in the sense that they are consumed almost daily. They are rarely if ever sold, though they may be given away. Bananas and other fruits which mature at different times are usually picked and consumed as they ripen. Garlic and onions are ready in about four months. Tobacco is not planted until August and is ready for harvest in January or February.

Given the variety of plants, they normally harvest one or another plant nearly all year-round. But in June very little is harvested and this is the time of greatest scarcity. By July the earliest maize begins to ripen, and late-maturing maize in October or November. But by February, when coffee is being harvested, the supply of maize begins to dwindle and some families have to barter coffee for maize. Alfonso commented that a *carga* (200 lbs. of maize in the kernel) might last him a month — then he had a family of five, and that not everyone has maize so those who have must share theirs. However, they do not consume maize everyday, even when it is available, as it is considered the best crop for food and is portioned out rather carefully. But there is no careful planning of the quantities needed for consumption of each crop, although they know well their minimum requirements. It appears that maize, beans and tubers are the staples, and that maize is preferred to the tubers but less available. However, tubers were and are the guarantee against starvation.

Riding through the settlement, I have been impressed by the small tracts of subsistence crops. Most of the cultivated land is now given over to coffee groves. Much of the terrain, however, is mountainous pine and oak forests — some of which, in recent years, has been felled by various lumber companies. The land which is not cultivated or in secondary growth is considered unsuitable for cultivation, as are some of the plots with secondary growth. The types of vegetation on these plots, mostly scrubs, indicate whether or not the soil is rich enough for planting.

In order to compensate for the scarcity of land and increasing sterility of the soil, confronted as they were with an increase in population, the Indians began planting coffee trees probably in the early 1930s. This innovation permitted a more efficient use of the land than shifting, slash-and-burn, agriculture. Although four to six years are necessary in this area for coffee trees to mature, they bear fruit for thirty or even fifty years. So while the Indians still had to cope with their subsistence problem, they now had a cash crop which would yield continually for several generations. In years to come, coffee almost entirely replaced maize as the cash crop. At times they failed to produce sufficient maize for their own needs and bartered coffee for maize.

The introduction of coffee cultivation generated a series of transformations which were to affect their entire culture, mode of living and way of relating to one another. The coffee groves were not communal property;

they were not worked as the large milpas had been. The settlement pattern was rapidly transformed from several nucleated units into a dispersed pattern of what I term "clusters" of huts. In 1972 there were some twenty clusters; here, members of an extended family lived and cultivated coffee groves, as well as tuber gardens and their milpas. The cluster began when a family or related families planted a coffee grove and as the family grew, the married sons built their homes near their parents and a few more distant relatives often joined the little group. This situation is still the typical pattern so the present tense may be used. The oldest man, or the most active of the elders, usually organizes the work among his brothers, adult sons, nephews and sometimes sons-in-law. He also deals with the merchants, some of whom come on horseback directly to his cluster. The heads of family plant their groves and tend their separate milpas with the help of the other adults in the cluster; they work together in what I have termed a communal form of labor. Leopoldo Martínez, who lived about a two-hours' ride from the entrance — east section, once explained to me:

> I am chief here. I give the orders. Below, at the chief's cluster, Doroteo is chief. We always agree. With my people here, I am chief. Here we all work together; when my field is done, we go work in his [pointing to his brother]. When we finish there, we go over there [to his brother-in-law's plot].

Leonor, then chief of the west section, referring to his cluster, commented:

> We all work together. Each of us has his own coffee grove. I have mine, Julio [his son] also, Fausto [his brother] likewise, but we all work together.

The dispersal of the community and the formation of clusters is largely still prevalent, given the need to be located as close as possible to the coffee groves. It substantially transformed the power relations, as the caciques lost some of their authority and the heads-of-households of the clusters gained increased autonomy. Another consequence of this dispersion was of course the isolation of the families, which tended to undermine the group and moiety solidarity. However, most of the members of the respective moieties still have the surname Martínez, for the east, and Soto, for the west, although more and more the Tolupans adapt surnames from their *ladino* neighbors.

The huts and fields of the members of the corresponding moieties, for the most part, lie to the east and west of the Guarabuqui River which bisects the settlement. As stated above, moiety affiliation is determined by place of birth and is not considered in the choice of marriage partners;

however, the idea of marrying "out," to as distant a relative as possible, is sometimes interpreted as favoring the opposite moiety. In reality, the consanguineous ties are by now so close that, except in the *ladino*-Tolupan families, those of the sixth and seventh generations are nearly all either siblings or cousins. Outside mating is more and more common and any rule of exogamy would have little or no effect on degree of in-breeding. The Tolupans are, as noted above, adamant about respecting the prohibition of incest of the nuclear family, although, very rarely, children are born of father-daughter or brother-sister parents.

With respect to the residence: traditionally, an individual remains a "member" of the moiety where she or he was born and nominally under the authority of its chief. Residence was patrilocal in the first and most of the second generations. It became neolocal in the second and third generations, when the communal fields were abandoned and the families dispersed through the territory in clusters. It then reverted to patrilocality, as most of the available land was occupied and as recently married couples tended to construct their homes near those of the husband's parents, that is in patrilocal cluster. Temporary matrilocality following marriage is usual, in that during the first few years of marriage, the son-in-law is expected to work for his father-in-law. Therefore, the couple lives with the bride's parents in her cluster, if the parents are still alive. Moreover, once this period of bride-service is completed, and the couple takes up residence in the husband's cluster, he should lend a helping hand to his wife's parents for as long as either of them live. This is the norm which, however, varies in terms of the groves and milpas accessible and their productive capacity to support a limited number of "mouths."

Poverty is clearly an ally of the tradition. With more favorable conditions, the poorer youth would be able to dress "presentably," and be encouraged to seek certain improvements in their life style. In the measure that the land is productive and available, the trading attractive and the possibilities for raising a family better than at home, some *ladino* men, as in the past, will probably seek a Tolupan wife, with the intention of settling in the community. Also, very likely, the traditional Indians will continue to distrust such unions. This "mentality" is dramatically expressed in the fear of "temptations"; (chapter VI) notwithstanding the Tolupans are becoming increasingly assimilated to the *ladino* ways but the inverse is very rare.*

---

*The group as a whole is becoming less endogamous, as the years pass and as the young people, especially the *mezclados*, free themselves from the domination or persuasion of their Indian kin and seek a *ladino* spouse.

Huts are square or rectangular in shape and are usually built to accommodate two families, each of which has a separate fireplace and bed. The walls are made of oak uprights, crudely hewed by axe and machete. Spaces between the uprights are partially filled in with small trunks and long branches but even so the huts are extremely drafty. The door, usually a large cedar plank, is simply inserted in the space provided for it in the wall. The roof, made of the *suyate* palm, is supported by four posts made of the *guachipilin* tree. No exit is provided for the smoke. When I returned in 1964, I recall that the then young chief, Cipriano, of the east section, proudly showed me his new house — the first adobe hut with a tiled roof constructed in the settlement by a traditional Tolupan. The missionary, Mr. Otrogge, had helped him build it. The latter and the *ladino* families in the Montaña had such houses but still, even today, the majority of houses are made of uprights and thatched roofs, probably because they are easier and cheaper to build than the adobe tiled-roofed huts. In most instances, the fireplace is situated in the middle of the hut, or when there are two, near both ends of the hut. It typically consists of three large rocks set on the ground. When the house is sufficiently large, entire trunks are inserted between the rocks and pushed toward the center as they burn. The bed is made of three cedar planks, wider than those used as doors, set on logs and gives the appearance of a huge three-sided box. The open side faces the hearth and is used as a sitting area during the day. The size of the family. determines that of the "box-bed." Cowhide, deer and other animal skins serve as mattresses and thin cotton coverings are bought from the *ladinos* or in the towns.

In January and February, the temperature drops to almost 0 degrees Centigrade during the night, so it is understandable that one sleeps in one's clothes, as I often did. There is usually just one table in the hut, that which supports the "stone" for grinding. It is also made of cedar, highly valued, and passes from mother to daughter. Rectangular in shape, crudely made, its two front legs stand higher than the rear ones, in order to drain off the water used in grinding maize or coffee beans and to facilitate the downward movement of grinding. The traditional Tolupans use no chairs or benches. They either sit on the bed or in a stooping position on the ground. Hammocks may be used for babies, but the older children sleep with their parents. Maize is stored in specially built bins near the hut and other dry foods are kept in canoe-shaped bins inside the hut. Domestic wares and personal belongings are placed in baskets, nets and gourds which hang from the rafters. A storage platform is often built by laying planks across the rafters in one section of the roof. Water is kept in the large pottery jars or in gourds having a narrow opening.

Coffee is virtually exclusively destined to be traded with the *ladinos*. It is not strictly speaking a "cash crop," as it is often used in barter with the merchants. It is consumed in small quantities by a few of the Indian families; the *ladinos* and *mezclados* who live in the settlement do drink it. During my many visits to the west section, the more conservative of the two moieties, I was never offered a cup of coffee, although occasionally I was given one or two tortillas with *cuajada*. Leonor, the chief of this section, once commented, "I can't both drink and sell coffee." In the other moiety I was sometimes offered a cup but only once did I see them drinking it themselves. During my trips back into the mountains, I was never offered any coffee. Anticipating this, I used to take some with me. One day, upon arrival at a hut, a woman kindly offered to prepare it for me. She did this by boiling the ground coffee directly in water and proffering a cup so thick with grounds that it was impossible to swallow. This was perhaps her first try and I thanked her for the effort.

It proved difficult to obtain precise, detailed data on the size of the coffee groves and their yields. Most of the Indians simply said they didn't know the size of their groves, nor had they ever counted the trees, nor did they know how much they harvested because they exchanged it in small quantities. But they are certainly aware of its importance, as illustrated by the following comment of José de los Angeles, "Coffee supports me, without it I would die." Most of the cluster groups possess two or more groves, either in common or as individual tenure by the male heads of families. The majority of groves are now fifty or more years old, though trees are planted from time to time. The groves are situated on a mountain side, among larger trees whose foliage and branches shade the coffee trees. A grove is cleaned of undergrowth with a machete once or twice a year. A cluster of four to five huts produces from five to ten *cargas*, 200 lbs., yearly, that is 1,000 to 2,000 lbs. In 1972, about one-third of the population produced less than this and only three or four clusters more.

The groves are scattered throughout the *ejido*. Usually there is a grove near a cluster, though some may be several hours' walking distance. Nearly everyone is active during the harvest, usually a few weeks for a grove, from January to March. The women remove the pulp from the beans by soaking them. They then lightly grind them on the stone and sort out the beans from the mass of wet pulp, whereupon the beans are sunned in front of the hut for a few days. During this time, the women stir them so that they dry evenly. The coffee is usually sold in this form, with only a thin parchment remaining on the beans. To avoid this preparation, coffee is sometimes sold as it comes off the tree, obviously at a lower price. To the contrary, less frequently, it is sometimes sold at the most favorable price ready for roasting, "in gold," the parchment removed by being pounded with a pestle in a wooden mortar.

With the introduction of the coffee groves, the milpas were much reduced in size, although their numbers increased and they were located as close as possible to the groves. But the milpas and tuber gardens still had to be rotated about every two years, and left fallow for five years or longer. Consequently, eventually the residences were relocated, from time to time, to reduce the distance to the milpas. Given this inconvenience, a few families in the east moiety opted to move to their chief's, Cipriano's, cluster at one of the entrances to the settlement and to walk some distance to the cultivated fields and groves. At the same time, the population continues to augment despite the increased mortality rate. The settlement pattern became one of a number of clusters of huts — about twenty in 1972 — dispersed throughout the mountains in the vicinity of the groves and rotating milpas. Each "cluster" consisted usually of three or four huts inhabited by members of an extended family, now owners of one or more coffee groves. The chiefs continued to live at the two entrances to the settlement with a number of other families. The extended families acquired increasing autonomy with respect to their chiefs, even though they remained officially subject to them. Also, more *ladino* men were marrying Tolupan women, thus forming a larger sector of the community which was inclined to scorn the traditions of respect and submission to a chief, as well as the norms of reciprocity. The *ladino* traders with their mule trains began penetrating the *ejido*, often bypassing the chief of the moiety, going directly to the clusters of huts to trade and barter for the coffee harvests with the producers.

Another aspect of these transformations of the traditional ways is the increase in economic inequality which is principally determined by the possession of a coffee grove and then by its size and productivity, in contrast to some heads of families who have no groves at all. The latter, though they usually have a milpa, often work for pay for their more fortunate companions, harvesting the coffee beans or maize. This sort of inequality is more apparent among the "affluent" *ladino* residents and "mixed" families than among the "rich" traditional Indians, who also have large groves, as these tend to be more generous with their companions than the others. The very poorest are usually sick, dress in rags, are constantly searching for work and sometimes beg for themselves and/or their children. The pattern and ethics of the capitalistic, individualistic society, small scale though it may be, is replacing the communal-reciprocal norms of the former society.

The Tolupans were not interested in money, accumulating property or acquiring display goods. There was a strong in-group, Tolupan awareness.

In years past, although the Indians had to sell, they rarely appeared anxious to do so. "They have to be begged" [to sell] was a frequent complaint of the *ladinos*. One day, while returning to the ranch, Don Genaro told me of a *ladino* who years before had come to buy maize from the Indians. He was a friend of Genaro's but a stranger to the Indians. Genaro accompanied him to Beltrán's section — the west moiety — where the stranger asked an Indian to sell him a *carga*, 200 lbs., of maize. The Indian refused, saying that he didn't have any. Genaro tried in vain to induce him to sell and finally the potential buyer became angry, protesting that he came this far to buy maize and that he intended to do so. The Indian still refused, for the same reason. The stranger departed, very much annoyed, to sleep over at Genaro's house. The following day, the Indian sent word to Genaro's ranch that he was willing to sell him forty *manos*, 200 cobs, of maize, adding that the stranger couldn't have had much need for it or he wouldn't have left so quickly. The stranger thereupon complained to Genaro, "I haven't the patience to sit around waiting and begging them to sell." He departed without buying. Moral — persuasion should be exercised by a stranger who is not a regular customer.

The community could not exist without trade, without acquiring certain indispensable goods. It is important to examine the character of these goods. With the exception of salt, all have been acquired by the Jicaques since the Spanish conquest. I suggest that trade has been the most important factor of acculturation since the Conquest. Most of the Spanish or *ladino* material traits of the present-day culture are commodities. The obvious exception being coffee, which is African in origin, transmitted by the *ladinos*. Recall that the Jicaques never were a trading people. Since the Conquest, and probably before, they obtained certain items through trade. However, they were never middlemen or itinerant merchants. And even today, they buy and sell very little among themselves.

The following comments are relevant, though they date from the late 1950s.

Leopoldo
Martínez: Money doesn't please me much here in the mountain [where he lived]. I might take a little, but I do need cloth. We don't make any cloth. I have to treat my friends right [referring to selling the *ladinos* coffee] so they can drink coffee, then God won't punish me.

Alfonso: God doesn't like us to buy maize or cattle. If you want to eat, ask, this is what the mouth if for, to ask. If you want to eat beef, ask for it. It's alright to sell to the *ladinos*, but not among us. If I want something, someone will give it to me.

Cleto Martínez [as if he were talking to another Indian, referring to something already purchased by him from the *ladinos*]:

> Why buy it again, if it's already been bought? If it's already paid for, why pay for it again? I already bought it, so why spend more money? Nothing is paid for among friends.

Coffee, as we have seen, is almost the exclusive trade crop and was first cultivated in the 1930s. The main commodities for which coffee is exchanged are: salt, machetes, firearms, cloth, matches, domestic pottery and sometimes maize. Salt, as mentioned, may have been obtained in trade in prehispanic times; machetes were introduced very early, in the seventeenth or eighteenth century; firearms and cloth date from the nineteenth or early twentieth century; matches, or cigarette lighters, are recent. Just when pottery was first used is not known. This item is doubly important because of its relation to maize and the tortilla. The Tolupans may well have cultivated maize in prehispanic times, but they could not make tortillas without the *comal*, the large plate on which the tortillas are cooked. The *comal* must be made of pottery or tin. I have the impression that both the tortilla and pottery are relatively recent acquisitions. As noted, few Tolupan women make pottery and still prefer to purchase it from the *ladinas*; the "stone" on which the tortillas are ground was selected from the river beds, that is, it is not a true "*metate*," although it serves the same function. Maize, if cultivated in prehispanic times, was probably consumed as a vegetable.

Of all the items mentioned maize is unique in that it is produced by the Indians and sometimes bartered for coffee, or, in times of dire need, given to them through government channels. (chapter II) As we have seen, it was formerly the principal trade crop, and now it is often obtained because the production is insufficient for the consumption requirements. This shift in the trade-subsistence relationship of maize has, I think, its importance. It should be kept in mind that although maize is a subsistence crop, it is, one might say, necessary for a certain prosperity but not essential for survival. Tubers are the buffers against starvation. Coffee and maize are both indispensable in the long run, but weeks or months might pass without coffee being traded or maize consumed. Tubers are the almost everyday requirement though not a trade item. This dependence on tubers reflects, I think, a prehispanic tradition; for despite the many and profound alterations in their indigenous culture, the Tolupans still retain certain basic traits of their aboriginal heritage. As we shall see later, fundamental aspects of the social structure and especially the mythology also had survived. These ancient survivals, together with certain posthispanic elaborations, are the fibers of the present-day culture, such as it is. Once they are snapped or worn away, the uniqueness of the Tolupans, except perhaps for their language, will melt into the rural *ladino* culture.

Today, most are poverty stricken. The first and most of the second generation in the Montaña were more prosperous, in that they produced greater quantities of food, obtained most of their other necessities from nature, and traded sparsely. Today, their poverty is caused not only by the critical sterility of the soil, the lack of sufficient land and the ecological deterioration but also by their dependence on trade, which, as we have seen, is due to the shift from maize to coffee as the exchange commodity. During the early period, from 1866 to the beginning of this century or somewhat later, maize was indispensable, essential for trading and bartering. The low price it brought, coupled with the few items exchanged for it, did not tempt the Indians to vary this pattern. A balance between subsistence and trade economy was maintained. The changeover to coffee upset this balance and, while temporarily mitigating certain difficulties, it created a predicament. Coffee brought a higher price than maize. Most of the Indians now receive a greater amount and variety of goods and cash than was previously the case. But they are not a trading people. They cannot prosper if they continue to increase their dependence on trade to the detriment of subsistence farming. They have neither the know-how, nor sufficient or quality, commodities, nor the motivation — the "Protestant Ethics" — necessary to orient their economy in terms of trade.

The shift from maize to coffee has had dire effects on their standard of living not because it was originally economically unsound but because their culture, their "Weltanschauung," cannot cope with this great dependence on trade. One might assume that a more highly valued trade crop would bring increased prosperity; however, the opposite may well be true. This is not to say that their poverty does not have other economic causes as well. But to understand this cause, we should look more closely to the effects of the shift to coffee and the nature of the commodity.

An obvious point is that maize was both a staple and a trade item, while coffee is not a staple. Maize may be eaten, stored or sold over periods of many months. Coffee must be sold, is consumed in small quantities and stored only for a short while, under conditions in the Montaña. It must be harvested on time and should be sold quickly. Therefore, the nature of the two plants as crops and food affects the conditions under which they are traded. Maize was a bank account, coffee is not. Coffee brings a higher price than maize because it is a luxury food, but it makes the farmer-seller dependent on a dangerous market — dangerous because it fluctuates anonymously and often without warning.

This "price-making-market" situation characterizes most single-cash-crop economies and is inherent in the Tolupan economy. But it is latent because much of the coffee is consumed locally and, therefore, its price is not always affected by the rise and fall of the international market, as is the case, for example, farther to the north in the coffee production regions of the Department of Yoro. The coffee produced by the Tolupans is mostly consumed locally because the Montaña de la Flor is located on the southern limit of the Yoro coffee area and faces plains where very little coffee is cultivated. So it is not so much the "cash crop" aspect of the coffee trade which has impoverished the Indians, as their greater dependence on selling, which in a large part is due to the fact that coffee cannot be made into tortillas. To conclude these remarks, it may be reiterated that although necessary, given the difficulties they confronted, the shift from maize to coffee as the "cash" crop, the crucial dependence on trade which ensued, coupled with a decreased subsistence production, the ecological deterioration of their area and the lack of viable alternatives have increased their poverty.

The second chief of the east moiety, Domingo Martínez, died sometime in the early 1930s, and his brother, Fidelio, also a son of Juan, took office. Fidelio was the best known of all the "Jicaques." His angular build, typical Tolupan long, thin curved nose, and traditional tunic impressed even the most jaded of city folk. Fidelio, who could be aggressive and moody, was uncompromisingly Indian yet accessible to strangers. Accompanied by his companions, he would visit Tegucigalpa from time to time to interview the current president and other high officials, usually concerning the problem of the *ladino* intrusion into their territory. Upon such occasions the "Jicaques," as they were known, would be given presents and interviewed by the press, whose reporters delighted in inciting comments from their exotic countrymen. With their classic Maya-like features, framed by long, black hair, their elegant though rustic tunics and pouches of wild animal skins — puffing at their tiny pipes, they presented an image that could not fail to excite sympathetic curiosity.

During the 1930s and 1940s, the chiefs received occasional visitors from Tegucigalpa: government officials, doctors, journalists, adventurous youths and more rarely a priest or missionary. In late 1938 and early 1939, the explorer- anthropologist, Wolfgang Von Hagen, spent several months living in a hut built for him by the Indians near the *ladino* family with whom I always stayed. It was his monograph that introduced me to the Tolupans of the Montaña de la Flor.

When Fidelio died in 1954, his brother-in-law, Doroteo, though a former member of the opposite moiety, became chief because Fidelio's sons were too young to assume leadership and all of his brothers had died. When Doroteo passed away, one of Fidelio's sons, Cipriano Martínez, was designated as the chief, and office which he still holds. He also lives at the entrance to his moiety with a few other families. Like his father, Cipriano has always been accessible to outsiders and speaks Spanish quite fluently. He is particularly open to contacts with government and private persons who might aid him in safeguarding the possession of the *ejido* lands and in improving the economic, health and sanitary conditions of the families of his section. He has always been extremely attentive, to and involved in, the many problems which his section and the community as a whole have confronted. He was also eager that the youth learn to read and write. These aspirations apparently also motivated him to accept the offers of the missionaries of the Summer Institute of Linguistics.

These missionaries, different families of which have alternated living near or in the east moiety, Cipriano's cluster, since 1960, have enjoyed greater success than their predecessors, mostly Catholics, because they settled among the Tolupans for long periods, learned their language, and offered some medical aid, other services and distractions. At different times, they took several youths to their regional headquarters in Guatemala for intensive linguistic interviewing and courses on the Bible. Moreover, their endeavors were supported by those, like chief Cipriano, who aspired to better their lot by increased contact with the outside world.

Shortly before or after Cipriano became chief, he put aside his *balandrán* and adopted pants and shirt, as has his eldest son, Anastacio. By this time, the 1960s, the east moiety consisted of almost two-thirds of the population, which numbered, in 1972, over 400 people and about 600 at present. At Cipriano's request, the Ministry of Education assigned a teacher to the east moiety in 1987 and another school as been established in the other moiety.

With respect to the west moiety, the second chief Beltrán, son of the founder, Pedro Soto, was succeeded in the 1940s by his son, Leonor, who died about 1962. When Julio Soto, the latter's son, became chief, he moved to the interior of the settlement and the palisade disintegrated. This move was motivated by his desire to avoid contact with the linguistic missionaries and other visitors, although he has maintained friendly relations with some *ladino* neighbors and goes to Orica, the municipal seat, when summoned, as does the other chief, Cipriano Martínez, more willingly.

The cultural conservatism of the community, in so far as it still exists, is and certainly was a function of its geographical and cultural isolation which began when it was founded. Other factors contributed to the retention of the ethnic identity: reluctance or refusal to adopt extraneous religions, eluding strangers and hiding the women and children from them, minimizing contacts with the *ladino* merchants, not caring for money beyond the needs of the present, and refusing to drink alcoholic beverages. The drink, called *guaro*, made from distilled sugarcane, was and is still proffered to them by the neighboring *ladinos*. The Tolupan consider it absurd to be drunk. They deride the *ladinos* for their propensity to get drunk, quarrel, wound and even kill one another with machetes or firearms during drinking bouts. (myth 7) Formerly, the Jicaques, like the great majority of cultivators in Mesoamerica as well as Central America, made a fermented beverage commonly called *chicha*, homemade with either maize or tubers. If *chicha* played the vital role in the rituals among the ancient Jicaques that it does even today among the traditional Lencas of Western Honduras,[26] its prohibition was the most immediate cause for the loss of their rituals. Possibly the Jicaques adopted this prohibition as a result of the missionaries' admonitions. If so, apparently only those of the Montaña de la Flor learned the lesson well, as those of Yoro are reputedly *guaro* consumers, as most of the *campesinos* elsewhere.

As noted above, since 1960 North American evangelical missionaries, graduates of the Summer Institute of Linguistics, have been active in the Montaña. They translated portions of the New Testament into Tolupan, which they call "Tol," and have published several primers as well as a bilingual dictionary.[27] Some converts, particularly young men of the east moiety, were taught the rudiments of reading and writing. By about 1976, the missionary family of Ronald and Margaret Dennis was no longer living in the settlement, although Ronald continued visiting the Montaña from his home in the nearby hamlet of La Joya or more recently from the United States. In La Joya, other North American missionaries have established a clinic and treat the mestizo population, mostly *campesinos* of small towns, from the surrounding area as well as some of the serious cases of illness from the Montaña. Certain of the more apparent effects of this prolonged missionary endeavor in the east moiety became clearly visible during my visit one Sunday in March of 1988. Then I attended the service, in the newly rebuilt "chapel," directed by three of the proselytized youths, including the eldest son of the chief, who read passages of the New Testament in Spanish and Tolupan, sang hymns and preached vigorously. The young men seemed determined to indoctrinate their less enthusiastic peers. When I returned in 1991, this enthusiasm had apparently spent itself and had been reapplied, so to speak, to the Federación de las Tribus de Yoro.

The increased sterility of the soil has resulted in lower productivity year after year. The depletion of the forests, birds and game is due most recently to the cutting of large quantities of trees by private lumber companies.[28] The pollution of the water has evolved into a crucial problem; it is caused, I was told, mainly by human and animal excrement. In 1991, a number of latrines had been built in Cipriano's cluster by the Ministry of Public Health with the aid of the interested parties.

Sickness occupies a great deal of time. The ailing person is often confined many weeks to the hut and when the illness takes a turn for the worse, the patient is often transported in a hammock or on a makeshift stretcher to the clinic, mentioned above, in La Joya, some three to four hours away. Death being so frequent, any illness provokes impassioned apprehension. The common cold, previously called "the plague," is still perhaps the most feared disease and there is full awareness of its contagious nature. Amoebic disorders take the greatest toll of lives, although epidemics of measles are quite frequent and tuberculosis is endemic. Sometimes the latter is treated in Tegucigalpa, in the specialized hospital. But there is a reluctance to transport sick persons there, because many have died in the hospital; the usual reason given is that they are taken there when the disease is too advanced for possible cure with the available facilities. Apparently the traditional cures have been forgotten. The Tolupans employ herbs and undertake empirical treatments recommended and sometimes administered by the neighboring *ladinos*. In so far as I could ascertain, the Tolupans have no theory of the causes of diseases other than contagion from a carrier and that of fetid vapor (*vaho*) from corpses. Now they are more fully aware of the dangers of the various sorts of pollution, lack of hygiene. inadequate diet, and so on. There is obviously an urgent need for routine and efficient medical assistance, adequate housing, clean water and more hygiene.

In 1972, as far as I could discover, there were 14 deaf-mutes in the living population of 409 individuals, including *ladinos*. But this count does not represent the reality because, given the high infant-mortality rate, an unknown number of babies who were so affected died before the parents became aware of the abnormality and recall that my genealogies are not complete, especially for this sector of the population. In any event, an analysis of the total Indian population from 1866 to 1972, including those of one *ladino* parent, gave the number of 968 of which 68 were deaf-mutes, that is 7½ percent, which is a high ratio. This abnormality, clearly present in the second generation, is probably due to the propagation of a recessive gene for deafness carried by one of the seven founders of the colony and the subsequent high degree of inbreeding. The gene pool being extremely small, it is not surprising that a malignant recessive gene soon became dominant, which resulted in this unusual percentage of congenital deafness and hence muteness.

The genealogies also showed a startling mortality rate. Of the total 1,100 individuals registered — five generations and the beginning of the sixth generation — 356 Tolupans by both parents belonged to the fourth generation in 1972. Of these, more than half, 192, had died — the great majority from diseases. Of these 192 deceased, 144 were children and unmarried adults. More accurate figures would show an even more critical situation.

There are also the usual serious complaints about the "invasion" of *ladinos*, who now have even planted coffee groves on land the Tolupans consider rightfully theirs. The chiefs have been requesting for decades — since the time of Fidelio in the 1930s — that the *ejido* measurements be completed and the land usurped by these *ladinos* be returned to them. However, some of the *ladinos*, who settled near the periphery of the Montaña many decades ago, as the López family with whom I lived, maintain friendly relations with Tolupans and are not in any sense considered intruders.

In the opinion of the Indians, all the land suitable for farming is either in use or fallow. They complained of this lack of sufficient land and the many miles they have to walk from their homes to reach some of the fields. The convenience of being close to the fields, especially the coffee groves, has greatly contributed to the dispersal of the population throughout the *ejido*, in small groups of extended or related families, which I termed "clusters." But there has also been, more recently, a movement toward the clusters of the present-day chiefs, especially those of Cipriano in the east moiety, called San Juan and sometimes termed a *pueblo* (town); however, this is a misnomer, as in reality it is only a group of houses now with a large school — adobe with a cement floor — used also as a meeting hall and sleeping quarters for welcomed visitors. Usually when the families are located too far from the milpas or groves, a temporary shelter is built in the fields where the head of the family, his wife or wives and children live for several or more days, while he tends the crops. This dispersal and that of the clusters sometimes makes it impossible for the parents to send their children, especially the girls, to either of the two schools located in the respective chiefs' clusters. An identical situation would prevail, were a clinic to built in one or both sections.

Harsh disputes and antagonisms between members of the moieties have created additional very serious problems. The power ambitions of one or more mestizo Tolupans, the impact of the missionaries — evangelists and other denominations as well — and the "proselytizing" of certain political — usually right-wing — parties or factions from Tegucigalpa further undermine the solidarity of the community and inhibit the possibility of reenforcing their identity as Tolupans in a multi-ethnic nation. This aspiration, if it exists, will hopefully find encouragement in the texts which follow.

The myths, as related by Alfonso Martínez, are extremely vivid and often humorous, as the divinities have human frailties for which they are reprehended and even punished by Tomam the Elder, although he does display leniency. Throughout the mythology, the powerful message of reciprocity is constantly reiterated. It includes all of nature: human beings, the humble maize plant, all animals including snakes, whose master is very wise. All must respect one another because we live in one world. Even the chiefs should work and refuse gifts unless they reciprocate in some way. The moral or ethics of reciprocity, the ideal is that of an egalitarian society, of living as an integral part of nature. The difficulties of living in society which the mythology elicits are, among others, those of hierarchy, of acknowledging or accepting the need for authority. The masters of the animals must be obeyed, as they safeguard the perpetuation of the species they protect, so also the supreme deity and likewise the chiefs in human society. Although authority is where the weight of give and take is balanced, it does generate hostility; it may err but it should always return to its center of gravity. Neither arbitrary nor self-fulfilling, it is personified by Tomam the Elder, also called the "Master of Authority."

The Tolupans often refer to themselves and to humanity in its entirety as "The Children of Death" or simply the Dead (*Muerto*) because of our destiny. In this English edition, I have translated *Muerto* as Mortal, which is justified in so far as the *Muerto* is invariably contrasted to the *Malomsano*, the "Immortal." Although the really dead person becomes immortal, he/she, not being a divinity, is not considered an Immortal. Only the divinities and the other supernatural beings are spoken of as the "Immortals." Once really dead, the person is still called a Mortal (*un Muerto*).

The concept that fetid vapor (*vaho*) of the cadavers of human beings and of animals — including meat under certain circumstances — spreads over the world causing death is a predominant theme in this tradition, so familiarity with the concept is essential for an understanding of these texts. Strangely enough, it is accounted for by a myth (#3) inspired by the Biblical story of the death and resurrection of Christ, Our Lord — the name Jesus Christ never appears in these myths — as told or heard about either from the *ladinos* or perhaps the missionaries of the last century. The fetid vapor emerged from "Our Lord's" corpse. He dies of his own doing and is buried by the Indians, following the advice of some *ladinos*. The Indians do not kill him, but they do stand guard over his tomb to make sure he is really dead and will not emerge again alive. Our Lord revives in the tomb but has to wait ten days before he can emerge. After ten days, the guardians become tired and go home. Our Lord then rises from his grave and escapes but not before leaving the fetid vapor in the pit. When the guardians return, peering in astonishment into the empty pit, they become contaminated with this fetid vapor and all but one die. So it was that death was propagated the world over, condemning humans and animals alike to a mortal existence. The plants are also victims of this fetid vapor which the clouds release in the form of frost. (myth 12) Alfonso once commented, "Frosts are like the blood of dead Indians mixed with the clouds."

The fetid vapor of *ladinos* is said to be more potent than that of the Indians. The most vulnerable are the sick and wounded, pregnant women and children. This is why the latter don't go to funerals and why the women, especially pregnant, are cautioned not to go either and all who do assist should wash and change their clothes afterwards.

Formerly, the Tolupans abandoned the house in which someone had died, as a further protection against the contagion of the *vaho* of the recently deceased. Cleto Martínez told me that the fetid vapor of his wife, who had died a year before, was still under the bed where she had passed away and for this reason he had not slept there since. But even so, the fetid vapor had caused the cold which he then had. And again an old lady, Juana Soto, was said to have died from the fetid vapor of her son, with whom she lived, who had died just a week previously.

Animals such as peccaries, cattle and even monkeys have strong fetid vapor. If an animal which is killed bleeds a great deal, it is believed to have dangerous fetid vapor — even so, it would be eaten. However, the death of one of the chiefs, Doroteo, was attributed to the fetid vapor of a bull whose meat he had eaten the day before he died. One of his relatives commented to me, "He only ate a small piece of the meat but even so it killed him. He died just like the bull, vomiting blood from his mouth and nose."

The reader will notice beginning in chapter III that I make the distinction between "myths" and "narrations." The former compose the tradition as it has been transmitted and modified from generation to generation, while the "narrations" are mostly Alfonso's existential experiences of this tradition, his interpretation of the tradition in his imagination and daily life. They refer to real people, Alfonso and others, or to actual events or describe a supernatural situation which lacks action.

If one were to ask just when these myths were told in the community, I refer to Alfonso, when he comments on inquiring of his father to tell him "stories" and obtains the following response, "Buy yourself an axe, a machete, this much more I can tell you. This is your story..." But finally, he did tell some stories, mixed in with advice. (chapter II) Given the loss of rituals and ceremonies, there would be no specific context in which the myths might be told or recited. The older people probably appealed to Tomam, the masters of the animals and other divinities and told these "stories" whenever a circumstance arose which brought them to mind. They probably told them in response to the questions and doubts of the children, seeking to understand how the living world was created, why people, even babies, die, what happens after death, why the *ladinos* get drunk so often, and so on.

To what extent the tradition may evoke a response in the young generation was illustrated a few years ago by students of the National University of Honduras who are presently involved in linguistic and ethnographic studies in the Montaña de la Flor. One Sunday, while the Summer Institute of Linguistics missionary was giving a sermon to a group gathered in the "chapel" of the east moiety, the students outside began reading excerpts from the Spanish edition of this book to a number of young Tolupans.[29] Their reactions were enthusiastic and that day, or the following Sunday, the students enacted some of the myths dressed in *balandranes*, the native tunics. These texts lend themselves to theatrical presentations, especially those written in the form of scenes, dialogues or monologues, as Alfonso related them to me. I was told that the young people laughed a great deal and seemed interested and involved. This does not mean that the oral tradition will survive and be reinterpreted — but it might be, especially now that a number of young Tolupans have learned to read and write. If it does take place it might well have a positive affect, encouraging greater solidarity in their community and pride in their heritage. But it cannot make a decisive contribution to day-to-day living unless this same theatrical technique also dramatizes actual problems. If so, the young people, themselves, could provoke discussions, stimulating cooperation among the families — especially between the two now antagonistic moieties — and with their *ladino* neighbors. Thus, the young people might also inspire their chiefs, alert the local and federal governments and concern the public at large with the urgent necessity for more efficient economic assistance and medical services, in return for a more viable, productive and creative Tolupan community.

NOTES

1. Adams 1957: 629. See also Von Hagen (1943: 32) quoting Squier (1958) calculates the total number of Jicaques about 1850 as approximately 6,000.
2. Jiménez Moreno 1978. With reference to the Pipiles, same author 1959.
3. The reference for the prehispanic and early periods is my Ph.D. dissertation (Chapman 1958), where numerous sources are cited, which unfortunately has not been published but is available on microfilm at Columbia University, New York. More available are Conzemius 1921–23, 1927, 1932; Kirchhoff 1948; Jiménez Moreno 1978. For a recent excellent study on the decline of the Indian population in Honduras as a result of the Spanish Conquest and its aftermath, see Newson 1986.
4. Chapman 1957.

5. Bright (1956), Greenberg and Swadesh (1953), classify "Jicaque" as Hokan. Lehmann (Vol. II: 641) and Squier (1858) considered it to be a Chibchan language; Sapir (1914) a Penutia language and Johnson (1948) and Rivet *et al.* (1952) described it as isolated or independent.
6. Oltrogge 1975.
7. Campell 1978.
8. Greenberg personal communication.
9. Chapman 1957, 1958, 1978a, 1985, 1986.
10. Juarros 1936, vol. I: 34
11. Anguiano 1946:128.
12. Annoyava 1813.
13. Conzemius 1921–23: 164.
14. Chapman 1958; Conzemius 1921–23; Lehmann vol. II, 1920; Squier 1855, 1858; Stone 1957 and Von Hagen 1943.
15. Chapman 1962 (article in French); 1971 (in Spanish).
16. See also Chapman 1961 (in French); 1971 (in Spanish).
17. Gaceta Oficial de Honduras en Centroamérica 1865; Davidson 1984; Vallejo 1893: 88–89.
18. In the original Spanish as follows:
   La Santa Misión a los jicaques los conquistó.
   Con cariño y amor los bautizó.
   La Santa Misión a los jicaques los conquistó.
   Y su entrada en el cielo no se astrasó.
   La Santa Misión a los jicaques los conquistó.
   Mas de diez años no necesitó.
   La Santa Misión a los jicaques los conquistó.
   Y poca después Dios a su paraiso lo llamó.
19. Data from the author as mentioned in the text; also several numbers of the Gaceta Oficial de Honduras en Centroamérica; Vallejo 1893 and Von Hagen 1943: 36.
20. Chávez Borjas 1984; Tojeira 1982.
21. In more recent times, the Tolupans planted many kinds of fruit-bearing trees, among them: papaya, aguacate, zapote, guava, *anon, guamo, manzanillo, matasano,* and nut- and date-producing palm trees.
22. Long after bark was replaced by cotton for the tunics, it continued to be used in the construction of the huts, to tie the beans together, and to cushion the heavy jars or gourds full of water the women carried on their heads. Bark was also used as chest bands for securing the burdens the men carried on their backs and as belts for the tunics.
23. Pozol is made from the corn mass, to which water and sometimes unrefined sugar are added, while *pinol* is prepared for roasted corn grains, ground and mixed with water.
24. The poorer *ladinos,* who cannot afford a casket, take their deceased to their cemetery in a similar fashion.
25. *Título del Terreno "Montaña de la Flor"* 1929.
26. Chapman 1985, 1986.
27. Dennis, R., and M. Royce de Dennis 1980a, 1980b, 1983.
28. See Cruz Sandoval 1984.
29. Chapman 1984.

CHAPTER II

ALFONSO MARTINEZ, HIMSELF

"Jicaques" the *ladinos* say but we are Tolupans. We call the *ladinos* "mak." They belong to one nation and we to another, like the English, the gringos [North Americans, USA], the Spaniards, the *ladinos*, the Indians; animals, too, have their nations, the tigers, monkeys, deer, snakes, cows, buzzards, the Devils, too. Nompwinapu'u made all the nations. (myth 1) The Indians of Aninkenen are the First Nation.

CHILDHOOD

Before I got a name, my mami just called me *natam chiquai* ["youngest son"] or "hey, little boy, come here," or "go bring me some water," or "go fetch some firewood."

My cousin, Ricardo, gave me a name. He said, "Without a name, you can't claim to be an Indian." I don't know how old I was then, about six I think. The old people didn't give it to me, the late Ricardo did. I don't know why. Because maybe he just thought of it. I've never changed it. I've always kept the same old name. Ricardo said, "There are no Alfonsos here. We'll name you Alfonso, for Alfonso Sanchez. He'll be your namesake."[1]

Alfonso Sanchez is a *ladino*. He didn't care. Later, I heard he raped one of our women and then another. There were witnesses. He went to jail but not for long. It's not with me, it's with the women that he turned out to be a rascal. He never acted badly with me. Whenever he came here he always gave me something. Later, when I was older, he bought maize and coffee from me — no bad words.

When I was very little, I wore the long shirt the mamas put on us. When you don't like the shirt anymore, you have to ask for a *balandrán*.[2] I, myself, asked for one and right then I started to wear it. I remember when I asked for it.

We brothers and sisters would roll around, playing all the time. I was a regular axe, tearing up my *balandrán*. We'd pull each other and fall all over, rolling around. We'd always be tearing our clothes. Once my mama said, "Why are you always tearing your *balandrán*? The *balandrán* is not to be torn but to be taken care of."

She'd take it off me when it got torn and sew it up again. But all the time, I was climbing everything, rolling over and over on the ground, tugging on the *balandrán* with my brothers and sisters. Then once, when she sewed it up again, she said, "This time I'll forgive but not the next. The next time, you'll get a bit of a spanking."

Then, I knew, I'd better watch out. I didn't tear it after that, as she warned me. She hardly ever spanked me. Scold, yes, every minute she'd scold me. But spank, not much.

When I began to stand up and my teeth started coming out, she tied a little gourd around my neck for me to suck on, to dry out my mouth. When you begin to stand up, it's not good to lose too much saliva. Sometimes you die if you lose a lot.

Some babies start eating at ten months. The boys are the slowest. Sometimes it's two years before they eat much. If a baby gets sick with a lot of tapeworms, it'll get skinny and then get a cold; so then it's given something to eat and, right away, it gets fat. The *ladinos* are healthier than we. They begin eating at nine months.

When the mother is big in the stomach again, she must wean the last one. When the next is already formed in the stomach, the last one is likely to get sick or have an accident, especially if it's a boy. The milk gets dirty when another is already formed. Then the milk is no good. The baby should be taken to another house to be weaned, sometimes for a month. It should be given something to eat, little by little, and often: tortillas, coffee and tamales, if there are any. After a year, it can eat anything: pozol [drink made with roasted and ground maize], camotes, yucca and bananas, when there are some, little birds, animals, everything. Pacas should not be given to a baby, when it's still nursing, or coati [similar to the raccoon]. Monkey meat is bad too [for babies]. It has a lot of *vaho* [fetid vapor].

Once I lost a pocketknife, a long time ago. It cost me twelve reales [1.50 US$].[3] I got really mad. I said to myself:

> I'm really angry with myself because I don't know where I lost it. I know I climbed that orange tree and ate some oranges and when I had my fill I came home.

At home my mama said to me:

> Lend me your knife to cut the tamales, to slice them, to heat them over the fire.

Then when I looked for it, I couldn't find it.

Mama: Where did you lose it? You just bought it yesterday or the day before.

I said: So now you're going to scold me! I bought it with my own money, not with our sweat, with my own sweat.

Later she said, "Go fetch me some oranges." I went to get them but instead I found my knife where I had climbed the tree, where I had been eating the oranges.

Mama: Did you find it?

I said: I did. I found it by going on the errand for you.

Mama: You're really lucky to have found it on my errand. You turned out to be a great loser of things.

I said: If so it's because you nursed me too long. I got this way from too much dirty milk; so if I lose things, it's your fault, not mine. When you weaned me you should have sent me to another house. It's your fault that I drank so much dirty milk.

She was quiet for awhile. Then she said, "What if you do lose a lot of things — if that's the way you want to be."

Once my mami put a switch to me. She whipped me for making arrows. So the next day I didn't make anymore. Why do it? I already knew my mama was delicate about this. She didn't whip me much, just a little.

When I was fighting, fooling around with my brothers and sisters, she would shout:

> I'm getting after the older ones (that meant Margarita [his oldest sister] and me). The older children should teach the younger ones to behave.

She never spanked the others. She only scolded them with her tongue. When she wanted to spank me I'd run and hide in the bush and wait until my papi passed and come home with him. Then he would say:

> Why whip your children? You must have patience, a good temper to dominate them. In the presence of God, you cannot strike your children.

Then Julia, my mami, would get a bit angry. As I was ordered about by the father and Margarita by the mama, she got more whippings than I. Besides I'd run away.

Why should I spank my children? My papa, Mateo, never whipped me, nor my mama, hardly ever. Mateo raised me very properly, with patience and good temper. He taught me to work. He was very nice. He never hit his children, never spoke badly to them. He only taught me good things, never to fight. He'd say:

> You must respect women, men and the little ones. Treat them all as brothers, never fight.

When my mami spoke badly to me, Mateo scolded her:

> When the children are naughty do not hit them. Teach them patiently, God will give you strength so that you can domesticate them. The Law of God [Tomam:chapter IV] is watching.

This is how my papa advised me. I don't hit my children either. I've seen fathers who are delicate in this way, mamas who are even more delicate. My wife, Todivia, is the same as I, so was Beltrán, her father. He only scolded with his tongue.

After me, a little woman was born. She died when she was two, just when the next was born. They say she ate *lo wa' eha*, a poisonous weed. She went to the creek alone and found it there and ate some of the leaves. Kids are full of mischief. She was always playing around in the bush and in the yard. We already had our maize in the granary but when she died we moved back into the mountains [where they had just harvested the maize]. We figured it was an unhealthy place as she had died from the poisonous weed. She didn't last at all, only three or four days. She was already eating it when she came back into the yard. We went to look where she had eaten it and that's how we knew.

This weed is a remedy for snakes. They eat it and then bite a horse and that's the end of the horse. The Master of the Snakes gave it to them. When he first put the Nation of Snakes on Earth they would bite a deer but it wouldn't die. So the Master asked Tata Dios for this poisonous weed. [myth 32]

The old people would say:

> It should not be overdone. You should not learn too much. The more stories you learn the sooner you'll die. Why go around contradicting God [Tomam]? When you learn to count the months, you condemn yourself. You die all the sooner when you know how to count.

Mateo taught me a little but he would say:

> You only want to work for me for stories, not to work for eating. I'm going to teach you how to grow maize, build fences. These are the stories you must learn, to work, to eat. This is your story. The stories about Tomam should not be told too often.

Anyway, he told me a few: about Nuestro Señor ["Our Lord"], about Nomwinapu'u [the son of Tomam the Elder] and Tata Dios ["God Our Little Father"], so that I live with a clean heart. He would say:

> The cattle and the horses belong to Tata Dios. They must be respected. You must fence in your crops in order to live as little brothers with the cattle. You must work with your fellows so that we all live as little brothers with the cattle, the horses, the gringos, the *ladinos*, so that all go smoothly. Neither the *ladinos* will harm you, nor the Indians, nor the gringos if you live as an honorable man. Then you will have no trouble at all. You should never touch [make love to] a woman just because you want to. Touch her just because you like her? No. You must ask first. If she is willing, then you can touch her. You should never speak bad words against the women. This is what I can tell you. Buy yourself an axe, a machete, this much more I can tell you. This is your story, your right — to work, to eat; clean the fields, build fences, plant maize. You don't have to learn anything else.

Anyway, papa would always tell me some stories but I didn't learn much from him. "I don't like stories much," he would say. "You should not learn against God — Tomam. It is not permitted." I wanted to learn a lot but it is not permitted. The old man [his father] was against it. He did tell me a

little when I as a kid [*cipote*] about Our Lord, Saino Jamayón — the
Master of the Peccary [white-lipped peccary] and about Aninkenen. This
much he did tell me. I'd say, "Papa tell me another story." He'd say, "No.
Well, I'll tell you just a little one." I'd ask, "Where does this Señor live, the
Master of the Peccary?" He'd tell me, "In Aninkenen, under the Earth, in a
mountain — in a far-away hill." While we'd be working, planting tobacco
or clearing a field, Mateo would say:

> What's in it for you, if I do tell you a story? When you plant
> tobacco, you'll have a fine smoke. When you build a fence
> around the milpa, you accomplish a lot for your food: beans,
> maize, squash. But a story? It won't teach you. It won't be
> of any use to you. How to tend the milpa, sharpen a machete
> — these are the stories that are good to eat, the others no.

When I was a little boy, Julián Velázquez [chapter VII] was not in the least
unwilling to tell stories. The truth is, that's all he did when he came here to
visit. But now the *ladinos* say that the Indians don't know any stories. The
old people used to tell the *ladinos* stories but no more. Mateo only told
stories in our language, never to the *ladinos*.

We'd go out together, I and Mateo, to hunt monkeys, with Feli [Fidelio],
Matías, Terrencio [Alfonso's uncles] to the place of the monkeys. Sometimes we'd be gone two days, until we found some. Sometimes we'd find
them the same day. When we had killed enough, we'd come back. Sometimes we'd stay in the mountains, roast the monkey, eat it there and keep
on hunting. When we'd bring some back, we'd have them boiled at home.
When we'd stay overnight, we'd build a shelter of palm leaves to sleep in.
Once in awhile, women would come along to gather snails. Then if we
found a monkey and shot it we'd eat it, if not we'd eat snails.

Once when I was a kid, we went hunting deer and the men hollered at
me:

> If you don't want to get into those brambles, get where it's
> clear, where the deer will pass. We'll put Alfonso in the
> center and the old men will take care of the sides.

Then, sure enough, the deer came out where I was. I killed it with an old
shotgun, first shot. Feli said to me:

> The youths are shooting well these days. I don't know why.
> You can't kill a deer just any old way. You have to learn
> first, to practice on the tree.

I said, "I'd rather practice on the deer. Trees aren't food." He got sort of
mad. That same day, I killed two. But when I didn't kill, another would.

When I didn't have any, they'd invite me to [have] some of theirs. When they didn't kill and I did, I'd give some to them. I used to buy gunpowder at fifty cents the ounce.

I killed a tapir with a twenty-two when I was just a kid. I haven't killed hardly any since. I was all alone going down to Pancho's [Alfonso's brother] house when I saw one in the bushes. I yelled to Pancho and immediately he lent me his shotgun. I shot and killed it and gave him half. I sold the hide for fifty cents, seventy-five cents, I don't remember how much. Lauriano Echevarría [a *ladino* neighbor] bought it. Tapir meat is darker than other meats. It has more of a stink, too. Another time I killed another. It was the month of June, during the waning moon. It came to the edge of a bush, near the house. When the moon is full, they stay inside the forest. Full moon — they don't like to move. Waning moon — they'd come close to the houses but only the tapirs.

Peccary [white-lipped species] can be killed in February, not just any time. They eat snails along the creeks, palm nuts, too. Sometimes there are 200 in a herd, at least 100. I killed two the first time when I was a kid.

I was just a kid when I first went to Leopoldo's, to Tamagazapan,[4] to eat squash. I went without telling my papi. Then I thought, "He will scold me." So when I passed my uncle Terrencio's house, I asked him to tell the old man so that he would know that I was visiting my cousin and not out just for fun. He said, "Don't worry, I'll tell him so that he won't act silly waiting for you." When I came home, he didn't scold me. As I was domestic,[5] I shouldn't have left home without saying goodbye to my parents. I did. But I was looking for something to eat. I stayed at Leopoldo's for a day and a night. When I left he said, "You cannot leave without having another meal." I ate tortillas, *elotes* [young ears of corn], squash. Then he said, "The maize is very tender in the milpa. Take some to eat when you get home." He gave me ten hands of hard-grain maize, two hands of *elotes* and two squashes.

When Uncle Domingo [Leopoldo's father] was alive, I visited them often, but that was a long time ago. This man, Leopoldo, is pure affection. When there is no maize, he gives away *arum* [an edible root], yucca, camotes. This man isn't miserly. When there are no bananas, he'll offer maize. He's affectionate with everybody, *ladinos* and Indians. I have no complaint against this man. To everybody who comes to his house, he offers something. If today he kills a deer, a peccary, a monkey, he'll give away some of it. Cleto is the same. I can't complain about him either. When I go to his house looking for a few ears of maize, he'll give me coffee and camotes, too. Doroteo [former chief of the east moiety] was the same, like Cleto, like Leopoldo. They'd always give whatever they had. Leonor [former chief of the west moiety] is the same.

COURTING

Only once did Leopoldo treat me badly. He said, "Do you have a woman?" I said I did. Then he said, "If you have, come to my house, if you already have. Come and I'll give you a shawl for her." But when I went, he backed down. He didn't give me any shawl. He deceived me. He didn't give it to me, sold or as a gift. He only gave me a lie. Then I said:

> The word of a man is worth more than money. Money can be paid back a little at a time, slowly. The word of a man has to be kept, once and for all.

He got offended. We got offended. I was young then. He was about twenty-five and I about twelve. I wanted the shawl to make a present to a woman, any woman I could find. I wanted to go courting and this is why I said to myself, "I'll get the shawl and then I'll go courting."

I tried to court Maria but I didn't get far. She told me she already belonged to someone else. She said, "Aren't you related to Mateito?" I said, "I will respect my Uncle Mateito. I won't do him a bad turn." By then Maria had already given Mateito hope, so I told her, "I will look elsewhere." The next day my Uncle Mateito told me, "I have the word from Maria."

The *ladinos* say that it's forbidden to marry cousins. The old people didn't say this. They only said not to marry in the family. They said you must look further than the family but you cannot touch other nations — *ladinos*, gringos, dogs, cattle, deer — as each nation prohibits it by law. Who can you marry then? How not to get into trouble? My sisters are for others. I'm not allowed to touch them. I must choose from only one nation, ours. So I went to the other side [the west moiety] to do my courting. There the family is a bit more distant. Julia and Mateo [his parents] advised me. Mateo said, "Go to the other side but not with the *ladinos*. On the other side, the family is not so close." The families of the late Domingo, Feli and Mateito[6] are very close. The daughters of Abrán are second cousins. This is why I did not touch them either. I took the advice of the *ladinos* and the Indians. Mateo said, "First cousins you must not touch. Second cousins you may." The *ladinos* say, "First cousins cost 100 even 150 pesos."[7] How can a poor fellow like me pay this? Mateo said to me:

> You should not look up the deaf-mute girls. If you do you'll have deaf-mute children. Treat them as sisters. Respect them. Don't speak badly of them. If you do, you will have a deaf-mute child. This is God's [Tomam] doing. Even if a person is deaf-mute, you must respect him [or her]. If you like a deaf-mute girl, say so today. If you marry one, it will

be for your whole life. That's up to you. If you like a *ladina*, the same. You have to choose. But don't be confident with the *ladinos*. You will have more confidence with an Indian woman. You might come to like a *ladina* or a deaf-mute. This is why I am giving you this advice. If a woman gets offended with you, don't insist, don't go back and look for her.

That's the way it was with Margarita [his sister who married a deaf-mute]. She only had a few deaf-mute children. She has one alive. She had a little woman deaf-mute who died. She has a baby now nursing. We don't know if it is a deaf-mute or not. If she doesn't behave, it might turn out to be one.

Leopoldo used to do all his courting in the bush. Once he said to me:

> Women are very sloppy. Babies are always crying, defecating, urinating. Babies are very sloppy, too.

That's why he didn't want to marry. That's why he got old first. He got married old. He didn't want a woman in his house, only in the bush. He lived with his sister, Elena, and his brother-in-law, Eustacio. His brother, Ramón, was very foolish too. He said the same:

> Women are very sloppy. How can I ever get married? They get everything dirty. They're very sloppy.

Then I would tell him:

> I, myself, would never be without a family, without a woman. You have to choose. Babies are always sloppy, *ladino* babies and Indian babies.

Ramón talked like a fool for years. He used to say, "Indian women are very sloppy. The *ladinas* are better." He talked like a fool and did his courting in the bush. But he liked Rafaela. She's Indian.[8] He hung around her house, hoping to get her out in the bush. That was all he wanted. He liked her but he didn't want to get married. Before she married Cipriano, he used to sneak around her house, spying on her. One day I met him on the trail.

Ramón:	Now I've found the way.
I said:	You're lost. You haven't got a chance.
Ramón:	I had a chance but Cipriano took her away from me. I'll get him yet.
I said:	If you want trouble, that's the way to do it.
Ramón:	You're right. I'll go eat some mangos.
I said:	Where are you going to get them?
Ramón:	I'll go to the late Domingo's house, take a look at his trees.

Finally he married a *ladina*. He changed to *ladino* clothes and went to live below on the plains with a *ladino* family. He married a *ladina* and that finished him off. He went crazy. He only lasted a year down there. No good can come of living with *ladinos*. For a long time, he wouldn't marry at all, Indian or *ladina*, only in the bush. Finally, he married a *ladina* and that was the end.

The three brothers were all alike. The other, Damacio, was the same. He walked alone, just like Ramón and Leopoldo. Once

He said:	I'm going down below on the plains to live with the *ladinos*.
I said:	It's up to you. As for me, I want to die in my *balandrán*. I'll stay Indian, just the way my father lived — Indian. I'm not going over.

Damacio got a little mad when I said that. Then

I said:	You've already gone over some.
Damacio:	As the Indians don't like me any more, I'm going to live with the *ladinos*.
I said:	If you go, it'll be because you want to, because you're a fool.

The truth was that Damacio didn't want to get married. He only wanted women in the bush. He was talking to hear himself talk. He finally did get sort of married.

When Leopoldo asked me for advice,

I said:	Leopoldo, I can't give you advice. You work with your hands. You have work. You have food. But who will cook for you? I would never be without a woman.
He said:	Elena [his sister] cooks for me, tamales and everything. But if I find a woman, I think I will take her. When I get married, I'll let you know.

Leopoldo is a hard worker. Once, he had 300 pesos. I said to him, "What good is all your work and your riches?" He finally did get married.

The old people warned me about women who don't take care of themselves, when they're big in the stomach, who keep running round just for the fun of it. I wouldn't commit myself to just any woman. I did choose. I chose my wife. It makes no difference if she is young or old but if the little angels [children] die, that's something else. If they die, they go tell lies to Jefe Segundo [Tomam the Younger].

I fled from women like a shy deer for a long time. I was about twenty-five before I had the courage to say hello to a woman. About that time, one day, Juana, wife of Pancho, stopped me on the trail.

Juana:	Why did you run from me the other day?
I said:	I didn't see you. I must have had something on my mind.
Juana:	I don't believe you.
I said:	Have it your way. If I take your word for it, I'll contradict myself.
Juana:	The truth is that you were fleeing from me.
I said:	I'm not ashamed about it. I've fled from you twice already.
Juana:	That's alright. I'm not offended.
I said:	Why be offended? There's no reason at all.

The truth is that I was scared. I was afraid of women.

I said:	You have a couple of daughters. Be my mother-in-law.
Juana:	Now you tell me! How are you going to be my son-in-law if you run away all the time. Besides, you shouldn't be looking for a mother-in-law. That will come later. I don't believe you anyway.
I said:	Get mad then. That's alright. The truth is the truth.
Juana:	Go ask my daughters. See if one will have you.

I did that the next day but neither would have me. A few days later, I ran into Juana again.

Juana:	Well?
I said:	They won't have me.
Juana:	Then try again.

I figured then that I wouldn't look anymore. What good did it do? I thought neither of these girls would do as a wife. I asked them just out of curiosity. I was just wondering how long they would live. The *prueba*[9] told me that both will die young.

I was courting a couple of women at the same time but they didn't pay much attention to me. First, one of Abrán's daughters, Prespinde, but she still wanted to stay with her parents.

I said:	I won't take you by force. Only if you're willing.
Prespinde:	I can't give you any hope.

I stayed over at Abrán's house three days, when I was courting her, but she wouldn't have me. Later, she joined up with Pantaleón. I went there courting three times. The last time, another of the daughters, Prestación, said to me:

> I'm going to say good-bye to you nice. I can't throw you out.

That's how she said good-bye.

I said: You've given me no hope. Now I am mad. I won't come
                 back.

Sometimes, when I went to Abrán's, I'd come home the same day. Sometimes, Abrán would ask me to go shoot deer with him or gather honey.
Once, the two sisters, Prespinde and Prestación, said to me:

> You're only interested in old women. You're not interested
> in girls.

I got offended and

I said: Now you've cursed me, but I'll still give you both a little
                 advice.
Prestación: It's alright that you're offended. This means the truth is
                 known.

Then she told me she was giving favors to Juan, that she gave him hope.

I said: Now I'll tell you the truth — your choice is bad. Juan will
                 take his love away. Juan is going to die young. You'd marry
                 someone else, if you knew what was good for you.
Prestación: Then, I'll live with Daniel [Juan's brother] instead.
I said: You'll come out of that badly, too. You'll still be left a
                 widow. You'll be even worse off. Daniel will die even
                 sooner than Juan.

Anyhow, she joined up with Daniel. Then she quieted down. Daniel died
very young. Alfonso does not lie. After that, she joined Alejandro. She
asked me about Alejandro after Daniel died.

I said: That's fine. You have to keep yourself up. How can a
                 woman stay alone? What would she work for? Then, when I
                 come to your door, you'll greet me well? You won't be
                 malicious?

I was at Alejandro's a few days ago and she greeted me well.

MARRIAGE

The time I first saw Todivia [his only wife] she was in the hills cutting
down *suyate* leaves [a palm] to make a broom. She asked me if it was
alright to cut it there. I told her that the *suyate* is for everyone, that there is
permission to cut it down. While I was saying this, I was thinking, "Where
is this woman from? She must be from the other side."

    When I was thinking about looking for a woman, I built myself a house
near Don Mateo's [his father]. It took more than a month to finish.

Everyone said then, "It's no secret why Alfonso is building a house. He must be courting someone." The *ladinos* said, "Alfonso is already happy. You can bet he's not building a house for the fun of it."

The next time Todivia passed by, on her way back to the mountain where she lived, I joked with her.

I said:	Sell me those squash you are carrying. Money doesn't weigh anything.
Todivia:	I can't. They don't belong to me.
I said:	Quite right. You shouldn't sell what belongs to someone else. Take care, don't fall.

Todivia lived with Domingo and his mother, a *ladina* [Sabina]. Todivia already had two kids with Domingo when I met her but he liked the *ladinas*. Once I had a talk with him about women.

Domingo:	Indian women are great wanderers. They don't stay put. *Ladino* women are more generous.

I was listening quietly. I didn't say anything. Then

I said:	If something is on your mind, speak out.
Domingo:	Indian women are always going from one man to another.
I said:	That's well and fine but we have to choose where we want to die. We might die any day. Don't be too hard on the restless women.
Domingo:	I will think over what you have said. I will store your thought away. One can listen to what is bad but good advice should be well received.

I saw him again, another day at Feli's house.

Domingo:	You gave me some advice. I'm not complaining. I feel fine. I will take your word, Alfonso, whether you speak the truth or whether you tell a lie.
I said:	Don't think about women all the time. You have to work to eat, to kill a deer. When you go to work don't think about women. When you come home, that's the time.
Domingo:	That's a good piece of advice.

Then I asked him what ailed him. He said he had pains all through his body.

I said:	Don't worry about that. They're caused by tapeworms. You'll never die of that. It's a local sickness, an old one. But you may die of foreign diseases. If you take care of yourself, you'll be alright.

Domingo: You're right. Once I got very sick from worms but I didn't die, just like you say. We'll talk again another day.

I said: Beware of your left hand. You can only be sure of the right one.

Domingo: I won't forget that. It's enough to want to eat deer to find only a snake.

The next time Todivia passed my house, I joked with her again.

I said: Why don't you get married. You're always carrying food: bags of maize, squash. You're really silly. Why don't you marry? Then you'll have a home and your man will bring food home to you.

Todivia: I don't think of that right now but a little later I may take your advice. I will come again, on the fourth of January, and maybe we can reach an agreement. Right now I can't leave Sabina, with Domingo sick. But when he gets well, I'll return.

After that, I was laid up with a snakebite so I didn't go out. The next time she came by.

Todivia: You shouldn't be courting when you've just been bitten by a snake. You must respect the women who pass by. It might harm you when they look at you [A belief held by the Indians and *ladinos* alike].

I said: Why are you so haughty? You don't have to stop to talk. You can go on your way.

Todivia: I'm not haughty! I just don't know you very well. I'm afraid.

I said: Stop for a minute.

I asked her if Domingo was better. She said that he was up and had already brought Sebastiana [a *ladina*] to the house and that she herself had separated from him and that he might bring in still another woman.

I said: It's up to you. If you want to separate you can. But don't get into a fight. You will only suffer with Domingo. It's not good to take up with *ladino* women. It's dangerous. It can easily mean death.

Todivia: I know a little. I've been around.

I said: I know a little, too, about *ladinos* and Indians. Only God can give advice. You must try to live as well as you can. It's better to stay with the Indians. Anything might happen with the *ladinos*. You should never get too close to them.

The fourth of January Todivia returned.

She said: It's not possible because of Sabina.

I said I understood.

Todivia: Now I'm going down to the other house to feed the chickens. The next time I come by, I will bring some clothes.
I said: Whenever you come I will be here. I don't always stay at home but I will now.

She didn't come back for a month and a week. Then, when she came, I was cured of the snakebite. Then she gave me hope to live with her. She said she would make my tortillas, pozol, *pinol* and coffee.

Todivia: I agree. I will fix the meals when there is something to fix.
I said: If we have enough to eat, we may not die right away.
Todivia: I have my little son with me.[10] If you don't want to raise him, you'd better tell me now.
I said: Don't worry. I can take care of him too. If there's enough to eat, I can raise him. When he is grown, he can decide where he wants to live.

This is the way it was. A month and three days later, Todivia came by again.

Todivia: I have come to ask if you have found another woman.
I said: I am still here alone.

That time she stayed. She brought her son, Santos, then ten years old. Todivia is still with me.

Domingo's mother, Sabina, was looking for a fight. She didn't want to give up Todivia. Feli [Fidelio, then chief of Alfonso's moiety] said to me:

> Stay here in my house, four or five days. We'll see if she wants to fight more. I called Pancho [Sabina's Tolupan husband] and Sabina to come down here. They didn't come, neither did Domingo or Vacho [Domingo's brother]. They don't have face. They come here and complain and then don't come to do their duty. I'm not looking for a quarrel with my nephew [Alfonso], as Todivia is with you because she wants to be. She can be in any house she wants.

Mateo, Juan José, Abrán, Ricardo, and Panchito [all Alfonso's kin of the east moiety] were my witnesses.

I said: If they [Sabina and family] are looking to argue, here I am. We want to get married. We'll get married.[11]

When a man gets married, he brings things for the house, for the kitchen. All the parents [of both spouses] give chickens, turkeys, things for the kitchen. They have to, as the pair is just beginning to live together. The man has to give animals of the forest to his in-laws — a lot, all at once, or patiently during two or three years. But when he likes his in-laws, he keeps taking them things until they die. Beltrán got a little mad when Todivia came with me but as the daughters are for others, not for the fathers, he conformed. What else could he do? First I gave him a little bit of cloth to make a *balandrán*. He wouldn't accept it right off. Then I gave him some deer meat, boiled and roasted monkeys. He asked me:

> Bring me some monkeys, armadillos, peccaries, deer. As I am plenty old, I can't hunt much. As for clothes, maize, I have enough. I only need meat. I want to eat animals of the forest. I won't charge you with anything else.

I would take him such things, when I had any. I'd send it with his daughter, Todivia. I worked for him, too, when he asked me.

Nowadays, so long as a man has a coffee grove, maize and bananas the woman is satisfied. The women don't want to marry a loafer. So long as he is a worker, it doesn't matter if he is poor. It doesn't matter if the cacique gets angry, so long as he is a worker. They want to eat. This is the way the women talk. The boys ask my advice, as I am old.

They say: Tell us. You know how it is to live, to work, to eat.
I say: You must notify the caciques. You have to let them know. You can't have a wife in hiding.

I asked the *prueba* of the knee and the *prueba* of the hills [chapter VII] before I decided on Todivia. If she hadn't wanted more children, I would have left her alone. If I didn't still like her, I'd leave her for another.

Todivia and I had already settled down when Fidelio sent for me, as he was my cacique, to come to his house for a few days. We went down, all the families went: my cousins, uncles and aunts, just about everyone, though some did not. Todivia's family went, too, except her mother who couldn't walk. We stayed there three days in Fidelio's house and visited Doroteo and Matías nearby. A pig was killed and we ate it roasted and fried, besides a turkey, chickens, eggs, tamales. I was given some things but I don't remember what. Todivia got some baby chicks and turkeys, gourds, a *comal*, jars, a lot of things like that.

Everyone gave me advice, my father-in-law too, but I don't remember what, as it was a long time ago [about 1935]. We fooled around a lot, uncles and cousins. Sometimes three or four men wrestled[12] and the rest stood around and watched. After awhile of wrestling, the chief would say,

"That's enough. Don't fight anymore." Sometimes we played with sticks about as long as an arm. Four or six men tried to hit the sticks out of the hands of those of the other team. Mine never got hit. No one got hurt, or just a little. When we got tired we left it. We like wrestling better. The chief watched but never joined in. He watched to make sure that no one lost his temper or was taking out a grudge, that there be no malice. Everyone has fun when no one gets mad in a fight. The chief said, "Even if you don't want to, you have to wrestle." You had to wrestle or run away. The women stood around watching. Sometimes Abrán played the guitar. Rosendo played a little too. I don't wrestle anymore, as I am old. When Facunda and Guillermo [his younger brother] got married, I wrestled a little. They played the guitar then too.

I, myself, am not afraid. I'd steal a woman alright, so long as she were willing. Let them fine me! Let them punish me! It doesn't matter. I'd steal her again, if the girl loved me. I'd steal her five, six times. Any old lawyer could save me. It's true that the law itself has a wife. The law itself knows well enough how to steal a woman. I have stolen. Well, I have a wife don't I? I was tried. They came to try me at Feli's house, at Beltrán's too [Todivia's father and chief the west moiety].[13] But I wasn't fined. Nothing happened to me because they asked Todivia. As she was willing, nothing happened to me. The law has a wife too, as God created women for men.

NEIGHBORS

When I go to Leonor's house [Beltrán's son, then chief of the west moiety], Teresa [Leonor's wife] runs out of the house. Maybe she doesn't want to greet me. Maybe she doesn't want to offer me something to eat. I don't know. Sometimes she doesn't have time to flee, then she'll talk some.

I asked:	Where are the men?
Teresa:	Working. They won't be back soon. What do you want?
I said:	Jars.[14]
Teresa:	I can sell you some.

But the wife of old Emilio Soto, women like her were not proud. The mama of my wife, Chabela, too, she was glad to converse, even when Beltrán [her husband] was not there. When I'd come by she'd say, "Come in. Sit over here. Here is where the visitors sit." Then she'd starting conversing with me. But Beltrán's other two wives, Papirona and Mariana, they wouldn't ever say, "Come in." They wouldn't say, "Get out." Nothing. Only the mami of my wife greeted me. When I first met her, she asked me:

What are your mama's and your papa's names? What's your mama's mama's name?

When I replied, she said:

We are related by your grandparents. Our families are a bit close.

You always have to make known your mother's and your father's names. Before Beltrán died, people brought many presents to his house [when he was chief]: snails, camotes, wasps, yuccas, maize, beans, deer meat, peccaries. After he died, Chabela grieved a lot. Once she said to me:

Now no one brings me anything. Leonor doesn't bring anything, or Lorenzo. Only Fausto brings something and Todivia a little. My sons and daughter treat me badly. Why? Since Beltrán died, the friendships have ended. I only get bad looks now.

She only ate old maize when she got sick. New maize upset her. She got sick to die. She was sick for four months. The last time I saw her she said:

I'm going to tell you something Alfonso, my son-in-law, so that you know me better. You must conform to my death. Don't think of your mother-in-law anymore.

Beltrán was malicious with me only one day. Soon after I took his daughter, I asked to stay overnight in his house.

He said:　Why don't you go ask to sleep in Panchito's house? Don't get mad at me, son-in-law.

I said:　I'm not mad, I'm conversing. I'm going to sleep in my own house [about two hours' walk from Beltrán's house].

But I already decided to go to Panchito's house.

Beltrán:　Be careful of the snakes.

I said:　When I ask God's permission, even if there are snakes around, they don't bother me. You are the cacique here on this side, not on mine. My cacique is Fidelio. This side is not my domicile. As you are the second cacique, you cannot bully me.[15] As Todivia is willing, it is her will to be with me, as women are made for men.

Beltrán:　That is true.

Beltrán didn't do anything against me for taking his daughter, as I answered him straight, according to the law. Later, I told Feli about what Beltrán had said and he said:

That's the way I like it, not hiding. No one should take a woman in hiding: out in the open, not in the bush.

But Martín had another opinion. He never even wanted a house of his own. He wanted to live in the late Doroteo's house and this is where he died. Not I, I want to live in my own house. Mateo advised me:

> Don't look for trouble. Build your own house. If you live in someone else's house, this means you are looking for someone else's wife. Each nation should get along well, women and men too. Otherwise, God will get angry.

Martín had another way. He was shameless. He would run away when I came. He always wanted to live in someone else's house. When Doroteo was still alive, he said to me once:

Martín: I'm not a woman chaser. I won't marry any girl who still wants to live with her parents. I won't steal anyone's wife either.

I said: You ask favors of other men's wives, to make tortillas for you. This means you are moving in on someone else's wife.

When he heard this, he ran out of the house.

Doroteo: I'm glad you scolded him.

When Martín was left an orphan, he went to live with Doroteo. He grew up in his house. Then he got mad at Doroteo and went to live with Alejandro. He got mad at Alejandro and went to Abrán's. He got mad at Abrán and went to Leopoldo's. But he made a milpa every year. This fellow was a hard worker. He had maize, tobacco, squash. He never missed a year. But he never had a house of his own. I think he only wanted other men's wives. I don't like other men's wives. I want my own family. If my wife wants salt, jars I have to get them for her. Mateo advised me, "You want a woman? Then get a grinding stone, buy salt, cloth."

I never saw Martín buying such things. He knew how to grind maize. When he got mad with a woman, he'd make his own tortillas. When the women refused to serve him, he'd run away to another house. But when Martín got very sick, Julia [Alfonso's mother] took care of him.

DREAMS

I dreamt last night that the *tikhuan*, the white tiger, was hunting a girl while I was harvesting maize. When I dream of a tiger, I don't go out the next day. It may mean a snake. Yesterday we were talking about tigers. Maybe this is why I dreamt of one.

When I'm going to hunt deer or monkeys, I dream of Prestación [Abrán's daughter, Alejandro's wife]. When I dream of her, a deer, an agouti, a raccoon, a monkey, a turkey-hen will surely appear the next day. When I dream of her, I never see a snake. But Prespinde, [Abrán's other daughter], she's no good for dreams. Snakes always appear. When I dream of her, I don't go out shooting. There are women who look like coiled up snakes.

When I dream of a *ladino* woman, female peccaries appear; when a *ladino*, male peccaries appear. I kill the female peccary more than the male. The meat of the male stinks.

I dream mostly of women: our women, *ladino* women, any women. Then the hunt is sure. But snakes appear with Prespinde. I dream I'm making love to her but really I am making love to a snake. With several women it happens this way but not with others. This is all nonsense. I don't know why I dream such silly things.

Sometimes, I am eating *guayabas* [fruit from the guava tree]. Right then, I begin to get a toothache. When I dream I'm healthy, feeling good, I wake up sick. The same when I dream of fire. When you dream of fire, you should take a bath right away.

The *zahorines* [shamans: chapter VII], they only have good dreams. The Mortals dream to die all the sooner. The *zahorines* don't have pain, as God [Tomam] helps them. They don't catch colds or fevers, as they have power. God separates them from the rest of us. They never ail. Only at the hour of death, then they may have pain. But they're never sick and never have bad dreams.

I dreamt Todivia was taking a bath with another man. The next day the deer were right there. Sometimes I dream that she's bathing with a woman. Once, I dreamt I was hugging Panchito's wife, Rosa, caressing her breasts. Then the next day I went to court the deer. Todivia tells me when she dreams I'm making love to another woman. Then I go right the next day and propose to a deer. The same when I dream Todivia is with another man, the same result, I always kill a deer.

What does it mean if I like another woman? Will Todivia get mad? She has no right to. What does it mean if she gets mad? Women get committed to other men. It turns out even.

When I dream of being burned alive or of pain in my bones, it's not good. When you have bad dreams, you shouldn't go out. If I dream of the dead, I don't go out either, as I am a child of death. You shouldn't overdo anything. When I dream I die and am not going to see my wife anymore, then I don't go off the trail. I take care of myself when I have bad dreams.

The same when If dream I am flying like a bird or falling, I don't got out the next day. After that, I walk more carefully.

Sometimes, when I'm looking for a deer, the next day I dream of deer, peccary, coatis. That means that there won't be any, so I don't go hunting anymore then. When I dream of a snake, I don't go out either or fish. I don't go until I dream of a woman. Then I go, even if I'm busy in the milpa. Too, if I dream I am hunting little birds, then I go out.

Sometimes, I dream the gringos are taking photographs of me. After this, I may find a Temptation of the Liauro [Devil: chapter VI], as God [here the Sun] is watching.

CHILDREN

We have four children. They're all here on Earth. God didn't want them to die. The old people: mama, papa, another — Julián Velázquez, another Félix Pérez [the latter two were shamans] advised me:

> Don't harm the little creatures. How can you let them die! Raise them well. Populate the Earth so that when Alfonso dies, they will stay on Earth working and eating.

Men and women are on Earth to procreate. If there were no women, men would suffer. Who would prepare their food when they go to work? If a man has no woman he suffers. He has to grind his own maize. I never wanted two wives, at least not up to now. I only wanted one woman. This is enough. I was courting Abrán's daughters but no more. Now, I don't even have enough strength to work.

My son, Lencho, said he wanted to be named after Lencho Castro. Lencho Castro said, "Why don't you name him Lencho Castro, Lencho Martínez, that's Indian." He was about eight then. Before that, he didn't have a name. When he was born, my mami bathed him. His cord was buried in the house. Outside it might get harmed [meaning some animal, dogs most likely, might dig it up and eat it]. I always bury them in the house. I bathed Celedonia [first daughter] myself, as none of the old women were around that day. I couldn't even find a sister, no one. I bathed Felipa and María [the third and fourth children] for the same reason. Sabina gave Celedonia her name, Felipa also. Sabina's daughters were here when Felipa was born but I didn't let them bathe her. I figured they'd charge me money, as they're *ladinas*.

When my son wanted to get married, I advised him.

I said: Set yourself up apart. You have to get along with your in-laws so set yourself up apart. You have to respect your mother-in-law like your mama.

Lencho: That's just the way it will be. I'll build a house, as soon as I can.

He's been with his in-laws for two years now. He's just there to get the girl, because he's courting, not because he likes it.

Lencho: So long as she loves me, I'll take her in January or February.

He notified the cacique a long time ago, last year. Awhile ago, I went to talk to Maria Jesús, the mother-in-law.

She said: It's alright Don Alfonso. He's here with our permission. He's not hiding.

But my daughter, Celedonia, is not the same.

Celedonia: I for sure don't want to set up apart. Why should I mistreat my old folks? When the mama is sick, I take care of her. She takes care of me. You have to pay four or five *pesos* a month for someone to come and help out when someone is sick. You don't have friends when you are sick. There are no friends without money.[16] I don't want to mistreat my mama, my papa. What the old folks advise, that's the way it will be.

I said: What the husband orders, that's the way it will be.

Domingo, her husband, agrees. He may speak against it but if he does, it's in hiding. When God says so, you die. Some die in childbirth. This is what Celedonia is afraid of.

When Ciriano came to ask for my daughter, Felipa, I told him he should ask her, not me, that if she wanted him it was alright with me. Afterwards, he talked to me again and said that she had given him hope. I said, "That's fine, so long as she's willing. My daughters are not for me. They're for others." Ciriano brought me a *cuartillo* [about 6 lbs.] of maize, some beans, and three packages of sugar and several yards of cloth for Todivia. Later she sold the cloth to Faustina, as a favor.

María [youngest child] is still too young to think of a man.[17]

THE CACIQUE'S ADVICE

Soon before the cacique Feli died [about 1954], he said to me:

Alfonso, you're just about the oldest now and you're the most awake of all; you have to give advice so that everyone get along well, so that no one fight.

MATEO'S ADVICE

If you are a friend today, tomorrow don't get mad. A friend is a friend until death.

OTHER ADVICE

The *mezclados* [mestizos inhabitants of the Montaña]: Tomás, Domingo, Facho, and the late Pancho and Sabina, long ago when I was young, would say to me:

Alfonso, you should learn commerce; take pigs and your coffee to the markets: to Tegucigalpa, to Yoro, Sulaco, Cedros, Talanga. Indians have rights, too. If you have eggs, sell them, if turkeys — likewise.

What advice! Yes, let the Indians die on the spot. Yoro is full of fevers, Cedros likewise, Tegucigalpa the same, Talanga less. An Indian comes down with the slightest fever and he is dead. The Indians don't know how to cure themselves. The *mezclados* know. But who knows how to read? It serves us right if we're treated like fools. I said to the *mezclados*:

How can Alfonso be cured, or ask for medicines? Also, he doesn't know how to sell. He'll be in for it, if he goes out trading; nothing good will come of it.

But they didn't leave me in peace. They advised me more:

Alfonso, man, you learn to trade! The stores sell everything cheaper than up here [with the itinerant merchants]. When you have coffee, why sell it up here sitting in your house? Take it down to the towns. Are you going to sit in your house all your life? But get yourself a passport;[18] if you don't, you'll be fined and your business will be ruined.

They were forcing me to learn commerce. But that's not for me. I don't like it. Later some big men came from Tegucigalpa. I don't remember who they were but I took their advice right away.

They said: Don't go out trading. Why do it? You're an Indian. This means you'll be accused of being an assassin. You'll take your machete along and go up to someone's door to sell something, the door opens and someone yells "assassin" before you open your mouth.

Mezclados: Why don't you go to the north coast to sell your pigs? There you can get fifty or sixty *lempiras*[19] for each. You can do a pretty business on the coast.

How can an ignorant Indian like me understand all this? Anyone can make a fool of me. I was calculating what they had advised, trying to figure out if I can do it, so long as I don't get thrown in jail. If I'm careful — maybe I can do it. I tried. It didn't work. I wanted to learn but it turned out badly. Later, a *ladino* came to my house with a herd of pigs.

He said: I'm going to the coast with these pigs. They're selling there for a pretty price.

I said: That's fine, Señor. Have a good trip. But if you have any sick pigs, you'll regret it. Sick pigs won't bring in the money.

He said: You're right and I do have some sick pigs.

Next time I saw him,

I asked: How did it go?

He said: Bad. I threw all my pigs to the buzzards on the way.

A PASSPORT FOR SULACO

Once, I went to Sulaco to sell some little things and buy [gun] powder. When I got there

I asked: Who's your mayor here? I want to take out a passport.

They told me Mercurias Barahona. Right then and there I called him.

He said: Why did you call me? What's the trouble?

I said: Here, I'm having a little mix-up. I left home without a passport and I was trading.

Mercurias Barahona: Without a passport? That's alright. You're only selling your own products. It won't do them any good to try to make it hot for you. Here, I'm doing you a favor so that no one bothers you. You people live apart. It's prohibited by the government to bother the Indians. You're only selling the products of your labor and that cannot be prohibited. Notice is being sent out to all the villages not to bother the Indians.

When they heard this, no one said a word. The mayor wasn't lying, the others were. He told everyone there:

> Anyone who harms this Indian will suffer for it. A fine for anyone who as much as touches him. Alfonso Martínez wants a pound of gunpowder. He has a right to it. The Indians don't fight their companions. Only our people go around killing each other. This is why Don Alfonso Martínez got into trouble. Why should anyone speak against him? Alfonso is a gentleman. He wouldn't touch anything that doesn't belong to him. He is only asking with his own money.

They tried to do me in for the powder but the mayor saved me. He didn't ask me for the passport either, as he knew me. He used to come to the Montaña to sell clothes and buy coffee. I stayed two nights in Sulaco, in Mercurias Barahona's house, with meals and bed. I bought three machetes — three *lempiras* [1.50 US$] each, some lead — six *reales* [75 cents USA] the pound, three or four lengths of white cloth for myself and my nana [mother]. I was single then so most of the cloth was for me. I spent all my money. And I never went back to Sulaco.

CEDROS OF THE COMPADRE [20]

Once, I went to Cedros with my uncles: Feli, Mateito, Sebastián, Raimundo and Juan José. I wanted salt and gunpowder. I had two kids by then. There, the *ladinos* told us:

> You had better stay overnight in the hills. You can't sleep here in town without a passport. You might get into trouble. One of the chiefs from Tegucigalpa might come here asking, 'And these Indians, what are they doing here? Looking for trouble?'

I said, if this happened, I would tell the chief:

> We have only come to get some provisions that we Indians need.

Anyway, we slept in the hills, out of town. We bought a cotton bedcover, there in town. We ate tortillas, beans and brown sugar with coffee that Emilio González, the secretary, gave us. He and I are *compadres*. He used to come here to buy hens, maize, coffee. He calls me *compradrito* Alfonso. He warned us not to sleep in town, that some bandits from Olancho had just raided Orica and might come into town and kill all us Indians. He told

us it was safer to sleep in the hills for the night. Anyway, I bought two
arrobas [50 lbs.] of salt there at two *lempiras* the *arroba*, thirty yards of
cloth at three *reales* the yard, to sell here to the neighbors at the same
price, and twenty more for Todivia and some for the kids. Also, a machete
and other things, I don't remember all. But no gunpowder. I spent all my
money, thirty-nine *lempiras*. Things are cheaper there. Here they are dearer
because of the mule freight, this is what the *ladinos* [merchants] tell us.

A PERMIT IN YORO

One April, I went to Yoro [the town]. I don't remember what year. It hadn't
rained yet. I already had a family, two kids. I went to get some powder,
some bullets and lead. My companions: my cousin, the late Vicente, my
uncle, the late Mateito, another cousin, Lucio, and a *ladino,* Manuel
Alemán, took me along as a hired hand. They took coffee [beans] along to
sell in Yoro and a packhorse to carry the coffee. It took two days to get
there and the same to come back. We passed the first night out in the hills,
in a little shelter we made from old logs. We took along tamales and
tortillas, with beans inside, and ground maize to make pozol. I went in
[wearing] my *balandrán*. Vicente, too, went in a *balandrán*. Later, when he
married Esteban and she told him she didn't like *balandrán* men, he
changed to *ladino* clothes. She was a *mezclada*.

When we got to Yoro, I went immediately to get a permit to buy the
powder. One of the employees scolded me:

	You, why have you come so far? Why didn't you go to Orica[21] to get your passport?
The people of Yoro:	You're a deserter, an assassin. We're going to throw you in jail.
I said:	I say that I am not a bad person. I am a little good, a bit correct and something of a gentleman.
Others said:	This is a good man. We can deal with him. He comes here because he needs powder for hunting. But if he hasn't brought any money, he won't get any.

I told them I came with money, sixty *pesos*. The employees sent me to a
gringo.[22]

| **Gringo:** | You don't have a right to a permit to sell but as you are an Indian, we'll make it out for you. But for the permit to buy the gunpowder — if you don't pay the tax, you won't have it. You're not in your own department now; you have to pay |

here — four *pesos* tax. But you have to see the commander for the permit for the gunpowder. Only he has the right to give it to you.

He figured this out because he knows how to read and write.

I said: Make it out on my order. I'll pay you whatever you ask.

Gringo: Indian or *ladino*, I'd do the same favor — with cash. If you don't pay me, I won't give it to you and the commander will throw you in jail. If you don't have the permit for the powder, this means that you're a killer.

I paid him like he said and the commander gave me the permit. He didn't throw me in jail either. The permit saved me. The gringo saved me, too. When he finished with me, the commander said:

Alfonso Martínez is a gentleman. It's not against the law to buy necessities, only for powder without a permit it's a bit bad. It means you're out for no good.

I liked it there but too much sickness. This is why I still have plenty of fevers and headaches. I got such a headache there in Yoro that I almost had to go to bed but I took some medicines and got better. I borrowed a place to sleep in for four *reales*; as there wasn't any family there, no neighbors either, I had to pay. For a meal they asked sixty cents: tortillas, fried pork fat, brown sugar and bread — only this. As I am poor, I don't eat much. Sometimes, I ate without paying, for friendship. Five nights I stayed there. They told me:

Plant your maize in March or April.

This is what they talked about. But they conversed a lot more that I didn't pay attention to, because I didn't like it. They talked about drinking *guaro* [a strong alcoholic beverage]. I told them I didn't want any.

I said: If you want to treat me to something, let it be tortillas made of maize.

They tried to force me to drink.

I said: I'll not drink it. I don't permit that.

I didn't taste it.

They said: You won't drink it! You're a coward. The man who doesn't drink *guaro* doesn't have balls.

I said: It's just the other way around. It's you who are fooled by the *guaro*.

They talked to me a lot there:

           Liberal Party or National Party — what's yours?
I said: God's Party. I belong to God's Party.

I told them I didn't like a lot of parties because they always fight. This is why I keep apart, quietly.

A Negro woman merchant[23] in Yoro almost got 80 *pesos* [*lempiras*] out of me. I gave her a load of coffee [usually 100 lbs.] and she wouldn't pay me.

Negro woman: The Indians are innocent. They don't have any village. If they get in trouble in a strange village, they are really in for it.

By the order of the chief [mayor] of Yoro she had to pay me. The work of the Indians cannot be lost. Maybe she didn't think she could get away with not paying me but she wanted to see. Foolish Indians can be taken in by everybody.

I brought back four pounds of powder at four *lempiras* the pound, one package of shells for ten *lempiras*, and two pounds of lead at three *lempiras* each that the Turks[24] sold me. You have to pay what is asked. Also, I got six little yards of cloth, two lengths at four fifty the length for me and for Todivia two lengths at two *lempiras*, two packages of brown sugar[25] at two *reales* the cake, two machetes at four fifty each. They took fifty cents off the machetes. No more. They turned out good — lasted three years. Then two *arrobas* [fifty pounds] of salt at twenty *reales* the *arroba*. All this weighed a lot. I carried it home myself. As I'm poor, this is all I bought.

I don't like to go to Yoro anymore. It seems to me that this trip finished off Vicente. After this, he got fevers all the time and finally died of them. This is why I won't go there again. I'd rather die of my own doing. Besides, there is no family there, no neighbors; everything is money. I don't go out to the towns anymore at all.

THE PARTIES

The Red Party is poor. Sometimes it goes against the Party of God. The Blue Party[26] is the Party of the Devils. It's the party to kill, to win souls. The National Party is like the Liberal Party. Each Party has its science. They want to kill each other with bullets. The Blue Party works with the Devils, this is why it has a lot of money. The Red Party is liberal. It's poorer. One-half of the Red Party is national; one-half of the Blue Party is national. This is meant so that they treat each other as brothers, so that they don't fight. But what kind of brothers! The one that wins is the brother.

The one that loses is dead. This is the way they think. The Liberal Party is run by civilians. It's liberal to kill its companions, to rape women. It wants to try all the women — Indians and *ladinas*. The Blue Party only bothers women if they're willing. It's Communist. The Communist law is the law of God. They say that to rape a woman is a crime; that to kill a companion is a crime; steal a cow is a crime. But no one likes the Blue Party. It learned to read with the Devils.

INSULTS IN COMAYAGÜELA

I went to Talanga once with Facho and Dominguito to take a herd of pigs — four days' walking. Domingo said to me:

> Say, man, Alfonso, do you want to make some money? Then come help me herd these pigs to Talanga.

I went for two or three *lempiras*. Domingo paid up. We sold the pigs there and then we went in a car to Comayagüela [sister city of Tegucigalpa]. We paid the chauffeur twenty *reales* there and the same back. As I didn't take anything to sell, I passed the time conversing. I was real young; now that I'm old, I don't go out anymore. When we got to Comayagüela, I went right away to a store to buy some little things. When the storekeeper saw me he got mad.

Storekeeper: What in the hell are you doing here! Everything is taken up there, where you live: salt, clothes, needles, thread, hats, skirts — everything you need. You only have the right to buy at home. Are you going to turn away the merchants who go all the way up to your mountain? Even though its tough, you have to work; plant a lot of coffee, maize, tobacco — make money. With the little bit of money you bring, you can't buy wholesale merchandise.[27] Even if you had 2,000 *pesos*, you wouldn't have enough to buy any of the merchandise here in Comayagüela. You have to buy a little at a time and retail. Any old poor man shouldn't come here. A little respect is called for. Besides, there is a lot of sickness here. You could die right here from the flu or a pain in your side. Where could you get money to pay for medicines? Here you have no brothers to put down the money, no one to buy medicines for you.

He balled me out good. He was right. I didn't have money for medicines. I did go to Comayagüela to buy some merchandise wholesale. I still have his advice stored away. I won't throw it away until I die. He balled me out some more:

> You've got a pair of huge fists, just like the rich!

I didn't get mad — just a little resentful. After awhile

He asked: Now let's see, what do you want to buy?
I said: I'm a bit offended. I don't want anything. I came here to buy but I'd rather buy at home.

I only bought one axe for three *lempiras*, one machete for four. He had lots of machetes for any price you want.

Storekeeper: Tell me, how much does a machete cost you at home?
I said: Four-fifty to five *lempiras*. That's already too high. But they go up to twelve when revolutions are being fought. Cloth, twelve *reales*, three *pesos* the yard.
Storekeeper: And your house, is it like mine here?
I said: No. My roof is all straw, sometimes palm, sometimes *suyate*.
Storekeeper: Then what are you doing here? You'd better go back to your pigpen.
I said: Go back? I came to a pigpen.

Then I got offended and went to find the chauffeur.

Chauffeur: Now where?
I said: Now, back to my country. I'm turning around here. Why should I let myself be offended in Comayagüela!
Chauffeur: Why did you get offended so quickly?
I said: Because they hate me here. They say bad things to me.

When I got home, I was asked:

> Ha! Why did you come back so soon?

I said: In Comayagüela they put the screws on me. As I am poor, and can't buy a lot of wholesale merchandise, I only bought a little. They offended me. It's no good to go to the wholesale stores.

FEVERS IN TALANGA

Once, when I went to Talanga to buy salt, a *ladino* asked me:

Ladino: Ha! What brings you here?
I said: Trying to keeping alive. For life.

Ladino:	What life?
I said:	The life of Castilla.
Ladino:	What do you mean the "life of Castilla?"
I said:	I'm here to buy salt. I don't like my beans without salt.
Ladino:	I have salt at twenty *reales* the *arroba*.
I said:	No deal. I'll give you eight cents the pound, no more. Twenty *reales*!
Ladino:	You're kidding!

I didn't buy any. Then I got sick from fevers. I called in a doctor. He spoke badly to me:

> If you don't pay me, as here you don't have any family or neighbors — if you don't pay me now you can die. No one will know. You'll be for the buzzards. The dogs will eat your flesh and the buzzards lick your bones.

We got offended. I figured, I'd just as soon die and let the dogs chew me up. I didn't say anything, as I wasn't going to pay him anyhow. The next day, another doctor came to see me.

Doctor:	Where do you have your production?
I said:	My production is in the Municipality of Orica.
Doctor:	An Indian whose production is in the Municipality of Orica has to be taken care of in the best possible way. We'll see if he turns out to be a gentleman. If he turns out to be a liar, we'll throw him in jail.
I said:	Here's my passport to prove I'm a gentleman.

This doctor cured me. He charged me four or five *pesos*. When I got better, I went to buy the salt.

Storekeeper:	Here's salt at two-fifty the *arroba*.
I said:	Then I won't pay. I'll give you eight cents the pound, not ten.

This is what I paid him. I was right. Two-fifty was too much.

SAN MARCOS FOR MAIZE

Todivia's daughter [by her first marriage], Luisa, went down to the plains about four years ago, with a *ladino*. When I passed through San Juancito on my way down to the *hacienda* of San Marcos[28] to get some maize, a *ladino* said to me:

Ladino:	There's a woman here that belongs to your people.[29] If you want, you can take her back.
I said:	No. She belongs here now. She's Indian but she's for you now. Our women are with us. She left with a *ladino* so she's for the *ladinos*. I won't take her back. She's not for us; she's for you.
Ladino:	Take her.
I said:	I'm not after a woman; I'm here for food, maize, that's what I'm after.
Ladino:	Want to hear some music on the radio?
I said:	No, thank you.
Ladino:	Why not?
I said:	I don't know how to play. How much is this music worth? It's worth nothing. I don't want to hear bad talk either. The radio sings bad talk from Tegucigalpa, from San Pedro, from anywhere. If you want to put it on, wait until I leave. Maize is what I want.

They waited. I don't like that music. Only the guitar is pretty, and the accordion. That's what I like to hear. But in San Marcos, they put the radio on. They didn't ask my permission. I listened but I didn't say anything.

Ladino:	Do you like this music?
I said:	No, I don't but as I have ears, I hear it.

I got fifteen *medidas*[30] of maize from San Marcos. They said the maize came from Tegucigalpa. It lasted about two weeks. In San Marcos, they told us:

> Now, don't come back again. We're giving you the maize now but only this once.

They told me too that the people of Pedernal [a nearby town] are very generous so we went on there. There everyone gave me five hands of maize [twenty-five ears]. When I asked how much, they'd say:

> Nothing. Why should we charge you, when you are so poor?

It was selling at one *lempira* the *medida*, as it was scarce. I stayed overnight there and they took a photograph of me.

They said:	You have legs. Why don't you come to visit us, now that you know us?

I said I would not return because many villages had offended me. The *ladinos* say that the Indians are doing mischief, that we walk at night so we can rob. We always leave before dawn, still dark, to get on with the trip and they always say we rob their fields [crops].

GENEROUS TEGUCIGALPA

The time I went to Tegucigalpa, I was pretty young. Don Tomás Neda was still inspector of the police. He was our friend; he offered us [gun] powder. This is why we went. We were six companions: three from this side [the east moiety] and three from the other. The chiefs stayed home. Only boys do stupid things. I was after powder, shells and lead and cloth. Tomás Neda took care of us. Lots of people photographed us. When we got there, he said:

> Here you have to wear pants [not *balandranes*] and we're going to send you all to school.

Tomás Neda was always kidding. I didn't say a word. I wasn't afraid. If they killed me, no matter. Then he said:

> The former president, Paz Barajona, left documentation for you all.[31] Since then, no government has the right to bother the Jicaques. There is documentation for the Indians. Only if they behave like rascals, I'll throw them all in jail. Rascals, don't have lawyers.

Always kidding, Don Tomás. Afterwards, we were taken to a beer factory, to visit. We were given beer to drink right there. The owner of the beer factory said:

Owner: I'm not offering you something bad. It's good. Have a drink.
I said: In the presence of God, I accept, as I can't refuse.

They gave us everything in Tegucigalpa: meals, sweet drinks, beef, pork fat, cheese, even beer. I drank it because they gave it to me with goodwill. They told us good things and bad things. A lot of bad things. But as the president was there, the jurisdiction was there, nothing bad could happen to us. They were very generous in Tegucigalpa. They talked [about] bad things but they always gave us something to eat. Tomás Neda told us a bad thing:

> The Indians are rascals, so they say in Marale.[32] Those from Marale are informing badly in Tegucigalpa.

A lot of people wanted to give us beer but I won't drink with just anyone. I only did with the owner of the beer factory. I got a little dizzy. Feli Martínez [future chief of the east moiety] was shy. He went for two days without defecating or urinating, too bashful to ask where. I wasn't. When I wanted to urinate or defecate, I asked permission. Why should you be bashful? A gringo [North American] who photographed me said:

Gringo: If you turn out to be a rascal, I'll take you to my country.
Tomás Neda: If he's a rascal, I'll take charge of him. I'll send word to his cacique not to expect Alfonso back and I'll let him die here in jail.

That was a close one! I just listened. General Neda was a great joker.

We stayed in Tegucigalpa two or three days, I don't remember which. But I remember we were three days and three nights in the *canton* station.[33] The sentry wouldn't send us home. I didn't talk much to him, as I was resentful because he wouldn't send us home. Don Tomás had told us:

> You won't be long at the *canton* station. When the car comes be ready, precisely at that moment. You must hurry home.

Hurry home! The sentry was always joking with me. Every few minutes he would say the car was coming. At last, I got offended and

I said: Now, I'm going and by foot, as no car will come and as I don't have any money.
Sentry: Maybe God will deliver you to your home.
I said: Maybe God will deliver me where my home isn't. You had better send me home. By myself I might get lost, as I don't know the way.
Sentry: Where there's lots of dust — that's your road home. But wait awhile. Don't get angry. I want you to accompany me for at least three days, to keep up the fun.

A little later, someone telephoned from Tegucigalpa, asking:

> Sentry, have you sent the Indians off home yet?

Sentry: No Señor, not yet. They're eating my food: tortillas, fried beans, pork. The boys are fine, they're not mad. After three days, I'll send them off.

He kept us there to pass the time away, to amuse himself. The next day Tegucigalpa phoned again:

> Have the Indians been sent off home yet?

Sentry: Not yet, Señor. They are very good Indians. I'm getting acquainted with them. I don't want to send them away, yet. They're being very nice.

The sentry was a great talker.

I said:	It won't do you any good not to lend us the car. If I get lost on the road, the sentry will pay for it. If I stay here, the *canton* will pay.
Sentry:	You won't die here, better in your own country. I'll notify the chauffeur to come and take you Indians back to your country.
I said:	That's alright, Señor sentry, so you won't send us home. Have it your way, I don't mind.

He liked that. He was very nice. Nothing happened to us, only jokes.

| Sentry: | The Indians are very pretty. Everyone says they're ragged but because there are no more Indians left around, God only left us these ragged ones. |

Finally, the third day the car came. The sentry said goodbye to us:

Sentry:	Have a good trip. You accompanied me three days and I am very grateful.
Chauffeur:	Sit back in your seats and hold tight. If you don't you'll be thrown out.

This is how we got home.

LA GRINGITA

Domingo Martínez:	The *gringita* [meaning the author] is conforming badly. She is photographing badly [excessively].
I said:	How can it be a bad thing? She knows how to work, taking photographs. She's here because she likes it here. She's not taking pictures for anything bad. I myself don't want to live without being photographed. If you respect me, I respect you. If you behave well, like Tomás [Domingo's brother], you'll be alright. I've not come looking for your daughters. I'm a man of work. The *gringita* isn't doing anything bad. She only wants to get to know the Indians.
Domingo:	Alfonso is communicating badly.
I said:	The *gringita* has been coming here for a long time and nothing bad has happened to me. She's not communicating badly.

Domingo didn't say anything more. I did.

I said: So you're going to flee. You know how to speak Castillan,
                 you dress in pants [not the *balandrán*]. You've been bap-
                 tized but you hide in the nearest stream.

Leonor
  Soto: [chief of the west moiety] Alfonso is communicating badly.
                 Cipriano [then chief of the other moiety] is asleep too.

Then there were five disputing with me.

I said: You hide your women. I, for me, don't hide my wife. I don't
                 hide my daughters either. On the contrary, I like them to be
                 seen. I have not come to speak against the *gringita*, nor
                 against Leonor, nor Domingo. I don't like to hear lies.

Leonor: I thank you for your advice.

That was it.

THERE ARE A LOT OF WAYS TO KILL

Tata Dios arranged it so that the *ladinos* kill each other: cut each other up
with machetes, throw bombs, any old thing, grenades, poison the rivers.
The same with the Parties. The Liberal Party is against something. The
Blue Party is against something else. Tata Dios arranged it this way. The
Party that wins will live. The Party that doesn't win will die. Tata Dios
gave them Parties so they fight all the more. All this he left for the *ladinos*
of death. Thirty thousand *ladinos* die; forty thousand more are going to die
but they won't be finished off, as there are lots of them. The world won't
be finished off. If the army of Honduras kills itself, the world will hear.
The military won't get cured until they die but more will be born. The
world won't die because there are chiefs: Tomam the Elder, Tomam the
Younger and the Tomam Far Beyond. They never fight but not so in
Tegucigalpa. If Tegucigalpa wants to fight Europe, Germany, the United
States, France — that's alright. If it wants to conquer the Indians, finish
them off — that's alright, too. Then Tomam will conquer them. This is
why I am confident.

The Sun gives notice that some nations are behaving badly, then Tomam
will know. The Law of Tomam does not like war, as there is no fighting in
the other world. Tomam doesn't work at killing his companions. Nor Tata
Dios. But as the Mortals want to fight, the fetid vapor was lent to them so
that they die. Tata Dios didn't want the *ladinos* to fight but they did. The
gringos make machetes, axes, bombs. There are a lot of ways to kill but
Tomam will not permit the nations to be destroyed.

I AM CONFIDENT

When I was young, I wanted to know [see] the whole world, this world of the Mortals. But now I want to stay at home. It's better that I be punished in the other world, not by the Mortals in this one. As I have hunted a lot: peccaries, raccoons, agoutis, I'll be punished in the other world. Their masters have the right to accuse me, when I die. God [the Sun] knows everything, as He sees everything. He notifies the other world when I kill a deer, an armadillo, when I kill an ant. If an ant bites me, I have the right to kill it, but it has the right to accuse me. I ask permission to hunt, to plant a milpa. If it rains the whole season, I won't harvest anything. I keep alive from year to year because I have hands to work with. When God, the Sun, sees that I am planting, he'll send me some rain. If I kill a companion, if I steal, if I don't work, I can be punished by the authorities here in this world. The laws must be respected. But if I am not punished here, by the laws here, I will be in the other world. If I am punished here, I won't be there. I am respectful, that's why I have confidence. At night, the Moon looks out after me, during the day, the Sun. When there is no Moon, the stars take care of me.

LEMPIRA
(Author)

Lempira, a *lenca* Indian, successfully organized an armed resistance of thousands of men and confronted the Spanish Conquistadores for over six months in the mountains of central Honduras. He was assassinated through treachery by Alonso de Cáceres in 1538, when he agreed to meet him for a peace parley. Lempira became the symbol of Indian resistance, throughout Central America. His name has been given to the Honduran money.[34]

LEMPIRA
(Alfonso)

The Spaniards closed in on Lempira. He shouted to all who could hear him:

> Today, the Indian, Lempira, will be finished. The Spaniards will finish him. Only the money, *lempira*, will remain in memory of the Indian, Lempira.

He was bidding farewell to this world, following the command of the Great Tomam, Tomam Pones Papawai. He was sleeping when the

Spaniards killed him. They photographed him to find out how he was fighting. Then they deceived him, in order to kill him.

The gringos like the *lempira*, money. Before, this money had a lot of different names but now this name will never be changed. The money, *lempira*, will remain so that everyone will talk about Lempira until they die.

NOTES

1. He refers only to the first name. Since then, however, some of the Indians also have adopted the surnames of *ladino* friends or acquaintances, contrary to the tradition of the moiety surnames: Martínez and Soto.
2. A poncho-like tunic made of cotton denim worn by the boys and men.
3. In the 1960s, a *real* was worth 12½ cents USA.
4. A cluster of huts where Leopoldo Martínez and his brothers lived, in the same moiety as Alfonso.
5. Domestic refers to a child who is still under parental care.
6. The first two were his father's brothers and the last his mother's brother.
7. Fee of dispensation allegedly charged by the Catholic Church for marriage between first cousins.
8. Rafaela, the first wife of Cipriano, chief of the east moiety after Doroteo, died about 1962, while still young.
9. Alfonso refers here to the "proof" or test of the knee. See chapter VII.
10. By the name Santos. Todivia's other child, by her first marriage, Luisa, was raised by Todivia's mother, who died a few years later. Whereupon, Todivia's oldest brother and family raised her.
11. With respect to a first marriage, once the couple agreed, the man had to obtain the consent of his future wife's parents and both moiety chiefs, if the two were from different moieties. Often, a man would live for a few years with his future wife and her family before and also after the marriage. However, this was not entirely the case with Alfonso and Todivia, as she had been married. At the time of their marriage, in the late 1930s, a celebration feast was still held in the house of the man's moiety chief but this practice was abandoned some years later.
12. Wrestling was a favorite game among the Indians of southern Central America, the Tropical Forest of South America, all the way to Tierra del Fuego.
13. Reference to the dispute with Sabina, Todivia's former mother-in-law, who did everything possible to prevent their marriage.
14. Leonor, one of the chiefs, sometimes acted as an intermediary between the Indians and the *ladino* merchants; he resold the goods at the same price he bought them for.
15. A defiance to Beltrán as chief of the west moiety which had, and still has, a smaller population than Alfonso's moiety.

16. Another example of the breakdown of reciprocal relations within the extended family. Matías, Alfonso's uncle, and Chabela, Todivia's mother, both complained about being left alone when sick.
17. In 1969, María died the same time as her parents, from the same epidemic.
18. Here, passport refers both to a permit for selling and an identification card which all Honduran citizens are required to possess. At the time the fieldwork for this book was in progress, members of certain Indian communities, as those of Montaña de la Flor, were not required to have IDs. Now, in 1991, they too are required to have I.D. cards.
19. At that time, one *lempira* was worth about 50 cents of the US dollar.
20. *Compadre* literally means "godfather." However, among the Tolupans, very few, it any, are Catholics. This sort of relationship is called *compadres de boca*, "godfathers by the mouth." For instance, a *ladino* might ask an Indian to be his *compadre* and, if the latter agrees, they will symbolically grasp hands by their little fingers of the right hand, while the *ladino* chants, *Compadre, compadre, ni mesquino, ni pelonero — hasta la muerte* ("Godfather, godfather, neither stingy nor a fighter — until death"). Thereupon, a third person separates their grasp by bringing the edge of his palm down on their hands. Although sometimes done in friendship, often a *ladino* itinerant merchant seeks, by this means, to gain favor of a certain Indian in the Montaña and thereby establish or cement a client relationship.
21. The seat of the municipality to which the Montaña de la Flor belongs.
22. Here, a light-complexioned person.
23. She was probably originally from the north coast of Honduras, where there is a large population of people of African descent.
24. Popular designation of Siro-Lebanese who throughout rural Honduras are proprietors of hardware and general stores.
25. A package or *atajo* contains four cakes of unrefined sugar.
26. Alfonso's allusion is to the two traditional parties of Honduras: the Liberal or Red (*Colorado*) Party and the National (*Nacionalista*) or Blue Party.
27. Most of the stores in Comayagüela deal in wholesale merchandise.
28. The *hacienda* of Tomás Neda, where maize had been sent by the government to distribute among the Indians of La Montaña de la Flor because of the exceptionally poor harvest that year.
29. The woman was Luisa, Todivia's daughter by her first husband, Domingo, whose mother was a *ladina*.
30. A *medida* is a measure of five pounds of grain.
31. Reference to the land title of 1929 which granted the Jicaques portions of the land of the Montaña as an *ejido*, a communal holding, when Paz Barajona was the president of Honduras.
32. A neighboring village in the Department of Yoro. The *ladinos* there were encroaching on the land occupied by the Tolupans. It was to curb such invasions that the land grant was made in 1929. Notwithstanding, it did not halt the encroachments and these and other neighboring *ladinos* have taken possession of much land the Tolupans rightfully claim.

33. At this time, at each main entrance to the capital there was a *canton* (municipal) station, where the military personnel on guard checked incoming and outgoing cargo — sometimes for tax purposes and other times to search for weapons. Alfonso and his companions were lodged there as a courtesy on the part of General Neda.
34. See Martínez Castillo 1987; Chapman 1978a.

CHAPTER *III*

ORIGINS

MYTH 1
THE CREATION OF HUMAN BEINGS

The monkey, Ts'iu, is our mother.[1] The mouse, Namütsis, is our father. They are the First Nation of people.

A long, long time ago, when the First Nation [existed in the world], the monkeys were like us. They had hands and feet like us, but they were hairy and had tails. The First Monkeys didn't know how to climb or jump around in trees. They only stayed a little while in the trees. And since they had to walk on the ground, the tigers and coyotes were always after them, bothering them all the time. One monkey spoke to Grandfather Tomam, "Why don't you kill us all?"

Grandfather Tomam: No, I kill no one. But I am going to change you all, that is, all except a female monkey [Ts'iu, named above], you. I'll keep you just as you are. And I'll give you Namütsis as a husband. I want you to make men and women: Tolupans, Indians, people.

Then Tomam changed the feet of the other monkeys so they could climb in trees and escape from the tigers. He changed them all, except Ts'iu. He didn't like the Nation of Monkeys. He wanted a Nation of People. This is why he kept Ts'iu, to marry her to Namütsis.

Grandfather Tomam gave orders to Nuestro Señor [Our Lord] to change the feet of all the monkeys, all except Ts'iu. But Our Lord wanted to fix Ts'iu too. She didn't like this. [She complained]:

Ts'iu: Why does he want to change my toes? I want to stay on the ground. I don't want to climb, jump around in the trees and perch on the branches where a hunter can kill me.

Grandfather
  Tomam: (to Our Lord) Why are you abusing Ts'iu? You have to leave a female for reproduction. Isn't that right?
Our Lord: Well, if you say so. I'll leave one.

And so it was that the Immortals left her just as she was, in order to make the Nation of Indians, with hands and feet like their mother's.

Then Grandfather Tomam ordered his grandson, Nompwinapu'u, to fetch the mouse, Namütsis, from under the Earth, where there is no *vaho* [fetid vapor]. Nompwinapu'u entered the underground level looking for a mouse who wasn't quarrelsome. He found Namütsis but even he immediately responded badly.

Namütsis: No, it's not true. I do not speak against you, Nompwinapu'u. Why should I?
Nompwinapu'u: If you do, we will become enemies.
Namütsis: How? Enemies! All the Nations are ruled by you. They all belong to you. No one can disobey.

That was as it should be. Then Nompwinapu'u took him up above to meet Ts'iu.

Nompwinapu'u: Does this monkey please you?
Namütsis: Indeed she does. I'll never leave her. If no one takes her from me, I'll marry her right away.
Nompwinapu'u: No one will take her from you. She will be your wife, forever.
Namütsis: What do you want of me?
Nompwinapu'u: I want a Nation of People, not of four-footed monkeys. I want only two feet, hair only on the head and no tail at all.
Namütsis: But why do you marry me to this female?
Nompwinapu'u: Because I want a Nation of Indians. Now I'm going to make you grow until you are the same size as Ts'iu.

And so it was.

Namütsis: Now I am ready. I'll see if it works. If not, I'll kill myself.
Nompwinapu'u: Don't fret. I'll not harm you.
Namütsis: Where are we to live?
Nompwinapu'u: Here, for now. Later, I'll send you both elsewhere. I'll come back in a year. You understand, Namütsis, don't make a mouse or a monkey. This is prohibited. I want a Nation of People — Indians. If you make a monkey, I'll beat you with a club. I might even kill you. I'll kill the both of you. Do you agree? Are you going to produce as I order?

The firstborn was a little woman, the Nation of Muymuy [grandmother], the Nation of the Moon. When Nompwinapu'u returned a year later he saw the little woman nursing.

Nompwinapu'u: You both did a beautiful job. Now we need a little man. This is all that I want. Then I'll send you off to the other world.

The next year the little man was born, Nation of Gokoy [grandfather], Nation of the Sun.

Namütsis: Now, are you going to find a good place for us to live? This world is full of fetid vapor and I never want to die.

Then Nompwinapu'u sent them to a place where the wind never blows, where fetid vapor never enters. Namütsis departed with his wife, Ts'iu. When they left, the Nation of People remained all alone. The little woman and the little man started working, looking for little roots to eat. But they were still lacking something.

Nompwinapu'u [of the East Heaven] created women, the vagina. Tyaj Guatecast [of the West Heaven] did likewise for the men, he created the penis. The two conversed:

Tyaj Guatecast: How are you going to finish making these "monkeys"?
Nompwinapu'u: I don't know but I'll do it somehow.
Tyaj Guatecast: I am a true *maestro* [master]. Do you know how to make a penis? I myself, I do, for a man and for a woman.
Nonpwinapu'u: Are you kidding?
Tyaj Guatecast: I repeat, I can make a penis for a man and a penis for a woman.
Nompwinapu'u: Alright. You do the documentation for the man; I'll work for the woman.

They agreed. Tyaj Guatecast and Nompwinapu'u are the first *maestros*. With the permission of Grandfather Tomam and Tomam the Elder [his son], they made the man and the woman.

Nompwinapu'u: I'll make the Nation of Women so that the women fall in love so much that they will die and when the men court the women, they will die, too, because all the caressing will make them so weak that they'll die.

Tyaj Guatecast: When the women are not enjoying themselves, they'll miss it so much that they won't work. They'll want to be amorous all the time and the men will be even worse.

Nompwinapu'u: I'm going to make the women ugly, the body very ugly, then maybe they won't be so restless.

Tsik'in Guatecast: [brother of Tyaj Guatecast, in the East Heaven] I'm listening. Why should I bother to make sexes for the Mortals? I'll have nothing to do with the Mortals. I won't do any favors for the Nation of the Dead. The women will die young. None will last for long. I myself prefer to do favors for the Immortal Women.

Nompwinapu'u returned to his home in the East Heaven, to his father Tomam's abode. He went to make love to the women there, to caress them, embrace them, to suckle the breasts of the women of the East Heaven.

Nompwinapu'u: Ladies. Do I have your permission to make love to you? I want to embrace you all, to kiss you, too, to possess you, like it or not.

Women: Why shouldn't we like it? We all belong to the same Nation.

Tomam: [to his son] You're doing well, creating the sex of women.

But Nompwinapu'u had not finished. Tomam sent a message to Grandfather Tomam because Nompwinapu'u wanted to talk to him.

Grandfather Tomam: How can I be of help to you, my grandson?

Nompwinapu'u: I want to make a Nation of Indian Women, from our own women.

So Grandfather Tomam handed it [the female sex] to him and said:

I'm only giving you a little, as the Indians will want to die. I'm only giving you this little bit because the Indians will behave badly, asking to die.

Then Nompwinapu'u went to visit the women of Grandfather Thunder [Tatico Trueno]. He embraced them, caressed them, and enamored them. Then he departed in search of Grandmother Moon.

Nompwinapu'u: I want to embrace the Moon. I want to caress the breasts of the Moon.

Moon: Why are you so ill-mannered? When you say you want me, you are being insolent. Why do you want my caresses? For whom do you want to make love to me?

Nompwinapu'u: Grandmother, I want to make women for the Nation of People.

Moon: I thought you wanted me for yourself.

Nompwinapu'u: No, not for myself. I want you for the Indian men so they can have women on earth from this immortal world. They don't want a Nation of Monkeys, or one of Mice. Each Nation wants its own women.

So the Moon permitted him to make love to her.

Nompwinapu'u had to take a little from the women of all the immortal nations: the Nation of Tomam, the Nation Gokoy and the Nation of Muymuy. A little from each. Then he returned to the earth to the first couple of the First Nation. There he met Tyaj Guatecast.

Nompwinapu'u: Just where are you going to place the penis?

Tyaj Guatecast took the penis between his thumb and forefinger, and pressed it against the inside of the baby's arm at the joint. He shook his head and said, "Not there." Then he tried the knee. But it fell on the ground and got dirty. It didn't stick there either.

Tyaj Guatecast: That's not a good place. I'll try here in the armpit. [It fell off there, too.] Not there either, maybe on the chin, on the chest. No, it doesn't stick anyplace. I'm going to throw it away.

Nompwinapu'u: Don't be so miserable. It has to be put in the middle of the body, there only, in front so that the men be pleased.

Tyaj Guatecast: Here it sticks!

Holding the vagina Nompwinapu'u turned to the other baby. He tried to make it stick on the knee, the neck, the arm joint and finally he found where it belongs.

This was all that was needed. Now the Mortals were saved. No one [no Immortal] would bother them again. Now they had sufficient to reproduce. They were born brother and sister like the fingers of a hand, but soon they weren't brother and sister anymore, they were husband and wife. Nompwinapu'u returned to his father's domicile.

Tomam: How did you make out with the Mortals?

Nompwinapu'u: Badly, very badly. For nothing, I made love to the Immortal Women. Only Mortals were born. They will only reproduce Mortals.

Tomam: Didn't I tell you so!

* * *

MYTH 2
THE FIRST NATION

During the time of the First Nation, no one ever died, everyone lived eternally. There were no sicknesses, no fights. Everyone lived peacefully. All the Nations had documentation. None suffered.

The First Nation had no machetes, knives, daggers or rifles — none of these. There was no coffee, tobacco, bananas, sugarcane or maize, either. The First Nation only ate wild camotes. Now only the peccaries eat them, now they belong to them.

The First Nation lived with the Tomams: Tata Dios, Grandfather Thunder, Noventa [brother of Tata Dios], the Stars, the Sun, the Moon. All these Immortals lived on the earth with the first humans, with the masters of the animals and their animals, too. The Devils were not here yet.

Afterwards, the Devils came to harm the Mortals [the people]. Tomam flung them here, to this world, so that they mix with the Indians and the *ladinos* so that they all be condemned to die. The Devils were being harmful where Tomam lives [in the East Heaven]. This is why he flung them here to this world so that they live with the Mortals. The Devils are immortal. Only Tomam can kill them; When the Mortals notify Tomam, he immediately fixes them; Nompwinapu'u kills them, too, with his lightning rod. But now there is no one to accuse the Devils, now that there are no *punakpanes* [shamans].

In the First World, the Nen lived in the lagoons. Then there were no streams or rivers. Nen had all the water, as he is the *amo* [owner] of the lagoons.

The Master of the *Saino* [white-lipped peccary], Saino Jamayón, is also the First Nation of the Indians. He lives in Aninkenen, in a mountain, in a cave, below the Earth. He's of clean heart and never fights. Now he lives with Our Lord. [myth 3] He will never die, as he belongs to the Immortal Nation; the same is true for the Master of the Deer, the Master of the *Quequeo* [white-collared peccary] and all the masters.

At that time, there were no guns, the *tigres* [here, pumas] killed many Indians. This is why Tomam created the English, the gringos [North Americans], the Spaniards, various nations, for rifles. Before that, the tigers ate a lot of people and the Little Old Man complained to Tomam. Tomam listened to him and asked, "But where does the tiger live?"

Little Old Man: He lives with Jo'popjil, the Master of the Deer.

Then Tomam notified Jo'popjil to punish the tiger, so that he respect others. The tigers also bothered the monkeys a lot. This is why Tomam sent them [the pumas] to the caves. [myth 39] Each nation has it own domicile.

During the time of the First Nation, the sky and the clouds were lower, much nearer the Earth.² Later, the clouds moved up a little because the smoke from the fires of the maize field bothered them a lot.

The Indians quarreled [myth 3] and the *ladinos* did likewise [myth 7]. This is why the Tomams, Tata Dios, the Moon and other Immortals fled into the heavens. They have never returned.

* * *

MYTH 3
THE DEATH OF THE INDIANS

Tomam sent Our Lord to the Earth so that we kill him. The Indians die for Our Lord and the *ladinos* for Tata Dios, because we fought with Our Lord and the *ladinos* with Tata Dios, so we are brothers — children of death.

When the *ladinos* fought with Tata Dios, he complained to Tomam the Elder and Our Lord complained about us to Tomam the Younger. We Mortals, ourselves, asked for death because we are troublemakers.

Our Lord gave us fetid vapor to spread sickness, to plague Indians forever after. He really fixed us, all of us. When we eat just a little bit, we vomit blood; blood usually means death. Our Lord didn't want people to live eternally.

In the times of old, people didn't die. During the time of the First Nation, there was no fetid vapor; people lived peacefully with Our Lord, with Tata Dios, with Tomam, with all the Immortals. But later, they all got very angry with us because we always fight.

Mother Earth gave Our Lord some advice:

> I advise you to die. Then they will make a reed mat, and dig a big hole to bury you. But in ten days, you will be out again. You can't leave on the ninth day, you must wait until the tenth day. The Indians will guard your grave. These caretakers, your enemies, will get hungry from

guarding your grave so long. Before ten days are up, they
will go home. By the tenth day, you can rise from your
grave and leave the fetid vapor.

Mother Earth advised him very nicely, and he fixed us in such a nice way.
He came here to our world an old man, with white hair, walking with two
canes. He went to the house of an Indian woman and asked her for something to eat. She gave him a tamale. The old man swallowed half of it but
the other half stuck in his throat. He tried to vomit it up but before long he
was stretched out on the ground, dead. No one killed him. He died because
of his own doing. Lo Chim Jamayón [Master of the Snakes] watched him
all the time from a hill and he saw that he died of his own doing. He had
been dead for three days but his body was still soft. Then a *ladino* passed
by and asked, "Who is this dead person? Or is he sleeping? Or is he dead?"

An Indian:	He's dead, alright. He is Our Lord.
Ladino:	You shouldn't leave him here. You must bury him. Learn to make a reed mat, dig a hole in a cemetery and bury him there. You have to bury him because he came here to die. You have to learn to dig a grave. You will bury him so that the Earth can eat him. There are chiefs here, employees, authorities, to give orders. The law says that the dead must be buried.

Hearing all this, Our Lord died more, saying to himself, "Let them bury
me, I don't care." So he was buried on the reed mat and they threw pine
needles over his grave. His body became stiffer and stiffer and he was
deader than ever. He laid with his arms stretched along the sides of his
body, his eyes closed. Then he opened his eyes and said:

Five days without dreaming, without moving. I am buried.
What a fix to be in! People are forever fighting and now
they want to finish me off. It's alright. They buried me.
That's as it should be. What a fix to be in. The Jews have
killed and buried me. No doubt about it, they really want
to finish me.

Jerking his head from side to side, he tries to raise it, saying:

The Earth is heavy on me. By order of the Jews, I have
been buried for five days and five hours. How can I get
out of here to go home? I must go to the city to the East
Heaven. Now I have been here six days. I was buried at
12:00 noon. I am really hungry. I want to eat. I want José
Hermunido [not identified] to come and get me out of

here. The High Commander [Tomam] should send José Hermunido to come and fetch me.

Still he jerked his head from side to side, the rest of his body lay stiff.

Eight days now, from 12:00 noon. Ten days, from 12:00 noon. Eleven days, from 12:00 noon. This is too much. I must go home.

The grave watchers kept a vigil for ten days in the cemetery, watching to make sure that he didn't rise and leave. If he rose, they were going to kill him, so that he be good and dead. He heard the guardians talking. He said to himself:

You will be sorry. My death will be your death, for all of you. No matter how the youth complain, how pitiful the woman, miserable the man, all of you, everyone, will die. But now, how can I get out of this grave? These Indians, the bandits, threw a lot of Earth on top of me. Ha! Ha ! Soon the Indians will be below and I will be above. I have to stay here for ten days to leave the fetid vapor. On the eleventh or twelfth day, I will be home.

The guardians stayed in the graveyard nine days, watching to make sure Our Lord did not escape. If he tried to get out, they were going to kill him again. Our Lord listened to all they said. He was not dead at all. He was alive. On the tenth day, the watchers had not eaten for nine days. They got hungry. They said:

By now, Our Lord is good and dead. He hasn't made a sign of life. Companions, let's go home and have a meal and make love to our women.

But when they returned, Our Lord had gone. He had escaped. When they left the cemetery, the voice of Tomam called to Our Lord saying, "Rise up." He answered, "I can't! The Earth is too heavy!" But with great strength, he pushed back the Earth and jumped out of the grave. Then he became a young man again.

The guardians punished him for ten days with hunger. They tried to kill him but he didn't die. Later they said, "Let's go back to the graveyard and have a look." When they arrived, they found the grave open, Our Lord gone. They looked into the pit saying, "Let's see how many excrements he left. If he left nine, if he left any turds."

They wanted to see how many times he had urinated and how many times he defecated. They wanted to see the nine turds, as he had been there for nine whole days. But they didn't find one single turd, not one drop of urine either.

While they were looking into the grave, they began to have aches in their bodies and very soon they died from headaches, from fevers, from all sort of sickness, from the fetid vapor Our Lord left in the grave. They all died, all except one. They dug the grave for Our Lord but it was for them. The guardians were the first people to die.

Tomam: I will not permit all human beings to die at the same time. When the elders die, the little angels [the children] won't die. And when the little angels die, the elders won't die. So this way, they will always be suffering.

When Our Lord jumped from the grave, he looked around and again heard the voice of Tomam:

Tomam: You had asked for tortillas, tamales and coffee?
Our Lord: I have been dead for eleven days. I want some coffee.
Tomam: Here, take some.

Our Lord drank it.

Tomam: What else do you need?
Our Lord: To cook the coffee, I want a can and cloth to strain it in.
Tomam: So you have learned to drink coffee! I will give you ground coffee everyday. Now go to the Indian Nation.
Our Lord: No. I won't go.
Tomam: You must go. You alone. Didn't they kill you? Didn't they bury you?
Our Lord: No, it was the Jews. Oh! Oh! what a headache I have! Only coffee will cure it. The Jews have coffee planted. How will I make out?
Tomam: Coffee belongs to the First Nation, to the Indians. And that is that. The Indians are not your enemy. They buried you by order of the Jews. Have you finished your coffee?
Our Lord: Not yet.
Tomam: Now everyone will have to learn to drink coffee. It will be the only cure for headaches.
Our Lord: How much will it cost?
Tomam: Two *reales* [25 cents USA] a pound in the shell. That will be the price. Every Saturday the *ladinos* will come to buy coffee.[3] And that is that. The Indians are not your enemy. They buried you by order of the Jews. Have you finished your coffee?

Later, Our Lord began conversing with the only guardian alive, the Master of the Peccaries, Saino Jamayón, the First Indian.

Our Lord: Now I have left the fetid vapor on the Earth. How are you, my enemy? Why did you bury me the other day?

First Indian: No, Señor, I am not your enemy. I am your friend. Find me a good place to live where there is no fetid vapor.

Our Lord: Now there is fetid vapor everywhere.

Our Lord became more angry with the Indian and said:

> You are my enemy. Why should I help you? Wait twenty years, and if I find a good place, then I'll let you know.

After he left, the First Indian said [to himself], "He will never return. Nothing will come of it." He wept, waited and wept. Three days later, Our Lord returned. He had forgiven his enemy.

Our Lord: Let us depart now. Get your things together, all your animals. It's true, you are my friend. It's alright. I've forgiven you and now, old Indian, you'll become my father-in-law.

First Indian: I agree. If you find a good place for me to live, I'll give you one of my daughters.

And so it was, he gave him a daughter. Since then, Our Lord lives with the Master of the Peccaries in the first level below the Earth, below the mountains, in Aninkenen. Tomam the Younger, the Second Chief [Lord of the West Sky] sent them there, so that they never die.

* * *

MYTH 4
OUR LORD ENCOUNTERS THE FIRST MONKEYS

When the Indians and *ladinos* began fighting, the Immortals fled to the heavens and never returned. And since that time, people have been castaways. Everyone, without exception, has to die.

The First Monkeys were enemies of Our Lord. They thought that he wanted to round them up and make them build a house for him near the Master of the Peccaries. But this was a lie. He really wanted to save them from the tigers.

Ts'ipaytsju, a little bird from Glory, a stranger in their land, heard them crying and asked, "Why are you weeping?"

Monkeys:	Because Our Lord is after us. He wants us to build a house where he lives with the Master of Peccaries. And you? Are you calling for the rain?
Ts'ipaytsju:	That's right. I'm asking for rain; I'm certainly not singing to make you cry. I'm singing to bring the rain.
Monkeys:	But why now?
Ts'ipaytsju:	So that it rain now. In September, I rise to Glory but there is still time enough for the rains to come.
Monkeys:	Our Lord is trying to pester us. What can we do? Where can we hide?
Ts'ipaytsju:	Make a canoe and hide under it. But don't forget, Señores Monkeys, to first turn the canoe upside down and then get under it. I am your friend. Our Lord will look for you in vain. He will have to find someone else to build his house.

When he finished giving the monkeys advice, the little bird fled to Glory so that no one would know what he had done. Finally, the monkeys hid under the upside-down canoe in the house of a women friend.

Our Lord looked for them high and low, through the mountains and hills, up and down the rivers and streams, in vain. He found no one, not one. He got angry, very mad, and shouted, "You monkeys are hiding in vain!"

He became so offended that he made the Earth swirl up and hit the clouds. So the canoe hit against the clouds and the monkeys were knocked around inside the canoe.

Monkeys:	Eh! Our heads are being crushed!

Then the world returned to its place. After a while the monkeys got hungry. Our Lord passed by the canoe very often, as he was asking for them in all the houses. But not a single one of the *cocineras* [women cooks] gave any satisfaction. Finally, he arrived at the house where they were hiding, asking, "What happened to the monkeys? Where can they be?"

Cocinera:	How should I know? They disappeared long ago.
Our Lord:	I am going to kill you. Well, I won't kill you but I must say I don't like gluttons. You eat too much. I think I'll take out your intestines.

The cook was only grinding maize, in order to feed the monkeys, as she was their friend. Every minute, Our Lord was asking what happened to the monkeys and was getting more and more angry.

Our Lord:	I am going to rip out your large intestine so that you will only have the small one, then you won't eat so much.

He did just that but she got well right away. He only took out half of her intestines.

Cocinera:	Why did you pull out half of my intestines?
Our Lord:	Because I don't like to see you grinding maize all day long. Now you won't eat so much. I don't like gluttons.

Suddenly Our Lord turned up the canoe and all the monkeys came out.

Our Lord:	Ah, my poor woman! I pulled out your intestines because I thought you were grinding maize all day because you're a big eater, but now I see that you're grinding maize for the monkeys.
Cocinera:	But don't kill the monkeys!
Our Lord:	No. I'm not going to kill them. I'm only going to change their fingers so that they can play and jump in the trees, eating fruits, and so the tigers won't harm them anymore.

This woman was very generous with the monkeys. Our Lord changed their fingers and sent them off to the mountains. He sent the cook away, too, I don't know where, perhaps to the other world or perhaps to the underworld. He sent her to a place where there is no fetid vapor, where she lives eternally.

*   *   *

MYTH 5
OUR LORD IN LOVE

Tomam the Younger:	Eh! So you like Indian women! But here [in the West Heaven] there are women, too.
Our Lord:	No thank you, Señor, I like the Indian women better. Now I'm going to the Earth to heckle the men and to embrace the women.

So it was. Our Lord came here to make love to our women. He didn't respect anyone. He got on top of them, embracing them, caressing them and making love to them. He did everything of that sort. But we Indians are jealous, just like the *ladinos*. In this we are brothers.

Then Our Lord fled, trying to hide from the men. He shouted to Mother Earth, "Open up for me!"

Mother Earth:	No. I won't open. Only the Mortals have the right to open me.

Our Lord:	Alright. If that's the way it is, you are behaving badly with me.
Mother Earth:	I'm not afraid. I repeat, only the Mortals have the right to open me. Go hide in the canyon. There, no one will harm you. I can't permit myself to hide you.

He fled away farther and hollered to the Cedar Tree, "Open up for me, Cedar Tree. The men want to kill me!"

Cedar Tree:	Enter. Enter.

The Cedar Tree opened up for him and hid him. The Cedar Tree is perhaps the mother of Our Lord as it protected him.[4] Grandfather Thunder doesn't have the right to harm the Cedar Tree because it saved Our Lord. He has the right to burn the other trees.

Our Lord still comes to the Earth to seduce the women and when he succeeds, they rot away. Therefore, he is our enemy. When the women go to fetch water, he appears as a Temptation. (chapter VI) Sometimes, he comes with his sons, the Devils, and other times, he comes alone. After he has made love to a woman, she may die within five days but she never lives more than a year. When he appears, it is the hour of death.

*   *   *

MYTH 6
OUR LORD QUARRELS WITH THE <u>LADINOS</u>

Our Lord didn't want to pay for food. He didn't like food that was bought. He wanted it to be given to him. This is why he fought with the First *Ladinos*. They wanted to be paid for everything. Our Lord would eat only through friendship. He wanted to live eternally. He said:

> The *ladinos* only eat with money. This is why they will be the Nation of Death.

He didn't like money. Maybe he didn't have any, as he never spent any. He said that only the *ladinos* could buy and sell only among themselves, as Tomam had ordered.

When they tried to sell him something he became angry. He quarreled with the vender.

The Rich:	Let him pay, if he wants to eat.
Our Lord:	I won't touch bought food, not one little piece. I'll pay you with death if you keep offending me. Here I am to say that I refuse to pay. How do you dare try to sell to the Nation of Indians, of Tolupans? You only have the right to

	buy and sell among yourselves, not with the Indians. And
	as for me, I'll only eat what is given to me.
Ladinos:	If you want to eat an egg, it will cost one cent. If you want
	a chicken, its price is two *reales*. Fifty hands [250 ears of
	maize] will come to three *lempiras*, a loaf of brown sugar
	is now one *real* each, a male turkey is selling for one
	lempira, a pig from ten to twenty *lempiras*, depending on
	the size.

Our Lord became offended with all this talk.

Our Lord:	I will only eat what is given to me, what grows from
	seeds, from breeding pigs and skinny hens. Chickens
	raised for sale, I won't eat. I step aside quietly. I won't buy
	love, either. If it's free, yes. There are women who sell
	themselves for three *lempiras*, others for five. There are
	contrabandista women who sell themselves for a few
	cents. They are available at any price, according to your
	pocket. But I will have nothing to do with bought love. I
	don't want to die.

The *ladinos* made fun of him.

Our Lord:	If the *ladinos* want to buy, let them buy. If they want to
	sell, let them sell. But me, not on your life, I won't com-
	promise with them. The *ladinos* have money, borrowed
	from Tata Dios. But if they try to force me to compromise,
	I'll hide. Where will they find me if I hide? I'll not eat
	bought food.

This is why the *ladinos* insulted him. Our Lord went home very angry.

* * *

MYTH 7
THE DEATH OF THE <u>LADINOS</u>

Ladinos misbehave. They rape women. They're always fighting. I [Alfonso Martínez] am not baptized. I don't get into fights, or rape women. Why should I abuse my fellows? It's better to live as brothers. Why should I drink this *guaro* [booze]? It's the sweat of the Devils, so the old people said. Tata Dios ordered that the *ladinos* pass their time fighting. Our Lord did not order it. Tata Dios ordered that the *ladinos* spend their time killing each other, shooting each other. They complained against Tata Dios be- cause he refused to pay taxes so he gave them Christmas Eve so they could celebrate, get together and drink a lot of *guaro*, spend all their money, fight with each other, be fined by the law and pay up, so there would be no way out. They have to die. Our Lord is more correct. He didn't do this. Tata Dios complained to the President in Tegucigalpa. He complained about the five *pesos* [*lempiras*] the ladinos tried to tax him for killing a cow or a steer, about the school tax. Then he complained to Tomam, in the other world.

When the *ladinos* behave badly, Tomam knows about it right away. The Law of Tomam doesn't like anyone to fight, as in the beyond [the East Heaven], everyone lives peacefully. There, no one is busy killing their companions. The gringos know how to make machetes, axes, rifles, bombs, this is what they study. They kill each other in lots of ways.

First the *ladinos* were against Tata Dios. Now they are against all their neighbors. They fight with any Mortal. Tata Dios wasn't looking to fight with the *ladinos* but they tried to oblige him to pay taxes: school tax, cattle tax.

Tata Dios: I don't pay because I don't choose to. And that is that. It's better that they kill me and then I'll pay with my corpse.

He refused, then he fled but they caught him and threw him in jail. Jívaro [the messenger of Tomam] went to see him.

Jívaro: Eh! How did you get here?
Tata Dios: Well, here I am! But I won't pay taxes, not even for schools.
Jívaro: Go and complain to Tomam.

He did just that. With no trouble at all, he got himself out of jail. No Mortal like us can ever get out of jail. They lock you in with seven keys and how in the world can you ever get out?

Tata Dios liked living in this world a lot but as the *ladinos* gossiped about him and threw him in jail, he fled to the world beyond. But before he left, he deposited the fetid vapor — great quantities of sickness for the *ladinos*, for the cattle, for horses and mules, as he is their master. Since that time, all these animals die. So to take more revenge on the *ladinos*, he left them booze, so that they get drunk and fight over women, over cattle, over horses. But they like this fine, as they compromised themselves. Today, they kill 1,000 of their own Nation, even 5,000 and today 1,000, or who knows how many more thousands are born. The *Ladino* Nation will never die out, even though they kill each other in great quantities. It doesn't matter if they fight, they are so many, and they like to fight. Let them have it their way. If they want to fight over cattle, horses or women, that's their business. Let them commit themselves all the more. When Tata Dios arrived at Tomam's domicile, he told him:

Tata Dios: I can't put up with the *ladinos* anymore. They want to make me pay taxes. They gossip about me.

Tomam: When the tax quota is posted on your door, you have to pay up.

Tata Dios: The *ladinos* try to force me to pay head tax, school tax, cattle tax. They threw me in jail. I have come to ask you for a good place to live.

Tomam: You're in charge of the *ladinos,* of horses, of mules and of cattle. Now you are prosecuting yourself with your own mouth. You've become gossipy. You're abusing the *ladinos* and behaving badly. You're a quarrelsome fake! You want to fight with the neighbors; you want to die! I'm going to throw you in jail, too!

Tata Dios got angry, too. He said, "I am a man of *de buena conciencia* [integrity]."

Tomam: I have no use for you here. Go live in Glory [the zenith]. I don't need you here. You can haul your dead *ladinos* to Glory. I'll send them to you there.

Tomam doesn't like the dead. He doesn't want them with him. He sent Tata Dios off to Glory so that he could fight there, if he wanted to. Tata Dios complained a lot. Our Lord didn't. He kept his mouth shut. Later, Tata Dios sent diseases to kill the livestock. He got mad because the *ladinos* branded his livestock.

Tomam: You are also to take charge of the dead livestock.

Tata Dios wanted to take all the cattle and horses to Glory, as he is their master, but Tomam didn't permit him.

Tomam: No, you will not take all the cattle, not all the horses. If the *ladinos* want to fight over them, let them fight.

Tata Dios: But that can't be! All of the livestock are mine, all!

Tomam: Leave them in the world for the Mortals.

Tata Dios: Leave them for the Mortals! But they are mine!

Tomam: Never mind, one day or another, every cow, every bull, every horse will die from the fetid vapor that you left on Earth and when they die, they will go to Glory for you.

Tata Dios didn't want to loan his animals to the Mortals. He only did because Tomam ordered him to.

Tata Dios:	I want to take all of my property with me, all of my belongings: cattle, horses, dogs. I want to take them all to Glory.
Tomam:	I will permit you to take a pair of each for reproduction: cattle, horses and pigs — two of each. The rest, you must leave for the Mortals, on Earth. It's better this way. Then the Mortals will keep on fighting and, besides, they'll have to pay taxes for each animal.

This consoled Tata Dios but not entirely.

Tata Dios:	I want a tiger as majordomo, Señor Tomam.
Tomam:	Eh! You are still annoying me! I'm going to throw you in jail. If you want a majordomo, why don't you make one yourself? Make a big dog for your cattle. To please you, I'm going to give the *ladinos* an iron so that they can brand their cattle. Then they'll have to pay taxes to the government, five *pesos* a head. They will have to pay because they are such fighters.
Tata Dios:	And I won't have to pay anything! It suits me fine to go to Glory.
Tomam:	You are not to let any branded animal enter Glory. But you can receive an unmarked cow that got bogged in the mire or a horse that died from a snakebite.
Tata Dios:	How do I climb up to Glory?
Tomam:	You must plant a *petok* [vine] and when it grows and reaches the clouds, you climb up it.
Tata Dios:	I'll plant it this minute.

He had just done so, when a tiger passed by.

Tiger:	Me too, I'm going to Glory.
Tata Dios:	You don't have the right. You're not the majordomo of my cattle. Tomam won't permit you. You only want to go to harm my cattle.

The tiger turned back and got down from the vine.

Tiger:	Alright, as you say. But when the *ladinos* are off guard, I'm going to kill the calves. I can't manage the larger cattle.

This is why tigers hunt so many calves.

Tata Dios went to look for his wife.

Wife:	How was it with the Head Chief?

Tata Dios:	I did very badly.
Wife:	Didn't you ask him for a good place to live?
Tata Dios:	That I did, I asked him.
Wife:	What place? Where?
Tata Dios:	I asked for a place where he lives. But it turned out badly. The Head Chief is a gossiper. But he'll give me another place. I'm leaving tomorrow.
Wife:	Really?
Tata Dios:	Really. I have had enough of this world, of fighters and tax collectors.

His wife also had livestock she didn't want to leave. They quarreled.

Tata Dios:	Alright. If you don't want to come with me, I'll leave you and the *ladinos* will finish you off. If you want to live with the Mortals, it's up to you.
Wife:	No. Don't leave me. Don't get me wrong; I don't want to die.
Tata Dios:	Let's be off then. Let's go with all the family to live in Glory, in liberty.

The vine had now grown very high. They climbed a little each day until finally they arrived.

Tata Dios:	I wanted to bring all my cattle, all my horses and mules, all my pigs but the Head Chief didn't let me. I had to leave them for the Mortals, for them to eat, to serve them. I only brought a pair of each so they can reproduce here in Glory, only six.

Tata Dios resented this.

* * *

NARRATION 1
ALFONSO COMMENTS

The Indians fought with Our Lord. They buried him, when they should have let him be. The *ladinos* fought with Tata Dios. This is where all the trouble started. The old men, Julián Velázquez and Félix Pérez, told me all this. They advised us to live apart, not to mix with the *ladinos*. One of the old men said:

> I am going to give you some advice. If the *ladinos* want to compromise [themselves], that's alright; but the Indians are apart. Don't mix with them. The *ladinos* want to fight

with the whole world. I'm going to give you some advice in a few words, don't compromise yourselves. It doesn't matter if the *ladinos* die, let them. Let the Mortals fight among themselves. You should see how some of them kill each other, even with bombs. Tomam sent the order. As they are Mortals, the sooner they die the better.

If a *ladino* spreads gossip on Earth, when he arrives in Glory, he gets thrown in jail. I might get thrown in jail, too, but in the East Heaven. That's where the documentation is for us. Our Lord wanted to live in this world but he couldn't. He was run out. Tata Dios liked it here, too, but he was chased out the same as Our Lord, though he went to Glory by the order of Tomam. Our Lord went into the mountains to the abode of the Master of the Peccaries, Saino Jamayón. Our Lord and Tata Dios left a lot of fetid vapor, a lot of sickness for which death is the only cure. We will see how I'll be punished in the other world.

*　　*　　*

MYTH 8
A RICH MAN ARRIVES IN GLORY

When a *ladino* appears in Glory, Tata Dios asks him:

What brings you here? I see that you are very rich. I have no use for you here. You had cattle, horses, money, as much as 2,000 *pesos*. You have some nerve coming here! Why did you abandon your cattle, your horses?

Tata Dios has no patience with the rich, or with gossipers, much less with tattlers.

Ladino:　　Why do you scold me for being rich? When I was in the world, it was only thanks to you, that I was rich. If it hadn't been for you, I would have been just another poor man. It is thanks to you, Tata Dios, that I became rich. You lent me horses, cattle, pigs and dogs. I had money and was well outfitted from sombrero to shoes, complete with a *pistola*. You lent me all this.

Tata Dios:　　Well said. You may come in. There's no argument.

They embraced and became friends.

Tata Dios:　　As you are so poor now, you are probably hungry. How would you like a little buzzard soup?

Tata Dios told his daughter:

Bring the gentleman a bowl of buzzard soup.

The *ladino* was afraid, thinking of the soup. Even though he didn't want to eat it, he had to eat it. How could he refuse the offer of the daughter of Tata Dios? When a dead *ladino* misbehaves, Tata Dios throws him back into this world so that he suffer at the mercy of the Devils. The Devils are also rich. It is more likely that the *ladinos* learned to be rich from the Devils [rather than Tata Dios]. This is why Tata Dios throws them back here.

Daughter of Tata Dios:	Don't you like my little soup?
Ladino:	Of course, and I'm going to eat it. I am a poor man. Everyone thought of me as rich but it wasn't true, as Tata Dios lent us all that wealth. He gave us his endorsement.

A little later, he ate the buzzard soup. It's punishment for the *ladinos*.

Ladino:	I would like to build a house for myself.
Tata Dios:	You are behaving nicely, even though you came here much too young; you are not behaving badly.
Ladino:	Sombreros, clothes, shoes, belts, spats: Tata Dios you gave me all this, how could I not be grateful! You lent me much livestock, how could I fail to thank you!
Tata Dios:	You can build your house here, on this little spot of level ground.

When he had finished his house, he returned to Tata Dios.

Ladino:	Will you give me a pair of cattle to breed?
Tata Dios:	I will, certainly, and a pair of dogs likewise.
Ladino:	Tata Dios, why do you keep those buzzards?
Tata Dios:	I am obliged to have them. I need them to eat the cattle, when they die in the fields. I'll tell you about it. There is only one kind of buzzard with a red beak. When cattle die in the countryside, this buzzard pulls out the dead cattle's eye and flies away with it to other buzzards so that they, too, go to eat it.

Tata Dios is the Master of the Buzzards.

* * *

MYTH 9
THE ORIGIN OF MAIZE

During the time of the First Nation, Nompwinapu'u [Master of Maize] brought maize to the world. Until then, the only food was the little roots of the First Nation. They seed by themselves. Now they belong to the white-collared peccaries. The Indians no longer have the right to eat those little roots.

The Little Old Man of the First Nation of Indians was searching for those little roots, as this was all there was to eat. He was twisting his magical cords to find them. [chapter VII] Nompwinapu'u was looking at him. Finally, he asked:

Nompwinapu'u: Hey fellow! What are you doing? Why are you twisting those cords all the time?

Little Old Man: I'm trying to live a little longer. I'm searching for the little roots with my magical cords.

Nompwinapu'u: Throw those cords away. They're useless.

Little Old Man: No, I won't. They're my secret to find little roots to eat.

Nompwinapu'u: What are you hiding in your bag?

Little Old Man: You don't have the right to touch by bag. It contains an ancient secret. If you want to help, bring me maize.

Nompwinapu'u: I was going to bring you some very good seeds, immortal maize seeds, but you're behaving badly with your useless magical cords. They won't get you anything to eat. I wanted to give the world turkeys, other nice fat birds, tapirs, monkeys. I wanted to improve the world. But you are advocating for a poor world with your secret cords so, Little Old Man, now you don't have any rights.

When he had scolded him enough, he added, "Alright, I will bring you five seeds of maize." This pleased the Little Old Man. Later, Nompwinapu'u returned.

Little Old Man: Why did you bring me so few?

Nompwinapu'u: These few are enough to plant. Plant one seed over there, another in the direction of that hill, another beyond the crest of that mountain, another toward that other hill. One seed in each direction [cardinal points]. Come back in four days to see how the plants are growing, if the stalks have sprouted. They should flower in six days. And in eight days you can harvest them. Later you will have two harvests each year. But now you will only harvest a little. You won't get any husks, only young ears but later when the maize ripens you can harvest the dry, ripe corn. First you will only harvest long-seeded maize, and later you will harvest round-seeded corn.

So it was. The Little Old Man got two harvests. He shared his seeds with his father-in-law. Nompwinapu'u returned again, "Didn't I tell you so? How do you like it?"

Indian: It's a beautiful harvest. But how can we eat this dry corn? It's too hard.

Nompwinapu'u: Make some clay pots to cook it, then you grind it on a stone. You can find a grinding stone in any stream nearby. The women have the right to make the tortillas and the tamales, while you men work in the milpas. Buy an axe to clear the field of bush and then plant. Work now, make plenty of money, enjoy living.

* * *

NARRATION 2
A FAMILY WITHOUT CHILDREN

A family without children does not harvest maize. Only when the elders are mixed in with the little ones, only then are the harvests good. When there are only old men and women, the harvest is never good.

* * *

MYTH 10
THE ORIGIN OF BEANS

Chiri Tsutsus brought the first *frijoles* [beans] to this world. She brought them from the caves of another nation. She harvested white beans from her head, from her hair, from above. These were for the men, food for the men. From below, from her skirt, she harvested black beans for the women, so that the women could eat.

She only stayed eight years in this world. She left because her brother-in-law killed her little son, and she became offended. Her kid [*cipote*] liked to go searching for *ts'astspiné* [honey]. He would leave with his uncles [brothers of his father] looking for honey. One day, an uncle said to him:

Uncle: Hey, do me a favor, nephew. Get that honey [high in the tree] for us so we can eat it.

The kid began to open up the hive.

| Uncle: | Put your whole arm into it, to get a good grip on the combs. |

He did so and got his arm caught in the hive. God [the Sun] was not pleased. Killing bees is strictly prohibited. The Sun watches to make sure that the laws are respected The uncles tried to free their nephew's arm by hacking at the hive but the axe slipped and cut off his arm and the kid died. This is why Chiri Tsutsus got angry.

Chiri Tsutsus:	I'm not going to live here anymore. The Indians fight all the time. I'm not staying here in the world any longer. The Indians are assassins. They killed my child, when they tried to get too much honey. They cut off his arm and killed him. I'm returning to my parents. Right this minute, I'll disappear.
Uncle:	Don't be angry, he died by accident.
Chiri Tsutsus:	How can you say it was an accident! It was not an accident. You cut off his arm with an axe.

She stayed angry forever. From that time on, she didn't greet or speak to anyone. Then she went into her cave and disappeared. She returned to her parent's place. Her husband couldn't follow her because she blocked the entrance to the cave.

| Husband: | Even though my wife fled, let's try to plant the beans she left. We have hands to work with, let's clear the fields of undergrowth and prepare it for planting. Let's plant *sinapopos* [lima beans], vine beans, northern beans. Tomam gave us these beans to feed our families. Come on, let's work. |

When Chiri Tsutsus became angry, she shook her head and the beans fell from her hair. Then the Mortals gathered them up and planted them. She only left the beans from her head. These were immortal. But later, they disappeared too. The beans we have now are all bought. The immortal beans disappeared because Chiri Tsutsus became angry with the Mortals. Her brothers-in-law are to blame; they killed her son.

* * *

MYTH 11
THE CHILD WHO CREATED PLANTS

A *cipote* [child or kid] got lost but then appeared where his father was working:

Child: Papa, I don't want to live any longer.

He didn't like to wear his *balandrán*. He wanted to go around naked, showing off his balls.

Child: Papa, I want you to kill me.
Father: Don't offend me. How could I kill a person, much less a child! No, I won't kill you.

The kid got angry. He was given a new tunic but he threw it away, too.

Child: Hey, papa, if you kill me, you will have camotes, *chayotes* [a vine fruit], to eat. They'll ripen right here. If you will only kill me, I will be born again and tobacco will grow out of my body and from my blood will sprout plants to eat — yucca, *malanga* [an edible root], bananas, *chayotes*.[5]
Father: No, I won't kill you. If you want to die, kill yourself.
Child: Alright, then I will kill myself and you will never see me again.
Father: You're talking too much.

The kid was thinking, wondering if Tomam had deceived him. He went to the other world to see Tomam and returned to the Earth with him.

Child: Papa, I still want you to kill me.
Father: What happened to the plants you promised me? I have cleared the field to plant them.
Tomam: You can't plant them yet. It's not the season.
Father: When can I plant them?
Tomam: The month of May, at the latest or the end of April.
Father: I'll believe you and hope that you're not fooling me.
Tomam: Don't search for this kid. I'll take care of him. Don't be sad for losing him.
Father: I agree.
Tomam: You will only lose this one child. I won't bother you anymore. I need this one alive.

The child returned to the other world with Tomam. When they arrived, Tomam gave an order to his [own] family:

> Take care of this kid for me. Don't harm him in the least. Let him go naked, as he pleases. With him, I am going to send seeds to the world of the Mortals. I will plant them in him. This is why I brought him here.

In late April, the kid returned to the Earth bringing seeds of bananas, of yucca, *malanga*, *chayote*, onions, tobacco. He took them all to his old father, planted them and disappeared again.

Tomam: [to the father] Soon they will sprout. You will be very proud of your son.

The man went home to tell his wife all that had happened.

Father: Now we will have all kinds of bananas, yucca, camotes!

The wife went to the field to see them.

Wife: But I am afraid. They may disappear just like our son.

The old father went back and forth from his house to the field. He wanted to make sure that no animal was harming the little plants. But the wife was doubtful.

Father: No, they will not disappear. Tomam gave his word. I still have confidence. I'm going to eat a little banana.

They began eating some of the products. They were sad because of their kid but they were eating reassured [that the new plants would not disappear]. Their other children all liked to be dressed. They never threw off their clothes; on the contrary, they took good care of them, as they didn't have many. They didn't want to go around naked. Tomam was spying on them.

Tomam: What do you think of the harvest? Did the plants produce well? Are you eating? Now you can harvest the tobacco. Now is the right time, it's ripe.

The man harvested the tobacco; a week later, it dried and he toasted the leaves. The next day, buyers came along, some *ladinos*.

Ladinos: Hey! Got any tobacco to sell?
Indian: No, the tobacco is not very good, the harvest was not up to par. I planted too much in one field.
Ladinos: Give us a little, to see how it is.

He gave them a few leaves.

Ladinos: This is enough to keep us going.

Then they bought some.

Ladinos: We also want to eat some *chayotes*.

The Indian went to get them and sold them a few pounds.

Ladinos:	If you have garlic, we'll buy some, too. It is a good remedy for worms and we'll have some onions to cook with meat.
Indian:	I'll bring only a few because they are not ripe yet.

He sold twenty-five heads of garlic and the same amount of onions. The *ladinos* were very gratified.

Many years later, the kid came back home. He was a grown man but he still went around naked. He didn't like the clothes of this world, clothes of the Mortals, clothes that only last a little while. When his little mother saw him, she thought to herself, "What a naughty child! He doesn't like our clothes."

Son:	Now I will never return again. Don't think about me. I am now settled in the other world. Now I am leaving papa.
Father:	Have a good journey.
Son:	I will never return again. I don't want to die.
Father:	Behave well with Tomam. This is the only advice I give you. If you don't behave well, he will send you back here.
Son:	Maybe Tomam will send me back here. If I don't behave as I should, I'll let him cool off.
Father:	Tomam is the Almighty.

He only came back to Earth to say goodbye to his old parents. He never returned again. And as we Mortals are the children of death, his old father and mother died.

*   *   *

MYTH 12
THE ORIGIN OF FROST

The Jívaros are messengers of the Tomams and owners of the frost. They made it, following orders of Tomam, to punish the Mortals.

A snake bit an Indian who was hunting deer. A Jívaro had put a snake in his path to bite him.

Jívaro:	Eh! Why are you alone all the time? I saw you. You have a wife. She is for you, not for your mother. But now [from now on], you can't go close to your wife because you have been bitten by a snake. If you do, you will surely die. Only if your little mother [*madrecita*] behaves herself, you won't die. But if she doesn't, a Jívaro will take you to the other world.

Little Mother: My son has the wanderlust. This is why that snake bit him. This is why his wife won't let him touch [have sex with] her. She grinds the maize to make pozol and tortillas. She does her duties but she won't sleep with him.

So God [Tomam] got angry. He intended that women be for men but the little mother didn't let her son sleep with his wife. The little mother behaved badly during five years. She really abused her son [it was then that Tomam sent Jívaro].

Jívaro: [to bitten man] Your little mother prohibited you from having sex with your wife. The punishment is frost, which will ruin your crops. Now go to your little mother now and ask her for your wife. If she refuses, you will die. But if you can keep your mother talking all night, you won't die — If she doesn't agree to talk, then you will die — without a doubt.

But the little mother didn't want to talk. She went to the stream to collect water.

Son: [to his mother] Come back. Send your daughter-in-law to bring water. Come back mama. Why should you carry the water? Send your daughter-in-law. Come back so that we can talk all night.

But the little mother didn't come back.

Son: Alright, mama, have it your way. If you don't want to talk to me, a Jívaro will send frost to ruin your crops. You won't have anything to eat. You'll be left with only the beams of your house.

The little mother didn't listen and went her way. She didn't even greet him. This was why, after that, she only had frostbitten, rotten maize, rotten camotes left to eat. The frosts attacked all her plants and roots [tubers]. Her son wanted to converse all night with her but the little old woman refused. This is why the frost ruined all her crops.

Jívaro: [to the son] Eh! Why are you always alone? Your wife is not meant to serve your mother. Your wife is for you but it turned out she is your mother's servant. Now your little mother will lose all of her crops: beans, camotes, maize, tobacco. All will be frostbitten.

Son: I'm not allowed to touch my wife. If I do, I may die. I refuse to disobey my little mother.

Jívaro: To the contrary, you will have sex with your wife, then
                    you will die. Blood will pour out of your mouth, you will
                    defecate blood [as a result having sex after being bitten by
                    a snake] and make the Nation of Frosts, so that all the
                    crops freeze.

Then the Indian slept with his wife. He embraced her and had sex with her.
She said to him, "Go ahead, I'm your wife. God [Tomam] created women
for men."

Jívaro was spying on them from a corner of their house. After the man
had sex with his wife, he vomited blood, blood seeped out of his ears,
nose, even through his skin, out of his whole body. He died. He died from
the snake bite when he "bit" his wife. Jívaro ordered him to die.

Then his neighbors and his in-laws came to bury him. His little mother
was angry, when she saw that her son had died. She got even madder,
when the in-laws came to the burial. One of them said to her, "Eh! Why
didn't you let me know, when your son was bitten by a snake?"

Little Mother: Because it is no business of the in-laws.

Then Jívaro ordered that all of her crops be frostbitten, because she had
behaved badly with her son. The in-laws harvested their crops as usual.

Little Mother: [to her in-laws] Now that the frost has ruined all of my
                    crops, you will surely give me a few ears of corn.

The little mother didn't have any maize, no camotes, no beans. All of her
crops were spoiled by the frost.

Tomam: [to the little mother] Why did you behave so badly with
                    your son? I intended that the women be for the men.
Little Mother: [to herself] I still have brothers and sisters.

She went to see them.

**The Brothers
   and Sisters:**   How did it happen? Why did you lose all your crops?
Little Mother: My son was bitten by a snake, that's the answer.
**The Brothers
   and Sisters:**   But why didn't you tell us? Maybe we could have saved
                    him. He was a good man. Why didn't you tell us? There
                    are lots of herbs to cure snake bites. You didn't even try to
                    save him. You behaved very badly with your son and your
                    daughter-in-law. Now you are punished for it. You cannot
                    prohibit a man from having sex with his wife.

This is how frost originated in the world. The Mortals themselves asked for it. The frost is blood of the Mortals, blood mixed with the clouds.

*   *   *

MYTH 13

THE ORIGIN OF THE RIVERS

In [during the era of] the First World, there were no streams or rivers, only lagoons.

Indians of the
First World: Let's go rob some water from the lagoon.

Then the Little Old Man appeared and spoke

Little Old Man: The Nation of the Indians is going to perish there in the lagoon. Nen [the Master of the Lagoon] will swallow them.

Three women were drowned in the lagoon. Nen swallowed them. Three gourds were floating in the lagoon. Then the First Indians sent a man to fetch water. The following day he was lost too. There was the proof — four gourds floating in the lagoon. They tried to gather water in their gourds, little by little, without making any noise. They wanted to steal some water without dripping any so that Nen would not hear them and remain sleeping on the bottom of the lagoon. But he heard them and he swallowed them, clothes and all. Only their gourds were left floating in the lagoon. Nen is the owner of the lagoon but he doesn't have the right to swallow people.

Nen: Anyone who tries to rob me: men, women, snakes, or cattle, I'll swallow them. Why are they such rascals? Why do they harm my lagoon? The Indian defecates in the lagoon, cattle the same.

Tomam the
Second: [Lord of the World of the Dead, to the new arrivals] How did you perish?

The Three
Women: We perished in the lagoon. Nen swallowed us. You haven't given us any rivers or stream so we had to steal water from the lagoon. You must make some rivers.

The Second Chief was ashamed. He said:

Without delay, we will create some rivers. But first, we'll
send a witness to find out if it is true that four were
drowned in the lagoon.

The Second Chief spoke to his brother, "Four gourds appeared floating in
the lagoon."

Tomam: Where? The Nation of Indians lost four Indians? I'll send
my son to find out the truth.

Nompwinapu'u: [the son] I don't want to go. I don't feel up to it. I don't
want to defend the Mortals.

Tomam: You must go.

Nompwinapu'u: First, a question. At what time of the year do the *guamas*
[fruit of the tree of the same name] ripen? I don't want to
waste my time. I'd rather not go at all. The world of the
Mortals is full of fetid vapor. I don't want to go to the
"dead" lagoon, not on your life. But alright, papa, I do
want to taste the *guamas*. I'll climb up the tree that's on
the edge of the lagoon and treat myself to the *guamas*.

Nompwinapu'u has a watch that tells when the fruits and crops ripen.

Nompwinapu'u: The *guamas* sprout in October, according to my watch. No
matter, I'll go mix with the Mortals. Papa, my watch tells
me that in May the *guamas* will be ripe. Now soon. I want
to eat the meals of the Mortals; maybe I'll like them better
than the food here. I'll be leaving soon now. It's not a bad
idea after all. I want to eat the *guamas*, even if I die in the
lagoon.

Tomam: You'll like them. They're nice and sweet.

Nompwinapu'u: Will you lend me your serpents and powder to shoot?

He arrived in this world coming down the hills, his serpents hidden under
his shirt.

Nompwinapu'u: [perched in the fruit tree on the edge of the lagoon, eating
guamas] Nen wants to kill me. [To Nen]: I'll kill you.
You're repulsive, swallower of Indians. I'll kill the lagoon
too. From now on, there will only be rivers and streams in
the world. Four days from now, I'll kill you. Then there
will be no more Nen, no more repulsive lagoons — only
rivers and streams, clean water to bathe in, to cleanse the
body and hair. Women get very nervous, if they don't
bathe. Women who are making love need to bathe. This is
why those three women perished, to get water. [To the

Little Old Man]: I beg your pardon, Señor Indio, I'm going to try to remedy this. Here, the tiger hunts women and if he catches one, he rapes her and then kills her. All the more reason why I should remedy the world. Let's see if I can. Even if I can't do it all, at least I'll make rivers and streams. It's worth trying. With your permission, Señor Indio.

Little Old Man: I want rivers and streams so that the lagoon doesn't make more trouble. He already swallowed three women and a man, four in all. This is why I'm against the lagoon.

Nompwinapu'u: If I can, I'll make the rivers and streams. Don't forget, I am under age. I don't give orders.

Little Old Man: Be strong. There are many harmful animals, tigers that hunt women. When the women harvest beans, a tiger carries them off.

Nompwinapu'u: You're complaining too much, old gossiper.

Little Old Man: I only complain of those who do harm. A word of warning, don't destroy all the lagoons. Only one is to blame. You must leave the Nation of the Lagoons and give us the Nation of the Rivers and Streams, too.

We need lagoons for the deer and agoutis to play in. The Little Old Man knew this and this is why he didn't present a complaint to Tomam against all the lagoons, but only against one.

Nompwinapu'u: Rivers and streams will be born in four days. Stay at home during these four days, curled up with your wife.

Grandfather Thunder threw his axes [lightning] four times, straight at the lagoon. During four days, it rained, thundered and the wind blew very strong. Grandfather Thunder was busy all the time throwing his axes. The Tomams dispatched the clouds. And when the storm was at its worst, Nen bit Nompwinapu'u's foot and swallowed three of his toes. Then Nompwinapu'u struck him in the mouth with one of his serpents, lashed out with the others, lassoed him like a monkey and finished him off. The storm lasted four days and so the rivers and streams were created — in those four days.

The Owner of the Rivers [also Nen][6] has a serpent [snake] in every river [or stream]. If the serpent dies, the river dries up; this is why it is prohibited to kill it.

* * *

MYTH 14
THE LITTLE OLD MAN DEFENDS THE EARTH

Nompwinapu'u: I want to fix the world of the Mortals. It has a lot of fetid vapor, vapor of *ladinos*, vapor of Indians. I want to destroy all the nations: *ladinos*, Indians, deer, armadillos, all and create another world, an immortal world.

Little Old Man: No, you can't do it!

Nompwinapu'u: What do you mean, I can't! I can easily make the immortal world.

Little Old Man: No, Señor. No order has been given to destroy this world. This World, the Earth, does not kill anyone. Only the Mortals are at fault. They fight because they enjoy it. Even I harm the rivers and lagoons, the deer, the agoutis. All nations are brothers of death but the Earth is not to blame.

He defended the Earth. And what does the Earth say! She doesn't say anything, she just eats dead Indians and dead *ladinos*.

Nompwinapu'u: Now you have offended me. You are wrong to advocate for the World. I will give you some advice, in two or three words, no more. Treat the Devil well; treat Tsëncley [Master of Many Animals] well, when he comes to harm your crops, when the armadillos feed on your maize, when the deer munch your beans. You're defending all of them.

Little Old Man: How can you speak against the Mortals: the Indians, the *ladinos*, against the armadillos, the snakes, the white-collared peccaries? You created all these nations. They are honorable. Only the Devil is a rascal.

Nompwinapu'u: Now I am really angry. You win. From now on, the Mortals will live on top of the Earth. The masters and the majordomos will live underneath the Earth, the armadillos, pacas and deer on top of the Earth. Each little animal will have its rights and when it finishes eating, it will go home to a cave.

Little Old Man: I am doing very well, defending this World.

Nompwinapu'u: Not so, you're behaving badly. Now I'm leaving. I'm going to defend my own World.

He left, resentful and angry. He climbed up a vine to the heavens. As he went, the clouds closed in on him so that we Mortals couldn't see him going up to the heavens.

* * *

MYTH 15
HOW THE FIRST FIRE WAS STOLEN

Grandfather Thunder agreed to give fire to the Little Old Man, the immortal fire which could never go out.

Grandfather
Thunder: [to the Little Old Man] Bring me that hornet's nest.

Grandfather Thunder took the hornet's nest home with him, to the heavens, and he gave the Little Old Man the eternal fire. But soon after that, Indians of the First Nation [of People] stole the fire. Then a great wind blew, sparks flew and set the robbers on fire. The Little Old Man pulled them out of the fire — smoldering ashes. Out of the ashes, came birds: from their arms — the wings, from their mouths — the beaks. Soon Grandfather Thunder appeared. The Little Old Man said, "Now, I will be blamed because you burned my companions."

Grandfather
Thunder: [the Master of the Fire] No, Señor, you're not at fault. From these ashes, I create the Nation of Wings: *merets* [a parakeet], *khiyu* [a white-faced parakeet], *ili'lis* [another parakeet], the *pokpok* [woodpecker], the red-breasted-*apep*, the *cerequeques*, and the *guaras* [not identified]. This is the punishment for the robbers of the fire.

Little Old Man: The robbers of the fire have no hands, only claws to eat raw maize and *guamas*. They won't need fire. They'll only eat raw food.

Grandfather
Thunder: So be it. But they'll feed on your crops, your maize.

The Little Old Man didn't like that. He said, "The maize is for my family."

Grandfather
Thunder: The maize is for many nations: for the parakeets, the *cerequeques*, so that the Indians not only work for their own families.

Before they stole the fire, the firebirds were the same nation as we are; they were punished for robbing the fire. Grandfather Thunder ordered the Little Old Man to make them into the Nation of Wings. The Nation of Crabs, Earth and Rivercrabs, were also made from the eternal fire.

Grandfather
Thunder: From now on, the immortal fire will only serve to make nations and confuse the Little Old Man.

The Little Old Man did not like that. He didn't like being fooled by Grandfather Thunder.

Someone: A couple of kids [a girl and a boy] got lost. But don't anyone search for them.

The children were burned up in the immortal fire. From the ashes of their little fingers, the earthcrabs appeared [were created]. But the *hop* [the rivercrab] was made from the ashes of the little fingers of an old woman and an old man. When they burned their little fingers, they ran to a stream to squelch the fire. Then the stream dried up and their fingers became the rivercrabs.

Deer came to the stream to drink. They complained that the stream had dried up. One of the deer pressed down on the bed of the stream with his hoof and almost crushed the crab.

Deer: What a stupid crab! It's your fault that the stream dried up. Why did you dry it up?

But when the deer saw that in the very spot where he stepped on the crab, water surged up, he forgave the crab.

Deer: The crab should be respected, not crushed. They are the companions of the water.
Deer: What's your name?
Rivercrab: My name is *hop*. What's yours?
Deer: *Pis.*

Then the *hop* swam deep into the stream.

When the Little Old Man died, Grandfather Thunder took the immortal fire home with him. Tomam said to the Mortals:

> From now on, you will cook with fire and you will get from the Spaniards. From now on, no animal will ever talk again.

So it was. Since that time, all the animals are speechless, none ever spoke again.

The immortal fire never goes out. Only Grandfather Thunder can kindle it. Now we only have a dead fire. When it goes out you ask for matches and if no one gives you any, you have to buy them from the *ladinos*.

*   *   *

MYTH 16
OPOSSUM AND THE FIRST FIRE

During the First Nation, there was no fire. The Little Old Man asked
Grandfather Thunder for it [for the eternal fire]. Grandfather Thunder gave
orders to lower a hornet's nest from the tree tops and [when he obtained it]
he changed [transformed] it into the eternal fire.

Some Indians wanted to roast an opossum. They killed it, scorched off
it's hair and threw it into a kettle over the fire. Then opossum began to
converse from inside the kettle, "You killed me in vain. You can't possibly
roast me." And later, "I'm still not roasted. I'm still alive and raw."

Opossum was making a nuisance of himself and the Indians were annoyed. He kept on talking, "I'm still not roasted. I'm still raw, green and
alive. Roast me some more." But they couldn't roast him. "He's not roasting," the Indians said.

Opossum: You'll never be able to roast me.

He was still raw. How could they eat him? After awhile, the men tried to
roast an armadillo but he escaped from the kettle and fled. Soon some
Señores *ladinos* passed by and asked, "What are you Indians eating?"

Indians: Beans.
Señores: Beans! So that's why you are farting. The Indians are
                 forever farting. They are really repulsive.
Opossum: They don't fart for the fun of it. They fart because they eat
                 too many beans and their stomachs swell.

The Indians told the Little Old Man:

> We're going to throw this fire away. It's useless for roast-
> ing. So they changed it for the fire of the Spaniards, fire of
> the Mortals.

The Little Old Man said to them:

> Choose whichever you like. I brought you this eternal fire
> to create parakeets, *cerequeques*, *guaras*: the Nation of
> Birds. That's what this fire is for, it's not for roasting.

Only the Little Old Man could roast with this first fire. But he didn't use it
to roast little animals. He wanted it to make the Nation of Birds. When he
created them from ashes, they would fly away singing, "cre, cre, cre," as
the parakeets do when they fly away over the hills. Grandfather Thunder
made the Nation of Crabs from the first fire and since then they have been
reproducing along the rivers and streams.

The fire of Spaniards can be used for roasting but not for making nations. The Little Old Man, the First Indian, had the right to roast with the eternal fire but those other Indians did not. That's why they got angry.

Grandfather Thunder took his fire back because he didn't like this world, where he could only create mortal birds and crabs [not immortal ones].

* * *

MYTH 17
THE WORLD ALMOST FELL DOWN

The old people said that four posts hold up the world, like the roof of a house.[7] There are two toward *tsik'in mo'o* (the east) and two toward *tyaj mo'o* (the west). During January, the world is on the edge of the posts and can easily be blown off and fall like a dead leaf. During February, it slides back almost into position and in March, it is firmly in place. From April on, there is no danger, except in June and July, when the wind blows strong.

The Mortals are really troubled when the wind blows because the world is in danger of falling [off the posts]. Grandfather Thunder warned that when the wind blows not to cut down any trees, to keep the wind from getting angry and blowing the world off its posts. Grandfather Thunder is the Majordomo of the Wind but sometimes it goes off by itself, without his permission.

If an Indian is mischievous or a rascal, he should be punished — not killed.

The First Nation of Indians didn't know how to make the strings for the guitar they wanted to play. Two mischievous brothers cut off the tail of a horse, to get hair to make the strings.

Indians: The horse is not food. Only its tail can be used.

They cut it off and the owner of the horse, a *ladino*, was so mad that he cut off their heads with a machete.

Ladino: These Indians were harmful, misbehaving and stealing.

But the death of these Indians endangered the world and that was the *ladinos*' fault. Then the Little Old Man, who was a *punakpan* [shaman], came from the West Heaven to save the world. He asked the *ladinos*, "Why are you so busy killing people?"

Ladinos: We *ladinos* don't kill people for the fun of it. But we defend our possessions. These Indians were offensive. They cut off the tail of our horse.

Little Old Man: Those Indians were stupid but that wasn't reason enough to kill them.

Then, following Tomam's orders, the Little Old Man made them pay a fine of 3,000 *pesos* to Tegucigalpa, for having cut off the heads of the Indians. If they refused to pay, the world would have fallen off its posts. The rich pay fines with money, the poor with chickens and pots.

The two dead Indians were sent to greet Tomam in the East Heaven and then to the West, to the World of the Dead, with Tomam Chikwai. There they saw the posts which hold up the world and they began digging under them so that the world would fall. The Sun saw them and notified Tomam, "There are some fellows there in *tsik'in mo'o* digging up the posts."

Little Old Man: What those again!

Tomam threw them in jail and then sent them to Oropang [the world beyond, where those who commit suicide or misbehave are sent].

NOTES

1. See Van Gennep (1906) for creation myths of human beings from monkeys and Pettazzoni (1954: 24–36) on the philosophical importance of origin myths.
2. A very common concept in the mythology of America.
3. The merchants often come to the Montaña to trade on Saturdays.
4. The cedar is a sacred tree among the Mayas and many other Indian groups. See Thompson (1958: 245–46); Karsten (1926: 302); La Farge and Byers (1931: 192).
5. See Zerries (1959a: 7, 1962 chap. III), with reference to South America for the concept of the origin of plants, as originating in the human body. Also, see Hatt (1951: 873, 878, 881).
6. Nen is also called "Sialpe" which is probably a derivation from the archaic Spanish word "sierpe" which signifies "serpent."
7. See Thalbitzer (1930: 83) for a similar concept among the Eskimos; Soustelle (1935: 174) and Thompson (1970: 347), among the Mayas. In Shaw (1971: 379–80) there is another version of this myth in English with transcription in Tolupan.

CHAPTER _IV_

THE HEAVENS

In the heavens, time passes imperceptibly; there, no one suffers, ages or dies and the laws are rigorously enforced. The Immortals, animals and plants all speak Tolupan and the language of the Immortals.[1]

THE TOMAMS
(Author)

Tomam Pones Popawai is the almighty. He reigns over the many "nations" — living beings — and all of nature. He is referred to as Grandfather Tomam the Greatest (Tomam Pones Popawai) and the Supreme Lawmaker. Although all supernatural power emanates from him, he rarely exercises it and remains detached from earthly occurrences and human affairs.[2] He delegated his power to his two sons. He is kind and imperturbable. His wife, Tomam Pones Namawai, is the _namawai_ (mother) of all that exists. Since they never age, they have children every few years, though only two of their sons are known.

Their eldest son also has various names: Tomam the Elder, Tomam Pones, First Chief, Head Chief, Lawgiver of the World, the Master of Authority, Tsik'in Tomam (Tomam of the East because he inhabits the East Heaven). He is also called simply Tomam or _Dios_ (God). He and his wife have many offsprings — the eldest being Nompwinapu'u — and many beautiful daughters who made love with their brother in order to create the Nation of Mortals, in particular, the Tolupans and by implication all humanity. (myth 1) One of the daughters agreed to marry the Little Old Man who was taken to the East Heaven by her brother. (myth 20) On another occasion, a daughter was sent to the Earth to marry a *punakpan* whose name was Gruperas. (narration 49) If a Mortal marries a daughter of Tomam, he acquires immortality, as do their children. Alfonso Martínez often said jokingly that he wished he were a *punakpan* so that he might marry one of Tomam's daughters and become immortal. (narration 3)

The world of Tomam, called *tsik'in mo'o* (eastern place or space), is mountainous and dotted with cultivated fields and houses. Fresh maize is available year-round, as are wild animals of all kinds who never age. The domestic animals which have died (cattle, horses, mules, and pigs) are in the zenith with Tata Dios (myth 7), while the deceased domestic birds are sent to another master, Noventa. (myth 33 and narration 12) When Tomam wishes to dine on one of these animals, he requests them from their masters.

Four suns and four moons shine in Tomam's world. It takes ten years to arrive there. Only a shaman (*punakpan*) can make the journey and he must be accompanied by a Jívaro, one of Tomam's messengers, so as not to lose his way. (narration 47) They start from the north coast of Honduras and proceed toward the east, crossing a sea the color of blood, beyond this world. They may return through the air.

Tomam, although subject to his father, is considered the "sovereign of the world." He reigns over all other Immortals, those of the heavens and of the Earth. Whenever a dispute arises among them, he applies the law. The same occurs when the Immortals abuse the Mortals. However, he is not especially partial to the latter. For instance, when the recently dead Mortals prolong their visit to him in the East Heaven, he does not permit them to remain at his side because of their cadaverous odor. (chapter VI) This is why he obliges his brother, Tomam the Younger, to take charge of the dead Indians and Tata Dios of the dead *ladinos*. (myths 3 and 7)

Tomam gave the Tolupans maize and the other cultivated plants, with the exception of beans which were lost. (myths 9 to 11) Nearly everything that exists in the Tolupan world has a master, an owner, who is directly responsible to Tomam or his younger brother, Tomam the Younger. Moreover, Tomam the Elder governs the Sun, the Moon, the Stars, and Mother Earth. The celestial abode of the trees, is called Lenko po and is situated close to his residence. He defends the trees, when they are being mistreated by the Wind. (myth 23) The forces of nature which originate in the east — wind, rain, thunder — are under his command, even though they be subordinate to other masters. Tomam sent sickness to the Earth, as only he has power over life and death. Diseases also have their special master. (narration 34)

Tomam dispatched the Devils to this world because they were being troublesome in the East Heaven. He confined them to caves and ordered them not to mingle with human beings but they often escape his control and win souls for their own "party." (myth 58) They can only be destroyed by Tomam or his son, Nompwinapu'u.

Tomam has messengers, the Tsik'in Jívaro (Jívaro of the East), and an assistant, Tsik'in Guatecast, who disdainfully refuses to take part in occurrences of this world. Humans are repulsive to him. (myth 1) Tomam exercises absolute dominion over the *punakpanes*, with whom he establishes contact through the Jívaros. If one misbehaves, he sends a winged snake whose bite is mortally poisonous. (myth 60)

Tomam maintains constant contact with the humans: through the Sun during the day and at night either the Moon or the Jívaros watch over them. So he knows all that is going on, including when and how anyone dies. (narration 9) Tomam does not disguise his antipathy for the baptized Indians. (myth 36)

Nompwinapu'u, Tomam's eldest son, is a first *maestro* because he created the "Nation of Women." (myth 1) He resides in the East Heaven with his parents and apparently is not married. He comes to Earth with serpents curled around his arm and hidden under his tunic. He employs these serpents to kill the Devils. Once, he used them to finish off Nen, the Owner of the Lagoon. (myth 13)

Nompwinapu'u created the rivers and gave maize to the humans, following instructions of his father. (myths 9 and 13) As Master of Maize, he defends his protégé and is very annoyed when the Tolupans harvest corn before it matures. (myth 19) He is also the Master of the *Guamo* Trees, whose fruit he loves to eat. (myth 13) When the First Humans became Mortals, he wanted to recreate the world so that humans live eternally but the Little Old Man forbade him from doing so. (myth 14)

Occasionally, Nompwinapu'u is sent to this world to kill the Devils. (narration 35) During an eclipse of the moon, he orders the *punakpanes*. (shamans) to tell the women to make noise by striking their wooden tables and thereby frightening the moon's enemy who is trying to devour her. (myth 28)

Tomam's brother is called Tomam Chikwai or Wowai; the latter words simply mean "younger" in the Tolupan language. He is also referred to as Tomam Tyaj. (Tomam of the West) or Second Chief. Although affable, Tomam the Younger is contrasted to his older brother by his negative attributes. He reigns over the World of the Dead in the West Heaven and is responsible for the winds, rains and thunder originating in the west, which are considered harmful. (myth 2) He, too, has a wife and children, although only a nameless eldest son is mentioned. (myth 21) The Tyaj Jívaro, Jívaros of the West, are his messengers and Tyaj Guatecast his assistant. The latter accompanies the recently deceased to the domain of the dead in the western heavens. He, like Nompwinapu'u, is a first *maestro* because he created the male sex. (myth 1)

*   *   *

MYTH 18
TOMAM MAKES THUNDER

The first chief saw his wife grinding maize and said, "My wife is working. I'm going to do the same. I'm going to make thunder so that the Mortals can hear me." When the wife is working, the husband shouldn't be lounging about. Tomam the Elder makes thunder from June to August [to bring the rain to the crops], while Tomam the Younger takes over during September and October and knocks down the maize stalks.

*   *   *

MYTH 19
THE LITTLE EAR OF CORN
COMPLAINS TO HIS MASTER

Nompwinapu'u becomes angry, when we fold over the shafts of the tender maize. The ripe, dry maize complains a lot to its master, when we fold over its shafts but the tender maize even more, saying:

> Why did that Indian fold over my stalks already? I'm still very young — only two months old. I don't want to be thrown into a corn bin. I don't want to be handcuffed [*mancuernado*: in the bin the ears of corn are tied in pairs by their husks]; I want to stand upright in the milpa. That Indian folded me over too soon. The Indians should not fold me over until I become dry and old, not before.

Nompwinapu'u: If you want to live longer, go ask my father for permission to live in his milpa. His maize never dries up.

The little ear of corn took his advice. When he arrived, Tomam said:

> You're welcome here. Go over there to my milpa. I won't fold you over, while you are still in flower. I won't tear off your tender stalks.

Tomam has ripe and tender maize in his bin all year-round. He can make *atole* [a drink made of new maize], whenever he pleases.

The little roots [tubers] also complain to their master, when they are dug up too soon, when they are still not ripe. But we only dig them up before they are ripe, when the white-collared peccaries and agoutis are eating them up. To save some for ourselves, we have to dig them up before they are ripe. Those animals don't have the right to eat all the crops of us Mortals, but sometimes they do. We don't feed in their masters' fields.

* * *

MYTH 20
THE LITTLE OLD MAN VISITS HEAVEN

Nompwinapu'u: Do you want to be my brother-in-law? I have many sisters. But now that I think of it, you offended me [myth 9] and I have changed my mind; I won't introduce them to you.

Little Old Man: Did I really offend you? I want very much to meet your sisters. Maybe, after all, you will advocate on my behalf. I want to court your sisters. Really, I would love to meet them.

Nompwinapu'u forgave him and took him to the other world. When the Little Old Man arrived, he became young again; all is immortal there, no one ages. He asked to meet the girls but right away he got angry.

Little Old Man: These women are great gossipers.

The daughters of Tomam became offended and got angry, too.

The Girls: This Nation of Mortals is terribly gossipy. Go, go back to your Earth.

Little Old Man: So, you're chasing me out! I'm not a dog. But if you want to order me around, go ahead. Eh! What made them so angry?

Tomam: [to his son Nompwinapu'u] What made you bring this gossipy Indian here?

Nompwinapu'u: Don't be offended papi, I'm going to take him home. He turned out to be a real tattler, that's true. He spoke against the women.

Nompwinapu'u agreed to take the Little Old Man back to the Earth. He had hoped that the Indian would marry one of Tomam's daughters, an immortal woman, so that he would never die.

Tomam: [to the Little Old Man] You spoke against the women! You came to my home and offended me! Who taught you to act in such a manner? The Immortals are gossipy, but the Mortals are even worse. Now, go to court your own women, the mortal women.

Daughter
of Tomam: How is it that the mortal men speak so crudely? How is it that this one dared offend us, we the immortal women?

Mother: But why are you so offended, daughter? Do you think a good husband is so easily come by? Besides, they all have the same penis.

Daughter: I refuse to compromise with a Mortal like this one. I won't allow him to court me. He spoke very badly to me.

Mother: You're talking too much. I'm about to punish you!

Tomam: He offended me, the father! This is a very uncouth Mortal!

Nompwinapu'u: [to his father] You have no right to touch this Mortal, much less throw him in jail. Besides, there are no jails for the Mortals here. I'll inform his chief on Earth that this fellow made a nuisance of himself, here in the home of the First Chief. It's my fault for bringing him. So punish me, not the Little Old Man. He came to insult us, here in the home of my father and mother. I never thought he would turn out such a gossiper.

Tomam: I agree and even though I have the right to punish you, this time I forgive you. Now take this gossiper back to his place.

And so it was. Nompwinapu'u brought the Little Old Man back to Earth.

* * *

NARRATION 3
ALFONSO WANTED TO MARRY
ONE OF TOMAM'S DAUGHTERS

Nompwinapu'u almost became my *napeiwai* [brother-in-law], because I nearly married one of his sisters. Nompwinapu'u spoke to me once:

> Alfonso, old fellow, let's go visit my nation, my father's home, so that you ask for one of my sisters in marriage, then we will be brothers-in-law. I have loads of sisters and all are very pretty women. There, no one ever dies.

* * *

MYTH 21
TOMAM THE YOUNGER CAUSES A FLOOD

An Indian misinformed Tomam the Younger [in the world of the dead]. He told him, "I was assassinated. This is why I died."

Tomam the
Younger: You died because you wanted to! I don't have any use for you here. I don't like gossipy Mortals. You were courting women from another nation, that's why you died. This I know. You are informing against your companions. Because of you, I'm going to punish all the Mortals.

He sent a telegram to inform the Head Chief [Tomam the Elder]. But right away [without waiting for an answer to his telegram], he sent a great excess of rain to the Earth and ordered the Earthquake to make the Earth tremble. Tomam the Younger only has the right to punish the Mortals — not the animals, not the peccaries, not the tapirs, not the tigers. But as they were wandering about on the shores of the rivers and streams lots were drowned. Some *ladinos* who lived close by were drowned too. Since we Indians live on the mountain tops, not one of us was drowned.

Tsëncley, the Master of the *Quequeos* [white-collared peccaries], and Tsets'em [Master of the Tapirs] complained to Tomam, "Why don't you give the order to stop these rains so that no more of our animals drown?"

Tomam: Where did all this rain come from?
Jívaro: Could be because of some gossiper.
Tomam: It surely must be the fault of the Mortals.

The Master Tsëncley said:

All the rivers and streams have flooded over. Many tapirs, tigers and peccaries have already drowned, all because of so much rain.

The Head Chief was very put out and said:

I'll send my son to find out what happened and bring me an account.

When Nompwinapu'u arrived on earth, he went directly to the domicile of Saino Jamayón [Master of the White-Lipped Peccaries]. Our Lord [his son-in-law: myth 3] came out to greet him.

Nompwinapu'u: Where are those peccaries who were drowned?
Our Lord: The boss is very angry.

Nompwinapu'u: Alright. I will send five witnesses to see if it is true that so many animals were drowned.

The entire pack drowned. The Second Chief applied the law badly. Why did he do such a thing? He only has the right to drown the Indians, the Mortals. Those animals were not to blame. The peccaries enjoy living, excavating, searching for food along the streams, for snails and *pacuca* [fruit of a palm tree]. Tigers were drowned, too, as they follow the paw prints of the peccaries. But the deer weren't drowned because they only stay a little while to drink along the banks of the streams. Nompwinapu'u returned to his father and gave his report:

What my uncle did is really criminal! Why did he pay attention to that gossipy dead Mortal?

First Chief: Tie up your uncle and bring him here. Why does he do such things? Several nations perished because of him.

The Second Chief and the Earthquake were brought with their hands tied to the East Heaven and thrown in jail. The nieces [daughters of Tomam the Elder] gave them food.

Tomam: Brother! Aren't you ashamed, eating as if nothing had happened? Aren't you repentant? You drowned many peccaries.

Tomam the
Younger: I won't do it again. From now on, I will only punish the gossipers who arrive at my place complaining and talking too much.

Meanwhile, Jívaro went to the Master Saino Jamayón to ask for something to eat, "Give me a peccary, I'm hungry."

Master: Are you a Mortal?
Jívaro: No, Señor.

They got into an angry dispute.

Jívaro: No, no, I'm not a Mortal. Do you intend to make a declaration against me?
Master: Only the Mortals have the right to eat my peccaries. You're not a Mortal, then why do you bother asking? You Immortals have no right to my peccaries.
Jívaro: Yesterday, I saw a lot of drowned peccaries. This is why I have come to ask you for one. You can't have eaten them all!
Master: No. I only have a couple of young skinny ones left.

Jívaro:	Why are you offending Tomam's messenger? I only asked for one. I have a mind to tie you up and take you to the Head Chief.
Master:	Don't be offended. Something else is bothering me. My peccaries and the animals of Tsets'em and those of Tsëncley are dead, drowned. Why did the Second Chief order so much rain? Why wasn't he more patient?
Jívaro:	They already threw him in jail.

The next day, a son of the Second Chief came to Tomam, saying:

	I am here to defend my father. He was misled by a gossipy Mortal. This is why he sent so much rain. Will you pardon him, this one time?
Tomam:	You are my nephew. You have the right to defend your father. The younger sons don't have the right, but the older ones do. Go, take care of your father. From now on, when a dead gossiper arrives at your place, your father should notify me, to avoid repeating such harm. If he does this again, he'll die in jail. This time, I'll let him go with you. I won't punish him anymore.

So it was, in this world there are laws. In the other world, likewise. This world cannot be remedied but in the other world there is justice.

* * *

NARRATION 4
THE JÍVAROS WATCH OVER THE MORTALS

Tomam sends the Jívaros to visit the Mortals. They come flying on a wooden board in the silence and darkness of moonless nights. Tomam sends them, when there is a little breeze. They squeeze into four corners under the roof of a house. Two Tsik'in Jívaros come together from below [the west]. They come to spy, to listen to what the Mortals are saying, to find out how they are behaving, if the man and wife are quarreling. If they are getting on well, the Jívaros won't bother them. The Jívaros only report to Tomam on those who are quarreling. Then their hour of death has come and they'll be taken to Tomam because he wants to meet them. If you behave well, you can live a few more years.

* * *

GRANDFATHER THUNDER
(Author)

According to the Tolupans, there are seven levels in the sky and several below the Earth.[3] Grandfather Thunder resides in the first upper level. He is said to be similar to people, wears a sombrero and pants. To make thunder, he throws stone axes with great force toward the Earth. (narration 6) He carries serpents encircled over his shoulder like lassos and employs them to make lightning. He destroys old decayed trees with his serpents and then sends the trees to the East Heaven. Tomam, as Master of the Trees, orders Grandfather Thunder to strike a tree so that it come to his domain. In this way, Alfonso explains, Tomam facilitates firewood for the Indians.

Grandfather Thunder is the majordomo of the wind because "when there is thunder and lightning, the wind blows hard." He has a great aversion to smoke. The old Indians were warned not to light a fire in their huts during a thunderstorm and, above all, not to roast maize during a storm because Grandfather Thunder's serpents have special dislike for the smoke of burnt maize and if they are bothered by it, they will surely strike the house with lightning.

This Grandfather is also the Master of the First Nation of Fire: the eternal fire from which "nations" of birds and crabs were created but which cannot be used for cooking. (myth 15) Grandfather's birds remain all year-around on Earth, while Tata Dios' "Birds of Glory" only stay during the rainy season. Grandfather Thunder is also the Master of Wasps. (myth 22 and narration 5)

MYTH 22
GRANDFATHER THUNDER,
MASTER OF THE WASPS

The wasps live on the first level with Grandfather Thunder. Once, when a wasp bit him on the forehead, he said to him:

> I'm going to throw you to the Mortals so that they burn you up.[4] This is a punishment for having bitten me so hard. Why did you bite me? Now you will have to die. If the Mortals don't burn you up, the *muhuh* [warrior ants] will bite the life out of you. If not, the *motetes* [anteaters] will eat you up.

*   *   *

NARRATION 5
WASPS HAVE LOTS OF ENEMIES

Wasps have lots of enemies: warrior ants, anteaters. We have the right to eat them, too. Once we have eaten them, they return to their master. If we don't eat them, the warrior ants will. They are their majordomos. These fellows [warrior ants] are military, like so many in Tegucigalpa. When they attack a wasp's nest, none escape. They are the majordomos of the frogs, too. They kill them, when they please. But they're our friends. They clean our houses. When you see a troop of these ants coming toward your house, leave the house and they'll clean it for you. One must respect these señoras. Only if one bites you very hard, should you kill it. They live in the first level above the Earth.

Grandfather Thunder punishes the wasps. They have a lot of enemies because they are good to eat.

* * *

NARRATION 6
GRANDFATHER THUNDER'S AXES

Sometimes, you find broken grinding stones and *tiesos* [pot sherds]. I leave them be. I think, "What can I use them for? They belong to the ancients." They show that people lived here before. I found polished stones. (*piedras afiladas* — axes), too, in the fields. They are blue-green, have a sharp end, six to eight inches long, are very well polished and sort of rounded.

The old people told us not to touch those *piedras*, to leave them be because they have a master, Grandfather Thunder. He throws them to this world when it thunders, breaking the branches of the trees. Once, I kept one, because they're pretty, but the old people scolded me, "You must leave it, where you found it. It has an owner." When Grandfather Thunder throws them this way, they go down deep into the Earth and little by little they rise. It takes them seven years to rise. When they get up on top of the ground, then they go off into the sky, back to their master.

* * *

NARRATION 7
GRANDFATHER THUNDER BRINGS THE LIGHTNING

When the rains begin, lightning comes to the Earth with its master, Grandfather Thunder, to play with the pine trees and other trees. If he sees a palm tree from a distance, he hits it. He can even hit cattle and horses. He has the right to strike everything, except deer. He'll strike a gossipy Mortal, if Tomam orders him to do so.

The old people said that during a storm, the men should not wear anything blue, the women should not wear yellow dresses and no one should wear anything white or new.

* * *

THE MASTER OF THE WIND
(Author)

The winds have the right to fell any dead tree except the cedar. (myth 5) Grandfather Thunder is the majordomo of the four winds of the cardinal points. Each has a master. Tomam is that of the eastern wind, called Tsik'in Lupu or Lupu the Elder. This wind brings the first rains of the spring in April and May. "It is very favorable to us Mortals." Tomam the Younger is in charge of the western autumn wind, Tyaj Lupu or Lupu the Younger. This wind has a bad reputation, as it blows over the mature corn in September and October just as it is about to be harvested. The north wind comes in the winter and is not liked because it brings cold weather. In the summer, the south wind is more favorable for the crops. The masters of these two winds were not reported.

In order to "suspend the wind," some Tolupans erect wooden crosses in their milpas to protect their corn. Alfonso explained:

> Each cross should have two little wooden sticks hanging from its arms, to make noise and scare the birds away from the corn. They think it is a hawk. I put crosses to protect the milpa against the parakeets and against the wind, too. If the bean harvest looks good, I put a woman's dress on a cross to keep the deer away. But this year I didn't put up any crosses. I thought that deer meat is better than beans any day.

* * *

MYTH 23
THE IMPERTINENT WIND

A healthy tree was knocked down by the wind and it complained to Tomam, "A lot of trees are falling down. That wind killed me. It blew me apart."

Tomam: Are you speaking the truth?

| Tree: | The whole truth. I don't go around lying. A wind finished me off. |

The Master got angry and right away sent the wind to jail. It stayed in jail for five months, left without permission and was gone before Tomam missed it.

| Tomam: | Get the wind who just escaped! |

Finally, it was caught and brought back, all tied up.

Wind:	I was knocking down maize, pine trees and other trees.
Tomam:	You have no right to good trees, only old rotten ones. You can only knock down dead timber. I am going to punish you, throw you back in jail.
Wind:	Let me go to roam through the hills. I want to go visiting.
Tomam:	No, I won't. I am very put out with you. Last year, too, you were knocking over maize and good trees. You're going back to jail.
Wind:	Let me go! I don't want to stay here.

The wind was very sad. He became very skinny. Then Tomam let him go. By then, he didn't have enough strength to knock anything down, except rotten trees.

| Tomam: | Healthy trees must be respected. |

* * *

EARTHQUAKES AND MOURNING
(Author)

There are only two Earthquakes: one in the East Heaven, called Tsik'in Chiquichi, and the other in the West World of the Dead, Tyaj Chiquichi. The former belongs to Tomam and is said to be less harmful than the latter, which is reputed to be very damaging and has Tomam the Younger as its master.

Earthquakes are believed to occur when someone who has died lies to Tomam the Younger. If he lies about how he died, accusing his family for not taking care of him, Tomam the Younger takes vengeance on the Mortals and orders his Earthquake to shake the posts which support the world. (myths 17 and 21)

Once, an old Tolupan woman told me that she was very frightened of Earthquakes. She shook a beam of her hut slightly, explaining, "The Earthquake is caused by the people below [in the World of the Dead]."

A grieving family is especially vulnerable and should take certain precautions to prevent an earthquake from striking their home, during the ten days after the death of an adult and five days following that of a child. By this time, the deceased is said to be installed in the world of the dead and unable to cause harm. The family should not keep water in the house from one day to the next but rather go fetch it everyday in a nearby stream or river. All the gourds and pots in the house should be empty of water. As the maize grains should not be soaked overnight to make the tortillas, tamales and *atole* [a beverage made with cooked corn], these foods are not to be consumed during the period of mourning. Nor should the grieving family drink boiled water as, "cooked water is dead water." All food should be either roasted or eaten raw during these days, not boiled. Water should be drunk only from leaves or corn husks and transported in a long-necked gourd or one with a small opening, to prevent it from swishing in the receptacle. Swishing would mean that the deceased is telling lies about the family to Tomam the Younger.

*   *   *

THE MASTER OF THE CLOUDS
(Author)

Tungsus, the Master of the Clouds, resides in the first level of the sky with his wife. He rides to Earth on a cloud to scatter rain. The Sun, who sees all that is going on in the world, notifies Tungsus when rain is needed for the crops. The clouds, *chiquihumel*, like the winds, are associated with the East and West Heavens.

*   *   *

MYTH 24
HOW THE CLOUDS WORK

When it is dry here on Earth, it rains where Tomam lives and when it rains here, it is dry there. When *Chiquihumel* turns his backside this way, it rains here; when he turns the other way, it rains there. When he brings us rain he says:

> Look at those Mortals; they are working and planting. I'm going to take them some rain so their crops grow nicely.

*   *   *

THE MASTER OF THE FROST
(Author)

Jívaro, the Master (myth 12), sends frost to the Earth cautiously so that it not destroy more than half of a milpa, or at least not an entire crop.

Frost is the color of blood and is the fetid vapor of the plants. There are two types: one is a yellowish red and the other, more harmful, is a blackish red. The yellowish frost comes to Earth hanging on the sides of a cloud, while the blackish frost fastens onto its tail.

The few magical practices that were still current in the Moñtana de la Flor were thought to protect the crops from the frost. The children should throw white, clean ashes at the yellow frost-bearing clouds. Ashes are considered medicine which cures the clouds from frost and makes them white again. Alfonso explains:

> Every dawn, we look to the east and if yellowish-red clouds appear, we order the children to throw white ashes to the east, four times, no more. If we don't, frost will descend and whither all our crops.

Another magical remedy consists of sprinkling the plants with Earth taken from the center of the milpa, to shield them from the frost. The frostbitten parts should be destroyed, to prevent the frost from contaminating the healthy plants. After these precautions are taken, the cultivator waits five days before returning to his milpa.

Some of the Tolupans have learned from the *ladinos* to make a cross with frostbitten corn stalks tied together with strings. The *ladinos* distinguished two types of frost: one caused by water and the other by the sun. To remedy the former, the cross is placed head down over a fire on the patio of the house; for those caused by sun, the cross is thrown into a well or a lagoon.

* * *

MYTH 25
A CLOUD GETS UPSET

If no one throws ashes at a cloud when frost is threatening the crops, the cloud gets angry and says:

> Why didn't that Indian throw ashes at me? He's behaving badly, I'm going to punish him. I'll send a lot of frost to ruin his crops.

If the owner of a milpa is asleep, his milpa may be ruined. But even if he does throw the ashes, the cloud might get angry and send frost. Only we Mortals are bothered by frost. It has no right to enter Tomam's domain.

*   *   *

NARRATION 8
ALFONSO ADVISES THE FROST

One day, when I passed the big cedar tree, there were the frosts. They were headed west. I said to them, "You're going that way for nothing; there aren't any crops in those fields. As we Mortals are lazy, no one planted there."

*   *   *

MYTH 26
THE STARS ARE "MONKEYS OF THE NIGHT"

We Mortals call them stars but they are really *micos de noche* [monkeys of the night: kinkajous, *potos flavus*]. They only come out at night, are dark-brown monkeys, *piaj* [in Tolupan language] and have a long whitish tail. They lived on Earth during the First Nation but the coyotes and tigers were eating them so they climbed to the first level above the Earth. In the sky, there are many mountains and trees: beech, pine, oak, cedar, *matapalos*. The monkeys of the night perch in the trees, feeding on fruit, and they eat so much that they defecate lots of seeds. Their *caca* [excrement] falls like red-hot coals. From the seeds, the beech, oak, pine, cedar, *matapalos*, vines, and *guamos* are born in this world. Nothing is lost of what these "monkeys" defecate. From their *caca*, trees are born and the winged creatures are fed. What we defecate is useless, as we eat a lot of cooked food.

You can't see them during the day; they don't defecate then, either. They pass the day sleeping. When it is daytime here, it is night above. During the day, the sky looks blue but it's not blue; it's full of trees that we Mortals can't see.

The *punakpanes* said the monkeys of the night give light to the Mortals. Tomam wanted to fool us Mortals, this is why we can't see them.

The Sun, the Moon and the Winds all have their *caminos reales* [royal roads] in the sky. Only the stars can go wherever they please, jumping from tree to tree, eating fruits.

Tyaj Haitecal is the first star to be seen in the west sky in the early evening. He doesn't have a belly button because a tiger ate it here on Earth, during the First Nation. This star leads all the others. The star which arises first in the morning in the east is his older brother, called Tsik'in Haitecal.

* * *

NARRATION 9
THE SUN WEARS GLASSES

Losakwai, the Sun, is a big man. He's in all the seven layers of the sky. We only see his face because his body is covered over by the layers. His knees are at the first layer; the rest is covered, except his head, which comes out at the seventh layer.

God, the Sun, is a *gokoywai* [grandfather]. He lives with his wife, has fields of beans, camotes and maize. If a dead Mortal misbehaves in the other world, he is sent to work in the Sun's bean fields. This man is not lazy. Every morning, he starts out again on his royal road. He's never sick and only sleeps a little while.

He wears glasses in order to see better. He can read and write and takes photographs of the Mortals, to discover how many years they will live. He's always looking down on the Earth at us Mortals. He sees everything: when anyone defecates, urinates, courts a woman. He has documentation on all the Mortals, on each dog, each cow, bull, ox — all the animals. When a Mortal dies or is behaving badly, he informs Tomam. If a *ladino* is trying to rape an Indian woman, he tells Tomam the Younger and this is the end of the *ladino*. The same is true, if an Indian is trying to force a *ladina* against her will.

The Moon notifies Tomam, too, but she is slower. When someone goes hunting, he should ask permission of the Sun, the hand of God, so as not to lose his way. God says:

> That poor Indian needs to kill a little animal to feed his family. He can't make a deer, or a pig, or a chicken. I'm going to put a deer or a paca in his path. The poor fellow only eats maize and beans and the beans often upset him. He has to plant coffee and sell it, to buy an old rifle to hunt little animals. I'll put one in his path now.

When you want the Sun to put an animal in your path, you should look up at him and say:

> Losakwai, as I am a child of death, as I have many contingencies, in the meanwhile before I die, I want to kill a little animal to eat.

But sometimes he doesn't provide a thing. The hunter shouldn't harm the little animals everyday. The Head Chief, Tomam, orders the Sun to look after us Mortals.

In order to hunt deer at night, one should ask the Moon for permission, "*Muymuywai* [grandmother], with your permission, I want to kill a deer. I need to harm it in order to eat." When there is no moon we use a flashlight. This is even better. The deer are not used to flashlights and come close to look at it. This means their end. On a moonlit night, the deer can see a long way and when it sees a hunter, it flees.

* * *

MYTH 27
THE FIVE SUNS

Tomam has four gods, four suns, to light up his world. With this sun, there are five. His four suns always go together.

God [the Sun of this world] set the Mortals' clothes on fire, even their hair. He tried to burn everything. The Mortals complained to Tomam and right then he gave the order, "Tie up this Sun and bring him here. I'll throw him in jail." But the Sun couldn't be tied up so easily. He burnt the ropes. Finally, struggling, he was tied up and thrown in jail, in Tomam the Younger's dominion. But the Mortals were even worse off because then Tomam sent his four suns to punish them, to shut their mouths so that they learn not to speak against God [the Sun].

When the four suns arrived here on Earth, all the water in the rivers and streams boiled, turned the color of blood and dried up. Everything dried up. The world became a plain... dust everywhere. The crops burned up without pity. The Mortals couldn't even step on the ground.

Tomam: That's good. That'll teach them to accuse the Sun.
Both Tomams: What can we do with God? The Mortals have made enemies with him.

The world was smothered with dust. It didn't rain. The Mortals were very upset. They said, "Maybe we can reach an understanding with the Head Chief."

Head Chief: What makes you think you are welcome here?

The Mortals were thinking.

Mortals: Take back your four suns. We can't stand it anymore.
Tomam: Request refused. Four are not enough; five would lighten your world even more. Eight would be even better. You

	can't sleep in the dark! Only foolish Mortals want to sleep in the dark.
Mortals:	We're no longer happy. The heat, day and night, is too much. We're to blame for being so bad.
Tomam:	Alright. I'll withdraw the suns, then you'll sleep in the dark. But I feel sorry for my brother [he lives much closer to the Earth than Tomam the Elder]. He won't like being in the dark at night.

He did call back his four suns and he stopped punishing the Mortals. Awhile later, he called for his brother and nephew. He told his nephew to free the Sun and fetch him.

Sun:	I refuse to return to the Mortals. They fight too much.
Tomam the Younger:	Now, why do you say that?

The Sun was sort of angry but he calmed down. He couldn't let all the Mortals die. When the cock crowed, he began his trip. The Mortals were overjoyed:

> Look at what this God has done! We should never contradict him. Now, the streams are nice and clear and the crops can be harvested.

* * *

NARRATION 10
AN ECLIPSE OF THE SUN

When the Sun goes into an eclipse, a man or boy may die. Nen [Master of the Lagoon] wanted to swallow the Sun but he couldn't; the Sun was too hot!

Even if Nen doesn't swallow him, when there is an eclipse, everyone should make a lot of noise — beat the tables — to save the Sun, just like when the Moon eclipses.

There was an eclipse when Feli Martinez was chief [of the east section]. When he got sick, there was an eclipse of the Sun, but as the Sun soon reappeared, we didn't beat the tables [make noises]. Maybe this is why he died [soon afterwards].

* * *

MYTH 28
AN ECLIPSE OF THE MOON

When the Moon goes into an eclipse, women and girls are in danger of
dying. They shouldn't look at her. Only the men have the right to look at
her. The old people told us to make a lot of noise so Nen doesn't swallow
her. The women should take their cedar tables⁵ out of the house so that the
Moon can see that her grandchildren are trying to save her. The tables
should be beaten with the *toto* [the sticks the men use to weave nets] until
the Moon is saved. Before [in former times], when an eclipse began,
Nompwinapu'u notified the Jívaro to tell the *punakpanes* to go from house
to house, ordering the women to begin the noisemaking. Now, there are no
more *punakpanes* so each family has to do it.

There are several Nens, not just one. The one who tries to swallow the
Moon is a big animal and has horns. His house is in the path of the Moon
so sometimes she bumps into it, when she passes by. He gets angry and
they quarrel.

Nen:	Today, I will swallow you. Can't you keep from bumping into my house? Today you will pay. I will eat you up and finish off with the world.
Moon:	I had to go through the canyon and there are so many rocks and stones that some bounced up and hit your house as I passed by.
Nen:	So be it. I'm still going to swallow you right now.

Then he jumped at her. Even though we make a lot of noise, sometimes
Nen swallows a little bit of her, but not all, as she is an Immortal. When he
swallows a little of her, immediately, she notifies Tomam and he gives the
order to throw Nen into the deep water where a shark will eat him up.

Moon:	Just try and swallow me! I'm going to denounce you with the Supreme Law [Tomam]. I don't bang your house for the fun of it. If I fail to come out on the nights that I should, the Mortals will die. Now, you'll be the shark's dinner or, at least, you'll be thrown in jail.
Nen:	No matter, I'm going to swallow you.
Tomam:	[to the Moon] Didn't your grandchildren do the favors for you [make noise]?
Moon:	Of course they did. They made a great racket but Nen didn't care and he swallowed a little of me. He got angry because I bumped into his house.

At times, Grandfather Thunder hits against Nen's house, as he lives nearby.
When this happens, Grandfather Thunder says:

I'm going to get even with this Señor Nen. I'm little but I won't be swallowed. The Moon is a big woman. Why does she let herself be swallowed?

Grandfather Thunder carries his axes and serpents with him and sets fire around his enemies. Nen is afraid of him.

*   *   *

MYTH 29
THE DEATH OF A YOUNG AND AN OLD NEN

Tomam first sent Our Lord to the Earth so that we kill him [myth 3], then he sent a young and an old Nen. When the young Nen arrived, he asked for food: tortillas, beans, meat. The *cocineras* [women cooks, euphemism for wives] got mad at him and said, "Let's kill this animal; he is a great nuisance." They cut his throat. So it was that the Mortals asked for their own death. When he got to the East Heaven, he was asked, "Eh! Why do you come back [so soon]?"

Young Nen: Because the *cocineras* cut my throat. The world is unlivable. I'm better off here, in my own country.

Then Tomam sent an old Nen to the Earth. He had hair all over his body. The Mortals set fire to his hair and burned him up. When he arrived back in his own country, he was asked, "Eh! Why did you come back here?"

Old Nen: They burnt me up, that's why I've come. And they set fires in all the hills. They'll all die because they killed me. Some will die young, others old.

He spoke a lot against the Mortals. These Nen are the same nation as the Nen who tries to swallow the Moon and the Sun but can't. He tries to swallow the Moon because the Mortals killed a young and an old Nen. The Nens want to finish off the Mortals and destroy the world.

*   *   *

MYTH 30
NEN TAKES REVENGE
AND SO DOES THE LITTLE OLD MAN

When the Mortals killed that young and old Nen, their nation sent a Ts'at'ekapan to the Earth. This Nation Ts'at'ekapan lives near the Nen, where the Moon rises. The Ts'at'ekapan has a tail like a raccoon and is the same color but he isn't a raccoon. Ts'at'ekapan wants to swallow the Moon, too.

He came to the Earth and cut a woman's throat, and drank her blood. Then the light of the Moon went out. Later, he went to lie in the Sun. The Little Old Man, the husband of the woman killed, was searching for him and found him stretched out in the Sun, covered all over with blood. He killed him, then sent for Jívaro and told him, "I want to notify the other world that Ts?at?ekapan killed my wife so I killed him."

Jívaro: You did the right thing.

*   *   *

TATA DIOS
(Author)

Tata Dios (God Our Little Father) lives in Glory, in the zenith, between the East and West Heavens, with his wife and domestic animals. [myths 3 and 7] Alfonso once said that he didn't know on which level of the sky he lives but assumed that he is not on the first level because one never hears his cattle bellowing. But later, he remembered that of the seven levels in the sky, Tata Dios is in the third level. God, the Sun, and the Moon are in the seventh.

Tata Dios, the God of the Christian *ladinos*, is also the Master of the Domestic Animals of European origin brought to Honduras by the Spaniards: cattle, horses, mules and pigs. This concept is also found among the Boruca Indians of Costa Rica.[6] Moreover, Tata Dios is the Owner of Money and Master of the Dogs and Buzzards.

*   *   *

MYTH 31
TATA DIOS IS THE MASTER
OF THE DOGS

Tomam created dogs but Tata Dios is their master.

Tomam: Dogs don't have hands so they have the right to live off
the Indians and the *ladinos*. They should take good care of
them and never kill them.

When a dog arrives in the East Heaven, Tomam says to it:

                    You lived as a brother with the Indians and the *ladinos*,
                    now you have to guide them across the river.

After greeting Tomam, the dog goes to Glory. Tata Dios has the right to dogs in afterlife. Dogs complain to their master, if the Mortals do not give them enough to eat.

*   *   *

MYTH 32
TATA DIOS AND THE MASTER OF THE SNAKES

Long ago, the snakes bit animals but the bite didn't hurt them. Lo Chim Jamayón [Master of the Snakes] spoke to Tata Dios, "Be smart. Give me something for my snakes so that when they bite your animals, the animals die right away." Tata Dios agreed. From then on, his buzzards could eat the cattle bitten by a snake. The buzzards can't kill the cattle by themselves. Tata Dios gave the master *lo wa' eha*, a poisonous weed for his snakes.

Tata Dios: I am going to kill a cow.

Lo Chim
  Jamayón: Don't you bother, I'll send one of my snakes to kill it. He'll take a quart of blood for himself and leave the rest for your buzzards.

Tata Dios: I agree.

Snakes have the right to bite the cattle, horses and mules but not the Mortals. Buzzards have the right to eat all the animals who die in the field but not the dead Indians or *ladinos*. Sometimes the buzzards share half a dead cow with the tigers. The buzzard with a red beak pulls an eye out of the dead cow or bull, flies away with it and shows it to the other buzzards. They have white beaks so they, too, can feast on the dead animal.

*   *   *

NARRATION 11
"LET THE LAZY INDIANS WORK"

The *ladinos* have cattle just to annoy the Indians. "The Indians are a great nuisance," they say. "Let them build fences, every year, to keep our cattle out of their maize fields. Let the lazy Indians work. Let them eat cows' dung." The *ladinos* keep their cattle and pigs up here [in the Montaña] just to make trouble for the Indians.

God created the Nation of Indians and *ladinos* so that they respect each other: not go around killing and making trouble. He didn't want the *ladinos* to mix with the Indians. Each nation should keep to itself: the Indians are one nation, the *ladinos* another. The *ladinos* are great fighters. They like to fight all the time. They drink *chicha* [made of fermented maize] and increase their herds of cattle. Tata Dios ordered that they own all the cattle so as not to make trouble with other nations. The Indians have no right to cattle.

*   *   *

NOVENTA
(Author)

Noventa is Tata Dios' brother but "they don't love each other as brothers." He is said to be dependable, not a gossiper like Tata Dios. Noventa is the Master of Chickens and Turkeys, makes firearms, especially pistols, and has an armory in the cave where he lives in the second level underground.

*   *   *

NARRATION 12
NOVENTA ADVISES THE WILDCAT

Noventa lent his birds to the First Nation of Indians. Since then, he only retrieves them when they die so he rejoices when they do.

Noventa: [to the wildcat] Do you want to eat a hen or a turkey? Then go to Alfonso's, he has a lot.

Wildcats [small felines] are great hunters of hens. But we Indians harm the wildcats, too. We make bags from their skins. We show these bags to the hens to scare them, to keep them from running into the thicket, where the wildcats can catch them.

*   *   *

MYTH 33
NOVENTA SCOLDS A HEN

Indian: [to the hen he is about to kill] Poor little hen, I am going to harm you, with God's [Tomam's] permission. I am about to kill you, in order to eat you. I raised you with my maize so I have the right. Now, don't go and complain to your master.

But the hen did just that, "I wanted to live a little longer but the Indian didn't respect me. He grabbed me and killed me."

Noventa: You are food. You belong to the women's kitchens. How can the Indian work, if he doesn't eat? He has the right to eat a cooked hen or a boiled turkey and if he wants to eat eggs, that too.

NOTES

1. Alfonso said he only knew a few words of the language of the Tomams. For instance, the word for tapir, in Tolupan, is *nam*, while the Tomams say *pim-pim*.
2. This notion of a Supreme God, who after having created the world and living beings retires and concerns himself very little, if at all, with human affairs, is documented in very different cultures. See Pettazzoni (1954: 34) and O'-Connell (1962).
3. The concept of levels above and below the Earth is common in America and Siberia, as well. The Mayas also conceived of several levels above the Earth, and five below. See Thompson (1970: 195).
4. The Tolupans build a small fire below or near the wasps' hive, to make the wasps flee, and appropriate their grub which they consider a delicacy.
5. These tables, which support the grinding stone, are valued and passed on from mother to daughter.
6. Zerries (1959b: 145).

Alfonso Martínez, 1956

Alfonso Martínez, Todivia Soto and their family, 1959

Daughters of Alfonso and Todivia: Felipa and Celedonia and baby, 1959

Don Jésus López, my *ladino* host, 1959

Doña Nieve Montés and her son "Chico," 1958

Leopoldo Martínez, 1959

Leopoldo Martínez in front of his house, 1959

Lupita, 1971

Cipriano Martínez before he became chief of the east moiety, 1956

Cipriano Martínez, chief of the east moiety, and his son Anastacio, 1972

Petrona Soto and her baby, 1957

Maria Soto and her baby, 1971

Alfonso Martínez offering a basket, 1959

Apolonia Martínez and her brother Victorio, a deaf-mute, 1959

La Montaña de la Flor

Ladino girl with her parakeet

Leonor Soto, then chief of the west moiety, and son, 1957

Julio Soto before succeeding his father as chief of the west moiety, 1957

Tolupan youth, 1978

Hermenegildo Martínez, 1956

Hermenegildo Martínez, his son and wife Angela, 1972

Domingo Martínez arriving home with a load of maize, 1959

Alfonso Martínez and his mother Julia, 1959

Hermenegildo, José de los Angeles Martínez and the author. Photographed by
Alfonso Martínez, 1959. (The author owns the rights to this photo.)

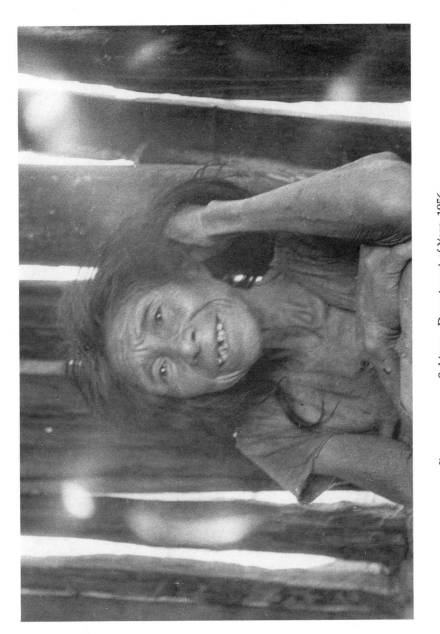

Jicaque woman, Subirana, Department of Yoro, 1956

CHAPTER _V_

MOTHER EARTH
AND THE MASTERS
OF ANIMALS

MOTHER EARTH
(Author)

The Tomams are the masters of Mother Earth [Nosiskier Namaywai]. Tomam the Elder created her, as ordered by his father, and Tomam the Younger cares for her.

Mother Earth is generous; she nourishes all living creatures. She is also vindictive. People make her suffer incessantly — digging into her to plant crops, for clay to make pots, building fences. When a big tree falls down, this hurts her too. Even walking on her may be painful. So, of course, she rejoices when a person dies, anticipating the fine meal she will soon have. Animals stamp on her with their hoofs, dig burrows in her, scratch at her endlessly. So when any living creature dies, she is consoled; as some part of it will surely be for her.

MYTH 34
MOTHER EARTH IS THIRSTY

When the Earth is thirsty, many cracks appear; these cracks are her mouth asking for water. The Sun sees them and bids Tomam to dispatch the clouds.

When it hasn't rained for a long time and the soil is very dry, these cracks appear. Sickness comes out of them as smoke or vapor. Then we Mortals have to be careful walking. These cracks are a sign that the Earth is asking for our death. But when she drinks, we are safe. She drinks water, also urine and eats *chinchin* [excrement] too.

*   *   *

MYTH 35
MOTHER EARTH COMPLAINS TO TOMAM

Whenever maize, yucca or beans are planted, the Earth complains, "What a torture! These Indians and *ladinos* are forever jabbing me." But this is our food so the Earth will just have to put up with it. When we build fences, she complains:

> Cows, pigs, horses, mules, Indians, *ladinos:* everyone is always digging into me, striking me, trampling on me!

It's all true. The Earth is forever being hit and struck. People are always planting crops and felling trees. This is why the Earth is so shameless; she is always eating the dead. When maize or beans are frostbitten, the Earth eats them. She consumes everything — deer, snakes, bones of all animals. When someone is buried, the Earth says:

> Ha! Ha! This one is for me! I only wish more would die: old women, young fresh women, dried out or unused, I don't care.

This is why God [Tomam] warns us:

> Be good Indians, *ladinos* and gringos all, because you all have the same death.

When cattle, horses and mules die, the buzzards have the right to their corpses, to their flesh and the Earth to their bones. Tomam speaks to the Earth:

Toman: There is no excuse for you to complain so. I give you pacas, peccaries, coatis, birds, and all sorts of other little animals. They never stop bearing young so that you will always have

	a supply of food. When they die, you eat them. Reproduction never ceases. Tell me, Earth, how can you complain? You have it rather easy. You are well paid for your wounds. You will always have something to eat.
Earth:	Ha! Ha! I will eat! Let the Indians and *ladinos* die soon, so I can eat them!
Tomam:	When dogs die, you eat them and so it is with all animals — pigs, peccaries, curassows — you eat them all.
Earth:	Ha! Ha! Let the cattle die! I'm going to eat them, too.
Tomam:	That's the spirit. They're all yours. So why complain?

Still, the Earth returned to complain, but she had gone too far. Tomam said, "Shameless one! Glutton!"

When she first heard about the Nations of Indians and *ladinos* she got mad and said to Tomam:

Earth:	Why should there be so many nations? These nations will be planting maize every other day. They'll work all the time, jabbing and sticking into me.
Tomam:	Never you mind. All the fruits of their labor will be for you. Everything, sooner or later, rots on the Earth — everything, that is, except the *ladinos* and Indians. They'll be buried because they have families and the families won't let the buzzards eat their dead.

Cattle don't have families. They have four hoofs but they don't have hands. They wouldn't know what to do with a machete or an axe. Women, the poor dears, they have huge tits, wonderful to embrace, to live with; they, too, have to be buried when they die. This is the order of the caciques. The Indians won't live for long and they'll only eat a little bit. Some of them boast, "I'll live to be eighty years old!" That's a laugh. Maybe some will live to be fifty. In Heaven to the East, this is not the case. There 100 years is a day. We should behave properly toward one another: Indians, *ladinos* and gringos. We all have the same death.

When anything is planted, the Earth makes a face as if sniffling. When we dig a grave, she doesn't like that one bit either. This goes on all the time; people are forever jabbing her and she's always complaining.

Tomam:	Stop! You are eating, aren't you? You eat soup and stew of Indians and *ladinos*. If you keep up this complaining, I will throw you in jail and fine you, too, and it won't be a small sum.

The Earth got mad and turned her back.

Tomam: Here, look at me! Turn around.

The Earth obeyed but she was still mad:

Earth: I want to go away. I don't have anyone to defend me here. It may be alright for the Mortals but not for me.
Tomam: What do you mean, you don't have anyone to defend you! You don't know when you're well off.
Earth: I'm sorry. I spoke out of turn. Still, it's true, I don't have a chance here. All the time, every minute, I am being hit, spiked, dug into, stamped on.
Tomam: Not a chance! That's a laugh.

*   *   *

NARRATION 13
MOTHER EARTH, THE GREAT PROVIDER

The Earth doesn't have a right to speak to the Mortals. Where Tomam the Second lives, to the west, is the domicile of the Earth. He is the Master of the Earth, the Earth's cacique. He gives orders to her here [in this world] but he receives complaints there in the west, where we Mortals go when we die. The Earth is the great provider. She sustains me. When I plant a grain of maize, a little later it sprouts. Here it comes! This is why I always ask the Earth's permission. As I am a child of death, I am very harmful.

*   *   *

NARRATION 14
"I AM AFRAID OF THE EARTH"

The Earth is *namaywai*, the mother, of all us Mortals. She nourishes us. The maize and yucca plants are happy to be born, as *namaywai* nourishes us all. She is my *madrecita* [little mother] until I die and the next day I'll be buried so she can eat me. I'm afraid but I'll die with this fear. I'm afraid but there is no escape, as I'm a child of death. Even if I had lots of money, I would still have to die.

When I was a *cipote*, I asked old León Soto, "Why do the young, the old and even babies die?"

León: It's that the Earth wants to eat them. She most likes eating Indians, *ladinos*, cattle and snakes. If the Earth takes a fancy to eat old people or little angels [children], they can't last. The Indians hunt monkeys, coatis, peccaries, guinea hens. The Earth eats Indians, *ladinos*, bones of any animal. The

Earth is a glutton, the Indians and the animals, likewise.

Tsëncley [the Master of Many Animals] pillages the maize of us mortal Indians. This is why every Indian and every *ladino* has the right to kill the animals of Tsëncley. The Earth is harmful, so are the Indians and animals, too. The animals of Tsëncley damage the crops of the Indians. This is why each Indian, each *ladino* has the right to kill Tsëncley's animals. Each is shameless with the other, that's because we live together in just one world.

* * *

NARRATION 15
"BUT I JOKE WITH HER"

The Earth gets mad because we are always digging into her but she will eat everything in the end — she has no right to complain. I joke with the Earth. When I'm ready to plant, I say to her:

> Look here, Earth! Now don't get mad, I'm going to stick you a little bit to plant my maize. Believe me, it's in your own interest that I die fat. Then you can really feast on me. Now, let me plant this yucca, so that when I die, you will have a nice fat Alfonso to eat. You wouldn't like eating just skin and bones, would you?

Then she says:

> That's quite alright, Señor Mortal Indian. God [Tomam] ordered that you not have the world in your hands, that your hands only serve to damage things. With your death, you'll pay me back.

If the Earth gets out of sorts, seeds dry up right away, nothing sprouts. The old people used to advise us that when someone dies, the Earth be given a month to rest, that after the grave is dug, we should not stick or jab her during a month. But this advice is not right. Imagine a month without working! How could I eat? In order to eat, I must work and that is what I do. The Earth will have to put up with us; she is going to eat everything sooner or later, anyhow.

* * *

NARRATION 16
THE EARTH DOES NOT LIKE TO BE DUG INTO

The Earth doesn't like to be dug into so I don't want Todivia [Alfonso's wife] to make jars. The Earth is harmful; when you take out the clay, coldness enters [the body] through the hands. She doesn't like being jabbed into and much less when the soil, itself, is taken out of her. I always buy jars from the *ladinas*, let them work the clay. If they ask a *peso* for a pot, I say to them, "Alright, I'll pay the price. Let the Earth get mad at you and not at me." When the *ladinas* hear this, they don't like it one bit.

* * *

THE MASTERS OF THE ANIMALS
(Author)

The masters or guardians of animals, like that of Mother Earth, is a very basic religious and philosophical concept among the American Indians. It is, or was, prevalent in many other parts of the world, especially in hunting and gathering societies. (chapter VIII)

In the Tolupan language, *jamayón* is the term for "master." They are said to be "like people" — either dwarfs or giants as tall as pine trees. Supposedly, they are married, though we only know the wife of the Master of the [White-Lipped] Peccary and of the Master of the Tapir and Bee. (myth 43) Most inhabit caves, in the first level underground, where it is light during the night and dark during the day. They live in houses, sleep in hammocks, keep their animals fenced in fields. They eat one or two of their herds and they toss the bones out of their cave entrances, where they accumulate in piles. A hunter knows when he sees such a pile in front of a cave that it is inhabited by a master and he should avoid approaching it.[1]

Some of the masters are in charge of just one species, while others have many more. Each master has an assistant called a *maritomo* [majordomo] — a real animal, usually a feline or a bird of prey, who in reality hunts the species of which it is in charge. The majordomo guards the entrance to the cave to prevent the animals from escaping. He accompanies them when their master lets them out into the world. Now and then, a master permits his majordomo to eat one of his animals but often the majordomo does so on his own, permission or not.

Not only does the master eat his own animals, he sometimes kills them, as punishment for some wrongdoing. But when they die, he receives their spirit.

The master allows the Indians to kill his animals for his family's nourishment, in exchange for the right to feed them on their crops. However, if an Indian hunts in excess, or wounds an animal, the master takes vengeance and the hunter will die from what appears to be an accident.

The wounded animal returns to its domicile, where its master attempts to cure it. "Each little animal has its master, who looks after it and prevents the hunter from killing too many."

According to Don Jesús Lopéz, many years ago, old Ulofia Soto, son of Pedro, one of the community's founders, said that every animal has its master, who allows the hunter to kill a few of his animals. He added that if the hunter kills many, the master gets angry and takes revenge against the hunter. Don Jesus commented:

> That's true. If a man kills animals all the time, he ruins himself. His clothes get to be rags; he doesn't want to plant; he only wants to hunt all the time.

The masters do not permit baptized Indians or the *ladinos* to kill their animals, although they do so, anyway, without the masters' consent. The Tolupans contend that only they have the right to the wild animals, the "animals of the forest."

Traditional Tolupans either ask for the master's permission to kill an animal or to be pardoned after making a kill. They explain to the master that they did so only because they were hungry. This custom is the survival of a very ancient hunting rite and still prevalent among some Indian groups: the Mayas, others in North and South America, and in Siberia. (chapter VIII)

* * *

BONES OF THE GAME TIED TO POSTS IN THE HUTS
(Author)

Preserving the bones of the game in deference to the master is also a very archaic custom among hunting peoples. Some of the Tolupans I visited tied the skulls and large bones of the game with vine ropes around a post inside their huts. The small bones were wrapped in corn husks and tied with the others. Revered in this fashion were bones of deer, a small black feline with a long tail, both species of peccaries, monkeys, pacas, rats, mice, squirrels, agoutis, raccoons, opossums and guinea hens. Almost all the game — except the bones of small birds and fish.

I never saw more than two posts hung, in any one hut, with animal bones in this fashion. I was told by several older Indians that the object of this custom is to attract members of the family, whose bones are so exhibited, nearer to the huts so that they may be killed more easily. I rather doubted this explanation, partly because I had been told many times that they did not like the majordomo felines — now virtually extinct — to come near the houses, for fear that they might attack the children who often play thereabouts.

With the passage of time, when the bones disintegrate and fall to the floor of the hut, they are gathered and thrown at some distance from the house.

*   *   *

THE MASTER OF THE WHITE-LIPPED PECCARY
(Author)

Saino Jamayón is the Master of the White-Lipped Peccary (*saino* in Spanish). He was the only Indian of the First Nation that Our Lord pardoned, for having kept him buried for ten long days and nights. Furthermore, Our Lord married one of his daughters and, thereafter, they lived all together in the first underground level. (myths 3 and 21)

The master sends his animals out of his cave from December to April and the rest of the year he keeps them in corrals underground. These peccaries are described as fierce animals who live in large packs, each of which has a chief, a white-headed peccary, the oldest of the herd. The master allowed the Indians to kill the "troops" and the "scouts," even the young ones, but not the chiefs. And when the Indians and *ladinos* began killing them, anyway, the master got so angry, he ceased to let any of his peccaries roam on earth. This belief is undoubtedly an allusion to the extinction of these animals in the area. Alfonso stated that while he had killed only three, his grandfather, Juan Martínez, some eighty-five years earlier, had killed about fifty such peccaries with a bow and arrow.

The Tolupans contend that, formerly, when a peccary escaped from the cave, the master would send his majordomo, the jaguar, to kill it. Now, the master carefully guards all his animals underground, "because in this world there is so much fetid vapor."

*   *   *

NARRATION 17
ALFONSO AND THE MASTER OF THE PECCARY

My cousin, José de los Angeles Martínez, used to say, "Saino Jamayón is my brother."

God [Tomam] sent him [Saino Jamayón] from the other world so there would be food here for the Mortals. I can't ever meet Tomam, not until I die, but once, I went looking for Saino Jamayón. Naturally, I didn't find him. I searched all through the hills, when I was hunting peccaries and monkeys, but this was not for me. I could never find him, never meet him. Only the *zahorines* can make his acquaintance. A little fellow, like me, will only get into trouble, if he tries. No one is permitted to enter his domicile without a permit, like everywhere else. When I leave home and go below to the towns, I must have a passport [I.D. card]. If I don't, I'm asked, "What are you doing here? You are probably a bad man. If you don't have a passport, this means that you are up to no good."

Peccaries, coatis and raccoons are forever getting into the crops. This is what their masters want. We must share our maize with them. We cultivate half for them and half for ourselves. We eat them and the Earth eats us.

* * *

MYTH 36
THE MASTER OF THE PECCARY
AND THE BAPTIZED INDIAN

Saino Jamayón [the master] to a hunter who just killed one of his animals:

Saino
Jamayón: Eh! Eh! Why did you come here, quarrelsome good-for-nothing Mortal? I'll kill you. But no, I've changed my mind. Here, the laws are for everybody. Even so, I have the right to scold you.

Indian Hunter: I am a baptized Indian.

Saino
Jamayón: Then you have no right to my animals. You say you are baptized, then go eat with the *ladinos* and mulattos from their plate. Away with the likes of you! Only unbaptized Tolupans have the right to my animals.

Indian: I am baptized. I'll not take your animals. I won't bother you anymore. You have scolded me enough; I'll not touch your animals. I haven't two faces; I have only one.

The hunter got angry, too, and was about to leave, when the master gave him a peccary and more advice:

Take it, it's yours. If not, the *ladinos* will kill it and you won't have a thing to eat.

The very ones who baptized him, harmed him. When the *ladinos* baptize a poor Indian, they should take care of him. They have quantities of cattle and pigs. All the masters, Tsëncley [and others], too, say this. Those who are baptized don't have a right to national [wild] animals. They have to eat with Tata Dios. The *ladinos* don't care about the masters, so they can't complain to them.

* * *

THE MAJORDOMO OF THE PECCARY
(Author)

This Majordomo is a male jaguar, called a tiger, whose mythical name is Japay. The jaguar is known to follow packs of peccaries, attacking those which lag behind. The mythological female jaguar is the wife of Tsets'em Jamayón, the Master of the Tapirs and Bees. (myth 43) The Majordomo is allowed to kill peccaries for his own nourishment and he also does so without permission. (myth 53) Jaguars are extinct in the region. Alfonso said that he had never seen one.

* * *

THE MASTER OF THE DEER
(Author and Alfonso)

The Master of the Deer, Jo'popjil Jamayón, lives in caves also in the first layer underground. When Tomam sent the deer (red brocket) to the world, he said, "The poor little Indians, they don't have money, let them kill deer and coatis to feed their families." Francisco Martínez, a cousin of Alfonso, told me:

> If the master wants us to kill his deer, he sends them here on Earth. But if we kill them and don't eat them, he doesn't approve. If a wounded deer returns to his domicile, his master cures it and sends it back to the Earth.

Mateo advised his son, Alfonso, not to kill more than a 100 deer in his lifetime. Alfonso commented:

> But my father killed more than 1,000 and nothing happened to him; he died an old man. At times, he killed five or six in one day and shared them with his friends and neighbors. He was a good shot. But it is true that if you kill a lot at one time, the master gets mad. When you have killed 100, it is best to wait awhile before hunting again. If you kill too many, a snake may bite you, and finish you off.

Julián Velázquez, a *punakpan*, said that if a hunter kills more than five at once, the dead animals complain to their master and shortly thereafter the guilty hunter will fall into a ravine and be killed — as if it were an accident. Julián Velázquez gave this advice, "If you kill a deer today, tomorrow go work in the fields. You should not bother the master everyday."

* * *

THE DEER'S MAGIC STONES
(Author)

The Tolupans say that the small yellow-tinted deer have stones in their stomachs and worms in their noses who smell the "scent" of the stones. Alfonso commented:

> If a hunter can get ahold of one of those deer stones, he can kill deer easy. The deer smells the stone and comes to get it and let itself be killed. God gave these stones [to the deer] for us.

When the deer is killed, the hunter should look for the stone which may be in its intestines or throat. He should tie the dead deer's snout so that it doesn't vomit it up. If the deer has one but the hunter doesn't find it, other deer will come to the spot where it was killed and swallow the stone. Those who have worms in their noses follow the scent of the stones and find them first. If the deer has a stone but not the hunter, the deer are skittish and can't be killed easily. But if the hunter has one and the deer also, the latter becomes stupid.

When a hunter finds a stone, he should put it in his shoulder bag without showing it to anyone, especially women; otherwise, he will miss his shot the next time. He can lend it to another hunter, bag and all, without taking it out of his bag. The hunter who borrows one should not look at it; if he does, the stone will jump out of the bag and break. A stone may last three or four years, before it falls to pieces. Cattle also have stones but no other animal has them.

Don Jesús López, the *ladino* neighbor, explained:

> Some deer have a canine tooth, a mole or some other sign. They're a yellowish color, have worms in their brains or in their hoofs, which alert them when a hunter is close by. Who knows how they [the worms] do it? Maybe they bite the deer or just move about a little. These deer don't let themselves be killed so easily. Some of these deer have stones too in the stomach, I think. When one of these is killed the stone comes out of their snout and enters another deer. If the

hunter picks it up it will bring him good luck but only if he doesn't tell anyone. He has to feed the stone; he carries it in his bag and each time he kills a deer he feeds it with the blood of the deer he has just killed by rolling the stone around in its blood.

This complex of beliefs and practices has been reported for the Brunka of Costa Rica.[2]

* * *

MYTH 37
THE MASTER OF THE DEER SCOLDS A HUNTER

Deer don't hunt. They only eat little leaves and beans. They don't harm the maize, either.

Too many deer were being killed so Jo'popjil [their Master] went to the house of the hunter. He wasn't home. Jo'popjil spoke to his wife, "I don't like the Señor here. He's doing too much damage. All he does is kill my deer."

Wife: I'll kill him myself. No, I won't. I'll let him die of his own doing. He gets into enough trouble by himself. If you want to kill this Indian, go right ahead. But I won't touch him. God might punish me if I did. The law also applies to him.

The hunter arrived home trailing blood from a deer he had just shot.

Jo'popjil: You're shooting every minute! Always bothering my deer! Just because you'll only live for a little while, you think you have the right to wound all my deer.
Hunter: I hunt for food. Right now, I'm going to eat a little deer meat.
Jo'popjil: I am very angry.
Hunter: God [Tomam] left me deer to eat.

The next day in the forest, Tomam spoke to him, "What you are doing is not good. I warn you, but today I will pardon you; now, go home."

Hunter: But I can't get into my house. My wife bolted the door.
Tomam: You can't die here. You must go to die where God told you. Now get out of here!

The next day, Jo'popjil returned to the hunter's house.

Jo'popjil:	You Indians are only going to live a little while. Tomam scolded you aplenty. I won't punish you because he forbade me to.
Hunter:	I won't hunt any more deer.
Jo'popjil:	I've had a lot of wounded deer lately, with broken legs, with bullets in their ribs. Who is going to cure them all for me? When you want to eat deer meat, take a good aim when you shoot. I'll forgive you this time but if you do it again, you won't have anything to eat and you'll have to go begging from house to house.

The stupid hunter didn't take his advice. He kept wounding deer. Then, Tomam put a deer near him to test him.

Tomam:	You are really a miserable man!
Master of the Deer:	Hunters should not kill deer just for the fun of it. Such hunters won't find any. God offered you a young deer but you couldn't even hit it. How can you eat, if you don't know how to hunt?
Hunter:	Curse it, I didn't hit it! I'm going to eat my ass.
Tomam:	Why scare the deer, if you can't shoot straight?
Hunter:	No, Señor Dios, the next time, right now, I will kill one.
Tomam:	Liar!

He shot and missed again.

Hunter:	Pardon me, God, I shot for nothing.
Tomam:	You must aim straight, if you want to eat; if you can't, then eat your ass, eat empty tamales. Why bother hunting? What are you going to take home to your family, excrement?
Hunter:	You have scolded me enough. Now, I'm going to eat my ass.
Tomam:	Have a good time. But I'll give you another chance. I'll put a deer in your path, when you come close to your house.
Hunter:	That's fine. Maybe this time, I can kill it.

He was ashamed of himself. Later he hit the mark. Tomam ordered Jo'popjil to put a deer near his house and make it easy for him to kill. If the masters don't want their animals killed, the hunters hunt for nothing. They fence in their animals underground and they doze in a hammock, while the hunters look high and low all through the hills, all for nothing.

*   *   *

NARRATION 18
THE DEER HUNT AND DREAMS

When there are three shooters on a deer hunt, they go to three separate points near where the deer [already sighted] will pass. Others beat against a tree to scare the deer. When there are more than three shooters, one goes ahead to where the deer is. A doe will flee but the male deer won't; he'll turn on the dogs and fight with them with his horns and often kill some.

When a deer is killed, each hunter gets a share. The one who killed it takes the head, the tail, the insides and the hide. The others get the legs. If there are only two hunters, the deer is divided in half. If someone asks for hide, he's given it. Sometimes, I might get the horns; sometimes, the noise-makers get them. It's divided right where it's shot. If there's a stream nearby, it's taken there to wash off the blood. At home, the women cook it and we all are invited to eat it. Sometimes, a deer is killed without a gun, just with dogs, but this is very hard.

Last night, I dreamt I entered a house and propositioned two women but neither would have me. I dream a lot of silly things. When I dream I'm with a woman, deer appear right away the next day. When a woman won't have me, the deer flee. Sometimes, too, when I dream of pretty women, they turn into deer.

* * *

NARRATION 19
ALFONSO MEETS THE MASTER OF THE DEER

Once, I met Jo'popjil, or maybe it was the Devil. He asked me:

> *Natam* [elder brother], do you know why the deer are hiding?

Alfonso: I belong to the party of God [Tomam]. Answer me by the law of God. Each Mortal has the right to kill a deer to eat. The children of death only live a little while but we have our rights.

I turned to look at him. He spoke to me out of a cave but I didn't see him, not on your life! I said:

> I won't hunt your deer anymore. I'm going home empty-handed. You spoke badly to me. You may belong to the party of the Devil. Why are you contradicting me, a Mortal? Maybe you are the Devil. I know where you live and I'll get even with you! But alright, I won't hunt anymore. I don't

> care if there's nothing to eat at home, if my wife scolds me.
> I'll find a squirrel or a wild hen, if not we'll eat beans.

This is what I said to him. Was he the Master of the Deer? Or was he from the party of the Devil? I don't know. But he didn't come out of his cave, not on your life! I said to him:

> If you belong to the party of God, come out. If not, better that you don't come out.

He didn't come out. He heard me, alright, and took the advice of a Mortal.

* * *

THE MAJORDOMO OF THE DEER
(Author)

The Majordomo of the Deer is the *tigre de léon*, also called simply a tiger. In reality, it is the puma which is now extinct in the area from overkilling, principally by the *ladinos* and owners of cattle ranches. The Tolupans said that no deer can escape from such a "tiger," that the male has the right to kill the doe, while the female can kill the male deer. But the Tolupans contend that the pumas don't usually hunt doe so that they can raise their young. Sometimes, the hunters do likewise. Alfonso once said to me:

> Yesterday, I saw a little baby deer but I didn't shoot it. The poor mother, I thought; better leave it to grow up and then I can eat it.

* * *

MYTH 38
THE MASTER OF THE DEER SCOLDS HIS MAJORDOMO

Sometimes, the Tiger [the Puma, Majordomo of the Deer] escapes from his Master to hunt armadillos, agoutis, cattle, peccaries — though he only has the right to hunt deer. When the Master finds out, he punishes him. He ties him up in his cave for five years.

The Master also scolds him when he doesn't obey, [as] when he doesn't a kill a deer for him.

Master: Now, you came back empty-handed! You loafer! You don't want to bring me any deer.

Tiger: They run away very fast. When they smell me, they take off before you know it.

Master: Alright, if you don't want to kill the deer and bring him to me, he'll die by himself and the buzzard will eat him.

*   *   *

MYTH 39
THE MAJORDOMO OF THE DEER KILLS A HUNTER

The "Tiger" [Majordomo of the Deer] killed an Indian. The Little Old Man went looking for him. When he found the Tiger, flat on his back eating the hunter, he said, "Eh! I'm going to report this to the Superior Law!"
    He did just that, taking the Tiger and the [dead] hunter with him.

Tomam: The Tiger has authority too. He can harm the deer. Let us call in his Master, Jo'popjul.
Jo'popjul: Who sent for me? Who killed this hunter?
Tiger: He got himself killed.

The Majordomo didn't respect the hunter and killed him with its claws. The Tiger has no right to hunt Indians.

Tomam: Let me advise you, Señor Master Jo'popjil. The poor are allowed to kill deer. There is no law against it. But, there's a law for the Indians. You shouldn't get angry, if an Indian kills three or four of your deer, but you may not kill an Indian.
Jo'popjil: I don't go around killing Indians. I don't go out looking for Indians. The Tiger did. He got away, without my permission.

Tomam ordered the Tiger to be punished. The Tiger complained:

Tiger: I'm no deer to be shot at. That Indian shot to kill me. That's why I killed him first.
Tomam: Let me give you some advice. Go live in the caves, where the hunters never pass by.
Tiger: I'll do just that and see if they don't shoot at me there.

The tigers [pumas] now live at their ease in the entrances to caves. No one bothers them. They live at liberty but they only have the right to kill deer. Jo'popjil said to him:

You'll have the right to eat half of a deer. You must leave the other half for the buzzards.

*   *   *

NARRATION 20
ALFONSO AND THE MAJORDOMO OF THE DEER

Once, I met the Majordomo of the Deer, the yellow-reddish tiger, in my milpa. I spoke to him:

> Well, Señor Tiger, a little deer is causing a lot of damage and he won't let himself be shot. He only comes at night and he's eating up my beans. Go notify the master and find out why he lets the deer do this to me. You are his majordomo. If I can't kill the deer, I'll shoot you full of holes. Night after night, he comes to eat. You are his majordomo, he belongs to your domicile.

The Tiger was listening. He made signs with his tail:

> Be patient, Señor Indio, I'll give notice. If the master doesn't give me orders to kill him, I'll frighten him so that he comes close to where you are and you can shoot him.

The Tiger was making signs with his tail, wagging it one way then another. The next day when I returned, my dog had him up a tree. I said to the Tiger:

> You're a man of your word. As you got rid of that harmful deer, I will pardon you.

Tiger: If the deer gives you any trouble when you plant your crops next year, I'll kill him. I'll do this favor for you every other year, but don't shoot me.

I tied my dog and came home. After that my dog didn't get him up a tree.

Dog: I got that tiger up a tree for you, yesterday, but you didn't do anything.

I said to him, "Listen, old dog, I didn't ask you to get him up a tree." The Majordomo was listening. He laughed and went away. We meet every once in awhile.

*   *   *

THE MASTER OF THE WHITE-COLLARED PECCARY, THE COATI, MONKEYS AND VARIOUS BIRDS
(Author)

Tsëncley Jamayón has more species of animals than any other master. He has the white-collared peccary (*quequeo* in Spanish), the coati (*pisote*), the long-tailed monkey, the olingo, the wild turkey, the pheasant, the guinea hen, and various species of wild doves. Tsëncley lives in two caves in the Montaña de la Flor. One, called *Petrokpok* in Tolupan, Peña Blanca (White Rock), is located in the western section, and the other, in the eastern section, is named *Carichamoo.* It is believed that if you enter these caves, you will surely die. Alfonso said, "The old people told us never to go near those caves so I never do."

The ocelot is the Majordomo of the White-Collared Peccary, the harpy eagle of the coati, the olingo and the monkey; another eagle is that of the wild turkey and guinea hen. The Majordomo of the Doves was not reported.

*   *   *

<h3 style="text-align:center">NARRATION 21
"THE WHITE-COLLARED PECCARIES ARE A NUISANCE"</h3>

The peccaries, agoutis and others don't even try to have their meals in their masters' fields because their masters don't permit them to damage their crops!

Tsëncley: [Master of the White-Collared Peccary] No matter if the Mortals die. I'm letting my peccaries loose in the Mortals' fields. Let them get mad. I want to fatten my peccaries to eat them roasted.

And they do get fat! September and October is the time when these peccaries tear up the milpas. Last year [1959], I went after a pack of about 200. We were three companions: I, my shotgun and my machete — four, that is, with my shoulder bag. I went alone so as not to make noise. But I went at sundown so when I got there, I couldn't see a thing. But by dawn, about 5:00 a.m., I saw them alright, in my milpa. They had been there about three days. The milpa was full of them and they had already eaten about two *medidas* of maize. I sneaked around the edge of the milpa, spying on them. I killed two, a male and a female, only two! All the rest ran away. First, they scented me and began to flee and when they heard the shots, they ran about a league away. They didn't come back because they knew I was on guard, so I ran to where I thought they would pass. But they didn't.

During the day, they are wilder and harder to kill than at night. When they scent gunpowder or blood, they run like hell. It is best to kill the scouts. If you kill three scouts, they won't return. The scouts may be male or female. The females are best to eat; the males have a strong stench. That time I thought:

> I won't kill too many so that they can reproduce more. Their
> master might get mad at me. You have to work hard so that
> the white-collared peccary can eat, too.

So I only killed a couple. These peccaries are great pests but so are the
raccoons, the pacas and the coatis.

*   *   *

NARRATION 22
"LAST YEAR I KILLED THREE COATIS"

Year after year, the peccaries, coatis, raccoons and others, too, come into
the milpas, when the maize is tender. They eat all they please and in
January they're fat. What can I do? I have to sleep sometime. The coatis
make nests of branches. Sometimes, I catch them sleeping there. They
grow fast. I only kill the oldest, never the little ones.

Last year, I killed three coatis: a male and two females. There were
about seventy, together, in my milpa. When they first saw me, they ran like
hell. I said to myself, "Tomorrow, I'll come back and kill at least one."

Then I went for some help. My brother, Guillermo, lent me his rifle
which the late Mateo had left him. I said to my cousin, Juan José:

> Man, my cousin, the coatis are sleeping now in the thicket.
> Let's sneak up on them.

So we went but we only killed three. We ate them; they're good food. I
always eat what I kill, if it's edible.

*   *   *

MYTH 40
THE COATI COMPLAINS TO HIS MASTER

As soon as a coati is killed, he goes straight to his master.

Tsëncley: What happened to you?

Coati: I was eating maize, when the owner of the milpa appeared
and he killed me! He killed me for eating an *elote* [young
ear of corn]!

Tsëncley: That's fair enough. You were damaging his maize. You were
being a bothersome coati. The owner of the milpa had the
right to kill you. He feeds my little animals and keeps them
nice and fat so he has the right to kill one to eat, now and
then. I'm not mad at him.

Tomam recommended the Indians to Tsëncley.

Tomam: The Indians only live a little while. You, Tsëncley, you live forever. What could be better, the Indians work so that your coatis and peccaries grow fat. Each lives off the other. You shouldn't get mad at the Mortals. You should be brotherly with them because they're in a sorry state. They don't know how to make chickens or any animal, for that matter. They only borrow them. You, Tsëncley, can make coatis, peccaries, monkeys, turkey hens.

*   *   *

MYTH 41
THE HARPY EAGLE OF THE HIGH CLIFF

Tsitsih-pine [harpy eagle] is as large as a turkey but has claws like a tiger. During the First Nation, he hunted people — killed as many as four in one day. He lived high on a cliff in a cave among the rocks, where there were heaps of bones of cattle, horses, coatis, monkeys and people he had hunted; he hunted everything.

Jívaro was sent to spy on him. He got into a corner of the cave and was spying. Then Tomam sent two little brothers as witnesses. He wrapped them in a cowhide and sent them up to the rocks high on the cliff near where *Tsitsih-pine* lived. *Tsitsih-pine* grabbed them and took them into his cave, cowhide and all. When he got there, Jívaro was spying on him. He [Jívaro] told the brothers to get ahold of a leg bone of an Indian and kill *Tsitsih-pine* with it, before he killed them. The brothers killed him, alright, then they climbed down from the cave on a vine and returned to their mama.

From that time on, the *tsitsih-pine* never hunt people. Tomam sent them to the mountains to hunt monkeys, raccoons and coatis and so the *tsitsih-pine* became their Majordomo.

*   *   *

THE MASTER OF THE MICE
(Author and Alfonso)

Mütsis Jamayón, the Master of Mice and Rats, is a dwarf, the size of a two-year-old boy. He has a wife and lives underground. The Majordomo of Mice and Rats is the house cat.

The *nam-mütsis* are real mice, not to be confused with Namütsis, the husband of the monkey. (myth 1) Real mice and rats were created after Namütsis and his wife departed to the underworld.

Alfonso: The First Nation of Namütsis, this is how the mouse is called. He is the father of the First Indians, the husband of the monkey Ts'iu. They live in the other world. All the mice of today were made after Namütsis went to the other world. These are good to eat, especially roasted. Some are called *matates* [nets for carrying maize] because they have a net in their mouths for carrying grains of maize. They take them back to their master to eat. Other mice are called *comerciantes* [merchants]. They only come out at night from a hole in the earth. They aren't afraid of the light of a flashlight.

If a Mortal squashes one or even so much as touches one, he won't harvest his maize. We don't kill these "merchants." We let them feed on our maize. The only other one that we can't kill is called *puzuts*. These stay in the hills, they don't come into the houses or anyplace nearby. If I bother the mice a lot, the master will know about it and I'd better watch out. I've killed 50, even 100, with little short arrows. But we don't use arrows anymore, now we buy traps from the *ladinos*. I have the right to kill them, when they do a lot of damage, but they, too, have a right to the maize of the Mortals.

The old people said that they should not be caught by their tails, to avoid a failure of the maize crop. Since they feed on the corn stored in the bins, their master permits the Indians to kill and eat them.

*   *   *

MYTH 42
FOUR BIG ANIMALS WAGER

Four little animals wanted to be big animals: a *til-kota* [mouse] wanted to be a *til* [tapir]; a *nam-mütsis* [another species of mouse] wanted to be a *nam* [white-collared peccary]; a *pu'p* [weasle] wanted to be a *japay* [jaguar]; and the *tsats* [squirrel] wanted to be a *piyon* [paca].

Four big animals were betting who could fart the biggest animal. The jaguar and the tapir bet against each other. *Til*, the tapir, let out a strong wind but all that came out was a little animal, the *til-kota*, a tiny mouse, all covered with *chinchin*, and very, very smelly. He became his namesake but he was very puny. *Japay*, the jaguar, let out a strong fart, too, but all that defecated was a weasle. He looked at it and said:

> You're smaller than I and you're not my namesake but you have a nice long tongue like mine.

Little Weasel: But I am the same as you are. I'm a jaguar, too. I can kill cattle, tapirs, peccaries and even people.

This was a lie; he was just a puny weasel and he could only kill little animals.

The jaguar and the tapir stayed on awhile chatting. Then, the tapir went to the mountains and the jaguar to the sources of the rivers. The weasel and the little mouse stayed on to see what would happen.

Finally, the paca and the peccary made a bet. *Piyon*, the paca, wanted to make another *piyon* but all that came out of him was the little *tsats*, a squirrel. He fell out covered with *chinchin*, even in his eyes and mouth. He was very, very smelly. Then *nam*, the white-collared peccary, said, "I am going to make a *nam*, just like myself." He farted strongly but he only let out a little mouse, a *nam-mütsis*, who only resembles him by his name and the color of his hair.

Only these four animals wagered. Only they got together. Only they were talking like this.

*   *   *

THE MASTER OF THE TAPIRS,
BEES AND DOVES
(Author)

Tsets'em Jamayón is the Master of the Tapirs, Bees and Red-Breasted Doves, called *tikme* in Tolupan. His wife is a *japay*, the female jaguar. The male jaguar is the Majordomo of the White-Lipped Peccaries. In the cave where Tsets'em and his wife live, each tree has ten beehives.

Tsets'em is as tall as a pine tree, strong enough to carry two tapirs, one on each hip, and can swallow people whole. He kills his tapirs with a very large blowgun, using ammunition the size of an avocado seed.

The Majordomo of the Tapir is the *tigre prieto* [black tiger]. The Majordomos of the Bees and Red-Breasted Doves remain to be discovered.

*   *   *

MYTH 43
THE MASTER PROTECTS HIS BEES [3]

With Tsets'em's permission, an Indian took two muleback loads of honey from some hives . As the Indian knew how to find honey, a *ladino* said to him, "I'll give you a cow to eat, if you get me some bees' wax."

The Indian agreed. He ate the cow and went looking for the wax; but then the master ordered that no hive be found. As the Indian couldn't find any, he went to see Tsets'em on the first level underground.

Tsets'em: Eh! Eh! What are you doing here?

Indian: I'm after white honey for myself and some wax to sell to the Spaniards [*ladinos*]. They need it for candles, to keep vigil for their dead.

Tsets'em: If you want some honey and wax come to my house.

The Indian spent a whole year in one of Tsets'em's houses. He wouldn't let him go. Then Jívaro said to Tomam the Younger:

> An Indian got lost. With your permission, I'll go look for him everywhere, on top of the Earth and below.

When he got to Tsets'em's house, he heard his wife, Japay, saying:

> Swallow this Indian; I'm tired of grinding corn for him. He's not my husband.

Tsets'em: I'll swallow this old offensive Indian tomorrow.

Then Jívaro went to the house where the Indian was prisoner and said to him:

> Tomorrow, Tsets'em is going to swallow you. I'll give you some advice.

In order to deceive Tsets'em, Jívaro made an Indian out of wax: the arms, the head, the hair, even the penis and the anus, just like a person. He gave the Indian an blanket and told him to hide under it in the corner of the house.

Jívaro: Tsets'em must be killed because he wants to kill this Indian.

The next day, when Tsets'em came to the house, he told the Indian to kindle the fire. As the Indian didn't reply, Tsets'em said, "You won't answer me! So I'll swallow you."

He thought he swallowed the Indian but, instead, he swallowed wax.

Tsets'em: [to himself] This dead Indian is stirring around a lot in my belly. I feel cold. I'm going to kindle a big fire to warm myself.

So he did. But instead of warming himself, the wax boiled in his belly and pum! He fell down like a tree trunk, dead. Then Jívaro said to the Indian:

You still have enemies here — the wife, Japay, and the family. You must kill them all. If you leave even one alive, he [or she] will be after you.

The Indian killed them all, as he was ordered by Jívaro who was sent by Tomam. So it was that Tomam punished them for harming the Indian.

Then the Indian returned home to die. He took along two mule-loads of wax for the *ladinos*, so that they might make candles to keep vigil for their dead and to scare away the temptations. When he arrived, his wife gave him something to eat. While he was eating, she said, "You came back a big eater!"

Indian: I learned this from Tsets'em. He was a very big eater. He swallowed gourds full of tamales, tortillas, pozol [drink made with cornmeal, sugar and water]. He ate heaps of food.

His wife didn't want to grind so much maize.

She said: You came back stinking like Tsets'em and Japay, too. You came back really filthy.

Tomam: Well, Indian, it seems your wife doesn't love you anymore. Your own nation doesn't love you either. Today, I'm going to kill you. Tsets'em was right.

Indian: How are you going to kill me?

Tomam: Go harvest a lot of maize and when you come out of your milpa, you will trip and fall into a ravine and choke yourself on the ropes of your carrying bag.

Later, when he was leaving his milpa carrying a big load of maize on his back, he saw Jívaro.

Jívaro: How did your wife treat you?

Indian: She said I stink of Tsets'em and that I came back a big eater.

Jívaro: Now that you have become your wife's enemy, you had better kill yourself.

So it was. He killed himself by falling down the ravine with his load of maize.

Tomam: The Indian vied against his wife. Tsets'em vied against the
                Indian. They both condemned themselves.

The Indian was taking too much honey out of the hives, killing too many
bees. He wanted to make a lot of money with the *ladinos*. This is why the
master got angry. He was right, but the master shouldn't have tried to kill
the Indian. This is why Tomam gave orders to Jívaro to have the Indian kill
Tsets'em and Japay and then the Indian had to pay for their deaths. It is
prohibited to fight for what nature gives us; this is for the poor.

From that time on, Tsets'em never fights with us Mortals, even though
we take a lot of honey from his hives. But still, we must take it carefully
so as not to kill the bees.

*   *   *

NARRATION 23
MUST ASK PERMISSION
TO EXTRACT HONEY FROM A HIVE

Honey has to be taken out of a hive with care, as a friend, with permission
of the Master, saying, "With your permission, Mr. God, I am going to take
this honey, as I have a yearning to eat it."

When the Master sees the hive empty, if he approves, he says, "That
Indian took this honey carefully; we are brothers. But when he crushes my
bees, we are enemies."

The old people advised the young not to kill the bees and not to eat too
much honey. To avoid offending the Master, you should not take honey out
of a hive when the entrance faces west, toward *tyaj momoras* [the World of
the Dead]. After taking it, always leave some honey for the larvae. If the
bees are killed, the honey becomes poisonous and eating too much honey
gives you attacks.

*   *   *

NARRATION 24
THE MASTER OF THE BEES PUNISHES ALFONSO

Mateo: Alfonso is a fool. All he does is eat honey. You have to plant
                sugarcane, if you want to eat so much sweets!

Once, I killed all the bees, when I tore at a hive to eat *zunteco* honey.[4] The
Master punished me. What nation isn't going to get mad, when all his
animals are killed by someone who is greedy? The Master has to punish.

When this happened, I died many times. I don't know how many. Mateo, my father, and the old people took care of me. My uncles — Terencio, Sebastian, Mateito — and old Juan José chopped down the tree but it was I who tore out the hive and I ate the *zunteco*. They didn't eat any. They said, "You want to eat honey? Here it is."

This *zunteco* honey is poisonous, if you eat a lot of it. It's a punishment. My papa often ate it but he only got a stomachache; his [tape] worms stirred up; he never got drunk from it. Only I went crazy. Mateo scolded me, "You can't eat much of this *zunteco*. It's poisonous."

I was dead for hours at a time. I vomited blood. I went out of the house and hid under the bushes so that my old folks and brothers couldn't see me. Only my body would stay inside the house. This was a bad sign. I was dead. And when I came to again, everyone was crying, my mother more than anyone. Each time, I died for many hours, with each attack. I couldn't find the road to Tomam the Younger, to the other world. That's why I came back to this world. I don't remember anything else. Later, they told me that my father held me down by my legs when I got the attacks. He laid me with my head toward the west so that if I died, I would go straight to the other world. The old people said:

> It's an attack mixed with an old illness. It didn't come on by itself. He's doing this [on purpose] to bother the old people.

They offered me food: tortillas, eggs, beans. I said, "I don't want the food of this world." They said, "If you don't eat you will die." My mother was the most cowardly, she didn't eat either. Mateo wasn't worried, or just a little. I said:

> Mama is crying for nothing. This is only punishment. I won't ever eat *zunteco* again. I'm not that crazy.

In fifteen days, I could stand up. Then Mateo said:

> Take good care of this patient so that he doesn't fall in the fire [in the hearth in the center of the hut]

After a month I was well. Then Mateo was glad. He said, "Now, when your mama gets sick you take care of her."

*   *   *

THE MASTER OF THE SNAKES, ARMADILLOS, OPOSSUMS AND PACAS
(Author and Alfonso)

This Master has two names: Lo Chim Jamayón and Ladate Chim Jamayón, meaning master (*jamayón*) of two supernatural snakes.

Alfonso: The Master and his family live in the first level underground, very near the surface of the Earth. He's black and like a Mortal. He carries his snakes rolled over his arms He whistles and they come. He's dependable, doesn't fight, is rich and has lots of children. One day he eats snakes and the next, opossums.

Snakes may bite cattle, other animals and humans, also, if they are stepped on. But when they escape from their Master, they bite whomever they please.

Only the *punakpanes* are never bitten, except if they misbehave. In which case, Tomam sends a *pomjantsip*, a plumed serpent, to bite them as punishment.

Certain parts of a snake may be eaten by the Master and others by humans. The Master has the right to the head and from the head down to the measure of four times four fingers. People can eat only the middle part, measuring four times four fingers from the tip of the tail, as well as the head. In order to eat it, one should open one's mouth very wide and place the snake meat directly on the tongue without touching the lips. If it does touch the lips, the individual will die.

Tobacco is thought to be poisonous to snakes and to their Master as well. Tobacco is rubbed on the feet, to avoid being bitten, and on a snake which has bitten someone.

Ants, any insect, have the right to eat dead snakes.

The snakes' Master is also their Majordomo, the ocelot is that of the opossum, a feline (*tigre mortete*: not indentifed) that of the paca. The Majordomo of the Armadillo was not reported.

* * *

MYTH 44
THE MASTER OF THE SNAKE
AND THE LITTLE OLD MAN

Lo Chim Jamayón [Master of the Snake, Armadillo, Opossum and Paca], said:

> The Mortals are really filthy. They smear my dead snakes with tobacco resin, so I can't touch them, then they bury them and the Earth eats them.

An Indian was clearing his field [to plant] when a snake bit him. But just before this happened, he had sat down to rest with his companions and the Little Old Man, his father-in-law.

His Com-
panions: Well, enough for now fellows, let's sit here for awhile.

Little
Old Man: Which one of you will pull this thorn out of me?

His companions pulled it out. These fellows were very attentive and generous with him. Then the Little Old Man returned to work some more. The fellow who was about to be bitten by a snake, said:

> Look, that snake is still there. I'm going to catch it; if I don't, it might bite me.

The Com-
panions: Let's go home, now. We've had enough work for today. [To their companion who was about to die from a snakebite, they said] You're sure to die here in the bushes, if you keep pestering that snake. You won't even be able to clear half of your milpa.

So it was. Then the companions called the Little Old Man.

Little
Old Man: Why are you calling me? You are all so capricious!

The Com-
panions: No, Señor, we called you because of a snake, a *barba amarilla* [a yellow-chin snake, very poisonous], who just passed by. It didn't bite anyone; it just passed by.

This was a lie. When the Little Old Man looked around, he saw his son-in-law bleeding. Soon afterwards, he died. Then the Little Old Man got angry and said, "He's really dead!" He reported this to Tomam [the Elder]. Then Jívaro came.

Jívaro: Lo Chim is going to be condemned for this. Nompwinapu'u [son of Tomam] is not going to like this. Lo Chim and all of his family are going to die. I want you to make a declaration against the Master of the Snake. Who did the snake bite? And what was he doing here?

Little Old Man:	The snake bit my son-in-law and I'm keeping him company.
Jívaro:	He was trying to catch a snake that was already in its hole. This means that the man was at fault. Why did you let him get out of hand?

Jívaro scolded the Little Old Man, who replied:

> The Second Chief [Tomam the Younger] must be informed. I want to know why the Master allowed his snake to bite this Indian.

Jívaro:	I can give you an answer the day after tomorrow, not tomorrow, nor today.

But don't think that Jívaro went to report to the Second Chief. Instead, he went directly to the Master of the Snake and said to him:

> Get going and fast, and ask the Old Indian to forgive you. He just might. If not, the day after tomorrow, you'll be good and dead. By then, he will have complained against you to the Second Chief. Go fast, go tomorrow at dawn, while it is still dark.

Very early the next day, the Little Old Man went hunting for deer. But don't think he found any. As he was old, his knees got tired and he sat down to rest. Then he took out his *cabuyas* [magic strings] to ask them where he might find a deer nearby. He twisted the strings a little bit this way [toward the east] and then that way [toward the west]. But the strings told him something else.

Magic Strings:	A black man is going to come.
Little Old Man:	Who sends him?
Magic Strings:	He will come to find out why you are against him because of the man who just died.
Little Old Man:	Why, I'm against him because of an Indian who just died?
Magic Strings:	It's because of the snake in a hole in the bushes, a snake who bit a man.
Little Old Man:	And why is he coming?

Magic
Strings: So you can forgive him.
Little
Old Man: I can forgive once.

He went to another hill, sat down again, and asked his strings some more questions. He still wanted to know where the deer was but the strings told him the same thing.

Magic
Strings: There are no deer today. There is only Lo Chim Jamayón who is looking for you.
Little
Old Man: What does he bring?
Magic
Strings: He's carrying a snake curled around his arm. He's treating it like a criminal because it killed a man.
Little
Old Man: I will ask him to kill that snake like it killed the Indian, my companion, my son-in-law.

His son-in-law was a very good man and this is why the Little Old Man was so angry. Finally, the Master arrived with the snake curled around his arm.

Master: Señor Little Old Man, I have come today to beg you to pardon me, for this once. I don't go around harming and killing Indians. Only snakes who escape from their Master kill people. So you shouldn't be too angry against the Master. This snake is the real criminal. You're really obliged to pardon me.
Little
Old Man: Give me the snake so I can kill it, just as it killed my son-in-law. I'm going to kill you, too, with one arrow shot.
Master: [pointing to the snake] This is the killer. But I won't give it to you. I, and I alone, have the right to punish it. And don't go and complain to the Second Tomam or to his employees.
Little
Old Man: Set it right down here so that I can kill it.
Master: No, no, I won't let you.
Little
Old Man: Well alright, I'll pardon you this one time. It is true that you don't go around killing people. It was this snake that killed my son-in-law. But I order you to control your snakes and to

punish this one. One death is not so bad but if there are two, then I will present a complaint.

So the Master was ordered to condemn the snake. Then the Master and the Little Old Man became friendly.

Little Old Man: When I pardon, I really mean it once and for all time. May God witness, I do pardon you.

So they became friends.

Lo Chim: When will you come to visit me, to my house? Can you come tomorrow? I'll give four armadillos, even eight.

The Little Old Man got angry and replied, "Are you trying to damage my reputation? I don't even know where you live."

Master: You can't say I live very far away, I live right in the middle of your milpa. I see you when you harvest and when you pile up your corn. I live just a little way this side that stack of corn. You work on the top of the Earth and I on the first level below, in your own field. Why don't you come! Now that we're friends.

Very early the next day, the Little Old Man went to visit the Master.

Master: Do come in.

Soon afterward, he gave him some tortillas and slices of snake meat to eat.

Little Old Man: How does one eat this meat?

Master: Open your mouth widely so that the meat does not touch you lips. If you put it inside your mouth, it is not poisonous.

Little Old Man: On second thought, I'll take this portion home to my wife.

Master: Before you leave, I'll give you some armadillos to take to your family. If you take home this snake meat, you might kill your whole family. Eat it here. Finish it off right now. You can only eat snake meat if I, myself, hand it to you. [The Little Old Man ate it.]

The Master called his daughter to take away his plate:

Master: Bring him some water to wash his hands. He must not go without washing, as he touched poisonous meat.

She brought the water.

Little
  Old Man: Now, I have washed my hands.

Then he took a pipe out of his pocket to have a smoke. He found the wick and the pipe, all that he needed.

Daughter: Look out, papa! He is about to kill us with the smoke of his tobacco!

Master: Don't light that pipe! Don't smoke!

Little
  Old Man: Alright, one word suffices. Advice should be given with just one word.

He didn't smoke. He put his pipe back into his pocket to smoke it at home. He said, "Señor Master of the Armadillo, now I'm off."

Master: Don't leave just now. Wait a minute, I want to give you four armadillos. You can carry two under each arm and your wife can cook them. This is good meat. Snake meat can kill, if it doesn't come directly from me. If you want to get rid of your wife, take her some snake meat — if not, take these armadillos. The armadillo is a very reliable animal, very healthy. I hope now that you won't speak against me because of the death of your son-in-law.

Little
  Old Man: I have pardoned you. But if you do it again, we will be enemies. Then I'll kill you and all your family so that you don't go on killing people. You must control your snakes. I have pardoned you this time. Now we will say goodbye as friends.

The Master Lo Chim paid for the death of the Indian with four armadillos. As the father-in-law was old and ate little, he only gave him four.

Little
  Old Man: In eight to ten days, or say nine days, I will return so that you pay me another four armadillos, four each visit.

So the Master paid eight armadillos after two visits, sixteen after four visits, until the Little Old Man died.

The Master doesn't ever order his snakes to bite the Indian Nation. The son-in-law stepped on the snake and this is why it bit him and it had the right to do so. The Indian was to blame and this is why the Little Old Man forgave the Master.

*   *   *

NARRATION 25
ALFONSO BITTEN BY A SNAKE

When Mateo saw me bitten, he got mad and said:

Mateo: That's what you get for not looking where you walk! So you were burning your milpa and it bit you! You know, if you don't work, you won't eat. So now, what?

Then

I said: I didn't ask the snake to bite me. It was an accident.

Mateo: It was no accident. You let yourself be bitten. You'll die right here and now, if that snake gets away. You'll swell all over.

I said: Have it your way.

I ran, grabbed the snake and

I said: "Eh! You bit me when I was working."

When a person doesn't die right away, the snake won't either. If you don't die right away, you must kill it but that takes courage. A *urulan* bit me. It's not big. It's like any small snake. But, anyway, if the bitten person doesn't kill it, it will come back and suck blood from its [the victim's] nose. Sometimes the tail has more poison [than the mouth]. Sometimes heaps of *barbas amarillas* [yellow-chin snakes] and rattlesnakes come. If you don't kill the snake, he'll surely come running back to finish you off. I wrapped it up in a rag and bit it, like it bit me. The teeth of Mortals are poisonous for snakes. Mateo finished it off; I was too dizzy. Later, he hung it from a rope and brought it home. Sometimes, we tie them up alive and bring them home. You have to bring them home so they see who they have bitten. I buried this one near the house. You should have a cemetery for all the snakes that bite you. When Mateo killed it, I called my brothers to come and see me. Mateo was still mad.

Mateo: You boys don't want to work. Why are you always getting sick? Why should I support you?

I got a little mad at Mateo.

I said: Papi, don't come close to me. I'll go look for another place to work, where the snakes don't bite. You scolded me and this is why I'm speaking badly to you. You may get bitten, too.

Mateo: I will think over what you have said.

Later, he asked me, "How would you like to work over there?" I said that I would like for us to work close-by. All the top of me swelled up and when I got home, I was swollen all over. The next day, I was given the bark of the *chinquite* tree. I drank some ground, mixed with water, and it was rubbed on me. And for three days, I was rubbed with tobacco leaves. Anita, a *ladina*, the wife of the late Lauriano, came to massage me with tobacco leaves. I told her I wasn't bashful about her being a *ladina* because I was sick. Mateo left my brothers, Guillermo and Panchito, to take care of me. He came to see me all the time.

Mateo:	You don't want to live. You are doing your best to die.
I said:	I haven't eaten for three days but I won't die yet because my blood is good. I want to eat a roasted *ayote* [squash].
Mateo:	You can't eat that; it will make you even sicker. There's nothing worse than ayote.
I said:	Then give me some roasted castillan bananas. I have a real yen for them.
Mateo:	Not yet. Bananas are bad food.
I said:	How could they be bad food, if God put them on Earth?

Mateo got a little mad.

Mateo:	You already have food. Tell me, why don't you eat what I brought you?

I told him that the food he brought me upsets me. He only gave me tortillas and snails. Later, I asked my brothers to bring me some squash and bananas, without telling the old people. Right away they brought me a "hand" [five] of bananas. Guillermo said they couldn't bring more because Mateo might come back any minute. We roasted them, where the old people couldn't see. Later, they brought me a whole box of bananas and two squashes. Then Mateo came back.

Mateo:	I've come to take a look at you and find out why you haven't eaten.
I said:	That food you brought me upsets me.

They brought me *curarina* [a medicinal plant] to drink. Mateo had gone to get it. He came back and when he counted the tortillas he got mad again.

Mateo:	They're all still here! You're killing yourself. There's no doubt, Alfonso wants to die.
I said:	I ate. Really, I did eat. I won't die for at least two days.

He left and took all the tortillas, saying:

Alright. I'm going to give these to the dogs. If the dogs don't die, they might find a peccary for me.

That evening, I asked Panchito [the other brother] to bring me some more squash. I couldn't eat tortillas yet, nor chicken, nor eggs. Anita [the *ladina* neighbor] massaged me for three more days and then I could eat tortillas. After a week, I could walk a little and in two weeks, I was well again.

*   *   *

NARRATION 26
OLD ANTONIO BITTEN BY A SNAKE

A long time ago, a *barba amarilla* bit my uncle, Antonio. He was a deaf-mute and already old. This happened when I was just a kid, when old Juan Martínez was still alive.

They tied the snake to a forked branch. Juan squeezed the head between the fork, while others got ahold of its tail. They tied it, branch and all, to a slat of wood and brought it home [Antonio's house]. They hung it up on the outside wall to punish it so that its master would be sure to see it. It didn't bite Juan but Juan was scared of it. He took care of all this because the snake had bitten his son, Antonio.

Three days later, it got loose; they hadn't tied it well enough. When it fell, it coiled up and the pigs got after it but it killed five pigs, some chickens and turkeys. Everyone it bit died right away. The deaf-mute Antonio died seven days later. All of his teeth fell out and he vomited blood. The snake lasted three days without eating. The man lasted seven days without eating. The man lasted longer.

*   *   *

MYTH 45
THE OPOSSUM AND THE ARMADILLO
ENCOUNTER THE TIGER

During the time of the First Nation, opossums and armadillos went around together. They don't anymore. Then the tigers [jaguars] were killing them.

Tiger: Hasn't anyone seen a *macoyac* [tiger of the First Nation] around here?

Opossum: One just went by. Look, here are his paw prints.

Tiger: Eh! And you, what do you eat? You're so skinny!

Opossum: As I am very poor, I eat *coyoles* [a fruit of a palm tree and euphemism for testicles]. This is why I'm sort of skinny and puny. You are a big animal. You hunt a lot, lots of deer, lots of tapirs.

The Tiger was looking at the Opossum, ready to spring on him.

Opossum: Let me show you how to eat *coyoles*.

He pretended he was eating his own *coyoles*. So the Tiger did likewise. He cut off his *coyoles*, ate them and died on the spot. He killed himself; the Opossum didn't kill him.

Opossum: [to Armadillo] Now let's pull out his fangs to make a *sokia* [necklace].

This they did.

Mother Earth: Are you killing the tigers?
Opossum: No, Señora. This one killed himself. He cut off his *coyoles*.
Sun: The Tiger killed himself. The Opossum is innocent.
Opossum and
Armadillo: Yes, Señor. We are only guilty of pulling out his fangs. We pulled them out because they're so pretty.
Opossum: [to Armadillo] The Tiger is a big hunter! Big as he be, little me taught him a lesson. And I'm going to kill all the tigers who pass by here. I won't kill the tigresses so that they suffer, searching for their husbands, so that they weep.

A Tigress passed by.

Tigress: Have you all seen a tiger around here?
Opossum: One passed by awhile back. If you hurry, you can catch up with him.

The Opossum and the Armadillo went along with her sniffing for the paw marks of the Tiger. But how could they ever find them! The Tigress got mad. She sent a convoy of warrior ants to attack the Opossum and bite the hell out of him. But he fled with the Armadillo.

Tigress: Go, convoy of warrior ants, and bite them hard!

But the Opossum and the Armadillo dug themselves underground and hid. They stayed there well hidden.

Tigress: I'm going to lie in wait for them and attack them. And for revenge, what's left of them I'll leave the buzzards. But I'll only leave Armadillo's bony plate and Opossum's hair. I, myself, will eat the meat and bones. This is how they'll pay for the death of my husband, whom they taught to eat his balls.

The Tigress proved to be a liar. But ever after, she was the enemy of the opossums and the armadillos.

The Tigress was searching for food, when she passed by and heard the death chant of her husband. Opossum was wearing the necklace of the Tiger's fangs and was singing his death chant. The Tigress heard it.

Tigress: [to Opossum] Now I'm sure that I heard it. Confess now, by your own mouth. Now I know the truth.

So the Opossum closed the door of the house, where he was hiding, and fled through the window. He went with the Armadillo to hide in a cave. Then the Tigress sent her hunters [warrior ants] but they couldn't catch them, as the Opossum threw earth up as he went underground through each layer.

After the Tiger had eaten his balls, he presented himself to Jo'popjil [his Master] to complain about the Opossum and the Armadillo.

Jo'popjil: You're a liar. You're a big hunter but you're such a glutton that you eat your own balls! Aren't you ashamed? With so many deer and rabbits to eat in the bush!

The Tiger had punished himself. But Tomam punished the Opossum and the Armadillo for having pulled out the Tiger's fangs. He had them whipped seven times with a tiger's tail.

The Rabbit is the only one who doesn't get caught by the Tiger. [myths 50 to 55]

*   *   *

NARRATION 27
"I DO HARM THE ARMADILLO"

The armadillo doesn't harm anyone but I don't want to eat my tamal empty, my tortilla empty. I want to eat them with armadillo meat, because of this bad habit of eating.

The Master of the Armadillo doesn't do me any harm but I harm his animals. It is better that I die, then I'll be condemned for having hunted so many animals. Then I'll pay for what I've done.

*   *   *

THE MASTER OF THE RACCOONS
(Author)

The Master of the *Mapachines* (raccoons) is only known as Mapachin Jamayón. His majordomo is the *tsitsih-pine* (harpy eagle).

* * *

NARRATION 28
ALFONSO AND THE RACCOONS

The peccaries, coatis and raccoons: all these little animals are very harmful for the crops. This is what their masters want. The maize is also for them. We cultivate half for ourselves and half for them. We eat these little animals and the Earth eats us.

I sent some raccoons to their Master, Jamayón. They asked for death. I killed the mother and grabbed the young ones. They were twins, a male and a female. The dogs got them up a tree and I killed the mother with a shotgun. I wanted to raise the little ones but they got into my milpa, fell into a trap, and both were killed. I didn't eat them. I left them for the buzzards and sent them off to their master. When I took them out of the trap I said:

> Raccoons, you are dead. You didn't want your master to receive you alive. You caught the fetid vapor of the Mortals and now you'll feed the buzzards. You wanted to eat too much of my maize and sugarcane and this is why you died. When your master asks you why Alfonso Martínez killed you, you tell him that you were being pests, just like your mommie, eating my maize at midnight.

The Indian is harmful and so is the raccoon. I give advice to each animal I kill — deer, peccaries, to all, so that they know how to present themselves to their masters.

* * *

THE MASTER OF THE AGOUTI
(Author)

The Master of the Agouti is the Giant. He lives in the caves with the Nens and the Chichinites. (myths 56, 57) Like the latter, he is covered with hair. He doesn't leave his cave often, because he fears that his hair might catch on fire. He swallows people and likes naked women.

The Majordomo of the Agouti is the *tigre mortete*, who is also that of the paca. He takes care of the agoutis during the day and the pacas at night.

* * *

NARRATION 29
LEONOR AND THE AGOUTI

One day, Leonor Soto [then chief of the west section] said to me:

> The agouti is bad, the white-collared peccary, also, the coati and raccoon, likewise. When I'm sleeping, the agouti is excavating in my milpa. A while ago, I planted 400 stalks of maize and he ate them all. Then I got sick but he kept on eating. When I'm harvesting my coffee, the agouti is harvesting my maize.

* * *

THE MASTER OF THE SNAILS
(Author)

Zozots Jamayón is the Master of the Earth and the River Snails. It lives in the river as a snail but when it comes on land, it transforms itself into a being, quite like a human.

If the people gather too many snails, the Master makes them very scarce and defends his snails by fatiguing those who search for them.

* * *

THE MASTER OF FISH
(Author)

The Master of the Fish, Bagre (Catfish) Jamayón, also lives in the rivers and streams together with his Majordomo, the river otter.

* * *

MYTH 46
THE MASTER COMPLAINS OF POISONING HIS FISH

During the First Nation, the Devils created *zopi*, a poison.[5] Many Indians died of this poison. One who didn't complained to the *zahorín* and he notified Tomam:

> The Devils are poisoning the Mortals. They are betting
> against you, Tomam, to win souls.

Right away, Nompwinapu'u ordered the Devils to be tied up or to be killed
on the spot.

The Indians learned to fish with this poison. They were poisoning too
many catfish and eels without mercy. Their Master got mad and complained [about the Indians] to the *zahorín*. He, too, got mad and said:

> Better they die on the shores of the streams. When they eat
> fish they will vomit blood. Why are they poisoning with the
> *zopi*?

*   *   *

NARRATION 30
ALFONSO AND THE MASTER OF THE FISH

When I was a kid, I used to fish for eels night after night. Once, I found an
enemy instead of a meal. It was an eel a yard long. It bit me like a snake;
I thought it was a snake. I struck it with my machete without pity, but I
didn't kill it. It was wounded and I thought it had drowned in the deep part
of the stream. Later, I told the old folks about it and went back with them
to show where it had drowned so they wouldn't say I was offending the
Nation of Snakes. I jumped into the deep part to get the snake but I didn't
find it. The old men got mad.

The old men: Now you must go to the domicile of the snakes and excuse
yourself with the Master. Why did you let yourself be bitten? Why don't you look where you're going! Were you
sleep-walking?

I said: I didn't see the animal that bit me. But I'm sure it was a
snake.

The old men: We're going to punish you. Go look again.

I jumped into the stream again. Then, I did get ahold of it.

The old men: What a liar! It's food. It's an eel! What do you mean a
snake? Every night you've been pestering the Nation of the
Eels. You pester them too much, that's why you were bitten.

As I was a kid, I had a yen for eating all the time. With other kids, I had
been fishing every night.

I said: I'm not going to eat these animals anymore. If I had been
bitten by a snake, I would be dead by now.

The old men: What do you mean "dead!" You liar!

I said: Look where it bit me. It's bleeding just like a snakebite.

The old men: It's your fault. The Nation of Fish were against you. This is why the eel bit you. Why did you say a snake! What a liar! Soon the eel will go to his Master and make a declaration against you.

Then the old people pardoned me a little. It was six to twelve days before I got well.

When you scare an animal, you should not eat it. It may be a Temptation [a Devil]. Sometimes deer get scared. Any animal may get scared and want to talk to you but only to take your life. Julián Velázquez [one of the last Tolupan shamans] warned me about this.

* * *

NARRATION 31
ALFONSO SCOLDS THE MASTER OF THE FISH

Once, the Master of the Fish spoke to me, like a person, in Tolupan:

What has happened to all the catfish? They haven't come out yet from under the rocks?

I said: What party do you belong to? You're offending me! I'm bothering your fish because I don't have any meat. I'm going to report you to the other world. Master of the Catfish, I say to you, each nation has its laws. I tell you who I am. I'm going to report to God [Tomam], to find out which party you belong to. Why are you offending me? You should invite the Mortals [to eat your fish]. When I overdo it then you can kill me, you can report me to the other world so that I die, but not unless. The Mortals have their rights, too.

It fled. It hid under the rocks in the stream. It was the Master of the Catfish, alright. I scolded it, that's why it fled.

* * *

THE MASTERS OF CERTAIN BIRDS
(Author)

The "Birds of Glory" come to the Earth during the rainy season. The rest of the year, they are said to live in the first level above the Earth. Among them are the red-collared dove and various species of humming birds.

Their Master is Tata Dios. Other birds, mainly hawks and owls, remain on Earth all year. The Devil is their Master. They are not edible.

* * *

THE MASTER OF THE COCKROACHES
(Author)

Totarapei, the Master of the Cockroaches, is like a small person. He lives in the underground levels. The little cockroaches emerge to the surface of the Earth, defecate in the bees' honey and often get stuck there. They eat the honey but they die. This is how the bees punish them.

* * *

MYTH 47
THE MASTER OF THE COCKROACHES IS GENEROUS

A *ladina* didn't have any money to hire a maid. She didn't have any money but she had a mouth. Totarapei [the Master of the Cockroaches] said to her:

> So, if you wish, I'll give you a male and a female. And they will reproduce.

He gave them to her as a gift. Later the neighbors said to her:

> You really scrub well. Your house is so nice and clean.

Ladina: It's not I, it's thanks to the cockroaches; they work for me.

The Master had deceived her. Awhile later, instead of cleaning, the cockroaches dirtied everything and one day they ate her face, her ears and her whole body. They ate her all up. Then her husband moved. He burnt down the house and built a new one.

* * *

MYTH 48
THE MASTER OF THE COCKROACHES IS DECEIVING

A *ladina* and an Indian woman spoke [to Totarapei, the Master of the Cockroaches]:

Indian woman: We don't know how to scrub. You really know how. Your gourds [used as plates] are nice and clean, really pretty, all white on the inside.

Totarape: No, my ladies, it is not I; it's thanks to my cockroaches. They clean them for me. This is why my gourds are so nice and shiny.

Woman: Then give us one [a cockroach].

Totarapei: I'll give you a pair: a male and a female so they can reproduce.

This was how he fooled them. The *ladina* paid for them but he gave them to the Indian woman, as a present. But instead of cleaning the gourds, the cockroaches defecated and urinated in them. Totarapei really tricked these women.

Indian woman: Cockroaches, filthy old things. All you do is defecate all day.

The women asked for it, as they have a mouth to speak with, they got what they asked for.

* * *

NARRATION 32
THE EARTH IS THE MASTER OF THE BEETLE

The *ronron* [black beetle in Spanish] comes onto the Earth. He lives by working the *chinchin* so that it not be wasted. Tomam put a lot of nations in this world so that nothing be wasted.

I don't defecate in vain, nor do the cattle, nor the horses, there's the *plame lup* [the black beetle in Tolupan], he's really repulsive.

* * *

MYTH 49
THE MASTER OF THE LICE IS INSIDIOUS

The *ladinos* are loaded with *piojos* [lice], the Indians with *pulgas* [fleas] and the gringos with *piojillos* [bird lice]. The Devils are the Masters of Fleas, Lice, Ticks, Bedbugs, Bird Lice, and the like. This is the story of a rich woman, a little old *ladina* woman. She didn't have anything to do. She didn't do anything. She was bored. The Devil came to console her.

Devil: Why aren't you working? Everyone should work. I can sell you some fleas or ticks. Why not purchase some with your money? Then you will have some work to do. You can work all day, scratching yourself. You can also buy some bird lice, ordinary lice, or bedbugs.

She brightened up a little. She had money; she could buy anything. First, she bought a pair of each: male and female — a pair of lice, another of ticks, and sent them off in all parts of her body, all over herself. All day and night she scratched, even her tits and her anus. Finally, she got tired and angry. She said to herself:

> The Devil fooled me. All these ticks and fleas and lice are sure to kill me. I will die and no one will know.

The pests made nests in her knees. The Devil consoled her, "Why should you suffer? Better that you die."

Ladina: Now I have the fetid vapor of the ticks, lice, or fleas; I'm going to die because I was stupid. You told me to buy them so that I die. I spent my money for this! My body is all swollen; these pests are eating me up!

She died.

Devil: The *ladinos* are children of death. So I lend them my little animals to help them die sooner. Why should they be so healthy? I will lend them to both Nations — to the Indians and the *ladinos* so they can all die sooner. The women will scratch themselves all over, while they are working, cooking, preparing tortillas. The little old *ladina* lady died for them, for the *ladinos* and the Indians.

The ticks practically eat us up. Fleas and lice bite us day and night. The Devil is very endearing with us children of death. The little old *ladina* died for us. When she died, the ticks, fleas, lice spread all over the world.

* * *

NARRATION 33
THE DEVILS ARE MASTERS OF THE MINES

The Devils are rich, have lots of money and storehouses full of weapons, just like in Tegucigalpa. They fight with the gringos for the mines. As the Devils live in caves where the mines are, the mines belong to them. But the gringos have a right to the mines, too, because they study them: they know how to make money [metal coins] and weapons. Even so, when the gringos take gold from the mines, the Devils get mad because they ruin their homes. Then, right away, the Devils complain to Tomam. He scolds them:

Why get so mad? Let the gringos excavate to make money out of gold. They have families to support. If they want all of it, let them take it. Then you'll have to look for another cave. Let the gringos work, as they know how to make lots of things. But if they don't ask me permission, a chunk of mine will fall on them, as they, too, are children of death. If they don't behave well, they'll pay for it when they die. Sometimes, the Devils kill the gringos on their own, without permission. But then Tomam will fix them. The Gringo Nation should be respected too.

*   *   *

THE MASTER OF SICKNESS
(Author)

Tusmai, the Master of Sickness, lives on the first level below the Earth, on the north coast of Honduras.

*   *   *

NARRATION 34
SICKNESS FOR SALE

Tusmai is the enemy of us Mortals. He has sickness in his house, wrapped in little pieces of paper, stuck between the beams.[6] He offered them for sale. He used to trade a cold or measles for a cow but now he gives his sickness away for nothing. This year, in September, the son of Fabían gave me his cold for free because I let him stay overnight in my house. The *ladinos* give me their colds for nothing, too. My papa used to say that if Tusmai gives you a cold and you don't pay for it with a cow, then the cold will kill you. But I don't hear anyone say this, now. A cold won't kill you, if you have good blood. The Devils' sickness is sure to kill you, not Tusmai's. But if your hour has come, any old sickness will kill you.

Toman ordered Tusmai to bring us colds, measles, smallpox, fevers, flu, sickness for cattle and pigs, so that we Mortals stop fighting, so that we die all the sooner. Tusmai doesn't approve of fighting, either. We fought with Our Lord and with Tata Dios and this is why, ever since, we have to die.

*   *   *

RABBIT THE GREAT TRICKSTER
(Author)

Rabbit is neither a Master nor part of the ancient Tolupan tradition, although he has been well incorporated into it. The following stories of Uncle Rabbit, very probably told to the Indians by their *ladino* neighbors, have acquired a distinctive Tolupan flavor.

* * *

MYTH 50
RABBIT AND "TIGER-WITH-A-BROKEN-MOLAR"

Rabbit climbs up a *zapote* tree [sapodilla] to eat some fruit.

Rabbit: I'm going to teach my enemies to eat *zapotes*.

Tiger passes by.

Tiger: What are you doing up there, Uncle Rabbit?
Rabbit: Eating *zapotes*. Want to try one?
Tiger: You bet. Throw me a nice ripe one.

Rabbit chooses a nice ripe one and throws it right into his mouth. Then, Tiger asks for a riper one.

Rabbit: Open your mouth good and wide. If you don't, you will lose this one.

But Rabbit throws a stone into his mouth and breaks one of his molars.

Rabbit: Now you are Tiger-with-a-Broken-Molar for being so greedy. Bye-bye Tiger-with-a-Broken-Molar.

Then, Tiger becomes even more of an enemy with Rabbit.

* * *

MYTH 51
RABBIT DROWNS TIGER

Tiger is hunting for Rabbit, while Rabbit is at home — thinking.

Rabbit: (to himself) I'm going to take revenge on Tiger. First, I'll teach him to play the guitar and to sing. Then, I'll give him a big piece of curd cheese [*cuajada*] and a little bit of meat so that he not eat me. As I know how to buy and sell, I'll teach Tiger how to work so that he can buy himself a cow. Then, I'll show him how to fence in a pasture [for his cow].

Rabbit hangs his hammock over the lagoon for Tiger. He gives him a blanket and teaches him to play the guitar and sing. Tiger relaxes in the hammock, playing the guitar and singing.

Rabbit: Señor Tiger, you see I'm your friend; I taught you to play the guitar. Now, you can woo the Indian and *ladino* girls, when you meet them in the milpas. But remember, I only lent you my blanket, hammock and guitar. Now, I'm going to the bean field. When I've had enough beans, I'll go eat some watermelons.

He departs but comes back soon.

Rabbit: Here I am again, Señor Tiger. Are you tired of singing?
Tiger: Not yet.
Rabbit: Not yet! Vacate my hammock, right away. I want to swing in it myself and sing. Alright, you can stay just a little while longer.

Rabbit cuts the ropes which hold up the hammock and Tiger falls into the lagoon and drowns.

Rabbit: That's one less enemy. Now, Sialpe [same as Nen, Master of the Lagoon] can eat tiger meat.

* * *

MYTH 52
TIGER HUNTS MONKEY AND COATI KILLS TIGER

Sh-sh-sh-sh, whispers the Monkey.

Tiger: As I didn't eat the Rabbit, I'll eat a Monkey.

He went looking up a stream.

Tiger: Monkey, hear me! Today, I will eat you!
Monkey: Catch me, if you can. Here I am, swinging way up in this pine tree.

How could he ever catch him?

Monkey: You'll be sorry, old Starving-to-Death-Tiger.

Later, Coati passes by. Monkey hollers to him.

Monkey: Be careful!

Coati: I'm going to get even with this Tiger. I'll slit his throat.

Coati lays down on his back, as if dead. Tiger comes up to him and Coati jumps up and bites his throat. Tiger flees bleeding.

Monkey: Let me tell you, Uncle Tiger, if you don't want to die, why are you bothering every animal who happens by? Coati is not that easy to kill.

Tiger doesn't go far, as he is wounded, and awhile later he dies.

Coati: I fixed him forever. I slit his throat. But he did me in, too, with his claws. I'm going to Master Tsëncley so that he cure me.

Tsëncley: Eh! What's the matter?

Coati: Tiger wounded me.

Tsëncley: What happened to Tiger?

Coati: He's dead.

Tsëncley: That's fine. That Tiger was a glutton. He was forever eating my coatis, my monkeys, my [white-collared] peccaries. Come in. I won't send you back until you have healed.

Coati recovered a month later.

*   *   *

MYTH 53
RABBIT TIES UP TIGER AND PECCARY KILLS HIM

Tiger: I won't give in until I kill Rabbit.

Rabbit is splitting some lianas.

Tiger: Why are you splitting those lianas?

Rabbit: Eh! A big strong wind is coming any minute and sweep everything away! The world will be lost!

Tiger believes him — first a little, then more, then a lot.

Tiger: Tie me down, right now. I'm your friend.

Rabbit: I'm no friend of yours. We're enemies. And, Señor Tiger, we'll die enemies.

Tiger: Not so, Señor Rabbit. I repeat, we are friends. Tie me down, right now.

Rabbit: Well, alright. Hug this tree and I'll tie you to it. The wind storm is coming any minute. The world will soon be lost. I was splitting these lianas for my poor old mother, so the wind not sweep her away.

He ties Tiger to the tree.

Rabbit: Now, you are in a fix. You're all tied up because you are really stupid. You're going to bake in the sun because you're so envious. You're the one who'll be lost, tied to this tree trunk. The wind won't kill you but the lianas will and you'll make a fine meal for the buzzards.

Tiger: Why did you deceive me?

Rabbit: I did not. It's true a strong wind is stirring and the world will be swept away. But if it doesn't come, I'll think of something else.

Monkey is in a tree nearby, eating fruit. Tiger sees him and hollers.

Tiger: Señor Monkey, I'm your friend. Why don't you untie me?

Monkey: Not on your life. You might eat me. Better stay there roasting [in the sun].

Tiger: I promise; I won't eat you. I'm your friend.

Later, the stupid Monkey unties him and is eaten for being so stupid.

Tiger: What a silly Monkey! You're a meal now. I was days without eating, so many days tied to that trunk. This I owe to Rabbit.

But Tiger is still hungry. He lies there, spying on the monkeys who are jumping in the tree tops. He can't reach them so he stays on, lying there, until later a [white-lipped] peccary passes by; he bites his throat and kills him right off. Then, the peccary goes to his master, as he's afraid that another tiger might kill him. He stays with his master for thirty days.

All animals hunt the monkeys, a lot. This is why it was ordered that they walk around in the trees, so that the tigers and coyotes could not catch them. The tigers and coyotes want to hunt all animals, any animal whatsoever. This is why some nations have claws to climb with or to dig holes and make caves. And God made dogs to chase the tigers up the trees so that they could not kill Indians and *ladinos*. And he gave the chickens wings. God is no fool.

*   *   *

MYTH 54
RABBIT AND "COYOTE-WITH-A-BURNT-BACKSIDE"

Rabbit goes to a field to eat beans and watermelons. He eats some beans and goes to find some watermelons.

Old Father
Priest: What a messy Rabbit! Why are you shitting on my watermelons?

The Little Old Priest goes home but Rabbit stays on, conversing with Coyote. Rabbit is an enemy of Tiger and Coyote, too.

Coyote: What are you doing here?
Rabbit: I'm waiting from some *piñuela*, the Little Old Priest is going to bring me. Why don't you wait and have a taste?
Coyote: What's *piñuela*?
Rabbit: It's curd cheese mixed with cattle urine. The Little Old Priest is very generous. He'll bring some, soon. Stay and see.

When the Little Old Priest comes, Rabbit runs away. Instead of *piñuela*, he brought a hot stone to throw at Rabbit. Coyote stays on to converse with the Little Old Priest.

Old Father
Priest: Eh! Rabbit, so now you've turned into a coyote!

He throws the hot stone at him.

Old Father
Priest: Now, get out of here, Coyote-With-a-Burnt-Backside. This is your reward for shitting on my watermelons.
Rabbit: (to himself) I got away. Enemies come in handy. Coyote saved me. It's not only the *ladinos* who can do a lot of things; I can, too. It pays to be friends with your enemies.

*   *   *

MYTH 55
RABBIT GOES TO GLORY[7]

After Tiger and Coyote, Rabbit's only remaining enemy is Buzzard. Rabbit is hiding in a cave.

Buzzard: Eh! I see you there, in that cave! Just wait, you'll pay me with your death.

Rabbit: Open you eyes good and wide, Señor Buzzard.

He does so and Rabbit throws dirt into them and flees. Then, Buzzard goes to Glory to complain to Tata Dios.

Tata Dios: Where's that Rabbit hiding?
Buzzard: In that cave down there.

But he had left, so Tata Dios has Buzzard killed for being a liar and, the next day, sends another Buzzard.

Buzzard: Tata Dios desires to hear you play your music.
Rabbit: But how can I get to Glory? I don't have wings. If I did, I'd come with pleasure. It's true — I play the guitar and can sing, too. If you take me to Tata Dios, I'll sing many verses for him and tell him many stories.
Buzzard: I'll take you up there, just as Tata Dios orders. He wants to hear your music and your verses, too.
Rabbit: (to himself) This is a trap, sure death. No Buzzard can fool me! I'm not a *zahorín* for nothing. He doesn't want to hear me sing; he wants to make me fall off Buzzard. I know the likes of this liar of a Buzzard. But if I'm enough of a *zahorín*, he won't [be able to] eat me.

He climbs on Buzzard's wings, with his guitar, and off they fly.

Buzzard: Señor Rabbit, can you still see the Earth?
Rabbit: Yes Señor, I still see it. (to himself) For sure, he'll try to make me fall at the door of Glory.
Buzzard: Can you still see the Earth?
Rabbit: Just a wee bit, now. (to himself) Now the moment of Rabbit's death has arrived.
Buzzard: Can you see the Earth at all?
Rabbit: I can't see it, now, anymore.
Buzzard: Be careful Rabbit, don't fall off my wings.

At the door of Glory, Buzzard shakes him off his wings, guitar and all. Slowly, he falls to Earth — like a leaf.

Rabbit: (while falling) I'm enough of a *zahorín*. I'm falling like a leaf, riding on the wind. I only lost my guitar. Now, Buzzard is really my enemy.

Later, Buzzard flies back to Earth, to feed on Rabbit. But Rabbit strikes him hard on the head and kills him.

Rabbit only lost his guitar, not his blanket or his hammock. He was punished for being such a prankster by losing his guitar. But he finished off his enemy. He proved that he was a real *zahorín*.

* * *

CHICHINITE [8]
(Author)

Chichinite is small, strong, likes naked women and walks with his feet backward "to fool his enemies." He is entirely covered with hair and eats his meat raw. He fears that if he lights a fire, he might set his hair on fire. Like the masters of the animals and the Giants, he inhabits a cave. If he is shot at, he simply lifts his hand and stops the bullet.

* * *

MYTH 56
CHICHINITE FIGHTS WITH THE <u>LADINOS</u> [9]

A *ladina* cried and cried because a Chichinite had hidden her in a cave. She had been there for so many years! She had a son who was pretty big and had hair all over his body, just like his father. Everyday, Chichinite left to hunt and blocked the entrance of the cave with a big rock. One day, when mother and son were alone, the kid (*cipote*) said:

> My father did wrong. Why is he mistreating the Nation of *Ladinos*? Mama, I'll get you out of this cave but I'll charge you eight *arrobas* [200 lbs.] of machetes and the same of axes. Also, I want to learn to read and write.

Everyday, her son pushed the big rock a little more. After ten days, he could move it a little.

Kid: Mama! I moved the rock a little!

Everyday, from then on, he moved the rock a little more.

Kid: Get ready, mama, soon I will take you home!
Mama: I've always been ready. I was only waiting until you were strong enough to move the rock.

Then the father arrived, carrying a peccary [which he had killed].

Chichinite: Take it and eat it.

They ate it — bloody and raw.

Kid: Mama, do you like to eat this raw meat?

Mama: I don't. I only eat it so as not to starve.

Kid: Get ready, mama! Soon you will be free. You won't have to defecate in the cave or quarrel with the Chichinite. Soon you will live in peace and have a good husband; that is, if only I can kill this Chichinite.

The kid was talking against his father. But his father didn't know. He was always out hunting for food. The next day, when the father left, the son said:

> Get ready, mama, now we are leaving.

Chichinite was out hunting a tapir. He didn't know it yet but, this day, he was going to bring meat for himself alone.

Chichinite: (to himself) What a kid! He moved the rock!

He followed their footprints, running after them.

Kid: Run, mama, run so that we get to your country! Farther on, there are some big trees, where we can slow down.

He looked back and saw Chichinite catching up.

Kid: Papa is going to grab us!

The mama stopped. Her son hollered at her:

> Hide behind me!

He pulled up a tree by its roots and, when Chichinite reached them, he struck him with the tree and killed him.

Kid: Now you have no more enemies, mama. We can walk slowly, now. I'm taking you back to your family. Sit down, mama. I'll get you some water, if you are thirsty. The danger has past.

When they arrived at the mother's house, her family invited them in. One of the family asked:

> Why did you bring this fellow along? Does he belong to another nation? Is he your husband?

Mama: He's my son. I won't let you kill him!

Kid: She's my mama but she doesn't belong to the Nation of Chichinites so I got her out of the cave.

The family gave him permission to stay but he refused.

Mama: Don't go away son. Try to make the best of it. They want to take a picture of you.

Kid: I don't know how to make machetes. All I ask is for 200 lbs. of machetes and the same of axes. Only this.

She gave them to him. She bought them in a factory [near-by]. The kid took one of the machetes and split a tree with it to test it. He liked it. He tested them all and then went to see his mama.

Kid: Now, I'm going to test the 200 lbs. of axes.

He wanted them to clear a field, to fell trees so as to plant maize. He tested them all and liked every one of them.

Kid: Mama, you have paid me. Now, I want to learn to read and write. Only this.

As he was living with his mama, he wanted to study but he got offended in school. The teacher said he was too much of a fighter and tried to throw him out of school.

Teacher: I'm going to punish his kid with a whip with iron lashes.

Kid: I don't even want to learn anymore. I'm going to kill you; then I'll dump you in a ditch.

He did just this. Then, the chief there grabbed him and threw him in jail.

Kid: (to himself) These are all employees of death. They're not to punish me anymore. I like the Nation of Chichinites better. Only the Chichinites have the right to punish me.

The Chichinite kid pushed down the jail, beams and all, and scared the employees to death.

Employees: Be gone with you. We don't need you here.

He did just that. He went back to his country. His mama stayed on with her family. The Chichinite kid never returned. Why should he?

Kid: I'm going to marry a woman of my own Chichinite Nation. Why should I bother with those quarrelsome Mortals!

*   *   *

MYTH 57
CHICHINITE FINDS A WIFE

Chichinite: (to the Giant) Why are you throwing dirt on my tamales? I'll kill you. By the hand of God, I'll kill you.

Giant: Why are you planting in my field? This is my property. You're the one who's making trouble.

They fought. Chichinite wounded Giant with his machete and Giant died. Then Chichinite went to Giant's house. In the cave, in a large hole, he saw Giant's wife. She called from below:

Why do you come here? You had no right to kill Giant.

She was a pretty girl and Chichinite liked her. He saw that she had a big bag of money. Chichinite's companion, "Knock-Down-Hills," was standing at the entrance to the cave. He, too, saw the girl and the big bag of money.

Knock-Down-
 Hills: (to himself) I'll kill Chichinite; then the girl and the money will be mine.

Knock-Down-Hills tied Chichinite by the waist with a liana and lowered him. First, Knock-Down-Hills pulled her up. He lowered the liana again into the hole; Chichinite tied the bag of money to the vine and Knock-Down-Hills pulled it up, too. Only Chichinite was still in the hole. Knock-Down-Hills lowered the liana again to pull him up.

Chichinite: (to himself) I'm going to test Knock-Down-Hills to see if he is a friend or an enemy. With your permission, Señor Tree, I'm going to strike you down.

He tied the tree trunk to the liana.

Chichinite: (to himself) He's not pulling the liana yet.

After awhile he said:

Now, he's pulling it with all his might.

Then, Chichinite looked for a reed to blow through and notify the Giants to come and get him out of the cave.

Reed: What do you need, Señor Chichinite?
Chichinite: Right now, nothing. In a little while, maybe something. I'm waiting to see whether Knock-Down-Hills is trying to kill me or not.

Knock-Down-Hills pulled the liana tied to the tree trunk almost all the way up; then he cut the vine. The tree fell back into the hole and he fled with the girl and the bag of money.

Chichinite:	Señor Reed, I'm not going to hurt you. I'm only going to blow on you, a little.

He blew and soon a couple of Giants arrived. From the entrance to the cave, they reached down the hole and pulled out Chichinite.

One of the Giants:	I'll give you some advice, Señor Chichinite, so that you not harm the Nation of Giants again. Go live in another mountain. We'll forgive you this time.

Chichinite ran away, caught up to Knock-Down-Hills with the girl and the bag of money. He grabbed him and shouted.

Chichinite:	I'll kill you, now.
Knock-Down-Hills:	How are you going to kill me?
Chichinite:	I'll cut off your head.

He did just that and Chichinite took the girl and the bag of money.

Girl:	Now, you are in for it. You won't last long. They'll hunt you down. Chichinite, you are a killer but if you kill me, you will be even worse off.
Chichinite:	I'll not kill you. I want you as my wife.
Girl:	That's alright. Women were born for men. Now, I'll give you some more advice. Let's go some other place to live.

They fled to Chichinite's country, with the bag of money.

NOTES

1. I have the impression that any cave, of the several in the region, may be considered to be the domicile of different masters.
2. Pittier de Fabregas (1941: 95).
3. See Shaw (1971: 147-48, 381-83) for a version of this myth in English and transcription in Tolupan.
4. *Zunteco* is the name of a bee, known in Honduras, whose honey may be toxic if consumed in excess.
5. In Honduras, *zope* is the name of a poisonous product of a tree called *zopolote*, not to be confused with *zopilote*, the buzzard.
6. The medicines, powders and pills which the *ladinos* sell to the Indians are usually contained in small envelopes and are tucked between the beams of the hut ceilings, just as Tusmai kept his sickness.

7. See Boas (1912: 205) for a similar story from Pochutla, Oaxaca, Mexico and Kunst (1915) for another version from the Chuh of Guatemala.

8. The name *Chichinite* is Nahuatl in origin, spelled *Tsitsimitl*. Myths and legends about it are reported among many groups in this part of Central America: for instance, the Chortis of Guatemala (Wisdom, 1961: 457); the Mayas of Guatemala (Gillen, 1954: 106; Thompson, 1932: 67); and the Misquitos of Honduras and Nicaragua (Conzemius, 1932: 168).

9. For another version of this myth from Tehuantepec, Oaxaca, Mexico, see Boas (1912: 241-45), in which "Juan Tiger" takes the part of *Chichinite*. Among other groups in Mexico, the personage is called "Juan Bear," as in Foster (1945: 227).

CHAPTER VI

DEATH AND AFTERLIFE

THE DEVILS
(Author)

The old Tolupans cautioned everyone to avoid the caves where the Devils (*Liauros*) live. These He- and She-Devils seduce people, to win souls for the "Party of the Devils" and their victims die soon afterwards.

When a man is all alone in the forest hunting, or gathering firewood, or working in his milpa — suddenly, a lovely Devil might appear and seduce him. Likewise, a handsome Devil might seduce a lone woman, while she is washing clothes or bathing in a stream.

These Devils are known generically as "Temptations" or *Chii*. Those who haunt the west section are called Toco *Chikwai* (Toco the Younger) and are the most dangerous. Those of the east, the Toco *Pones* (the Elder), are less bothersome, according to Alfonso, who belonged to this moiety.

* * *

221

NARRATION 35
SEDUCTIVE DEVILS

The Devils are like people, like us, like me, so the old people said. I've never seen one. Mateo never saw one either. But Félix Pérez [a *punakpan*] did. They don't bother me now but at my hour of death they might.

The Devils win more souls than God: souls of *ladinos* and Indians, too. They live mostly on Leonor's side [west section], underneath the earth. But they can't stay out after 4:00 p.m.

The women Devils are really pretty: fat, with large breasts and long braided hair. They wear yellow skirts, tight around the waist, and are naked above. They're young and haven't been used [virgins]. When a man kisses one, this means his hour of death is not far off; in five or eight days, he'll be in his grave. The old people gave this good advice:

> When you go to the field to work, don't think of women; only think of the work and watch out for snakes. The same when you go hunting — only think of the deer, if you want to live to a ripe old age. The hour of death can come in many ways.

Four women *Chii* might take a man into their cave. There, they offer him a fine meal: a leg of a peccary, *iscamote* [an edible root], all sorts of bananas, *patastilla* [the *chayote*, a vine fruit]. But this would only be to deceive him. When he gets home, he won't like the tortillas or pozol. Then the pains start: his guts swell, his stomach bloats, he vomits blood, he gets worms, measles, flu, fevers — all kinds of ailments. Then there's no more life, all because he ate that food in the caves. He's a goner. He'll never recover. I'd rather live, be poor, eat empty tortillas. Besides, if a man makes love to one of these women, all his children might die. The same holds true for women. If a Devil seduces a woman, he'll try to suck blood from her vagina and finally suck out all of her intestines and make sausages of them. Then she'll die soon, very soon.

During the time of the First Nation, there were no Devils here on Earth. Tomam the Elder sent them here to mix with us Mortals. They were bothering him a lot in his place, seducing the women up there. This is why he threw them down here.

They only die by the order of Tomam the Elder. Only the *punakpanes* can denounce them with the Jívaros. They alert Tomam who sends his son to Earth to kill them. But, now, no one accuses the Devils, as there are no more *punakpanes* and, besides, the old people are even afraid of the Jívaros. No more *punakpanes* — this means we all die a lot sooner.

*   *   *

MYTH 58
THE DEVIL GROUND-UP A DEAD MORTAL

When someone dies, you must close the door good and tight so that the Devil doesn't enter; he is betting with God [Tomam] to win souls. If the Devil does enter, the soul of the defunct might escape by climbing through the roof [made of straw]. But if the Devil captures his soul, he'll take it to his cave and grind it up in his sugarcane press.

When a dead Mortal doesn't arrive at the other world, the Sun notifies Tomam the Younger.

Tomam the
Younger: Where is that dead Mortal?

Then the word goes out that he's lost and to search for him in the caves. Guatecast [Tomam's assistant] is ordered to set fire to the Devils' caves so that they don't abuse the Indians. Tomam doesn't approve of Devils grinding up dead Mortals. They grind them like sugarcane, seven times ground up, so that they become one of their gang. When the Devil finishes grinding, he asks the dead Mortal:

Devil: Now, what party do you belong to?

Dead Mortal: I belong to God's party. You've ground me up seven times for nothing. I won't join your party. I belong to God's party. I'm going to notify Tomam the Younger. I'm going to present myself as I should. I won't compromise my soul with you.

Devil: Then go chase your tail. I ground you up seven times and still you won't join my party!

He chases him out. The dead Mortal goes to the world below, to the west. Guatecast greets him.

Guatecast: Why did you let yourself be chewed up by the Devil's sugar press? Now you'll have to present yourself to Tomam all ground up!

Nompwinapu'u: What happened to you, old ground up Indian?

Dead Ground
Up Mortal: I was captured by the Devils. I didn't grind myself up! But now, how will I have the strength to present myself to the Party of God [Tomam]? I'm at the mercy of the Devils, compromised by them.

Nompwinapu'u: But why did you compromise yourself with the rich, with the Devils?

Dead Indian: I didn't do it because I wanted to.

Nompwinapu'u: Alright. If that's the case, I'll take you to Tomam.

And he did.

*   *   *

NARRATION 36
THE ERROR OF TERRENCIO

My old uncle, Terrencio, died because he thought that a Temptation was his wife because both were deaf-mutes. He went out to get some firewood and a woman appeared. She embraced him and they made love, then she said to him with signs:

> You are my husband.

But when he came back home, he found his wife there. Then he knew that the one who appeared in the forest meant death for him. Soon after, I happened to stop by his hut. He already felt a little better.

He said:	Well, nephew! Let's go hunting monkeys.
I said:	You are really sick. I can tell from your eyes. Your hour of death is close by. I won't go with you without permission from our chief. If I do, I might get into trouble.

Awhile later, I asked to stay overnight.

Terrencio: You're welcome to stay here with your uncle.

During the night, the dog scented the odor of a person and ran out of the hut after him. A dog that flees in the night is a bad sign. His dog had a lot of fetid vapor. Then I told my uncle:

> Uncle, believe me, now we're in trouble. I can tell from your dog.

If Terrencio were to die, the dog would not. If the dog died, the man would not.

   The dog didn't die.

*   *   *

NARRATION 37
THE DEATH OF FELIPE

Felipe always kidded with me. One of the last times I visited him

He said:	Who's asking for me now? What's your errand?
I said:	My errand is to smoke.

Then we went into his hut and smoked his tobacco leaves. Then we ate some bananas. After awhile when we were quiet.

I said: It's not wrong to ask for a smoke. God gave us a mouth to ask for things.

Felipe: It's all yours for the asking.

Later, we worked cutting down tobacco in his field. That same day, Felipe gave me five leaves of tobacco. I took them home to smoke.

He said: I don't have much longer to live. I have a chill in my ribs.

Sometime later, he went searching for deer and he cut himself a little with his machete. Then he got a tumor. When he was laid up with the tumor, he said to me:

> I'm going to tell you something. Felipe is not well. All my joints are wobbly.

He got so swollen, he looked like a fat pig. He died fifteen days later. After he died, I was left thinking:

> Felipe was a good worker. He had everything: bananas, tobacco, maize, everything. Where could you find another like Felipe?

The last time I saw him.

He said: Send for my sons to come for the last service.

Three days later, his sons, Reyes, Paulino and Celestino, came.

I said: Your papi is dying. He wants all of you here for the last service. Now is the time for the last look.

His sons were very sad. Many of us went to bury him

* * *

NARRATION 38
MATIAS IS SEDUCED BY A FEMALE DEVIL

Once, when I was out hunting, I ran into my uncle, Matías.

Matías: Well nephew, did you find any deer? I shot one but didn't kill it.

I said: I killed some baby armadillos.

Matías: That's good. You'll share them with me, even if only a little. I didn't kill a thing. When God isn't willing, the shots miss.

I said:	That's the way it is. We have to kill in order to live a few more days. But if we don't behave ourselves, we die young.
Matías:	Without God's permission, you can't kill a thing.
I said:	I'm a good shot but I don't go against God. When I don't make a hit, too bad for me. The deer, too, have the right not to be shot all the time. I don't overdo this killing. Uncle, if you don't understand, too bad for you.

Matías stood staring at me; he got angry.

Matías:	Why do you speak badly to your elder?
I said:	You don't act right with me, uncle. Just because I'm young, doesn't mean you can ride all over me. You're going to die soon. A woman will appear in the hills and this will mean your death.

Matías got angrier:

Matías:	I'm going to report you to the eldest brother, to Mateo, so that he punish you. You should never quarrel with your elders.
I said:	We'll see. If my papi beats me, we'll be worse enemies. I'll report you to the chief and he'll fine you.
Matías:	Don't be angry, nephew. We'll just quarrel here in the woods. You're my nephew and you shouldn't accuse your elders, nor should I accuse the minors.
I said:	If you complain to your elder brother, I'll complain to the chief.
Matías:	Mind you, when a youth speaks badly, this means he will make a widow of his wife.

Matías was sick, when I next saw him.

Matías:	You were right. I'm sick now and have no friends. I have money to buy maize but no friends. I'm sure to die alone, with only my wife.
I said:	I'll inform the chief so that he notify your brothers to come and accompany you, now that you're committed to die. It seems that your nephew looks after you more than your brothers.
Matías:	So it seems.

All his brothers came to see him, as I pushed them. Matías died because he saw an apparition of his wife's sister, his sister-in-law. Some sister-in-law! A sister-in-law-take-your- life-away. She asked him for some tobacco to smoke. He fell in love with her and right away she said yes. After he made love to her.

He said: My lovely sister-in-law, let's go for a nice visit.

He wanted to take her to his house but she wouldn't go.

She said: How can I go visit my sister? I can't. I'm the elder and she owes me respect. Now that you were a man to me, I can't show myself with you. Now you go, go home and lie down to die. Go quickly so that you don't die before you arrive.

Matías: It turned out badly, sister-in-law. So you came to take my life, to win my soul. I made love to you with trust but I found death.

Temptation: Now that we have spoken, you must die. You got into this of your own doing. Now there is no escape. You'll not recover until you are buried.

He died five days later. He got swollen all over; it was *propicia* [sickness] of the Devil that killed him.

*   *   *

NARRATION 39
THE LAST DAYS OF JOSÉ

Cleto Martínez told me this. He was out hunting with his son, young José, when José saw a woman. He joined her and they made love. But when he got up and looked, he saw that she had become an animal without a tail. When José went into the woods to make love to the Temptation, his father thought that he had gone to defecate. But when he returned, his father saw the look of death in his eyes.

José said: Come, look papa, there goes an animal that I have never seen.

Cleto went to look but didn't see a thing.

José: Come, look papa, there goes an animal without a tail, the color of a tiger.

Cleto: You're seeing things. I don't like what you are saying. It seems that you want to die young.

José: Have it your way; I won't say more.

Cleto: What do you mean an animal! That's your death that's appearing.

José got angry.

José:	You're scolding me; I won't tell you anything more.
Cleto:	You're telling me a bad thing and I'm going to hit you with a stick. An old man can see bad things but not a young one. You don't want to die, do you? Abandon your wife?
José:	So what? You take care of her. I don't want to live any longer in this world.

Cleto told me:

> All animals have tails; and it wasn't a tiger so it must have been a Temptation. José wants to die young, so he let himself be tempted. Now he is doomed. He doesn't eat; he's going to die.

Only fifteen days later he died, as we are all children of death. He died of an infection from a cold.

*   *   *

NARRATION 40
LEONITA LIKED <u>LADINO</u> MEN

Leonita liked *ladino* men: first Pedrito. He was Indian but he wore *ladino* clothes. He lived with her for two years; then, I hear, he left her. Then she went to live with Silvestre, a *ladino*. Then she lived back in the mountains and used to pass by my house at times. Once, I ran into her on the trail and joked with her.

She said:	My man has a shirt that really looks like something.

She said a lot of other things, all meant that she didn't like Indian men.

I said:	You won't last long. You weren't born for *ladino* men. You're offending God; you'll die young. God has heard your words. You'll be buried a sick corpse. This is all I'll say to you, nothing more.
Leonita:	You can say what you please. I like *ladino* kitchens.[1]
I said:	You won't live long; you can bet on that. You're offending a lot of people. That house where you are is the last one you'll be taking care of. After that, you'll only find death. Neither man nor woman can live for long disobeying God. You cannot compromise with Him. You shouldn't mix with the *ladinos*.

| **Leonita:** | I like the kitchens of the *ladinos*. I don't like Indian men. |
| **I said:** | You won't be liking even *ladinos* for long. Only God knows what your death will be. |

Later, she got offended with Silvestre. Then she came to my house.

| **Leonita:** | Now, let's see if you will give me something to eat. |

I told her to come in and asked my wife to let her help make the tortillas. Awhile later, she said to us:

> Now you will never be rid of me. Now that you gave me permission I will stay here the rest of my life.

She left that very day. She was certainly a liar. I told her to stay at least two or three days.

| **She said:** | I'm going to uncle's, to Lucio's, to my cousins to live. It's my right. |
| **I said:** | The *prueba* [chapter VII] says you don't have any rights, that you won't last long. You'll be dead by the fifth of May. (I had done a *prueba* on her.) The fifth of May, the fevers will start. This is what the *prueba* said. |

Leonita didn't have any friends. She didn't have any rights [because she rejected the Indians and the *ladinos* treated her badly]. She could find friends but they were passersby. A few months later, Gerónimo González, Silvestre's brother, told me that Leonita was very sick. She was in Lucio's house. I ran into him near Lucio's house, in the mountains.

| **He said:** | Leonita is in agony. She is really bad, bad. We should begin the wake, to light the candles for her. |

The candles are of bees' wax and only last three or four hours. When they are lit, it means that death will follow soon. Little by little, slowly, it is sure to come. Four candles were lit for her. As soon as they were lit, she felt the light and

She said:	Why did you light the candles?
Someone:	In order to brighten the darkness.
Leonita:	My days are numbered. I don't want to live anymore — this sickness, the kidneys, the lungs. Go fetch Fermán.[2]
Someone:	He will never have time to get here. He just won't. Time is too short to bring Fermán.

Soon after that she died. Right away, Lucio left his house taking all his animals with him.[3] He was afraid of the fetid vapor. He won't go back there until February or March, after he has harvested his coffee. Lucio didn't want to bury her but she was rotting. Leonor [then chief of the west moiety] notified but only a few were going so I was asked.[4] She was laid on a stretcher and carried to the cemetery by four men. Vicente [Lucio's brother] and I carried her for awhile, then Lucio and Emilio [Lucio's cousin]. Four others went ahead to open the pit. They finished digging when we arrived. Afterwards, we all took a bath in the river so as not to pass the *vaho* on to the children. Leonor put a wooden cross over her grave and some jars on top, too.

*   *   *

NARRATION 41
FABÍAN TRIES TO TAKE HIS WIFE
TO THE OTHER WORLD

Fabían died vomiting blood. When I saw him the Monday before, he had death in his eyes. I knew he was going to die but he didn't say anything about being sick. He may have died because he made love to a woman Devil, when he was working in the milpa. The last day I saw him.

He said: Today, Alfonso, I send greetings to my sister [Alfonso's wife] — to all my brothers and sisters.

He was suffering all the time. He said to his wife:

Juanita, I leave you two or three little cows and a milpa so you can go on eating. I don't want to work anymore in this world. I can't keep anything down, vomiting all the time.

He wanted his wife to die with him, to accompany him to the other world, but she didn't want to go so he left her be and said:

Let her die as she pleases. Maybe she'll find another man. If she doesn't, she'll die alone.

Fabían wanted her to die so that she not be left to suffer alone. He wanted to take his kid, too. He wanted to make love to her, pass his sickness on to her, so that they die together but she didn't want to.

*   *   *

NARRATION 42
THE DEATH OF ALFONSO'S FATHER

I grieved a lot for my father — I cried. Just before he died,

He said:	My son, Alfonso, you are taking care of me. You give me food. Now I want to eat beef, snails, squirrels, deer, turkey-hens.
I said:	You must not eat those things. They have lots of *vaho*. That deer meat is very "hot."[5]
Mateo:	Nonsense. Bring me some; I can't eat an empty tortilla.

I brought him some squirrel meat.

| **Mateo:** | So you brought me *bukutnat*! |

I bought him good meat but even so

He said:	I won't eat it. I'm tired of living in this world. I don't want to accompany my wife and children anymore. I can't swallow. Nothing passes into my stomach.
I said:	Why did you fool me then? Here I've been out in the forest, trying to get food for you!
Mateo:	It's better this way. I'm an old man. My children are grown; they work on their own. Their mother will stay on with them. If they behave badly, God will know. If they take good care of her, God will send word to the east, to Tomam Mayor. If I don't want to eat, God will know that I died because I wanted to.
I said:	That's alright, papi. You don't want to accompany me anymore.
Mateo:	You didn't bring the sickness that is killing me. Why do you grieve then? There will always be sickness, but the natural sickness from here doesn't cause death. God didn't want people to live forever so he brought other sickness to Earth.

His sickness spread from his lungs. While he was dying, some *ladinos* came by.

| **They said:** | Alfonso, why don't you take your mother to your house? She's grieving too much for Mateo. |

When I came back,

| **Mateo said:** | What is that commission doing here? Or is it a military escort? |

He was talking crazy because his hour of death had come. The commission, the military escort, was not of this world.

| **I said:** | Tomorrow, you will wake up stiff. Tomorrow, you will say goodbye to your wife and family. Guatecast will come to |

	get you, by order of Tomam the Elder. The escort was not from here; it was from the other world.
Mateo:	Why are you talking so badly to me? If I had known, I wouldn't have told you. You are going too far.
I said:	I am the eldest son; I have the right to speak. I am speaking the truth. That commission was for the dead Mortals, from Guatecast, sent by Tomam the Elder.
Mateo:	Alright, Señor Alfonso, it's true what you say. Tomorrow, when the sun rises come to say goodbye with all my children so that they greet me for the last, final time. You will pardon me; I said bad things to you, to my children. The sickness has made me crazy.
I said:	Papi, you are forgiven. We all will speak badly at the hour of death.
Mateo:	My family is not here. It is in the other world.
I said:	That's alright, papi, so you have no family here. I won't be mad. I respect old people. It seems to me that Mateo is my father. You taught me to work; you raised us all. How can you say that you have no family? We were all brought up by you. Only Mateo raised me and my brothers and sisters.
Mateo:	You have spoken enough; I am tired now. Just leave me in the cemetery for the last service. I have lived enough in this world; God is calling me. You must grieve a little. For ten days, you shouldn't go around happy. Put on new clothes right after you bury me. Go on a diet for five days. And after seven days, it's alright to grind maize again. Don't try to diet any longer; the children might get sick.

At the hour of death

He said:	Why should I show you my death? We are fine Alfonso. But at the hour of death, a lot of little animals appear.
I said:	Let them appear. I'll do as you say and I might live a little longer; if not, I'll die whether I want to or not. I'll die anyway, now or later, as I am not God and we all belong to the Nation of the Mortals.
Mateo:	My death is not for you. My children will each have an hour of death, each in his or her own way. My death is for me; yours, Alfonso, will be for you.

As Mateo was old, he went to the other world as a baby. He's in a hammock now, still nursing. When someone dies already grown-up, he [or she] goes to the other world like Mateo, as a baby. When someone dies a baby, he goes grown-up. But whatever way you go, you always stay young in the world of Tomam the Younger.

* * *

NARRATION 43
THE DEATH OF HIS GRANDFATHER

I don't remember my grandparents, either Victoriano or Juan or Polonia or Mercedes. I was told it was bad, when Juan Martínez died. He told his daughters-in-law:

> My sons have offended me. They went hunting without my permission.

He got crazy from the sickness.

> They're acting mean with their father. My only family is in the other world.

He knew he was going to die. He threw everything out of the house, got mad at his daughters-in-law. Then he went to sleep. Later, when his sons Matías, Feli, Domingo and Mateo arrived, he quarreled with them.

He said:	I don't have any family.
They said:	You're the chief here and all your sons, all of us, are here.
He said:	I'm not going to bother you anymore. I'm leaving so now you can throw everything away.

He, himself, had thrown everything out of the house. Then he tried to go into the woods to die but his sons came in time and put him and everything — machetes, deer skins, baskets — back in the house. Then he made Domingo the chief so it was Domingo who ordered everything back in the house. When he was about to die, someone, like a woman, appeared; but it wasn't a woman, it was death.

Everyone said:	He's going to die now. Death has appeared.

* * *

THE GUATECASTS
(Author)

There are two brothers: Tsik'in Guatecast, the Elder, of the East Heaven, and Tyaj Guatecast, the Younger, of the Western World of the Dead. The latter is the chief of the dead Indians and it is his duty to guide their souls to the worlds beyond. After greeting Tomam the Elder, in the east, he accompanies them back to the cemetery to inspect their mortal remains. Finally, he escorts them to greet Tomam the Younger, in the West Heaven, where they remain forever. Unlike his brother, who has nothing but contempt for humans, Guatecast of the west gave the "first little man" his reproductive organs (myth 1) and cares for the dead mortals.

*   *   *

QUESTIONS AND ANSWERS
(Author and Alfonso)

1. What is the World of the Dead Like?

It's like a city but much larger than this world. There, everyone lives in harmony; each nation respects the other. The domicile of Tomam Wowai lies beyond. The Jívaros live near-by but only Tyaj Guatecast lives with the dead, as he is their chief.

When an old person, like Mateo, dies, he goes to the other world as a baby, but with no bones. There he grows up, nursed by his mother; his bones and teeth grow but not his hair. He has to return to the cemetery to get at least one strand of hair, then he goes back to the other world. He grows very slowly; there, 100 years is just one day. Once he is grown-up, he stays that way forever and never gets old. But when a baby dies, he [or she] goes to the other world already grown-up. There is no sickness there. Only here on Earth we are punished by sickness and death.

Everyone lives in a house and wears new clothes — they never wear out. Anything grows there. I don't know if they plant every year but there is always new [young] maize. Everything stays young. Besides, the plants talk. You can say to an avocado:

> Come down off that tree, Señor Avocado; I want to eat you.

He'll obey and let himself be eaten. The same with maize and beans. But it's prohibited to eat too much. The animals and fish converse and obey, too, just like the plants, though everyone is careful not to abuse any animal. It's prohibited to kill spiders or buzzards, as they are there to eat *caca* (excrement) of humans and animals. Anyway, they belong to Tata Dios. There, all the nations treat one another like brothers.

*   *   *

2. Up There, How Do They Know When Someone is About to Die?

The *caracacao* [a white-breasted eagle] cries out whenever someone dies. He is sent by Tomam the Younger just for this. The *guaca* eagle screeches when someone dies because of the Devil.

* * *

3. Why are the Dead Buried?

So that the Earth can eat them.

* * *

4. Why Do You Put a Jar on Top of the Grave?

For water. The dead one has to drink before he goes to the other world, to make his body clean.

* * *

5. Why Does the Jar Have a Hole in It?

Because the jar is dead, too. It can no longer be used in this world. A piece of jar can serve, the same.[6]

* * *

6. Does the Spirit Go Directly to the Other World?

No. The dead one stays in the cemetery for five days, to rid his body of all the ailments and filth. He makes a fire and heats the water in the jar, lets it cool off, then drinks it. This is what the old people said but it may be a lie, as I've never seen any signs [of fire on top of the burials].

After five days, the dead one is clean; he has thrown away his bones, too, and is ready to leave for the other world. But there are some who hide from Guatecast, who don't want to go to the other world, who want to stay here. Guatecast always ends up by finding them and sometimes he punishes them — throws them in jail when they arrive at the other world, as every place has its jail. But if the dead one doesn't hide, he [or she] goes off happily with Guatecast to greet Tomam the Younger.

* * *

7. How Does One Get to the Other World?

There are two ways: by the royal road or by the long road full of briars. If you go by the royal road, you have to pass the *hop* [the crab]. If the crabs grab you, this means that you are a rascal. Better go the long way, through the briars.

On the royal road, you might slip and fall in the well, where the crab is waiting with his jaws open. As you have to pass over the well holding onto a rope, you might lose your grip or the rope might snap. And BAMB you fall in the well! A recently dead person is very weak and can easily fall. There is not just one crab in the well; there are several: two males and two females and their families. When a dead person falls in the well, Tomam the Younger asks:

> Why hasn't that dead one arrived yet? I'm going to send Guatecast to look for him and bring him along.

Then Guatecast goes to spy on him and when he sees him in the well, he returns to inform Tomam:

| | *Hop* is eating him! |
| **Crab:** | He fell off that precipice. Now he's my meal. |

First he eats the knees; he breaks them at the joints. He puts away the rest for later. They are all gluttons and as big as a guitar or bigger. They only eat the gossipers and rascals who always want to fight. The Law of God put the crabs there so that we don't misbehave. But the truth of the matter, I don't really know but this is what the old people told us. The crabs punish two, three even six days but, then again, only for half an hour. When a dead one finally gets to the other world, Tomam asks him:

	What happened to you?
The dead one:	The crab caught me!
Tomam:	So, you're one of those gossipers!

The crabs don't kill; they just punish a little or a little more. Tomam might ask upon the arrival:

	Which road did you take? The royal road?
The dead one:	No, Señor, I came by way of the briars, through the thorns.
Tomam:	Are you telling the truth? You're not lying?

The dead one swears he's not lying.

| **Tomam:** | Then you're welcome here. You're not compromised by the crabs. You're an honest man. |

*   *   *

8. And the River that One has to Pass?

The river is called *hol ma sas' mo'o*, "the place where no one can pass." It's very deep and full of rocks, like the one here near-by during the rainy season. When you arrive at the edge and see that you can't pass, you begin to cry. Tata Dios hears you and sends one of his dogs to help you, as he is their Master. When the dog sees you, he says:

> Eh! You threw me bits of food. I'm your friend. Grab my tail. Grab it tight and I'll pass you. Don't let loose.

This is why you should always give the dogs bits of food so they remember you when you have to pass that river, to get to the other world. You can't pass without the help of a dog. And a good hunting dog should be buried when he dies so that the Earth, not the buzzards, eats him.

* * *

9. What Happens when Someone Arrives There?

The little angels go right away to greet Tomam the Elder and only later go to Tomam the Younger. This is why they must be buried with their heads toward the east, so they don't lose their way. The older dead should be buried with their heads toward the west because they go first to greet Tomam the Younger and afterwards go to greet the Principal Chief. Then they return to Tomam Wowai, the Younger.

When you arrive at the domicile of the Principal Chief, you have to bite a heated stone. You should open your mouth very wide so that the stone not touch your lips. You can only eat the food in the other world after your teeth have been heated by the stone. Before you bite the stone, you can't eat anything. Tomam the Elder hands you the stone, you bite it and then

He says: That's fine. Now go quickly. You smell very bad! You did right to come to greet me but you shouldn't have come when the wind blows this way.

Then the dead one returns to Tomam the Second, the Younger.

* * *

10. Why Does One Have to Return to get a Strand of Hair?[7]

The dead leave their hair, bones and teeth in the cemetery. When they arrive at the other world, the bones and teeth grow again but not the hair. Tomam the Younger says [to the new arrival]:

> Why do you come all bald like this? What did you do with the hair I gave you? You're really ugly.

The dead one:	I left my hair in the hole in the cemetery. That's why I didn't bring any.
Tomam:	Do you still remember where you went walking through the forests looking for firewood or snails or hunting deer? If you go there, surely you'll find a strand of hair that got caught on some branches. If you don't find any, don't bother to come back here. I don't want any bald, hairless dead here. If you just find one strand, one little hair, that will do; then you can come back.

The dead one returns and searches until he finds at least one little hair. He puts it on his head and right away all his hair grows back — on his head and other parts of his body.

Guatecast leads him back to this world, by the royal road. First, they go to the cemetery because the dead one wants to see his bones and the stretcher used to carry him there. But Guatecast doesn't enter the cemetery. He waits outside.

Dead one:	So, this must be where they buried me, as the stretcher is close-by. They tried to hide it from me but I found it. You can't deceive a dead one.
Guatecast:	Where's your stretcher? Are you sure you are dead?
Dead one:	I found it already. Now I'm looking at my bones.

Then the dead one takes Guatecast to show him his house. They aren't allowed to enter; they can only look at it from a distance.

Guatecast:	Eh! But why did you die? Maybe your family killed you.
Dead one:	No. It was God's wish. I died because we are children of death.
Guatecast:	Where is your family now?

He wants to know everything. He goes on talking:

	Now I see why you died. You lived in a ruin of a house. Sickness, frosts, wind entered it, no protection. No wonder you died. Besides, you went out working when you were sick. This is why you died. You may even have had to do with a woman from another nation. All the more reason for dying.
Dead one:	You're right. You can scold me if you want.
Guatecast:	I haven't finished. Everyone dies because they choose to die; that's the real reason. Now, you see your wife crying, all the family grieving. Aren't you ashamed?

But some of the dead don't like all Guatecast's scoldings.

Another
dead one: I planted maize, yucca, camotes. They died of frost; the wind blew them down; the peccaries ate them; the coatis ate them. How dare you ask me why I died! Aren't you ashamed?

Then Guatecast is humbled and doesn't scold anymore. Other dead are even worse. One might say:

You're the one who killed me! The camotes got frostbitten. All my crops were ruined. What could I do? I only lasted three or four days without eating. This is why I died.

With this, Guatecast is silenced. He doesn't scold anymore.

Yet another
dead one: I didn't die because I wanted to. My wife killed me.
Guatecast: Rise and follow me. We're going to Glory so that they send some wasps, *blanca petels.*

The wasps are sent and they bite this gossiper all over, for being such a liar, for accusing his wife.

Guatecast: Now you are compromised. From now on, you'll have to live with your wife, forever, or else go to jail.

Guatecast doesn't like to be made a fool of.

*   *   *

11. What Else Occurs When a Dead Mortal Lies?

When this happens, the Earthquake may shake the world. But at times, Guatecast asks:

A dead gossiper stopped in here. Did he come with your permission?

Tomam the
Younger: No. He's gossiping on his own.

Then Tomam orders Guatecast to shut the mouth of the gossiper. Guatecast whips him for good and even throws him in jail for awhile, half an hour. This teaches him and the Earthquake doesn't bother us Mortals.

At times, a little angel comes by and says to him, "My mama killed me. My papa killed me." This is a lie. How can anyone kill his own child? The little angel should not speak against his parents. Kids may die of sickness. They die, too, because we Mortals are always being punished. God Tomam ordered that we all live in peace, like brothers and sisters, but, no, some people don't agree. This is why we have to die. We should mourn when someone dies because even the older ones spread lies in the other world.

*   *   *

12. Why Do Children Die?

Children are innocent but they die for God. But some do die because their parents didn't take care of them. When they arrive in the other world and tell Tomam the Younger their story, he sends the Earthquake to punish the Mortals. (myth 21)

A little angel arrives in the other world.

Guatecast: Let's go [back to the child's home] so you can show me why your father killed you. He didn't have a child to kill but to raise, to help him, to do errands. When someone kills a little angel, they are neither man nor woman [not human] and will die soon.

Little Angel: My father lived badly; frost and cold and sickness entered our house.

Then Second Chief sends the Earthquake to stir up all the streams. I'd rather die before my little angels. I treat my stepchildren just like my own. I raised someone else's son as if he were mine. So God protects me. My crops produce a lot; I get good harvests. If you have children, your own or someone else's, you have the right to produce maize. Men are born to work, to support their children, women to protect them so that they live longer. I don't throw out the advice of the old people.

*   *   *

13. And Women Giving Birth?

They, too, are innocent. Guatecast comes to accompany them to the other world and there they give birth. Here, there are a lot of women, so God sends some to the other world to raise their children there.

*   *   *

14. And the Youth?

Sometimes they die to take care of their parents and grandparents, in the other world: to bring them water, firewood, to plant beans for them. A brother who had died might feel lonely in the other world, homesick for his family, and call for someone in his family to keep him company. When one brother or sister dies, another or two will certainly follow. But four would be too much of a punishment. They leave happily, singing. Why not? There they never age. There 100 years is a day. No one suffers. They have everything.

* * *

15. Why Do Some Hide in Caves?

Those who die belonging to the Party of God [Tomam] don't hide. But those of the Party of the Devils get themselves compromised and the Devils throw them in the caves.

* * *

16. How Do You Feel About Death?

I think that from under the rocks, in the caves, another nation is killing off the Indians. I don't have permission to die yet. My children are still young. I still want to live awhile longer.

Life is to be lived. To die is to die. When I am called to the other world, at the hour of death, I will go to the west when the Second Chief calls me. If I have misbehaved, God, the Sun, will give an account. If I have been harmful, he will report me. God gives an account of everybody.

* * *

17. Those Who Kill Themselves, Do They, too, Go to the Other World?

If you kill yourself, you don't have the right to go with Guatecast. If you cut yourself with a machete and die or fall off a cliff and kill yourself, you can't go to the city beyond. You have to go to a place called Oropang, the other side of the city. If you kill yourself with your own hands or hang yourself from a tree, this means that you are an assassin, a fighter and should go to Oropang. You won't be punished. There are houses there and all you'll need.

As God [the Sun] is forever watching us here on Earth, he knows when someone kills himself and says:

	Eh! Why did this mortal die?
Someone:	He died by his own hands.
God:	But why?
Someone:	Because he wanted to. Don't blame anyone else. He should be sent to Oropang.

* * *

18. Are the Dead Ever Born Again?

We Mortals are liars, busybodies and gossipers so the crabs punish us.
They eat us so that we die twice. Some are born and die three or four
times. They are reborn here on Earth as an *ururu* [or *ulula*, raccoon], to
tear up the crops of us Mortals, dig up our maize, pick our beans. Then we
Indians shoot them and they die and are born again, maybe three times.
They might also be born here as snakes, dogs or tigers; as *apep* [a little
bird with a red breast], *trul* [an eagle], or *ts'ts'al* [a tiny mosquito] — a
really disgusting animal. He spends his life urinating and defecating in our
pozol.

These are all punishments — making us be born and die so many times.
We have to be punished here on Earth; in the other world there is hardly
any punishment.

Sometimes a dead gossiper arrives in the other world and walks around
and around Tomam's house, without talking, and refuses to enter the
house. He walks like a crazy man, around and around. Tomam and his wife
look out at him. Tomam says to his wife:

> Look, that fellow is a real nuisance. I invited him to come
> in; the door is open, but he doesn't come in. He's really
> acting strange. This means that he misbehaved on Earth.
> I'm going to send him back there so that he be born again
> as a raccoon. Then the dogs will get after him; the Mortals
> will attack him; and the buzzards will finish him off. If the
> Mortals don't get him, a snake will certainly.

*   *   *

19. Can a Live Mortal Visit the Other World?

Yes, but you'll have to come back here to die.

*   *   *

NARRATION 44
CLETO RETURNED TWICE FROM THE OTHER WORLD

My cousin, Cleto Martínez, went to the other world two times and came
back two times. He's still alive. He'll be really old when he goes there for
good. The first time, he died near his house from a rattlesnake bite. He fell
down and an hour later he was dead.

**Tomam the
Younger:** I don't want you here now. When you're old is time
enough. I'll send you back now so that you kill that rattlesnake. He has no right to bite Indians.

If a snake flees after biting, that's his right but if not, he pays with his life.
God [the Sun] was watching: the snake got tired, went into a hole and
waited there until Cleto came and killed him. He buried him and then the
snake went to present himself to his Master, Lo Chim Jamayón.

Lo Chim: Why did you bite that Mortal? You don't have the right.

The other time, Cleto died of the flu. He wasn't buried right away because
his hands were still trembling and his stomach jumping. They mourned for
him four or five days. The family was nervous. The chief [then Domingo
Martínez] said:

> We won't bury him yet. His stomach is still jumping; he
> may come back. Watch over him; don't leave him alone. A
> Temptation might come near him. Bring in more
> pinewood to keep the fire burning.

Cleto arrived with Tomam the Younger.

Tomam: Why did you die? Don't you have a family?
Cleto: Yes, wives and kids.
Tomam: Then get out of here, go home. I don't want you here yet.
When you get home don't overeat, just a tortilla.

The *caracacao* announces there in the other world that a dead one just
arrives. The old people there come to see who it is. They saw Cleto.

Old People: What happened? How did you die? Did you hang your-
self?
Cleto: I came down with the flu, vomited blood. How could I
live?
Old People: We don't want you here yet. When you get home, ask for
some medicine and you'll get well right away.
Cleto: Give me something to eat.
Old People: No. We won't. If you eat this food, you'll never recover.
It's bad food for those who live on Earth, for the Mortals.
Go home and take care of your wives. How could you
abandon your little babies? You're really shameless.
You're behaving very badly by dying so young. Go fast
before they bury you. They're already making the
stretcher!

Cleto:	If you don't want to give me a tortilla or a tamale, let me suckle some milk.
Old People:	No. When you get home, ask for warm water to get well. Your stomach is sour; you have to urinate and defecate and your fever will pass through you with the warm water. You can't stay here now; you're too young. Your wives need you. You'll come back when you're old.
Cleto:	But I'll bury all my wives; they'll die young. I'll be left alone — a widower, suffering.
Old People:	What are you saying! You have sons. You'll have daughters-in-law. Maybe they'll take care of you.
Guatecast:	I'll show you the way back and steer you clear [of *hop*, the crabs].

They looked down at the crabs, their tremendous legs and jaws. Cleto was a bit nervous. When they got, back Guatecast said:

> No wonder you died with such a house, full of awful fetid vapor. Now you have to stay and put up with it because you misbehaved and wanted to abandon your wives. When they die, maybe you can live with your daughters-in-law.

And so he returned. When he entered his body again, he sighed and trembled.

One of his wives:	What do you want?
Cleto:	I want you to raise me up so that we can talk a little.

*   *   *

MYTH 59
THE MAN WHO FOLLOWED HIS WIFE TO THE OTHER WORLD

Sun:	A woman is killing herself! A cut-up woman will arrive soon [to the other world].
Husband:	What a lazy wife you are! Go get me some snails to eat.
Woman:	[to herself] I'm going to cut a slice off my leg and give it to him to eat.

She didn't want to work to feed her husband. This is why she sliced a piece off her leg. She wanted to die and [thereby] punish her husband.

Woman: Your mama came awhile ago and brought you this piece of paca meat.

He ate it without distrust. He didn't see that his wife was bleeding, as she was covered by her long skirt. She gave him some tamales, too. After he finished eating, she handed him a gourd full of water to wash his hands so that the fetid vapor from the paca not spread to the milpa where he was going to work. When he had washed his hands, she fell down; she fainted.

Husband: I see now. You're going to die! Why did you cook your own flesh and give it to me to eat? Why didn't you talk to me? Now I'll be punished in the other world for eating your flesh.

The next day she died. She bled to death, while she was digging up roots in the field. It wasn't his fault.

When Guatecast came to take her to the other world, the husband spoke to him:

Take me, too, alive as I am now. I don't want to die yet.

Guatecast: You loved your wife a lot? That's good. I'll take you alive. But as you ate a piece of your wife's flesh, I'll take you to her sister's place [in the other world].

The husband went with Guatecast and his wife, hidden under her skirts. When he got to his sister-in-law's place, she said to him:

I'm going to get water in the stream. You stay here in the house but don't dare touch my kitchenware, bedding, baskets or clothes. I don't like having a live Mortal here.

When she returned from the stream, her things were scattered all about — some thrown outside her house, broken or torn. The man had left. As he was still alive, he behaved like a rascal, just like he had in this world. He tried to kill all the little animals in the other world: the lizards, the frogs, the buzzards. It's prohibited to kill any animal there, except for food. All the animals can speak so they complained and got him in trouble.

When he felt the need to defecate, he asked permission to do so. After he defecated, a buzzard came to eat his *caca*. The man got angry and tried to hit him but missed.

Buzzard: What's the idea! All the *caca* around here is for us buzzards.

The buzzards scolded him, as should be. Then he met up with the Sun.

| Sun: | What are you doing here? This is no place for the living. But forget it; let's go along the stream, see if we can find any little crabs to eat. But first, come with me to light up the world. |

The Indian accompanied him for a couple of days, until he got tired. He wasn't given anything to eat at all. Then one night the Sun said to him:

Now we can go looking for those crabs.

The Sun gave him a pinewood torch already lit up [on fire]. But it went out right away. The pinewood was punishing him, too. As the Sun knew where to find the crabs, he took him where there weren't any. This was another punishment. He sent him to the big stream, the *jivaron pones*, saying that he, himself, would go looking along the small stream, the *jivaron chikwai*. Instead, he came to this world to light it up. The Indian wandered around lost. His torch blew out. Then he heard the "monkeys of the night" [night monkeys — *kinkajous*] hollering:

Night Monkeys:	Kulu, kulu.
Indian:	What's your name, Señores Monkeys of the Night?
Night Monkeys:	*Pistesi hus* but the Indians call us *kulu*. What are you doing here?
Indian:	I'm lost. Take me home. I want to see my family.
Night Monkeys:	You have your mama, brothers and sisters on the Earth. We'll get you out of here.

They did, they brought him home. But he was afraid to see his family, as he had eaten his wife's flesh. When he arrived, he was famished and cold from having tramped along the streams. He couldn't talk either. He couldn't greet his family; he could only make signs.

| His mother: | Climb up in that papaya tree and get a fruit for me. |

The man climbed the tree; then his mama cut down the tree with an axe and the tree fell — he in it. From the blow, he could talk again. He shouted:

| | My mama made me fall! My mama killed me! |
| Mother: | Why didn't you say hello? You were afraid? Why didn't you speak? This is why I made you fall, so that you could talk again. Why did you kill your wife? |

Indian: No. I didn't kill her. She killed herself. I only ate her flesh but I didn't know it was her's. She said it was paca meat that you had brought her. This all turned out badly for me.

His mother scolded him.

Indian: Now I have paid; I've been punished sufficiently. The night monkeys showed me the way home. Now I can die here in this world.

The next day he died. When he was alive, he was a rascal but as he was punished, he turned out a good man — in the other world, dead. His wife was punished, too — for killing herself.

NOTES

1. The *ladinos* cook on a structure made of earth, while the Indians cook on the fire on the hut floor.
2. A *ladino* who was allowed to live in the settlement with his family because of his reputation for curing. He employed herbs and store medicine and was paid in cash or kind.
3. Lucio was one of the few who had two houses: one in the mountains, near his coffee grove, and the other on the southern edge of the settlement, where he had his milpa.
4. The deceased, as well as Lucio, belonged to the west section, while Alfonso belonged to the east. Each moiety usually buried its own dead; therefore, Alfonso was not expected to assist in the burial of Leonita.
5. Reference to the culturally determined concept of food as "hot" and "cold" which is more prevalent among the *ladinos* than the Tolupans.
6. Wisdom (1961: 349) writes that the Chortis of Guatemala place a gourd full of water on the tomb for the same reason. Karsten (1926: 226) refers to the custom of placing a jar with a hole in it on top of the burials in South America.
7. According to Hultrantz (1953: 176, 296) certain groups in North America considered the hair to be a magical prolongation of the person. Karsten (1926: 46–47) states that in South America it is thought to be the seat of the soul.

CHAPTER _VII_

SHAMANISM
AND
DIVINATION

THE _PUNAKPAN_
(SHAMAN) (Alfonso and Author)

Alfonso: We say _zahorín_ because the _ladinos_ say that this is what _punakpan_ means. The _ladinos_ have _punakpanes_ also but I don't know who they are.

The _punakpan_ may be considered a shaman because he was a mediator between human beings and the supernatural "beings," a diviner and a healer.[1]

The last two _punakpanes_, Félix Pérez and Julián Velázquez, probably died in the early thirties. Alfonso knew them during his childhood and youthful years and recalled what the elders said about them. They made frequent visits to the Montaña, traveling through the hills on foot from their hamlets, La Laguna Seca and Los Planes, in the Department of Yoro.

When I visited these hamlets in the late fifties, I located relatives of Julián Velázquez who told me that Julián spoke fluent Tolupan as well as Spanish but he dressed as a *ladino*. He even worked for one of the banana companies on the north coast of Honduras. But despite his mixed culture, he was highly respected in the Montaña as a *punakapan*.

In the final period, if not traditionally, a *punakpan* was designated from among the eldest of the group, regardless of sex, by the oldest *punakpan*, when he felt his end was near. Julián Velázquez wanted to "appoint" León Soto, one of the founders of the settlement, as his successor. According to Alfonso, León was afraid; he did not have the courage to become a *punakpan*. He was so timid that he would not even say hello to *ladino* neighbors much less strangers. He did not like to converse. León's wife, Juana, the daughter of old Juan, was also too afraid. So Julián was unable to find anyone to succeed him.

The *punakpanes* had great prestige in their community and throughout the region of Yoro, where the majority of the Tolupans lived. For their services they received gifts: food, large carrying nets, machetes. When these two *zahorínes* visited the Montaña, several men had to accompany them home to transport all the gifts they received.

Traditionally, the *punakpanes* were proficient diviners, expert at performing the *prueba de la cabuya* (proof of the cord or string), by means of which they predicted the future, consulted and advised. They healed by sucking the sickness out of the body; or simply by blowing on the sore or painful part of the body; or effortlessly shaking the clothes of the sick person and "the sickness then fell off, like dust." They were reputed never to suffer pain or illness, were said to be immune to snakebites and to live to a very old age.

Alfonso explained, "As they had power, God did not let them suffer." Moreover, their dreams were always "pretty." They could defeat the Devils when they emerged from the caves to win souls. By the wind, they established contact with the Jívaros, messengers from the East Heaven, to complain about the Devils. Thereupon, Tomam the Elder would send his eldest son, Nompwinapu'u, armed with serpents (lightning) to smite them. The Jívaros notified the *punakpanes* whenever the moon entered into an eclipse so that they order the people to make loud noises to save her from being swallowed by the monster Nen. (myth 28)

They could converse with the masters of the animals and even visit them. This contact enabled them to locate the game and to send a deer or other animals to a hunter. As told by Alfonso:

> When Félix Pérez came to the Montaña and visited my family, he would say to Mateo, 'I'm a *zahorín*. I'm going to

> send a deer to cross Mateo's path so that he kills it, so that
> he be well fed when he works, as a present from Félix Pérez.
> Wherever he works there will be a deer.' And so it was. That
> man never failed.

The *punakpanes* were *sabeadores*, the most knowledgeable of the oral
traditions, mythology and legends. Alfonso commented:

> Almost all that I converse with you, I remember from the
> old *sabeadores* — Félix Pérez and Julián Velázquez. My
> papa didn't tell me hardly anything. He talked mostly about
> the hunting deer and peccaries.

*   *   *

NARRATION 45
ALFONSO WANTED TO BE A *PUNAKPAN*

[When the last *punakpan* died, Alfonso was too young to become one.]

Alfonso: I wanted to be a *zahorín*, to take out documentation with
Julián Velázquez but he never came back. He deceived me. I
wanted to visit the other world, Tomam, the Glory, too. But
now there are no more old people to take me, no more
zahoríness. So I stay here quietly with the mortal women. I
will die with them. Jívaro accompanied Julián Velázquez to
and back from the other world. Then they went beyond to
visit the levels below the world. But only a *punakpan* can do
this. Julián Velázquez met Nompwinapu'u. I never did, nor
did my papa. I wanted to meet Tomam's daughters, too, but
I'll leave my bones here, as I am only a Mortal.

*   *   *

NARRATION 46
THE BAD *PUNAKPAN*

One called Capitancito [Little Captain] behaved badly. A Mortal offered to
pay him so that he never die.

Capitancito: You paid me for nothing. You'll die anyway.
Indian: If you kill me, I'll not pay you anything. Well, Capitancito,
you are not behaving well with me.

The Greatest
  Power: [Tomam] If the *punakpanes* don't behave well, I'll punish
        them, dead or alive.

The Capitancito charged cattle, machetes, clothes for immortality. He
deceived the Mortals. The Coronelcito [Little Colonel] complained to
Tomam but he didn't pay any attention to him. Tomam said to let him be;
if he wants to kill or sell people, let him do it. But then Tomam sent him a
sickness that killed him. This Capitancito was a friend of the Devils. He
was compromised by them to make money. He sent the Devils to kill his
enemies but then the Coronelcito stopped him. This one was a good *punakpan.*

* * *

NARRATION 47
JOURNEY TO THE OTHER WORLD

Jívaro lives way that way [to the east], very far beyond the sky, on the edge
of the other world. He has permission to accompany the *zahorínes.* He
accompanied Julián Velázquez everywhere, to Tomam, to the Second
Chief [Tomam the Younger], to Tata Dios. Julián Velázquez said that this
world is very small; he, himself, told me. I, too, wanted to meet Tomam
but as I am not a *zahorín,* I can't. If I tried, I might die.

    Julián Velázquez wanted to flee from the Commission of Santa Marta
[the missionaries established in this hamlet]. He didn't like the conquest;[2]
he didn't want to serve Manuel Subirana. He didn't want to learn in school,
neither to read nor write nor pray novenas. He wanted to die stupid. He
didn't want to serve in the army; he didn't like to fight. He didn't want to
be baptized, either. This is why he fled.

    As he was a *zahorín,* he went to report to Tomam. He went with Jívaro
so as not to get lost on the way. He lived in Los Planes, near La Laguna
Seca, near Santa Marta. He went everywhere. It took them ten years to get
to Tomam's domicile; after twenty years, he returned home. He departed
with Jívaro on a board [of wood]. Jívaro stood at the front and he on the
back. They went under the world and returned above the world. They
traveled all sorts of ways: by air, by land, under the sea, as he was a
zahorín.

    First, they came to the shore of a sea where he saw a girl gathering
flowers. The flowers were falling on the sea: *tzem totak,* flowers of the
gourd of castilla, and she was gathering them.

Girl: I am working. This is my job [*oficio*].

Julían Velázquez wanted to embrace her, to make love to her.

Girl: You want to compromise me, Señor Indio?

She wanted to throw him to the sharks.

Julián
Velázquez: Why do you want to throw me to the sharks? I can take you by force. Are you going to comply? I won't bother you for long and only once. You are not of my creed but, with God's permission, I'll embrace you, as I am a *zahorín*. As you are working, I won't embrace you very long, only an hour.

They made love on the seashore and became friends.

Then they [he and Jívaro] went on by the seashore and came upon a nation with just one eye, the Zamba Nation, a people-eating nation. They were grabbed and thrown in a pigpen with three *ladinos*: a fat one and two skinny ones. They were being fattened up with unripe, raw yucca to be eaten later. These Zambos eat people just like eating pigs. They kill them with a knife, cut their throat, and eat the meat fried in lard poured from a bottle. They said that this meat is very good.

Julián
Velázquez: I can't eat this raw yucca. Shameless ones; I'm not a pig. When you're not looking, I'm going to escape from this pigpen. I'm not just any old Indian that you can fatten.

Tomam doesn't like the Zamba Nation. He says that only the Earth has the right to eat people. He gave orders to have people buried so that the Earth eat them. When the Zambos eat people, this means they are being contrary to the law.

Julián Velázquez was often in danger. He escaped from the pigpen by excavating a hole with his knife.

He said: I'm going to excavate far under the sea.

The *ladinos* are afraid of sharks and this is why he excavated far under the sea. He could have gone other ways, by air or land, but he wanted to take the two *ladinos* with him. The third *ladino*, the fat one, had been eaten. The two skinny ones were left to be fattened. When the Head Chief [Tomam] knew about all this, he ordered that the Zambo who had eaten the fat *ladino*, and all his family, be killed.

Julián Velázquez excavated under the sea like an agouti. On his way he met the Nation of Cayugas who live there. Julián Velázquez was not offensive; he always asked permission to visit.

The Cayuga Nation are not people-eaters; rather, they are enemies of the Zambos. They live in the deep sea but not the sea of this world. There are two seas: one of this world and the other, which is the color of blood. Julián Velázquez said to the Cayugas:

> I am not abusing anyone so we can be brothers.

The Cayugas: We will take you to Tomam. We will not harm the Nation of Mortals, neither Indians nor *ladinos*. We will give you a meal so that you have strength to arrive at your destiny.

Then they took them in a steamboat. When the Zambos saw that they had escaped they said:

> They can't be far; they must be quite near still, on the seashore.

While searching for them, they met the Cayugas and asked:

> Haven't you seen some agoutis pass by here?

Cayugas: A couple of *ladinos* and an Indian were here, selling their wares. They were going to meet the Head Chief but no agoutis passed by.

Finally, Julián Velázquez arrived in the other world. Tomam said to him:

> There are lots of employees here and three chiefs. I'm the one in the middle. What brings you here?

Julián Velázquez: The *ladinos* have offended me a lot. They want me to learn to read and write; to baptize me; throw me in the army.

Tomam: Are you a criminal? Is this why you are fleeing?

Julián Velázquez: No, Señor, I am not a criminal. I just don't want to learn.

Tomam: Why flee? You have to suffer, to live in peace with the *ladinos*. Also, you will suffer from sickness. But the law of the *ladinos* doesn't kill and you may even die without being sick. If the *ladinos* want to conquer the Indians, let them. If they want to compromise the Indians, let them. I am going to advise you so that you live in peace.

Don't look for trouble; look for work and live in peace with your wife, with all, among brothers. The *ladinos* make machetes, clothes, axes and have salt to sell. You should work and trade with them. They want to drink coffee; they want maize, camotes, yucca, tobacco, potatoes. Sell them all these crops. No one will harm you if you work. So don't flee. Return to your country.

This is why he turned to leave. Then Jívaro said to him:

> I'll show you where Tata Dios lives, where the Sun and the Moon pass by so that you can tell the Mortals all about it.

When Tomam sent them off, they went to the Glory to greet Tata Dios. There Julián Velázquez saw where God of the Sun and the Moon pass through the seven levels [below and above the world]. They stopped over to greet Tomam the Younger; then Jívaro brought Julián home again. He arrived safely. Tomam had given him good advice.

* * *

NARRATION 48
TRAVELING THROUGH THE AIR

The *punakpanes* traveled everywhere. Julián Velázquez would ride through the air, mounted on a tree trunk.

Tree: Be careful when you stand on me so that you don't fall off and be killed.
Julián: Why? Do you want to kill me?
Tree: Not at all. I'm inviting you to ride on me.

Julián got on.

Tree: Don't move around so much. Stand up and hold tight; if not you might get dizzy.

He stood steady.

Tree: Let's go greet the Mortals in Santa Marta and in La Laguna Seca and leave documentation there so the old people last a bit longer. If the oldsters die too soon, the fetid vapor gets worse and worse.

* * *

MYTH 60
THE PUNAKPANES AND THE WINGED SNAKE

Long ago, no one ever died from a snakebite; when a *barba amarilla*[3] bit someone, nothing happened. Then people only died from the bite of the *ponhan im chip*, by order of its master. The *ponhan im chip* has wings, is white and very long. This snake is reliable; it's not a fighter. You can't kill it. It escapes and flees back to its Master and only goes out to feed.

Long ago, the *ponhan im chip* would only bite a gossiper Mortal who complained to its Master; the Master would send the *ponhan im chip* to bite him. Now this is all changed; now you can die from the bite of any old snake, even if its Master doesn't give the order.

Now only the *zahorínes* don't die from a snakebite. If someone doesn't die from a snakebite, this means that he's a *punakpan*, a *zahorín*.

The late Félix Pérez was bitten by a *barba amarilla*. He killed it but even so he almost died. His whole body bled; he vomited blood. He was sick for six months but then he got well. Five or six years later, he became a *punakpan*.

Only the *ponhan im chip* has the right to bite the *zahorínes*. When they behave badly with the Mortals, the Head Chief [Tomam] orders the *ponhan im chip* to bite them, as a punishment.

A *zahorín* visited the Master of the Snakes to have one of his enemies killed.

Zahorín: Give me a *barba amarilla* to put in the path of an enemy of mine.

Then the Master notifies Tomam.

Master: A *zahorín* Indian just came to see me.
**The Law
of God:**   [Tomam] What's his motive?
Master: He's asking for a *barba amarilla* to bite an enemy, one of his own Nation.
Tomam: Send him a snake and we shall see.

Tomam then orders the Master to send a *ponhan im chip* to bite that *zahorín*.

*   *   *

A *BRUJO* NAMED "GRUPERAS"
(Author)

Gruperas was often mentioned among the mestizos of Tolupan descent, as well as the *ladinos* of the Department of Yoro. During the trip I made on horseback in Yoro in 1956, I visited a small hamlet named Gruperas, located on the shore of the Siguapa River near the hamlets of La Laguna Seca and Los Planes. The last *punakpanes*, Félix Pérez and Julián Velázquez, had lived here. The *campesinos* of the region assured me that a *brujo* (witch) called "Gruperas" had lived during the last century in this very hamlet.

A *ladina* of Santa Marta told me as follows:

Gruperas was an Indian who did many bad things; he robbed women and killed a lot of people. When the Santa Misión [the missionary Manuel Subirana] came, he was told about this *brujo*. He sent five Indians to kill him, to cut off his head. They were very afraid of him but the Santa Misión forced them to go after him in the cave where he was and kill him. After they cut off his head, it rolled around making noises like an eagle.

Another *campesino* from the hamlet of Las Vegas reported:

When I lived in Santa Marta, the people there said that Gruperas lived in a cave — that when he tired of the women he had captured, he cut off their heads. You had to enter the cave through a hole by climbing down a liana. Gruperas had a shotgun that he used to kill people. Finally, he was killed. A convoy of soldiers set fire to the cave. He was a very bad *brujo*.

In the hamlet of Subirana, a Jicaque woman had this to say:

Gruperas lived in a cave with all his women. In front of the entrance, there were many little sticks stuck upright in the ground with poison on their tips. If you touched the tip, you were sure to die. Only Gruperas knew the pathway through this jungle of sticks, but no one else did, as you couldn't see it. But one of his women captives followed him once and escaped. She notified the authorities and so they were able to enter the cave and kill him.

* * *

NARRATION 49
GRUPERAS MARRIED ONE OF TOMAM'S DAUGHTERS

Alfonso:	Why did Gruperas live in a cave?
Julián Velázquez:	Because one of his wives was the daughter of Tomam, so he had to live in seclusion. Gruperas had asked Tomam for her.
Gruperas:	I don't want any more mortal women, Indians or *ladinas*. I don't want to die. I want to live eternally.
Tomam:	I'll give you one of my daughters. But your children will not be allowed to live mixed in with the Mortals. You will have to live by yourselves. I am the supreme chief of the world

but it has much fetid vapor. I'll give you one of my daughters but I'll kill you if you abuse the Indians and *ladinos* again. Now you will have a wife and one is enough. Don't abuse the mortal women. Don't eat chickens, turkeys, pigs, cattle — all these belong to the Mortal Nation. You can only eat turkey-hens, guinea hens, pheasants, white-collared peccaries, deer and monkeys — only these.

Gruperas: I want to live where I was born, in this world.

Tomam: Agreed. I'm giving you a girl so that you live in peace. When you marry my daughter, from then on you will never die. I promise not to take her away from you. I will only give you one piece of advice: don't behave badly with the Indian or *ladino* women, the mulattos, the *gringas*, the Devils, the French, or the English. As you will be eternal, you will never be sick. When my grandchildren are grown, bring them to me.

Gruperas took the daughter of Tomam to a cave to live. But soon he didn't keep his promise. First he liked a *ladino* woman, then an Indian woman, then a woman Devil. He had women from these four nations. He became very offensive. He wanted to make love to women from all the nations. Soon after he arrived with the daughter of Tomam, he left to look for an Indian woman.

Gruperas: (to an Indian) Don't you have a wife? Why are you here alone?

Indian: Yes, I have a wife. She's at home. If you want to meet her, I'll bring her here. [He brought her.] Do you like her? If you want her, kill me; kill me and take my wife. You go around robbing women. You want to possess all the women. You'll pay for this with your death.

Gruperas: No one can tell me what to do.

Indian: If you want — kill me. Why waste time talking, if it's women you want, now that you have fancied an Indian woman, a mortal woman?

He took the woman and killed the man, threw him into a deep ditch and finished him off with his machete. Then he put the woman in his cave. He was offending a lot of people. Then Tomam's daughter escaped and returned to her papa's place. Soon Gruperas was killed through deception, immortal or not. A convoy of soldiers came to get him, surrounding the entrance. They split open his head. His head rolled to the entrance of the cave. But the next day, it grew back on his body, just as before, except face to back. They killed him a second time, split open from behind. When the convoy of soldiers had first come.

They said: Why did you misbehave? But we're not going to harm or kill you.

Gruperas: If you kill me, we will be brothers but if you capture me and take me all tied up, we are not brothers.

He was living in the cave with his four women. As he was a *zahorín*, he went wherever he pleased. But the daughter of Tomam escaped from him.

Gruperas: Why are you trying to give me advice? I am the one who has been offended, mistreated. If you don't kill me, I'll kill you all.

This is why they split his head twice, because he was a robber of women and a killer. Tomam sent him to Oropango.

Tomam the
Younger: (to Gruperas) Eh! Why did they split open your head? I know very well why, because you were a rascal, for taking that which is not yours. Each Nation has its rights. I'm sending you without delay to Oropango.

* * *

DIVINATION
(Author)

The Tolupans of the Montaña de la Flor believed that the future could be known but that it was not predetermined — that an adverse circumstance or series of events could be avoided and a desired outcome obtained. This was possible by means of two very different divinations, *pruebas* (proofs or tests). One, called the *prueba de la canilla*, the "proof of the knee or lower leg," is very simple. The other, the *prueba de la cabuya*, "proof of the cord or string," involves a complicated manipulation of four knotted strings.

The "proofs" are a means of communicating with and seeking the advice of the supernatural, especially Tomam. You could ask a question or describe something you plan to the *pruebas*. For example, a young person might inquire if he or she should marry one of several candidates, what would be the outcome of the marriages? Which of the proposed spouses would die young? Which would live a long time? Which marriage would result in healthy children? The *pruebas* would tell you if a sick person was destined to recover or die in the near future. You might want to know if a given day was propitious for hunting, visiting a particular person or plant-ing. The "proofs" were often asked to tell the whereabouts of a lost object or strayed cattle, or of game — especially deer.

As Alfonso explains below, the "proof of the knee" is only a matter of interpreting the meaning of tripping or falling — if this occurs when you start out to achieve a certain objective. For instance: hunting, visiting someone with a particular motive in mind or simply walking and thinking through a problem or project. If you trip with both feet, this is interpreted as an alert and signals that you should not persist in your objective. But if you trip with one foot, this signals the direction you should take, to the left or right, opposite the foot on which you tripped. However, this "proof" does not always involve tripping, stumbling or falling; you may just feel a twitch in a nerve in one or both legs — especially the lower leg, the *canilla*.

*   *   *

INVOLUNTARY CORPORAL MOVEMENTS
CONSIDERED OMENS IN AMERICA
(Author)

Among many groups of American Indians, from Canada to Tierra del Fuego, there are accounts of a wide gamut of uncontrolled movements of different parts of the body which are interpreted as messages from the world of the spirits — decoded or deciphered, described as omens or foreboding signals, in more or less everyday contexts.[4] The sources con-sulted refer to these involuntary movements as contractions, palpitations trembling, jerking, shivering, winking, buzzing in the ear, tripping and sneezing.

Without having done research on this subject worldwide, the question comes to mind, for example: why do many of us say, "God bless you" when someone sneezes? Such an expression may well be part and parcel of a very ancient "code" of involuntary movements which must somehow be neutralized or interpreted.

The following quotation from Bernabe Cobo, first published in 1610 about the Incas, is surprisingly significant with respect to the "proof of the knee" which I found among the Tolupans 350 years later.

> When the eyelids trembled or the lips or other parts of the body, or the ears buzzed or they tripped, they said that something good or bad was to happen or to be heard about; if it was the right eye, ear or foot something good, and bad if it was the left side.[5]

Among the Navajos of North America and the Paez Indians of Colombia, the interpretation of such phenomena was very elaborate. The Navajos practiced a ritual called "the trembling of the hands."[6] The Paez have a codified concept of messages sent from different parts of the body by such involuntary movements, whose interpretation plays a fundamental role in their method of diagnosing the sick.[7]

In Guatemala, Honduras and Colombia this type of divination is usually associated with shamanism. The interpretations of such movements is an attribute or a function of people described as diviners, witches (*brujos/brujas*) medicine men, wizards, *chimín*, soothsayers and *zahorínes*.[8]

Similar to the Tolupan "proof" is the technique referred to here executed by a Chorti diviner of Guatemala:

> The diviner obtains his information by formulating questions to the spirit *sahurín [zahorín]* (located in the right calf of the leg), by examining an egg which has been broken into a gourd, by taking the pulse or by looking into a crystal ball. The first method is employed with greatest frequency. He [the diviner] goes to the house of the patient and darkens the interior, as the diviners claim they cannot work well in bright light. He sits down beside the bed, chews tobacco, and rubs his saliva on his right leg and in a few minutes begins to work on the diagnosis. This consists in formulating direct questions to the spirit, relative to the possible causes of the sickness. The spirit answers 'yes' by making the muscles of the calf contract and 'no' by letting them remain in repose.[9]

* * *

NARRATION 50
THE "PROOF OF THE KNEE"

The knee feels [has a premonition] when something is going to happen. When I trip on the right side, I should go to the left to find a deer. When I trip on both feet, I don't go searching for deer, or a woman, or do I go work in the field. I had best not go anyplace that day. Once, I tripped but I didn't pay any attention and I went up a hill and fell down. Then my knee said to me:

> Go back home. Why look for a deer today? This is not the right time.

Once, I set out to visit Alejandro but as I tripped on the way, I went back home. My knee told me that Alejandro wasn't at home or that he wouldn't receive me well. Why should I take a chance if I stumble?

When I was young, I was courting two sisters but going to their house I tripped. The knee told me:

> These girls will die young. They'll leave you a widower. They're sick; they won't live long.

Sometimes my knee tells me that the *gringita* [meaning the author] or the *alcalde* [the mayor of the town of Orica] is coming to visit, even though I haven't received notice.

*   *   *

THE "PROOF OF THE CORDS OR STRINGS"
(Author)

The other "proof," that of the knotted strings, may be compared to the game known as "cat's cradle." It requires a rather long explanation and, in all likelihood, had been exclusive of the *punakpanes*. Since there were no *punakpanes* in the Montaña de la Flor, it was performed by certain *sabeadores*, knowledgeable men or diviners, while "proof of the knee" was done by any adult male.

Alfonso, among several others, willingly performed the "proof of the strings" without payment, when asked by their fellow Tolupans. There was, however, an aura of secrecy around it, an obvious reluctance to perform it in the presence of strangers, myself included. However, finally, Alfonso did agree to demonstrate it for me. Before describing it, I will attempt to situate it in its ethnographic context, participating, as it must have, in the larger Pan-American tradition of such magical practices.

*   *   *

STRING MAGIC IN AMERICA
(Author)

I have yet to find in the ethnographic literature a detailed description of the "proof of the strings" such as that practiced among the Tolupans of the Montaña de la Flor. However, Conzemius, author of several important studies on the Indians of Honduras, mentions an identical or similar divination technique among the Sumus, neighbors of the Tolupans. He writes:

> The Sumus seem to have utilized the *tapuá* [*cabuya*] for the same objectives as the Jicaques of Honduras. With its aid they pretended to be able to obtain almost any information concerning the future, the outcome of fishing, hunting and courting.[10]

As mentioned above, this technique is somewhat comparable to the game called "cat's cradle." Known throughout the world as a game, it is usually described simply as a distraction which requires a certain ability to form different figures with strings held between the fingers of each hand of the performer.[11] It is rarely documented as a magical practice, much less an attribute of the diviners or shamans.

But Jenness, who worked for many years among the Eskimos, found that almost all of them associated certain of their "superstitions" with the figures they formed while performing this "game" — cat's cradle. In Alaska it could be played only during the long winter nights. They associated the figures with an evil, harmful spirit. Jenness writes:

> The Eskimos of Hudson Bay have beliefs that are partially different from those of their relatives in Alaska. Captain Comer states that the natives of Iglulik played the cat's cradle during autumn when the sun revolves toward the south, with the objective of catching it in the webs of the strings and thus preventing its disappearance.

This same author declares that on the west coast of Hudson Bay:

> The boys should not play cat's cradle to prevent, when they become adults, their fingers from getting entangled in the strings of the harpoon. They may play this game when they are adults. They told of two cases of hunters who lost their fingers and in both cases they thought it was because they had played cat's cradle when they were young.[12]

While among the Wailaki of California, an expectant father performs this game in order to ascertain the sex of the baby. George Foster writes:

> He [the Wailaki authority] was incapable of explaining why the strings revealed the sex of a newborn [before it was born]. The secret resides in the separation of two parallel strings situated on the radial side of the small fingers. If the string on the upper part of the finger lies on the index finger, a masculine figure is formed; if the string on the lower part is in this same position, a feminine figure is formed. However, usually the strings are interlaced so that it is impossible to know which one is really above. Even knowing the key, it is usually impossible to produce the desired figure. Miss Isabel Kelly has recently informed me that the Southern Paiutes divine the sex of a baby to be born using figures formed from strings. Unfortunately, she could not see the figures and thus it is not possible to say whether or not they are identical to those of the Wailaki, or simply similar. These two cases of divination by means of string figures suggest that this practice is more diffused [in the world] and that specific interrogation on the part of the ethnologists who carry on fieldwork might well discover many cases which until now have not been documented. In any event, it is evident that here is a new type of divination.[13]

Closer to "home" in prehispanic Mexico, the Aztecs (Nahuas) and the Otomies utilized knotted strings or cords for divination.[14] The following references may be especially significant, not only because they are "closer to home" and the strings were knotted but also, because of the etimology of the word *tapúa* used by the Jicaques to describe the technique (see quote above from Conzemius). I cite Professer Jímenez Moreno who called my attention to it:

> An interesting case is that of the *tapúa*, the name which is given for the cords that were used to divine (also called "Cabuya") which is derived from *tlapoa* ("to count" in classical nahuatl) because this term may indicate a possible prehispanic contact, with reference to Anne Chapman's comparison of the actual practice of the Jicaques shamans with that of the *mecatlapouhquê* nahuas of Ancient Mexico.[15]

According to the great sixteenth-century Franciscan chronicler of Aztec life, Fray Bernabé de Sahgún, the diviners worshiped the "Mother of the Gods," also called "Heart of the Earth" and "Our Grandmother." He writes:

> This goddess was the goddess of medicine and of medicinal herbs. She was worshiped by the doctors, the surgeons and the blood-letters, also the midwives and those who administered herbs in order to abort and also the diviners who tell of the good or bad luck that the children will have according to their [date of] birth.
> They also worshiped those who augured by throwing grains of maize and those who augured by gazing into water in a crock and those who augured with little cords, which they tied one to the other, they called mecatlapouhquê.[16]

The German scholar Seler[17] relates this same operation of the strings described by Sahgún to the later text by the chronicler Fray J. de Torquemada.

> And consequently they had little strings arranged in a bunch like a key ring, where the women hung their keys; they threw [the strings] on the floor and those which were tangled they said was a signal of death. And if one or several fell extended they held it was a sign of life, saying that the sick person was already beginning to extend his feet and hands.[18]

Simeón defines the term *mecatlapouhquê*, employed by Sahgún, as "those who count or read by means of strings." This is evident by the meaning of the Aztec word *mecatl*, "string or cord," and *poa* (derived from *tlapoa*) — to count or read.[19]

In the first folio of the Codex Florentine[20] there is a representation of the two founders of the Aztec ritual calendar, the *tonalpohualli*. One, a female divinity named Oxomoc, holds several knotted strings and the other, a male divinity, Cipactonal, performs a divination with grains of maize.

Molina defines *tonalpuqui* as the "diviner or augur who casts lots" (*el adivino o agorero que echa suertes*), *mecatlapoami* — to cast lots with strings, auguring (*echar suertes con cordeles, agoreando*) and the *mecatlapuhque* as those who cast said lots (*los que echan dichas suertes*).

If the Eskimo and Wailaki divining techniques seem simple, derived as they may be from the game of cat's cradle, those of the Tolupans are relatively complex and are inserted in a cosmological context. But why is the Aztec string divination, which iconographically, at least, is represented as partaking in the very origin of the ritual calendar (the *tonalpouhualli*), so succinctly described? Further research of Nahua (the classical epoch) or Nahuatl (the post-classic) data may find even greater similarities of this "Aztec" technique with that of the Tolupan/Jicaque. It may be discovered to be an expression of these two cultures which, although they evolved along very different routes, may have shared a very ancient tradition.

* * *

ALFONSO PERFORMS THE "PROOF OF THE CORD"
(Author)

This technique is structured on the concept that the individual's future is shaped by the choices made among a limited number of alternatives and that a person may influence his or her "destiny" by communicating with supernatural powers [the Tomams] and discovering which alternative is preferable or most beneficial.

Tomam of the East Heaven is symbolized by the right hand of the diviner and Tomam of the West by the left hand. The former is indicative of all that is positive: the good life, health, success in all the various endeavors. The opposite is true of the latter, even though there is no connotation of evil here — Tomam the Younger is portrayed as kind and well meaning, although sometimes stupid.

The messages transmitted from the other world by four cords or strings (*cabuyas*) do not always respond to questions of the diviner. The cords may "speak" on their own, give unsolicited advice or make unwelcome comments, as related in the myth (#44) concerning the Master of the Snake and the Little Old Man with his *cabuyas*.

This involves a rather complex symbolism because in addition to the east-west dichotomy, the four cords employed have one to four knots on their extremities with which the diviner forms a loop, and should also be "decoded."

By twisting and pulling the cords, the diviner forms a loop on one of the cords whose message is partially decoded by its direction with respect to the cardinal points. The principal dichotomy of east and west is usually interpreted as described above. The reading of the north-south axis is apparently a function of the question put to the diviner. If, as will be shown, the diviner asks a question concerning himself and the loop falls toward him, to the south, this means a favorable outcome for himself and to the contrary, if it falls away from him, toward the north. If the loop falls in the direction of a cardinal point, it gives only one message; while if it falls between two points, it carries two messages. The diviner also considers on which of the four cords the loop has been formed. He should only do the "proof" a maximum of four times to answer a question concerning himself or his client.

The few Tolupans knowledgeable of this technique refused to show it to me and it was only after five years of coming to the settlement that Alfonso agreed to give me a demonstration. Thanks to him, I am able to describe it in some detail. I was living that year, 1960, on the ranch of the late Don Jesús Lopéz' family, a half-hour's horseback ride from the east entrance to the settlement. The day of the demonstration, as usual, Alfonso came to the ranch. He preferred to talk to me there rather than in his home in the mountains, where we were often interrupted by visiting neighbors. I quote at length from my diary of that day.

"Yesterday, Don Jesús selected four pieces of thin rope, each about a meter long. I put them aside in the hope that I might prevail upon Alfonso to give me a demonstration of the *prueba de la cabuya* (proof of the cord), which he sometimes calls the *prueba de los cerros* (proof of the hills).

"As soon as he arrived today, I brought them to him asking him to show me how it is done. He smiled and looked about saying, 'Maybe some people will arrive.' I replied that I didn't think so because they rarely come during the afternoon of a weekday. He smiled, as if he were deciding whether or not to do it. Then he took the strings saying, 'I'm going to show you.' He went through the operation five times, making comments all the time and answering my questions. I did not take notes during the demonstration, because I was too absorbed trying to comprehend, and also I felt he might be uneasy were I to do so.

"It so happened that a *ladino* did come to the ranch. He stood at a distance for a few minutes looking at us. Alfonso saw him but paid him no attention.

"After he took the strings from me, he was still reluctant. Smiling again, he looked about repeating, 'Maybe people will come.' Soon afterwards he began. During the five demonstrations, he would often look up saying, 'I'm doing this so that you don't think that I'm not willing. I'm only doing it so that you see it, not for the little animals [for the hunt].' He often complained about the strings, saying that the *prueba* would or did not come out because they were not good quality. As soon as he received them, he began smoothing them down and asked me to trim the ends so that all would be the same length. I did. He said he uses somewhat longer pieces, about two *varas* long [about a meter and a half] and made of the maguey [fiber]. He said his strings last two or three years and if well taken care of, five or six. The word for *cabuya*, cord or string, is *makel* in Tolupan.

"He explained that the knots are so that Tomam the Elder and Tomam the Younger can send the answers to the questions asked. At one end of each rope is Tomam the Elder, the Head Chief, and at the other end is Tomam Wo huai, the Younger — one rope, one knot at each end, another two knots, another three, another four. The first *prueba* is done with the rope with one knot. The second *prueba*, with the rope having two knots. The third *prueba*, the rope has three knots. The fourth *prueba* has four knots. 'There are four ropes to know about all in the world.' You should not do more than four *pruebas* at a time, to answer a question. If there is no answer the first time, you have to do it again but only four times.

"He sat with his right hand toward the east and his left toward the west. He began by laying each string over the upper part of his index finger of his left hand, one next to the other, ranging them carefully so that they doubled over his finger at the middle and hung down evenly on either side.

"Then he smoothed over each string several times, carefully drawing out the kinks. They laid in a specific order, the string with one knot on the inside, toward him, and thus consecutively. His legs being crossed, the strings laid partially on his thigh and in this position he had smoothed them out until each hung in this order over either side of his index finger.

"Then he raised his left hand, holding the strings up in a slightly vertical position, allowing the ends to hang in the air from the index finger and, taking up the ends with his right hand, he began twisting them.

"The twisting was always done toward himself. He commented on this when he saw I noticed saying, 'It's for me,' meaning that he was twisting the strings toward himself because he was demonstrating the *prueba* as if it were for himself, concerning something he wanted to know, or desired. He twisted the strings around themselves in short fast movements forming an apparent confused mass, though he held this twisted part in place by shifting his thumb and bracing it against the part of the strings which lay against his middle finger after each twist while the mass of strings got thicker. He did this one or two times for each *prueba*. Then he stopped and taunted them by raising his left index finger over which the four strings still hung. Then he raised up the twisted part of the strings with his right index finger, thus forming a small loop in the section of the twisted part.

This he did four times, making four small loops from the twisted part of the strings which he held in place with his left thumb against his left index finger.

"Once the four loops were formed, he straightened out the untwisted end so that they lay as from the start, the one knotted string toward him and consecutively. Then he chose four ends of two strings, the one- and two-knotted strings, and placed them between his left middle and third fingers so that they laid over the back of his hand, while the remaining two strings hung toward his palm. He always seemed to do this in just the same order, pairing them in the same way and placing them in identical position. Then, with his right hand, he tied the ends of one of the strings together. Three of the five demonstrations he tied the ends of the string with one knot at each extremity and during the other two demonstrations he tied the ends of the string having two knots. This he did without altering the position of the twisted parts of the strings. Then he laid them out again in order, now with one string tied tightly at its extremities. All this time he continued holding the punched twisted loops tightly with his left thumb. Having tied the one string and smoothed the other out on either side of his hand, he then pulled the punched part out with his right hand holding onto the untwisted extremes. He pulled quickly, tugging at the strings looped over his index finger which he held secure by his thumb. He tugged and pulled with his right hand and made several crunching movements into his left palm and then wound the strings around his right wrist, and unwound them twice. He always did this twice.

"After this he chose two pairs of strings from the opposite sides of his hand. Picking up these four ends with his right hand and the ends of the remaining untied string with his left, he then pulled his left index finger out of the loops, releasing the punched-up twisted string having four loops and pulled the strings apart. This he always did rather slowly.

"Now he held the strings out in front of him horizontally and began to examine them. First he carefully examined the middle section where the strings were now linked and, when the *prueba* was successful, the strings had formed another loop which stood out visibly despite the strings being stretched out rather tightly. This is the loop he now 'read.' He studied it carefully. When apparently there was no loop, he examined the linked section to make sure that there was not a tiny loop there not entirely visible. He always took a few minutes before looking up to me to give an answer. Three times he said that it hadn't worked and twice that it had. Often during the twisting he would say, 'It seems to me that this one isn't going to work.'

"I recall clearly the position of the loop one of the times it was successful. It was to his left, that is west of the middle where the four strings were linked and slightly turned inward, towards him. After the other successful operation he said:

> 'This time it says that I am going to find a paca, or maybe a peccary, if I take good hunting dogs; or even without dogs, I can find them but it will take me longer.'

"He further explained:

> 'When the loop faces outward, then I don't go out [hunting]. Why should I? I won't find anything. When it falls to the right of the middle, it's for me and when to the left, it's for someone else.'

"He went on to say that the direction of the loop also indicated where the game is to be found. He added:

> 'The *prueba* tells many little things. It's good for a lot of things. Just one *prueba* tells a lot, but you can't know about it. Now I am showing you a little so that you don't say that I am unwilling.'

"I inquired if the *prueba* could be used for courting [which of course I knew it could be, as he had said so several times]. He replied jokingly:

> 'As I am old now, why should I go looking? But when the girl is going to say yes, the loop is towards me. If it is towards the outside, I won't bother to look for her, as she will surely refuse.'

"A few days ago, he had said that young men come to his house to consult him, so that he do the *prueba* concerning the outcome of their courting or love affair. In the latter case, to find out if the girl will have a baby and if so the young man will want to marry her. He added now:

> 'They all come to see me. They come because they have confidence in me. Like you, you know how to read so they come to you so that you read them something. The same with we *sabeadores*. The *prueba* knows everything, has it all stored up. If I need something like game I have to do the *prueba*. If I need a paca, an agouti or any animal, the *prueba* will tell me if it's there [to be hunted]. If it says no, I don't bother. As each master has its animals in corrals, when the Indians kill a lot, the master keeps them shut in. So it doesn't do any good to look for them without asking the *prueba* first. The *prueba* tells about everyone: Indians, *ladinos*, gringos, Spaniards, French, English — when we are

going to plant the milpa, when it is going to rain. It might
say that it won't rain the whole month of April and that we
had better wait until May 15, then it will rain.'

"I asked if it ever tells a lie. He replied:

'Sometimes the *cabuyas* say a lie; then I throw them in the
fire. When they tell the truth, then I keep them for another
time.'

"I asked if it might be done anytime or place or by the women.

'Anytime it can be done, day or night, at home or in the
bush. But I have never seen a woman do it. They have other
tasks: to cook, to grind, to sew. I haven't seen them do it, as
they don't search for animals in the woods. They don't go
courting. Sometimes the *prueba* doesn't come out. Just like
you, you take photographs of me twenty or thirty times until
one comes out, the same with the *prueba*.'

"He affirmed again that the *prueba* of the rope and that of the knee are
equally effective that, 'Both are good.' I inquired if the *ladinos* know about
these *pruebas*. 'I don't know,' he said, 'but I think not. They have other
sorts of *pruebas*.'"

* * *

A *LADINO* SPEAKS OF THE *PRUEBA DE LA CABUYA*
(Author and Jesús López)

As far as I could discover, none of the *ladinos* knew how to do either of the
pruebas nor would it be expected, as the *pruebas* are very much a part of
the Tolupan tradition. However, some of them believed in them. Don Jesús
López, who knew some of the first settlers in the Montaña and their sons,
told me:

A few Indians still know how to throw the *cabuyas* but they
don't like to say so. Many years ago, when I used to go see
them often, my late wife would say to me, 'Without notifying them, you'll not find them at home' [meaning they
would be out in the fields or hunting]. But it wasn't true;
they knew when I was coming, without notifying them. Old
Juan [the first chief of the east moiety], his son, Domingo,
Ulofia [son of old Pedro, first chief of the west moiety], they
all knew how to throw the cords. When I got there, Domingo would say to me, '*Compadre*, I knew you were coming.'

> I would ask him how he knew. He would say, 'Well, a little
> bird told me.' But the truth is that he knew because the cords
> told him. Old Juan, Ulofia and the others said the same.

During my first stay among the Tolupan, Don Jesús told me that once,
years ago, when he could not find one of his mares, old Juan did the
prueba of the cords for him. He told him to return home and not to look
any farther, that in two days someone would bring the mare to him and ask
for some money. He also told him just where the mare had strayed, by
which streams, through which hills and where she was then. He said not to
worry; she would be returned just as he had predicted. And so it was. Don
Jesús also related that a certain Indian by the name of Facho, who had just
done the *prueba*, told him that there was a deer close by but that it was not
for him [for Facho], that someone else was going to kill it. So it was. Don
Jesús did kill it and afterwards gave some of the meat to Facho. He
laughed as he recalled this, saying, "The cords don't tell lies."

NOTES

1. I have insufficent data to ascertain by what means the *punakpanes* received
   their supernatural powers to cure and predict — by visions or by spirit possession during a trance. Nor do I have any reliable information on knowledge of
   the use of plant or animal derivatives for curing. The only data I gathered on
   this subject was *ladino* in origin. But the *punakpan* does fulfill seven of the
   eight criteria of the definition of the shaman enumerated by Furst (1976:
   151–52) as characteristic of the ideological context of Asiatic–American
   shamanism. The eighth criterion, for which I have no data, is the achievement
   of a state of trance.
2. The spiritual "conquest" carried on in the Department of Yoro by the Catholic
   missionary Manuel Subirana from 1856 to 1865. See chapter I.
3. A very poisonous snake whose lower jaw is covered with yellow scales, hence
   the name *barba amarilla*, yellow chin. It belongs to the *Crotalides Bothrops
   asper* family.
4. Chapman 1965–76; Flannery 1946: 256; Guiteras-Holmes 1961: 305; Jenness
   1930: 58; Madson 1955: 57; Métraux 1949: 585; Ray 1933: 214; Reichel-
   Dolmatoff 1951: 132, Roth 1915: 152; Swanton 1908: 459; Torquemada vol.
   II, libro VI, cap. 48; Vallis & Wallis 1955: 167.
5. Cobo 1983: 150.
6. Hultkrantz 1968: 130–132.
7. Villa 1954: 224–27.
8. Girard 1949, vol. I: 319–21; Oakes 1951: 178; Schultz-Jena 1945: 57;
   Thompson 1958: 237; Valladares 1937: 218–19; Wagley 1949: 72.

9. Wisdom 1961: 392–93, 451. The above quotation is not an exact transcript of the original text, as it was translated by Chapman from the Spanish edition.
10. Conzemius 1932: 135, translated by the author from Spanish.
11. Boas 1888; Furness 1906; Martínez Crovetto 1972.
12. Jenness 1924: 183, as translated from Spanish.
13. Foster 1941: 127, again translated from Spanish.
14. For the Otomies, see Carrasco (1950: 228) for the reference to *echar suertes con cordel* (cast lots with string) from a Spanish–Otomi dictionary published in 1640. See also Giard 1949 vol. I: 322.
15. Jímenez Moreno 1978: 17.
16. Sahgún 1969: libro I, capítulo VIII.
17. Seler 1926: 365. See also Seler 1900: 53.
18. Torquemada vol. II, libro VI, capítulo 48. See also Motolinia 1903: 126.
19. See Durand-Forest (1968: 14) for a mention of this technique documented in the Codex of Madrid.
20. Sahgún libro IV, capítulo I.

CHAPTER <u>*VIII*</u>

ANALYSES

HISTORICAL PROCESS:
MYTHOLOGY AND CULTURE

The Tolupan oral tradition lacks the resources of certain American Indian cultures because of the disintegration of its culture. In an ongoing culture, the mythical thought participates in the ritual actions; it lends its significance to ceremonies, dances, music, ornaments and other symbolic manifestations. In this small refugee group much of the cultural heritage, including shamanism, is now nonexistent. The myths may have become less complex, having lost their symbolic supports during the process of cultural disintegration.

Nevertheless, it would be an error to consider this mythology an empty shell, the remains of an ancient shipwreck. The oral tradition forms a coherent whole and probably, for the elders, it still expresses a faith, a morality and real sentiments.

In order to situate the Tolupan culture as it survives in the Montaña de la Flor, I propose two models of historical processes.

In Brazil there still exist Indian communities which, despite their small number, are heroically struggling to safeguard their identity — their territory, their social organization, their ceremonies. They resisted being con-

273

quered, assimilated as marginal laborers. However, many are being decimated by diseases resulting from contagion from people who have invaded their lands and from the destruction of their forests, the fauna and the fragile soils. "Savage" exploitation by large-scale cattle enterprises and multinational companies is only now beginning to be restrained. But, historically, these communities were resistant. They will either achieve a chance to perpetuate their cultures, though somewhat modified, or be destroyed, as their populations are decimated through assassinations and diseases, while the survivors become "assimilated" into the rural and urban poor.

The indigenous cultures of Guatemala are for the most part syncretic. Through the centuries since the Conquest they have incorporated much that is Spanish, especially on the political and religious levels. But despite the heavy hand of the Conquest and colonization, these communities maintained their linguistic identity. With their language, other ancestral traditions and the posthispanic transformations, they created original syncretic cultures.[1]

The Tolupans of the Montaña de la Flor survived a devastating historical process and have preserved their language and identity, although not to the extent of certain groups in Brazil. They did not, however, adopt the religion and political organization of the invading Spaniards and later colonists, as occurred in Guatemala. Therefore, this Honduran experience may be situated between the Brazilian and the Guatemalan "models."

The Tolupans did not assimilate the elements of Christianity, which form part of their mythology, but rather they utilized them in order to accentuate the differences between the *ladinos* and themselves. For example, the Christian God, "Tata Dios," is incorporated into the Tolupan mythic universe but "He" is subordinated to the God Tomam, assigned to look after the *ladinos*. This accentuates the distance which separates the Indians from the *ladinos*, who historically and culturally are largely the descendants of the conquistadores. Hence, the Tolupans proclaim their spiritual autonomy.

Also, recall that Tata Dios is not particularly indulgent with his devotees, the *ladinos*, who fight with him and he has an obvious disdain for them. He is disgusted by their excessive drinking and fighting and so offended when they require him to pay taxes, that he seeks refuge with Tomam, who finally sends him to Glory. (myths 7 and 8)

Our Lord, "Nuestro Señor," obviously Christian in origin, is however portrayed as the instigator of death on Earth yet the savior of the First Indian, the Master of the Peccary, whose daughter he marries. (myth 3) Then (myth 5) Nuestro Señor is portrayed as a seducer of Indian women, an enemy of the Indians and an ally of the Devil; yet (myth 6) he identifies with the Tolupans challenging the *ladinos*. Although his personage is ambiguous and completely transformed with respect to the Christian savior, certain of the themes as well as his name are indisputably Christian. Nuestro Señor and Tata Dios might even be thought of as parodies on these most cherished figures of the Christian faith.

MYTH AND REALITY

This mythology both reflects and transcends the society which has created it. The mythology reflects and defines the norms of behavior, that is, relations that the human being should maintain with his fellows and with nature. The economy, the social structure and historical experiences propose themes to the mythology but the latter does not limit itself to a simple elaboration of the infrastructure and the past on symbolic levels. It has its own dynamics and, in this sense, at times it transcends the society and may even contradict it. The functions of mythology and religion of course are not similar in all societies and not even within a given culture or society. But, in almost any culture, the mythology, as an integral part of the religion, attempts to resolve, on a symbolic or moral level, certain profound and fundamental problems of human existence. It attempts but it does not necessarily succeed, especially, perhaps, in a religion such as the Tolupan which is neither dogmatic nor ecumenical. It is not dogmatic in that disagreements with the divine precepts are incorporated into the mythology (myth 14, chapter VI, answer 10), not all the principal deities are paragons (myth 21), and what might be called the problem of evil, as exemplified by the Devil, is not resolved (narration 35). It is not ecumenical simply because it does not aspire to universality; it recognizes that other "nations" have different beliefs (and abilities). (myths 6-8, 37, narrations 1, 33 and 47)

For the Tolupans, human beings are "Children of Death." The theme of death is present in so many of the myths, that one might question if this be an obsession of the Tolupans of the Montaña de la Flor, threatened as they are by cultural disintegration and a high percentage of mortality. But these phenomena are recent, while the theme of death probably has been characteristic of the mythology since ancient times and may well be ontological, as it is a universal problem of human existence, the focus of all religious thinking and faith in one way or another. The Tolupan Mortal establishes a contract with Nature which obliges him to pay for his life with his life, to reciprocate by nourishing her in return.

PROBLEMS WHICH THE MYTHOLOGICAL
THOUGHT PROPOSES

The crucial aspect of this mythology lies in resolving the ontological problems of creation (existence) and death.

Here the gods order the mouse and the female monkey to make love and give birth to the first humans. (myth 1) But when the "little man" and the "little woman" are born, they lack something essential — their sexes. Then the gods and goddesses give them sexual organs. Nompwinapu'u travels to the far distant heaven to be given the female sex by the Great Tomam; then he makes love to his father's, Tomam the Elder's, women (his mother and sisters, supposedly), subsequently to those of the Thunder God and finally to the Moon herself. All the Immortal women lend their sex to create the female human. Tyaj Guatecast, Messenger of the West Heaven, is assigned to obtain the male sex, which the gods simply bestow upon him. The sexual act of the Mortals, therefore, involves complicity with the Immortals. However, this act is fraught with danger because if certain spirits (the Devils), disguised as seducers, succeed in making love to humans, death will result. Thus, the very act of creation (sexual intercourse) may destroy its creators.

Maize, like all plants, is another gift of the gods. However, in the moment of creation (planting), Mother Earth becomes indignant. "She nourishes us but she is rebellious. She demands our death in order to nourish herself with our body." (myths 34 and 35)

The paradox of existence: the sexual act and the right to nourishment are both gifts of the gods but are equally fraught with dangers.

In this mythology, nature participates in culture. The individuals of each kingdom (plant, animal and human) establish a contract, a relation of mutual dependency which permits them to live, although it condemns them to die. (chapter V)

The Tolupan mythology may be characterized in two words: reciprocity and hierarchy. (chapters IV and V) Between the two poles of life and death, reciprocity links the human being with the animals, the plants, the Earth and even the winds, the rains, the Sun and the Moon. Hierarchy guarantees that the rights of each and all be respected and the supreme deity, Tomam "the Master of Authority," ensures these rights.

The incessant relations among all these beings, both mortal and immortal, weave the fabrics of existence. But the threads of the weft are frequently broken, the rule of reciprocity transgressed, complications emerge, dramas are unleashed. Ambiguity makes its appearance: What is death? A complement of life or an intruder, a maker of disharmony? The mythology confronts this dilemma. Death is accepted, incorporated into a whole where reciprocity exchanges it for life, but death is also rejected, when it takes the form of a diabolic provocation. The Devil is the rival of the Master of Authority, Tomam, who claims to be all powerful. This mythology does not resolve the problem of being; it refrains from soothing the believer, it avoids reconciling him with his destiny, to close the circle. By eschewing dogma, it evokes uncertainty. The believer may or may not resolve the enigma.

MYTHOLOGY AS A CLASSIFICATORY SYSTEM

In an article published in 1903 entitled, "Essay on some Primitive Forms of Classification," its authors, Durkheim and Mauss, declare that, "Each mythology is basically a classification, which however derives its principles from religious beliefs and not from scientific notions."[2] We might add that the classifications and the logical operations which structure them are not conscious. And this is a radical distinction which differentiates mythological from scientific thought.

Two systems of classification are easily discernible in the Tolupan mythology: one is based on the concept of duality and the other utilizes the notion of master.

All systems of classification necessarily are composed of relations of reciprocity as well as those of hierarchy. That is to say, a classification is not limited to simply establishing an order of its similar or "reciprocal" elements into groups, or placing them in different classes under various rubrics, but also defines specific relations of hierarchy among the groups of which it is composed. According to the article by Durkheim and Mauss:

> Thus primitive classifications do not constitute exceptional singularities, without analogy with those in use among the most cultured peoples; they would seem, to the contrary, to be directly related to the first scientific classification. In effect, although in certain aspects they differ greatly from the latter, they do possess certain of their essential characteristics. On the one hand, they are constructed as hierarchical systems, just as the scientific classification. The elements are not simply ordered into isolated groups, but rather in groups which maintain certain defined relations among each other and form in their totality one related whole.[3]

THE CLASSIFICATION STRUCTURED
ON THE NOTION OF DUALITY

The pairs listed below have one or more shared characteristics and in this sense are reciprocal[4] but one of the paired partners (associated with the east and listed on the right) is almost always endowed with greater power or positive attributes than the other, thus creating an hierarchical relationship. Therefore, the pairs are at the same time reciprocal and hierarchical.

WEST

1. Tyaj moo (place of the west): West Heaven: world of the dead Indians and divinities that rule there.
2. Tomam the Younger, also called Tyaj Tomam, younger son of Tomam the Great: cacique of the dead Indians and reigns over the World of the Dead: responsible for the natural phenomena which originate in the west.

3. Eldest son of the above: no name given: a few positive attributes.

4. Thunder of the West: sent by Tomam the Younger in September and October: knocks down the crops.
5. Tyaj Chiquichi: Earthquake of the West: very destructive, may cause flood.
6. Tyaj Lupu: Wind of the West: blows in September and October: very destructive.
7. Tyaj Chiquihumel: Clouds of the West: bring excessive rains in autumn.
8. Reddish black frost: very harmful.
9. Toco Chikwai: Toco the Younger, a "very dangerous" Temptation.

10. Tyaj Haitecal: first star to appear in the western sky: younger brother of the eastern star.
11. Tyaj Guatecast: although younger brother of other Guatecast, he is paired with Nompwinapu'u as creator of the male sex. He guides the dead to and from the Earth to the West Heaven of Tomam the Younger.
12. Tyaj Jívaro: messenger of Tomam the Younger.
13. Tyaj moo ("place of the west"): also applied to the west moiety or section of Montaña de la Flor: however, it is in no way associated to the West Heaven.

EAST

1. Tsik'in moo (place of the east): East Heaven: world of Immortals.

2. Tomam the Elder, also called Tsik'in Tomam, eldest son of Tomam the Great. He is all-powerful (almost), creator of human beings (by order of his father) and of all animals and plants. He reigns over all the Immortals, all living beings, especially the Tolupans.
3. Eldest son of the above: Nompwinapu'u: created the human female sex, also gave maize and rivers to the humans.
4. Thunder of the East: sent by Tomam the Elder, June through August: announces good rains.
5. Tsik'in Chiquichi: Earthquake of the East: not harmful.

6. Tsik'in Lupu: Wind of the East: brings the first rains of spring.

7. Tsik'in Chiquihumel: Clouds of the East: bring beneficial rains in spring.

8. Reddish yellow frost: not so harmful.
9. Toco Pones: Toco the Elder, a Temptation but does not bother humans.
10. Tsik'in Haitecal: first star to appear in the eastern sky.

11. Tsik'in Guatecast: older brother of counterpart: does not wish to concern himself with humans, with the Mortals.

12. Tsik'in Jívaro: messenger of Tomam the Elder.
13. Tsik'in moo ("place of the east"): another term for the corresponding east section: allusions are made to its affinity with the East Heaven, although it is not deemed superior to the opposite moiety.

At first glance, it may seem strange that the feminine sex be classified under the east rubric (#3) and the masculine under the west (#11). In Tolupan society, the women, in general, are subordinate to the men. Yet the feminine sex is positioned under this superior rubric perhaps because of the great importance accorded to women's life-giving power in the creation myth. (#1) This is an example of a mythical concept which transcends and even contradicts the behavior current in the society. I suggest that because of their procreative gift, women were considered superior to men in the mythological sphere, despite their being socially inferior to them.

A "third dimension" served to incorporate Spanish and Christian (*ladino*) themes into the mythology and is situated between the two poles of attraction (the East and West), in the zenith, in Glory — the paradise of the *ladinos*. Here is the domain of the "Master" of the *ladinos*, Tata Dios, who is also that of the domestic animals brought to America by the Spaniards. This category includes another personage of Spanish origin or inspiration, Noventa (whose name may be derived from "novena"), the brother of Tata Dios. Noventa was the Master of Firearms (the present master — the gringos). Noventa's domicile is in the second level under the Earth, perhaps to keep company with the other masters of animals. He is also the Master of the Chickens, which were also brought to America by the Spaniards, and of the native turkeys as well.[5]

THE CLASSIFICATION BASED ON
THE CONCEPT OF MASTERS

The relations of hierarchy in this classification also conform to the criteria of Durkheim and Mauss and are manifested as essential attributes of the Tomams and the Masters, while the entire "system" functions in terms of reciprocity, of interdependence and mutual support.

1. **Tomam the Elder**: also called the Master of Authority. He is the presiding supreme deity, though he is said to follow orders of his father, Tomam the Great (Tomam Pones Popawai), who retired to the far heavens and rarely intervenes in earthly affairs. In effect, Tomam the Elder reigns over the Immortals and all living creatures: humans, animals and plants — usually through the lesser deities assigned to them. Moreover, he directs the natural phenomena which originate in the East Heaven and is said in particular to be the Master of the Earth.

> **Grandfather Thunder**: is the Majordomo of the Wind,
> whose masters are the two brother Tomams.

2. **Tomam the Younger**: governs the Tolupan World of the Dead. Hence, he is responsible for the Indians' behavior during afterlife and also

regulates natural phenomena proceeding from the West Heaven. He is the Master of the Earth together with his elder brother.

> **Tyaj Guatecast**: is the assistant of the above Tomam and particularly in charge of guiding the Tolupans to the World of the Dead.

3. **Nompwinapu'u**: by order of his father, Tomam the Elder, gave maize to the Indians, also the rivers and the *guamo* tree. As Master of the Maize, he is particularly vigilant concerning the well-being of the tender plants.

4. **Chiri Tsutsus**: she created the beans (*frijoles*) of the First Nation which she reprieved when her son was killed and since then, beans must be purchased from the *ladinos*.

5. **Grandfather Thunder**: controls the thunder, lightening, the fire of the First Nation. He is the Master of the "Firebirds," Crabs and Wasps, which he created.

> **Warrior Ants**: is the Majordomo of the Wasps.

6. **Jívaro**: Master of the Frost.

7. **Tungsus**: Master of the Rain (and clouds).

8. **Nen**, also called **Sialpe**: owner or Master of the Lagoons and Rivers.

9. **Namahuai** Mother Earth: the mother of all humans. She is also "Master" of the Beetles.

10. **Our Lord**: even though he left the fetid vapor on Earth which is the cause of death, he is sometimes identified with the Indians (myth 6) and called Jamayón ("Master" in Tolupan) of the Indians.

11. **Tata Dios** (God our Little Father): god of the *ladinos*, alive and dead, and is the Master of Cattle, Horses and Mules which have not been branded, as well as Pigs, Buzzards, "Birds of Glory," Dogs and Money.

> **The Dog**: Majordomo of the Cattle.

12. *Ladinos*: owners of the cattle which have been branded (have owners), of the fire lighted with matches and of beans whose seeds have been purchased in the stores.

13. **Noventa**: Master of Chickens, Turkeys, Firearms and, formerly, Mines. (See Devils and Gringos.)

14. **Saino Jamayón**: Master of the White-Lipped Peccary.

> **Japay** (the Male Jaguar): Majordomo of the same.

15. **Jo'popjil Jamayón**: Master of the Deer.

> **Tiger** (Puma): Majordomo of the same.

16. **Tsëncley Jamayón**: Master of the White-Collared Peccary, the Coati, Monkey, the *Gato Mora* (a small black feline), such birds as the Pheasant, Guinea Hen, perhaps the Wild Turkey, the "Mountain Dove" and the *Palomita* (a species of small doves).

> **Ocelot** (also called Tigrillo): Majordomo of the White-Collared Peccary.

> **Harpy Eagle** (*tsitsih pine*): Majordomo of the Coati and Monkeys

> **Eagle** *bikuk* (not identified): Majordomo of the Pheasant, Guinea Hen and perhaps the Wild Turkey.

17. **Tsets'em Jamayón**: Master of the Tapir, Bees and the "Red-Collared Dove."

> **Black Tiger** (Tigre Prieto): Majordomo of the Tapir.

18. **Lo Chim Jamayón**: Master of Snakes, the Opossum, Paca and Armadillo.

> **Ocelot**: Majordomo of Opossum.

> *Tigre Mortete*: Majordomo of Paca.

19. **Mapachin Jamayón**: Master of the Raccoon (*mapachin* in Tolupan).

> **Harpy Eagle**: Majordomo of the above.

20. **Giant**: Master of the Agouti.

> *Tigre Mortete*: Majordomo of the above.

21. **Mütsis Jamayón**: Master of Rats and Mice (*mütsis* in Tolupan).

> **Cat** (domestic): Majordomo of the above.

22. **Zozots Jamayón**: Master of the Sails.
23. **Bagre Jamayón**: Master of the Fish (*bagre*, "catfish" in Spanish).

> **River Otter**: Majordomo of the above.

24. **Totarapei**: Master of the Cockroach.
25. **Devils**: Masters of the Owls and Birds of Prey, Fleas, Common Lice, Bird Lice, Ticks, Bedbugs and the like. Also Masters of the Mines because they live in deep caves, though now the gringos are said to be.
26. **Tusmai**: Master of Sickness.
27. **Gringos** (North Americans): now Masters of the Mines and Firearms, as well as Coined Money.[6]

This classification, probably of prehispanic origin, has additions such as the recent last entry and besides those already commented upon of Spanish origin. Qualitative transformations may also have occurred. Some of the ten animals known to belong to the Master Tsëncley may have had other masters in former times. Also, the many small mammals, birds and certain aquatic animals may have had masters when the Jicaques inhabited a much larger region, which probably encompassed an area of the north coast of Honduras. (See chapter I.) Moreover, the above enumeration does not include all the plants cultivated and gathered by the Tolupan or all fauna of the Montaña de la Flor with which the Tolupans are familiar.

THE MASTERS OF THE ANIMALS IN THE WORLD

This concept has been reported from every continent and numerous groups. The terms may be misleading, as that of "master" is known by many different words translated into English: mistress, spiritual owner, lord, guardian, protector, proprietor, boss, spirit of the forest, elder of the species or elder of the kind, chief, king queen, father, mother, elder brother, and so on. Yet the relevant documents coincide, in that certain species of animals, or game in its entirety, and less frequently species of plants, have a "master" who protects them and takes vengeance on the human hunter if he kills in excess of his needs or on the cultivator if he harvests plants before they are mature. Frequently, the myths or beliefs are accompanied by propitiatory rites in honor of the masters, and, as among the Tolupans, by prayers or pleas in which the hunter begs the master to forgive him for the harm he has done, or will do, to the animals. He entreats the master to allow him sufficient game to nourish his family. In many cultures, these supplications are directed to the principal game animal.[7]

Recall that one of the few Tolupan rituals documented here consists of hanging the bones, especially the skulls, of the hunted animals on one or two of the posts inside the hut. (chapter V) This custom has been reported among the Tzotziles of Chiapas, Mexico,[8] in vast areas of North and South America, Europe and Asia.[9]

Often, the beliefs described are only vestiges of myths and rituals which in the past were probably complex systems. The fact that these vestiges are known to be more elaborate and complete among hunters, gatherers and fishing peoples than among agriculturalists indicates that this tradition has a very ancient origin, possibly in the earliest periods of human history.[10] In their mythology, the Tolupans preserved an image of themselves as a hunting people who, when they adapted cultivation, simply supplemented their archaic tradition of the masters with innovations, principally relative to maize and other domesticated plants.

Otto Zerries, in his detailed account of the supernatural protectors of animals among the indigenous peoples of South America, explains:

> We are dealing here with an assemblage of problems concerning the history of religions which is based on the civilization of the hunt (the most ancient in human history) in the broad sense of the term which includes fishing and gathering. In South America we find a striking situation that without doubt could be found in other parts of the world, which is revealed by the fact that even agricultural peoples are still profoundly marked by the concept of the world of hunters.[11]

The concept of masters of animals is found the world over and has been especially well documented among the hunters and fishing people of the immense region which encircles the North Pole — the Greenland Eskimos, the Siberian tribes, those of northern Finland and the Laps.[12] This concept is also known among the fishing/gathering peoples of the northwest coast of Alaska and Canada; among the hunters of the tundra and the forests in Alaska, Canada and the northern United States; and among such agriculturalists as the Algonquins and the Iroquois. On the plains of the United States, masters are documented for the Sioux and other former buffalo hunters, the gathering peoples of California, and such cultivators as the Hopi.[13]

In Mexico and Guatemala, the concept is also very widespread.[14] Haekel proposes that it originated among the Chichimec hunters/gatherers of northern Mexico and spread from there to the south, to the Mayas of Guatemala.[15] It appears in almost all the indigenous groups of Central America,[16] however, not as elaborate as among the Tolupans.

Several authors suggest that analogous concepts have existed in Peru since very ancient times.[17] And the tradition exists throughout South America, from the northern tropical forests and the savannas to Tierra del Fuego.[18] In an attempt to clarify the complex of beliefs and rituals concerned with this concept, I propose a model consisting of the following four traits which appear to be the most significant with respect to the Tolupan material and the sources consulted.

1. The masters of the animals communicate with human beings through the shamans.

2. The mythology functions as a code or norm of reciprocity which engages the hunter to refrain from overkilling and the master to supply him with game.

3. The hunter prays or supplicates, begging or asking for pardon of the masters for having killed their animals, and performs rituals that include offerings dedicated to please or placate the masters as well as the animals.

4. Analyses of the mythology often reveal this complex of themes to be a coherent system of classification.

The concept of the masters of animals is not simply one mythological theme among others but rather it expresses an awareness, a conscious recognition of what might be called our species responsibility with respect to nature. This consciousness is profoundly rooted in the culture and mentality of the hunting/gathering peoples. It also reveals that in this respect the so-called "primitive peoples" were much more advanced than "civilized peoples." Although they exploited Nature, they were aware of the damage they inflicted on "her" and sought to create a harmonious world in which all living beings had a legitimate right to existence.

FINAL COMMENT

One of the most cruel paradoxes of this century is the unrelenting discrimination against the American Indians, destruction of their cultures and even extermination of groups in South America precisely when they are gaining a greater recognition of the value of their heritages and are assuming a more decisive defense of their rights. Humanity could greatly benefit from their consciousness of what it is to be really "human," from their creativity as well as from their vast accumulation of knowledge.

For the Tolupans of the Montaña de la Flor and those of Yoro, it is not too late: a government program of intensive medical aid, and economic orientation and support could generate the necessary conditions which permit this people to forge a new future.

And now, finally, as a last homage to Alfonso Martínez and Todivia Soto, the hope that after the "hundred years of solitude" the Tolupans may be an inspiration, for all peoples, to create or recreate societies founded on the recognition of the need for reciprocity and an equitable hierarchy within our society and with Nature.

NOTES

1. These models are partially based on concepts of Ruth Benedict (1943).
2. Durkheim & Mauss 1903: 63–4.

3. Ibid. 66.
4. See Needham 1978: xxii.
5. The Tolupans may well have adopted the turkey from the *ladinos* and assumed that it originated with them; that is, the Tolupans were unaware that the turkey is a native American.
6. See narration 33. The founders of the Montaña de la Flor encountered some North Americans who came there in search of gold mines. They were armed and asked the caciques to take them to the nearby caves to examine them. Coined money is probably associated with them because they were looking for gold and also because of the reputation of the gringos as being rich.
7. For comparative data relative to the contemporary Mayas, see Thompson 1932: 141–42; 1958: 146–47; 1970: 308–09. For South America: Zerries 1959a; 1962: 384–85; and for North America and Siberia: Hallowell 1926: 55–58; Lot-Falck 1953: 88–89.
8. Guiteras-Holmes 1961: 26.
9. Heizer and Hewes 1940; Paulson 1959: 187; Zerries 1962: 390.
10. The hypothesis that the concept of masters of animals originated in such early times is found in many works: Campbell 1975, chapters 7–8; Hallowell 1926: 161; Haekel 1959: 67–68; Hultkrantz 1953: 508–10 and 1961b: 53, 56–59; Heizer and Hewes 1940; Paulson 1959: 188 and 1961: 261; Patte 1960: 123–33, 171.
11. Zerries 1962: 367.
12. Bogoras 1925: 224; Frazer 1926, chapter 9; Hallowell 1926; Jenness 1930: 59–61 and 1935: 22–23; Jochelson 1924: 144–50, 236; Lot-Falck: 1953; Paulson 1959: 187 and 1961, as well as Paulson, Hultkrantz and Jettmar 1965.
13. Alexander 1916: 30, 91, 292; Flannery 1946: 246; Hallowell 1926; 1934; 1960: 46–47; Heizer and Hewes 1940; Hultkrantz 1953: 509; 1961a; 1961b; Speck 1935: 37–38; Simmons 1942.
14. De la Fuente 1949: 349; Gillen 1951: 107; Girard 1949: 244; Guiteras-Holmes 1961: 26, 287; Hatt 1951; Johnson, L.B. 1939: 144–45; Landa 1941: 156–59; Redfield and Villa Rojas 1934: 116; Thompson 1958: 146–47 and 1970: 165; Villa Rojas 1945: 102–03; Wisdom 1961: 441–42, 452.
15. Haekel 1959.
16. Conzemius 1927; 1932: 79; Gabb 1875: 503–06; Pittier de Fabregas 1903; 1938; Schultz-Jena 1945: 24; Stone 1962: 47, 55–56, 64; Thompson 1932: 141–42; 1970: 165, 308–09; Zerries 1959a; 1959b; 1962: 367.
17. Alexander 1920: 289; Metraux 1961: 124–25.
18. Alexander 1920; Murphy 1958: 13–39; Roth 1915: 292; Steward (ed.) 1946–1950, vol. I: 123, 179, 470; vol. III: 91, 448, 462; vol. V: 566, 568; Wilbert & Simoneau (eds.) 1989, vol. II passim; Zerries 1959b and 1962. For Tierra del Fuego, see Gallardo 1910: 189; Gusinde 1931: 707.
    One of my principal Selk'nam (Ona) informants of Tierra del Fuego, Angela Loij, told me that the hunter spoke to the fox after killing it, asking for good luck in future hunts. The hunter also took special care when he killed a guanaco, cutting the meat with special attention and throwing the bones into the fire as signs of respect.

BIBLIOGRAPHY

Adams, R.N.
1957   *Cultural Survey of Panama-Nicaragua-Guatemala-El Sal-vador-Honduras.* Washington, D.C.

Alexander, H.B.
1916   *The Mythology of All Races*, North America, vol. X. Boston.
1920   *The Mythology of All Races*, Latin America, vol. XI. Boston.

Anguiano de, R.
1946   "Visita hecha a los pueblos de Honduras por el Gobernador Intendente Ramón de Anguiano, Año 1804." *Boletín del Archivo General del Gobierno*, Year XI, nos. 1–2: 113–50. Guatemala.

Annoyava, A.
1813   Manuscript letter. Archivo General de Indias, Sección Quinta, Audiencia de Guatemala, Legajo, no. 963. Sevilla.

Benedict, R.F.
1943   "Two Patterns of Indian Acculturation." *American Anthropologist*, vol. 45: 207–12.

Boas, F.
1888   "The Game of Cat's Cradle." *International Archiv für Ethnographie*, vol. 1.

1901   "The Eskimo of Baffin Land and Hudson Bay." *Bulletin of
          the American Museum of Natural History*, vol. 15.
1912   "Notes on Mexican Folklore." *Journal of American Folklore*,
          vol. 25: 204–60.

Borgoras, W.
1925   "Ideas of Space and Time in the Conception of Primitive
          Religion." *American Anthropologist*, vol. 27: 205–66.

Bright, W.
1956   "Glottochronologic Counts of Hokaltecan Material Lan-
          guages." *Journal of the Linguistic Society of America*, vol. 3,
          no. 1: 42–48.

Campbell, J.
1975   *The Masks of God: Primitive Mythology*. New York (8th ed.)

Campell, L.
1978   "Distant   Genetic   Relationship   and   Diffusion: A
          Mesoamerican Perspective." *Actes du XLII Congrès Interna-
          tional des Américanistes*, vol. 4: 595–605.

Carrasco Pizana, P.
1950   *Los Otomíes. Cultura e historia prehispánicas de los pueblos
          mesoamericanos de habla otomiana*. Mexico.

Chamberlain, R.S.
1959   "The Conquest and Colonization of Honduras." *Publication
          of the Carnegie Institute of Washington*, no. 598. Washington,
          D.C.

Chapman, A.
1957   "Port of Trade Enclaves in Aztec and Maya Civilisations." In
          Trade and Markets in the Early Empires, eds. K. Polanyi,
          C.M. Arensberg and H.W. Pearson, pp. 114–53. Glencoe, Il-
          linois.
1958   *An Historical Analysis of the Tropical Forest Tribes on the
          Southern Border of Mesoamerca*, microfilm. Columbia
          University, New York.
1961   "Mythologie et Ethnique chez les Jicaques." *L'Homme*, vol.
          1, no. 1: 95–202. Published in Spanish in *América Indígena*,
          vol. 31, no. 3. Mexico, 1971.

1962   "Survivances de l'organisation Dualiste chez les Jicaques."
            L'Homme, vol. 2, no. 1: 91–101. Published in Spanish in
            América Indígena, vol. 31, no. 3. Mexico, 1971.
1965–76   Ethnographic Journal: the Selk'nam, Tierra del Fuego,
            typescript.
1975   "Lupite, fille de la Montagne." *Les Lettres Nouvelles*, Sept.–
            Oct.: 170–85.
1978a   "Los Lencas de Honduras en el siglo XVI." *Instituto
            Hondureño de Antropología e História. Estudios
            Antropológicos et Históricos*, vol. 2. Tegucigalpa.
1978b   "Les Enfants de la Mort: Univers Mythiques des Indiens
            Tolupan (Jicaque)." *Etudes Mésoaméricaines*, vol. IV.
            Mexico.
1982   *Los Hijos de la Muerte: el Universo Mítico de los Tolupan-
            Jicaques (Honduras)*. Mexico.
1984   "Los Tolupan de la Montaña de la Flor: ¿Otra Cultura que
            desaparece?" *América Indígena*, vol. 44–3: 467–84.
1985   *Los Hijos del Copal y la Candela: Ritos agrarios y tradición
            oral de los Lencas de Honduras*, vol. I. Mexico.
1986   *Los Hijos del Copal y la Candela: Tradición Católica de los
            Lencas de Honduras*, vol. II. Mexico.

Chapman, A. and A. Jacquard
1971   "Un Isolat d'Amerique Centrale: les Indiens Jicaque du Hon-
            duras." *Génétique et Populations: Travaux et Documents*, no.
            60: 163–85.

Chávez Borjas, M.
1984   "La Cultura Jicaque y el Proyecto de Desarrollo Indígena de
            Yoro." *América Indígena*, vol. 44–3: 589–612.

Cobo, B.
1893   *Historia del Nuevo Mundo*. Sevilla.

Conzemius, E.
1921–23   "The Jicaques of Honduras." *International Journal of
            American Linguistics*, vol. 2, nos. 3–4: 163–70.
1927   "Los Indios Payas de Honduras." *Journal de la Société des
            Américanistes*, vol. 19: 245–302.
1932   "Ethnographic Survey of the Miskito and Sumu Indians of
            Honduras and Nicaragua." *Bulletin of the Bureau of
            American Ethnology*, no. 106. Washington, D.C.

Cruz Sandoval, F.
1984   "Los Indios de Honduras y la Situación de sus Recursos Naturales." *América Indígena*, vol. 44–3: 423–46.

Davidson, W.V.
1984   "El Padre Subirana y las Tierras Concedidas a los Indios Hondureños en el Siglo XIX." *América Indígena*, vol. 44–3: 447–60.

De la Fuente, J.
1949   "Yalalag, una Villa Zapoteca Serrana." *Museo Nacional de Antropología*, Seria Cientifica 1. Mexico.

Dennis, R.K. and M. Royce de Dennis
1980a   *Nin Mu'usus Ca Sin Pacj (aprender a contar)*. Instituto Linguístico de Verano. Guatemala.
1980b   *El Alfabeto Tol*. Ibid.
1983   *Diccionario Tol (Jicaque) -Español y Español-Tol (Jicaque)*. Ibid. In collaboration with the Instituto Hondureño de Antropología e Historia. Tegucigalpa.

Durand-Forest, J. de
1968   "Divination et présages dans le Mexique ancient et modern." *Cahiers des Amériques Latines*, vol. 2: 3–43. Paris.

Durkheim, E. and M. Mauss
1903   "Essai sur Quelques Formes Primitives de Classification." *L'Année Sociologique*, vol. 6: 1–72. Paris.

Flannery, R.
1946   "The Culture of the Northeastern Indian Hunters: A Descriptive Survey." In "Man in Northeastern North America," ed. F. Johnson. *Papers of the Peabody Foundation for Archaeology*, vol. 3.

Foster, G.M.
1941   "String Figure Divination." *American Anthropologist*, vol. 43: 126–27.
1945   "Some Characteristics of Mexican Indian Folklore." *Journal of American Folklore*, vol. 58, no. 229: 225–35.

Frazer, J.G.
1926   *The Worship of Nature*, vol. I. London.

Furness, J.C.
1906   *String Figures: A Study of Cat's Cradle in Many Lands*. New York.

Furst, R.
1976   "Shamanistic Survivals in Mesoamerican Religion." *Acta del XLI Congreso Internacional de Américanistas*, vol. 3: 149–57. Mexico.

Gabb, W.
1875   "On the Indian Tribes and Languages of Costa Rica." *Proceedings of the American Philosophical Society*, vol. 14: 483–602.

Gaceta Oficial de Honduras en Centroamerica
1865   Tome 6, no. 18. Comayagua.
1881   Serie 12, no. 116. Tegucigalpa.

Gallardo, C.
1910   *Los Onas*. Buenos Aires.

Gillen, J.
1951   "The Culture of Security in San Carlos. A Study of a Guatemalan Community of Indians and Ladinos." *Publications of the Middle American Research Institute*, no. 16. Tulane, USA.

Girard, R.
1942   *Los Chortís Ante el Problema Maya*. 5 vols. Mexico.

Greenberg, J.H. and M. Swadish
1953   "Jicaque as a Hokan Language." *International Journal of American Linguistics*, vol. 19, no. 3: 216–22.

Guiteras-Holmes, C.
1961   *Perils of the Soul*. Glencoe, Illinois.

Gusinde, M.
1931   *Die Feuerland-Indianer*, vol. I, *Die Selk'nam*. Mödling bei Wein.

Haekel, J.
1959   "Der 'Herr der Tiere' im Glauben der Indianer
        Mesoamerikas." *Mitteilungen aus dem Museum für
        Völkerkunde in Hamburg*, vol. 25.

Hallowell, A.J.
1926   "Bear Ceremonialism in the Northern Hemisphere."
        American Anthropologist, vol. 28: 1–175.
1960   "Ojibwa Ontology, Behavior and World View." In *Culture in
        History*, ed. S. Diamond, pp. 19–47.

Hatt, G.
1951   "The Corn Mother in America and Indonesia." *Anthropos*,
        vol. 46, nos. 5–6: 853–914.

Heizer, R.F. and G.W. Hewes
1940   "Animal Ceremonialism in Central California in the Light of
        Archaeology." *American Anthropologist*, vol. 42: 587–605.

Hultkrantz, A.
1953   "Conceptions of the Soul Among North American Indians."
        The Ethnographical Museum of Sweden, Monographic
        Series, no. 1. Stockholm.
1961a   "The Masters of the Animals Among the Wind River
        Shoshoni." *Ethnos*, vol. 26, no. 4: 198–218.
1961b   "The Owner of the Animals in the Religion of North
        American Indians. Some General Remarks." In "The Super-
        natural Owners of Nature," ed. A. Hultkrantz, *Stockholm
        Studies in Comparative Religion*, no. 1.
1968   "La Divination en Amerique du Nord." In *La Divination*, eds.
        A. Caquot and M. Leibovici, vol. II: 69–149. Paris.

Jacquard, A.
1971   "Les Isolats, Laboratoires Naturales." *Génétique des Popula-
        tions*, vol. 60: 1159–68. Paris.
1973   "Distances genéalogiques et distances génétiques: Applica-
        tion aux Indiens Jicaques du Honduras et aux Eskimo du
        Scoresbysund." *Cahiers d'Anthropologie et d'Ecologie
        Humaine*, vol. 1. Paris.
1974   Génétiques des Populations Humaines. Paris.

Jenness, D.
1924   "Eskimo Folklore. Part B. Eskimo String Figures." *Report of the Canadian Arctic Expedition 1913–1918*, vol. 13.
1930   "The Indian's Interpretation of Man and Nature." *Transactions of the Royal Society of Canada*, Section 2, Serie 3, vol. 24.
1935   "The Ojibwa Indians of Parry Island, Their Social and Religious Life." *Canada Department of Mines, National Museum of Canada, Bulletin 78, Anthropological Series 17.* Ottawa.

Jímenez Moreno, W.
1959   "Síntesis de la Historia Pretolteca de Mesoamérica." *Esplendor del México Antiguo*, vol. II: 1019–1108. Mexico.
1978   "Prefacio, Anne M. Chapman, los Jicaques y sus mitos," pp. 11–24. In Chapman 1978b.

Jochelson, F.
1924   "The Yukaghir and the Yukaghirized Tungus. The Jesup North Pacific Expedtion." *Memoirs of the American Museum of Natural History*, vol. 9. New York.

Johnson, F.
1948   "The Caribbean Lowland Tribes: The Talamanca Division." In "Handbook of South American Indians," ed. J.H. Steward, vol. IV: 199–204. *Bureau of American Ethnology*, Bulletin 143. Washington, D.C.

Johnson, L.B.
1939   "Some notes on the Mazatec." *Revista Mexicana de Estudios Antropológicos*, vol. 3: 142–56.

Juarros, D.D.
1936   *Compendio de la Historia de la Ciudad de Guatemala.* 2 vols. Guatemala.

Karsten, R.
1926   *The Civilization of the South American Indians.* London.

Kirchhoff, P.
1948   "The Caribbean Lowland Tribes: The Mosquitos, Sumo, Paya and Jicaques." In "Handbook of South American Indians," ed.

J.H. Steward, vol. IV: 219–29. *Bureau of American Ethnology*, Bulletin 143. Washington, D.C.

Kunst, J.
1915   "Some Animal Fables of the Chuh Indians." *Journal of American Folklore*, vol. 28: 353–57.

La Farge, O. and B. Byers
1931   "The Year Bearer's People." *Publications of the Middle American Research Foundation*, vol. 8. Tulane.

Landa, Fray D. de
1941   "Landa's Relación de las Cosas de Yucátan." In *Papers of the Peabody Museum of American Archaeology and Ethnology*, ed. A.M. Tozzer, vol. 18.

Lehmann, W.
1920   *Zentral Amerika*. 2 vols. Berlin.

Levi-Strauss, C.
1962a   *Le Totémisme Aujourd'hui*. Paris.
1962b   *La Pensée Sauvage*. Paris.

Lot-Falck, E.
1953   *Les Rites de Chasse chez les Peuples Sibériens*. Paris.

Madsen, W.
1955   "Shamanism in Mexico." *Southwestern Journal of Anthropology*, vol. 11: 48–57.

Martínez Castillo, M.F.
1987   "Los Ultimos Dias de Lempira y otros Documentos." *Universidad Nacional Autónoma de Honduras. Colección de Documentos*, no. 2.

Martínez Crovetto, R.
1972   "Distribución de algunos juegos de hilo entre los Aborígenes Sudamericanos." *Actas del XXXIX Congreso Internacional de Américanistas*, vol. 6: 268–92. Lima.

Métraux, A.
1949 "Religion and Shamanism." In "Handbook of South American Indians," ed. J.H. Steward, vol. V: 559–99. *Bureau of American Ethnology*, Bulletin 143. Washington, D.C.
1961 *Les Incas.* Paris.

Motolinia, Fray T. de Benavente
1903 *Memoriales.* Mexico.

Murphy, R.F.
1958 "Mundurucu Religion." *University of California Publications in American Archaeology and Ethnology*, vol. 49, no. 1.

Needham, R. (ed.)
1978 *Right and Left: Essays on Dual Symbolic Classifications.* Chicago.

Newson, L.
1986 "The Cost of Conquest: Indian Decline in Honduras Under Spanish Rule." *Dellplain Latin American Studies*, no. 20. Boulder and London.

Oakes, M.
1951 "The Two Crosses of Todos Santos: Survivals of Mayan Religious Ritual." *Bollingen Series*, XXVII. New York.

O'Connell, Father J.
1962 "The Withdrawal of High God in West African Religion: An Essay in Interpretation." *Man*, vol. 62, nos. 108–09. London.

Oltrogge, D.F.
1975 *Proto Jicaque-Subtiaban-Tequistlateca: A Comparative Reconstruction.* Photocopy of manuscript, Ph.D. thesis. University of Texas at Arlington.

Patte, E.
1960 *Les Hommes préhistoriques et la religion.* Paris.

Paulson, I.
1959 "Zur Aufbewahrung der Tierknochen in nördlichen Nordamerika." *Mitteilungen aus dem Museum für Völkerkunde in Hamburg*, vol. 25: 182–88.

1961   "Schutzgeister und Gottheiten des Wildes (des Jagdtiere und
            Fische) in Nordeurasien." *Stockholm Studies in Comparative
            Religion*, no. 2. Uppsala.

Paulson, I., A. Hultrantz and K. Jettmar
1965   *Les Religions Arctiques et Finnoises*. Paris.

Pettazzoni, R.
1954   *Essays on the History of Religions*.

Pittier de Fábregas, H.
1903   "Folklore of the Bribri and Brunka Indians in Costa Rica."
            Journal of American Folklore, vol. 14, no. 60: 1–9.
1938   "Apuntaciones Etnológicas sobre los Indios Bribri." *Museo
            Nacional. Serie Ethnologia*, vol. 1, part 1. San José.
1941   "Materiales para el estudio de la Lengua Brunka hablada en
            Borunca recogidos en los años de 1892 a 1896." Ibid. vol. 1,
            part 2.

Pison, G. and J. Vu Tien
1974   "Les Indiens Jicaques du Honduras, mise à jour des données
            généalogiques." *Cahiers d'Anthropologie et d'Ecologie
            Humaines*, vol. 2, no. 2: 131–41. Paris.

Quilici, J.C.
1975   *Structure Hémotypologique des Populations Indiennes en
            Amérique du Sud*. Toulouse.

Quilici, J.C. and J. Constans
1971   Informe acerca del Estado Sanitario de la Poplacion Jicaque.
            Typescript of the Mission du Centre Hemotipologie, Hopital
            Purpan. Toulouse.

Ray, V.F.
1932   "The San Poil and Nespelem: Salishan Peoples of North-
            eastern Washington." *Publications in Anthropology*, vol. 5.
            University of Washington.

Redfield, R. and A. Villa Rojas
1934   "Cham Kom, a Maya Village." *Publications of the Carnegie
            Institute of Washington*, no. 448. Washington, D.C.

Reichel-Dolmatoff, G.
1951   *Los Kogi: Una Tribu de la Sierra Nevada de Santa Marta,
        Colombia.* 2 vols. Bogotá.

Rivet, P., G. Stresser-Pean and C. Loukotkna
1952   "Langues de l'Amérique du Nord." *Les Langues du Monde,*
        eds. A. Meillet and M. Cohen, pp. 959–1065. Paris.

Roth, W.E.
1915   "An Inquiry into the Animism and Folklore of the Guiana
        Indians." *Annual Report of the Bureau of American Ethnol-
        ogy,* vol. 30. Washington, D.C.

Royce de Dennis, M.
1987   "Un Programa de Alfabetización entre los Jicaques de la
        Montaña de la Flor." *Yaxkin,* vol. 10–1.

Sahagún, Fray B. de
1969   *Historia General de las Cosas de Nueva España.* 4 vols.
        Argentina and Mexico.

Sapir, E.
1914   "Central and North American Indian Languages." *En-
        cyclopaedia Britanica,* 14th ed., vol. 5: 138–41.

Sauvin-Dugerdil, C.
1988   "The Biological Diversity of Human Populations of Central
        America." *Rassengeschiche des Menschheit,* vol. 12: 23–80.
        Munich.

Schultz-Jena, L.
1945   "La Vida y las Creencias de los Indígenas Quichés de
        Guatemala." *Anales de la Sociedad de Geografía e Historia,*
        vol. 20, nos. 1–4. Guatemala.

Seler, E.S.
1900   "Magic in Ancient Mexico." *Globus,* vol. 78, no. 6.
1926   *Fray Bernardino de Sahagún. Einige Kapitel aus seine Ges-
        chichtswerk Wortgetreu aus dem Aztekischen.* Stuttgart.

Shaw, M. (ed.)
1971   "According to our Ancestors." *Summer Institute of Linguistics*, Publications in Lingustics and Related Fields, no. 32. Guatemala.

Simmons, L.W. (ed.)
1942   *Sun Chief. The Autobiography of a Hopi Indian (Don C. Talayesva).* New Haven.

Soustelle, J.
1935   "Les Idées Religieuses des Lacandons." *La Terre et la Vie*, no. 4: 169–79. Paris.

Speck, F.G.
1935   *Naskapi. The Savage Hunters of the Labrador Peninsula.* Norman, Oklahoma.

Squier, E.
1855   *Notes on Central America: Particularly the States of Honduras and San Salvador.* New York and London.
1858   "The Xicaque Indians of Honduras." *The Atheneum*, no. 1,624: 760–61.

Steward, J.H. (ed.)
1946–50 "Handbook of South American Indians." *6 vols. Bureau of American Ethnology*, Bulletin 143. Washington, D.C.

Stone, D.Z.
1957   "The Torrupan or Jicaque Indians of the Montaña de la Flor, Honduras." In R.N. Adams, pp. 661–69.
1962   "The Talamancan Tribes of Costa Rica." *Papers of the Peabody Museum of Archaeology and Ethnology*, vol. 43, no. 2.

Strong, W.D.
1948   "The Archaeology of Honduras." In "Handbook of South American Indians," ed. J.H. Steward, vol. IV: 71–120. *Bureau of American Ethnology*, Bulletin 143. Washington, D.C.

Swanton, J.R.
1908   "Social Condition, Beliefs, and Linguistic Relationships of the Tlingit Indians." *Annual Report of the Bureau of American Ethnology*, vol. 26: 391–486. Washington, D.C.

Thalbitzer, W.
1930   "Les magiciens esquimaux, leur conception du monde, de l'âme et de la vie." *Journal de la Société des Américanistes*, vol. 22: 73–106. Paris.

Thompson, J.E.S.
1932   "Ethnology of the Mayas of Southern and Central British Honduras." *Publications of the Field Museum of Natural History*, Anthropological Series, vol. 17, no. 2. Chicago.
1958   *Grandeur et Décadence de la Civilisation Maya.* Paris.
1970   *Maya History and Religion.* Norman, Oklahoma.

Título del Terreno "Montaña de la Flor," Municipio de Orica
        Departamento de Tegucigalpa, Concedido en calidad de ejido a la tribu de Hicaques que la ocupa (1929). Copy of original document.

Tojeira, J.M.
1982   *Los Hicaques de Yoro.* Tegucigalpa.

Torquemada, Fray J. de
1943   *Monarquía Indiana.* 3 vols. Mexico.

Valladares, L.A.
1957   *El Hombre y el Maíz. Etnografía et etnopsicología de Colotenango.* Guatemala.

Vallejo, A.R.
1893   *República de Honduras, Primer Anuario Estadístico, correspondiente al año de 1889.* Tegucigalpa.

Van Gennep, A.
1906   "L'Idée d'Evolution dans les Mythes des Demi-Civilisés." *La Revue des Idées*, no. 15: 593–97. Paris.

Villa, B.
1954   "Medicina y Magia entre los Paeces." *Revista Colombiana de Antropología*, vol. 2: 211–64. Bogotá.

Villa Rojas, A.
1945   "The Maya of East Central Quintana Roo." *Publications of the Carnegie Institute of Washington*, no. 559. Washington, D.C.

Von Hagen, Victoria
1972   "Distance biologique et Endogamie." *L'Homme*, vol. 12: *Cahier*, 4: 85–96. Paris.

Von Hagen, Wolfgang
1943   "The Jicaque (Torrupan) Indians of Honduras." *Museum of the American Indian*, Notes and Monographs, no. 53. New York.

Wagley, C.
1949   "The Social and Religious Life of a Guatemalan Village." *American Anthropological Association, Memoires*, vol. 71.

Wallis, W.D. and R.S. Wallis
1955   *The Micmac Indians of Eastern Canada*. Minneapolis.

Wilbert, J. and K. Simoneau (eds.)
1989   Folk Literature of the Toba Indians. 2 vols. University of California at Los Angeles.

Wisdom, C.
1961   "Los Chortis de Guatemala." *Seminario de Integración Social Guatemalteca*, Publicación no. 10. Guatemala.

Zerries, O.
1959a   "Representaciones de Animales en Sudamérica." *Estudios Américanos*, vol. 18, nos. 96–97. Sevilla.
1959b   "Wildgeister und Jagdritual in Zentralamerika." *Mitteilungen aus dem Museum für Völkerkunde in Hamburg*, vol. 30: 144–50.
1962   "Les Religions des Peuples Archíques de l'Amérique du Sud et des Antilles." In *Les Religions Amériendiennes*, eds. W. Krickeberg et al., pp. 327–456. Paris.

INDEX

A

Afterlife, chap. VI. (221–248)

Agouti (cf. Hunting, Masters of Animals)

Agriculture (cf. Masters of Plants, Mother Earth), see also 13, 16–17, 28–29, 38–41, 48–54; Myths 9, 10, 11, 12

Alcoholic beverages (not consumed among Tolupan/Jicaques, although they are among *ladinos*), 12, 16, 22, 51–52, 56, 84–86, 91; Myth 7; Narration 11

Ancestors (cf. History and Prehistory), also Narration 6

Anteater, Myth 22, Narration 5

Ants (cf. Majordomo of Wasps), also 28

Armadillos (cf. Hunting; Masters of Animals), also Myths 16, 45; Narrations 27, 38

Ashes (as a symbol), 151; Myth 25

Aztecs, 14, 264–265

B

Babies and childbirth, 66–67; Narration 2; Q&A 13

Balandrán (tunic or poncho worn by the men), 16, 33, 35, 51, 56–57, 59–60, 74, 84; Myth 11

Bark cloth (formerly used to make the *balandranes*, still used to tie the poles together in construction of huts and sometimes as a belt), 16, 33

Barter, 17, 30–32, 36–37; Myth 43

Beans (cf. Masters of Plants, Meals), also 40–41; Myth 16

Bees (cf. Masters of Animals), also 17, 28

Beetles (cf. Masters of Animals)

Birds (cf. Masters of Animals), also 17, 21

Blowgun, 28, 33; Myth 43

Bones of the game, 169–170

Brazilian Indians as model of historical process, 273–274

Burial practices, 37–39; Myth 3, Narrations 40, 42; Q&As 4, 5, 6

Buzzards (cf. Masters of Animals), also Myth 59

C

Cats (cf. Majordomos of Animals), also 29, 34

"Cat's Cradle," 262–264

Cattle (cf. Domestic animals; Masters of Animals), also Narration 11

Cayungas, Narration 47

Cedar tree, 44; Myth 5

Ceremonies (cf. Burial practices), 12

Chichinite, 214; Myths 56, 57

Chickens (cf. Domestic animals, Masters of Animals), also 29–30

Chiefs (cf. Moieties), 5–6, 7, 17, 29, 36–37, 38, 42, 50–51, 76

Childbirth (cf. Babies)

Children, 37, 59–65, 74, 79–80; Myths 10, 11, 59; Narration 42; Q&As 1, 11, 12, 14
family without children, Narration 2

Christianity (cf. Missionaries, Myths (resumés), Our Lord, Tata Dios, Subirana), especially 273–275

Clothing (cf. *Balandrán*), 16, 33, 35, 51, 59–60; Myth 11

Clouds (cf. Tungsus)

Clusters (cf. Montaña de la Flor), 41–43, 45, 53

Coati (cf. Masters of Animals), also Narration 22

Cocinera (cook, euphemism for wife), Myths 4, 29

Cockroaches (cf. Masters of Animals)

Coffee 6, 11, 12, 25, 38, 41–42, 44–50, 53; Myth 3

Compadres (godfathers), 83–84

Communal work (cf. Labor)

Cooking, 33–34; Narration 40

Corn (cf. Maize)

Courting (cf. Dreams, "Proof" of the knee, "Proof" of the cords), also 66–78; Narration 40

Coyotes, 28; Myth 54

Crabs (cf. Masters of Animals), also Myth 59; Narration 44; Q&A 7

Crops (cf. Agriculture)

Cultural conservatism, 51–52

D

Deaf mutes, 8–9, 53, 66–67; Narrations 26, 36

Death (cf. Burial practices, Fetid vapor, Population, Sickness), also Myths 3, 7; chap. VI (221–248); 275–277

Deer (cf. Dreams, Hunting, Masters of Animals), also Myths 15, 39; Narrations 7, 9, 20

Deer's magic stones, 173–174

Devils (cf. Mines, Myths (resumés), Temptations), also Myths 2, 5, 7, 8, 14, 46, 49, 58; Narration 19, 33, 34; chap VI (221–248), 250

Digging stick, 30, 39–40

Divination (cf. "Proof" of the cords, "Proof" of the knee), 17; chap. VII (249–272)

Division of labor (cf. Labor and Women's work)

Dogs (cf. Majordomos of Animals, Masters of Animals), also 29, 34; Narrations 20, 36; Q&A 8

Domestic animals (cf. Bees, Cattle, Cats, Chickens, Dogs. Horses, Pigs), also 29–30

Dreams, 77–79, 176, 250

Drinking (cf. Alcoholic beverages, Meals)

Duality (cf. Moieties), also 276–279

E

Eagles (cf. Majordomos of Animals)

Earth (cf. Mother Earth)

Earthquakes (cf. Mourning), 149–50; Myth 21; Q&As 11, 12

Eating utensils, 34

Eclipses
of the sun, 12; Narration 10
of the moon, 12; Myth 28

Endogamy (cf. Moieties), also 8–9, 42, 66

Environmental problems, 25–26, 38–39, 49, 52–53

Ethnic identity (cf. Jicaques of Yoro), also 51

Ethnographic diary, 8

Evangelization (cf. Missionaries)

F

Families (cf. Courting, Marriage), 8, 12, 29, 32, 42–43, 45, 46, 54, 68

Farming (cf. Agriculture)

Fetid vapor (*vaho*), 53, 55–56; Myths 2, 3, 7, 59; Narration 1

Fire (cf. Grandfather Thunder, Matches), especially Myths 15, 16

Firearms (cf. Hunting, Gringos), 82–86

First monkeys, Myth 4

First Nation (cf. Human beings), Myths 1, 2, 9, 13, 45, 46; Narration 35

Fish and fishing (cf. Masters of Animals), also 17, 30

Flood, Myth 21

Franciscan missionaries, 15–16

Frost (cf. Jívaros), especially Myths 12, 25; Narration 8

Furniture, 44–45

G

Game (cf. Hunting)

Games, 74–75

Genealogies, especially 7–9, 53

Giant (Master of the Agouti), 200, 281; Myths 19, 57; Narration 29

Grandfather Thunder (owner or master of the fire of the First Nation; cf. Masters of Animals, etc.), also 146–148, 279–280; Myths 2, 13, 15, 16, 22, 28; Narrations 5, 6, 7

Grandfather Tomam (cf. Tomams)

Gringos (North Americans) (cf. Mines, Firearms, Money), 79, 92–94, 96, 280; Narration 33

Gruperas, 256–257; Narration 49

Guamo (tree and fruit) (cf. Masters of Plants)

Guatecasts
Tsi'kin Guatecast (of East Heaven) (cf. Myths (resumés)), 233–234, 278–279; Myth 1
Tyaj Guatecast [of West Heaven] (cf. Myths (resumés)), 233–234, 278–279; Myths 1, 58, 59; Narrations 42, 44; Q&As 1, 6,7, 10, 11, 12, 17

Guatemalan Indian communities (as a model of the historical process), 274

H

Hair (as a symbol), Q&As 9, 10

Hens (cf. Chickens)

Hierarchy (cf. Tomams, Chiefs), 54, 277

Historical processes (History and Prehistory), chap. I (11–58), 273–275

Honey (cf. Bees)

Horses and mules (cf. Masters of Animals), also Myth 17

Human beings (creation of), Myth 1

Hunting (cf. Dreams, Masters of Animals, "Proof" of the cords, "Proof" of the knee), also 17, 28, 29, 55, 64–65; Narrations 35, 38, 39

Huts, 17, 28, 32–33, 43–44

I

Illness (cf. Sickness)

Inbreeding (cf. Endogamy), especially 53

Incest (and prohibition of), 12, 36, 42

Involuntary corporal movements (as omens) (cf. "Proof" of the knee), 260–261

J

Jaguar (Tigre, Japay) (cf. Majordomos of Animals), also Myth 42 (Female Jaguar, wife of Tsets'em Jamayón), also Myth 43

Jamayón (defined), 168

Jars (cf. Pottery)

Jesuits (cf. Missionaries), 18–20

Jicaques (cf. Xicaques, Yoro), 13–26, 47, 51
  defined, 1, 13
  former territory, 15
  population, 11, 17

Jívaros (Messengers of the two brother Tomams, Master of the Frost) (cf. Frost, Myths

(resumés)), also 151, 250; Myths 7, 21, 25, 30, 41, 43, 44; Narrations 4, 47; Q&A 1

Jo'popjil Jamayón (Master of the Deer), 172–173, 280; Myths 2, 37, 38, 45; Narration 9

K

Kin terms and relations, 59, 76; Myths 21, 56, 59; Narrations 3, 14, 17, 19, 38, 41, 42

Kinkajous (Monkeys of the Night) (cf. Stars)

Knock-Down-Hills, Myth 57

L

Labor
  communal, 29, 34, 36, 41–42
  reciprocal, 34–35
  individual, 34–35

Ladate Chim Jamayón (cf. Lo Chim Jamayón)

Ladinos (mestizos) (cf. Tata Dios, Trade), 1–4, 9, 12, 34–35, 39, chap. VII (249–272); Myths 3, 6, 7, 8, 11, 14, 15, 16, 17, 34, 35, 36, 43, 47, 48, 49, 56, 57; Narrations 1, 9, 11, 14, 16, 34, 35, 40, 47

Lagoons (cf. Nen)

Laguna Seca (cf. Yoro)

Language ("Jicaque"), 14, 50–52

Lempira, 95–96

Lencas (cf. Lempira), 15, 51

Lice (cf. Fleas)

Lightning, Narration 7

Little Old Man (cf. Myths (resumés)), Myths 2, 9, 13, 14, 16, 20, 30, 39, 44

Lo Chim Jamayón (Masters of Snakes, Armadillos, Opossums and Pacas), 63, 189, 243, 280; Myths 3, 32, 44, 60; Narrations 27, 30, 44

López, Don Jésus, 2, 20, 39, 172–173, 266, 270–271

López family, 2–6, 8, 46, 53, 266

Losakwai (cf. Sun), Narration 9

Lupita, 7–8

Luquigue (cf. Yoro)

M

Magical practices (cf. Bones of the game, Divination, Frost, Eclipses (moon), Mourning)

Maize (cf. Agriculture, Masters of Plants), 33, 40–41, 47–50, 89–91; Myths 9, 19

Majordomos (cf. Masters of Animals)

Mapachin Jamayón (Master of Raccoons), 182–183, 200, 281; Narration 28

Marriage (cf. Courting, Endogamy, Moieties), 8, 12, 42–43, 66–67 marriage celebration, 73–75 polygamy, 12, 75

Martínez, Alfonso (principal informant for all texts), Preface, 6, 8–9, 12, 54, 56, chap. II (59–98), then *passim*

Martínez, Cipriano (present chief of the East Moiety), 4, 31, 43, 50–54, 67

Martínez, Domingo (second chief of the East Moiety), 38, 50, 65; Narration 43

Martínez, Fidelio (third chief of the East Moiety), 38, 50, 53, 74–75, 80–81, 83, 91–92; Narrations 10, 43

Martínez, Juan (first chief of the East Moiety 1866 to ca. 1910), Diagrams 1, 2; 26–27, 30, 38; Narrations 26, 43

Martínez, Leopoldo, 41–43, 47, 65–68

Martínez, Matéo (Alfonso's father), 56, 60, 62–65, 73, 77, 250–251; Narrations 24, 25, 38, 42, 43; Q&A 1

Masters of Animals (cf. Myths (resumés)), 55, *passim* in chap. IV (137–162) and chap. V (163–220), 277–284

Agouti, Master the Giant, 200, 281; Myth 19; Narration 29

Armadillo, Master Lo Chim Jamayón, 189, 281; Myth 44; Narration 27

Bees, Master Tsets'em Jamayón, 184, 281; Myth 43; Narrations 23, 24

Beetles, "Master" Mother Earth, 280; Narration 32

Birds (cf. Chickens, Turkeys)
"Birds of Glory," Master Tata Dios, 146; 203–204, 280; Myth 4

Birds of Prey, Master the Devil, 203–204, 281

Buzzards, Master Tata Dios, 280; Myths 8, 32, 35, 55

"Fire Birds," Master Grandfather Thunder, 146, 280; Myths 15, 16

Red Collared Dove, Master Tsets'em Jamayón, 203–204, 281

Other Birds, Master Tsëncley, 179–190, 280–281

Cattle (not branded), Master Tata Dios, 280; Myth 7

Cattle (branded), Master the *ladinos*, 280; Myths 7, 8

Chickens, Master Noventa, 160, 280; Myth 33

Coati, Master Tsëncley, 178–180, 280; Myths 40, 52; Narration 22

Cockroaches, Master Totarapei, 204, 281; Myths 47, 48

Crabs, Master Grandfather Thunder, 146, 280; Myths 15, 16

Deer, Master Jo'popjil Jamayón, 172–173, 280; Myths 2, 37, 38, 45; Narration 19

Dogs, Master Tata Dios, 158–159, 172, 280; Myths 7, 8, 31

Fish, Master Bagre Jamayón, 201, 281; Myth 46; Narrations 30, 31

Fleas, Lice and the Like, Master the Devil, 281; Myth 49

Gato Mora (a black feline), Master Tsëncley, 280

Horses and Mules (branded), Master the *ladinos*, 280; Myths 7, 8

Horses and Mules (not branded), Master Tata Dios 280; Myths 7, 8, 32

Mice and Rats, Master Mütsis Jamayón, 182–183, 281; Myth 42

Monkeys, Master Tsëncley Jamayón, 179–180, 280; Myth 52

Olingos, Master Tsëncley Jamayón, 179–180

Opossums, Master Lo Chim Jamayón, 189, 281

Pacas, Master Lo Chim Jamayón, 189, 281

Peccaries (white-collared), Master Tsëncley Jamayón, 179–180, 280; Myths 2, 9, 19, 21; Narration 21

Peccaries (white-lipped), Master Saino Jamayón, 170, 172, 280; Myths 2, 3, 4, 19, 21, 36; Narrations 1, 17, 21

Pigs, Master Tata Dios, 280; Myths 7, 8, 31

Raccoons, Master Mapachin Jamayón, 182, 200, 281; Narration 28

Rats (cf. Mice)

Snails, Master Zozots Jamayón, 201, 281

Snakes, Master Lo Chim Jamayón, 189, 281; Myths 32, 44, 60; Narrations 25, 44

Tapirs, Master Tsets'em Jamayón, 184, 281; Myth 21

Turkeys, Master Noventa, 160, 280

Wasps, Master Grandfather Thunder, 146, 280; Myth 22; Narration 5

Majordomos of Animals, 168–169

Ants, Warrior, Majordomo of Wasps, 280; Narration 5

Cats, Majordomo of Mice and Rats, 182–183, 281

Dogs, Majordomo of Cattle, 280; Myth 7

Eagle, Harpies, Majordomo of Coatis, Monkeys and Olingos, 179–180, 281; Myth 41

Eagle, Bikuk (not identified), Majordomo of Wild Turkey, Pheasant, Guinea Hen and Various Species of Wild Doves, 179–180, 281

Jaguar (male), Majordomo of the White-Lipped Peccary, 170–172, 280

Ocelot (or Tigrillo), Majordomo of the White-Collared Peccary and Opossum, 179–180, 189, 280, 281

Otter (river otter), Majordomo of Fish, 201, 280

Puma ("Tiger"), Majordomo of Deer, 177, 280; Myths 38, 39; Narration 20

"Tigre" (Black Tiger, not identified), Majordomo of Tapir, 184, 281

Tigre Mortete (not identified), Majordomo of Agoutis and Pacas), 189, 201, 280

Warrior Ants (cf. Ants)

Master of Plants
  Beans (of the First Nation), Master
    Chiri Tsutsus, Myth 10
  Corn (cf. Maize)
  Guamo (tree and its fruit), Master
    Nompwinapu'u, 280; Myth 13
  Maize, Master Nompwinapu'u, 280;
    Myths 9, 19

Matches (cf. Fire), 280; Myth 15

Matrilocality (temporary), 36, 42–43

Mayas, 14

Meals (cf. Cooking), 28, 33–34, 55,
  65, 74; Myths 44, 59; Narrations
  30, 35, 41, 47, 49

Medicines, 52–53, 81; Narration 40

Merchants (cf. Barter, Trade)

Mezclados (defined), 1

Mice (cf. Masters of Animals),
  182–183, 281; Myths 1, 42

Milpas (cf. Agriculture, Maize)

Mines (cf. Devils, Gringos), 281;
  Narration 33

Missionaries (cf. Subirana), 15, 18,
  50–52, 54

Moieties (cf. Chiefs, Duality,
  Marriage), 5, 17, 30, 47–51,
  53–54, 66, 76; Narration 35

Money (cf. Lempira, Trade), 46–47;
  Myths 6, 8, 57

Monkeys (cf. Hunting, Masters of
  Animals, Ts'iu), 179–180, 280;
  Myths 1, 2, 4, 52, 53

"Monkeys of the Night" (kinkajous)
  (cf. Stars)

Montaña de la Flor, 1, 2, 5, 11–12,
  26–28, 53–54
  population, 1, 8, 11–12, 30, 53
  ejido, 8, 39, 45, 53, 54

Moon, Grandmother (cf. Myths
  (resumés)), Myths 1, 2, 26, 28,
  30; Narrations 9, 47

Mortality rate, 12, 53–54

Mother Earth (cf. Masters of
  Animals, Myths (resumés)), 163,
  280; Myths 3, 5, 14, 34, 35, 45;
  Narrations 13, 14, 15, 16, 32;
  Q&As 3, 8

Mourning, 149–150; Narrations 15,
  40, 41, 42, 43, 44; Q&As 6, 10,
  11, 12, 14

Multifamily hut, 32–33

Music, 12, 37, 90

Mütsis Jamayón (cf. Master of Mice
  and Rats)

Mythology, 8, 12–13, 54–55
  Analyses, chap. VIII (273–285)

Myths
  defined, 56 (cf. Narrations)
  resumés, 54–56, 63–64, 137–140,
    168–169, 249–251, chap. VIII
    (273–285); Myth 2; Narration 1

N

Namahuai ("Mother," cf. Mother
  Earth)

Naming, 59–60

Namütsis, Myths 1, 42
  defined, 183

Narrations
  defined, 56

Necklaces, 33, 34; Myth 45

Nen (Master of Lagoons and Rivers)
  (cf. Myths (resumés)), 280; Myths
  2, 13, 28, 29, 30; Narration 10

Nompwinapu'u (son of Tomam the Elder) (cf. Masters of Plants, Myths (resumés)), Myths 1, 2, 9, 13, 14, 19, 20, 21, 44, 46, 58

Noventa (Master of Chickens and Turkeys), 160, 279, 280; Myths 2, 33; Narration 12

Nuestro Señor (cf. Our Lord)

O

Ocelot (cf. Majordomo of Animals of White-Collared Peccary and Opossum)

Old Father Priest, Myth 54

Opossums (cf. Masters of Animals), also Myths 16, 45

Oral tradition, 6, 12, 13, 56–57, 63–64, 273–275

Orica (municipal seat), 2, 8, 21, 31, 37, 39, 84, 89

Oropang (afterworld for those who commit suicide), Myth 17; Q&A 17

Otter, river (cf. Majordomo of Fish)

Our Lord (cf. Masters of Animals, Myths (resumés)), 274–275, 280; Myths 3, 4, 5, 6, 21, 29; Narration 1

P

Pacas (cf. Masters of Animals), 189, 201, 280, 281; Myth 42

Patrilocality (cf. Moieties), also 36, 42–43

Peccary, White-Collared (cf. Hunting, Masters of Animals), 179–180, 280; Myths 2, 9, 19, 21, also 40, 53; Narrations 21, also 29

Peccary, White-Lipped (cf. Hunting, Masters of Animals), 170, 172, 280; Myths 2, 3, 4, 19, 21, 36, also 40, 53; Narrations 1, 17

Pérez, Felix (cf. *Punakpanes*, *Zahorines*), 79, 249–251, 256; Narration 1

Photography, 9, 79, 80, 93–94

Pigs (cf. Domestic animals, Masters of Animals), 82; Myths 7, 8, 31; Narration 11

Pipiles, 13, 14

Pochteca (Aztec long-distance traders), 14

Political parties, 54, 86–87, 94

Population (cf. Montaña de la Flor), 1, 8, 9, 11–12, 30, 53

Pottery, 33, 34, 47–48, 75; Myth 9; Narration 16

Poverty, 34, 43, 46, 48–50; Narration 35

"Proof" of the cords, (cf. Divination), 12, 17, 74, 259–260, 262–271; Myths 9, 17, 44

"Proof" of the knee, (cf. Divination), 12, 74, 259–260; Narration 50

Puma (*Tigre*) (cf. Hunting, Majordomos of Animals), 64, 177, 280; Myths 38, 39; Narration 20

Punakpanes (cf. Myths (resumés), Shamanism, *Zahorines*, Velázquez), 17, 189; chap. VIII (249–272); Narration 35

Punishments, 29, 61–62; Myths 7, 17, 56

R

Rabbit (The Trickster), 208; Myths 45, 51, 52, 53, 54, 55

Raccoons (cf. Hunting, Masters of Animals), 182, 200, 281; Narrations 28, 29

Rain (cf. Tungsus)

Rats (cf. Mice)

Reciprocity (cf. Labor, Mother Earth), 47, 54, 95, 168–169, 172, 275–277, 284; Myths 15, 35, 37, 39, 40, 43; Narrations 9, 13, 15, 17, 21, 23, 24, 27, 28

Reincarnation, Q&A 18

Religious faith, 94–95; Myth 2; Narrations 1, 9, 11, 14; Q&A 16

Rituals (cf. Burial practices, Magical practices)

Rivers (origin of), Myth 13

S

Saino Jamayón (Master of the White-Lipped Peccary) (cf. Masters of Animals), 170, 172, 280; Myths 2, 3, 4, 19, 21, 36; Narrations 1, 17, 21

Sarsaparilla, 20–21, 24, 25, 26

Schools, 54

Sexual relations (cf. Courting, Dreams, Snakes), Myths 5, 12

Shamanism (cf. *Punakpanes*), chap. VIII (249–272)

Sickness (cf. Fetid vapor, Tusmai), 51–53, 71–72, 87–89; Myth 34; Narrations 36, 37, 38, 39, 40, 41, 42, 44

Snails (cf. Masters of Animals), 64

Snakes (cf. Lo Chim Jamayón, Masters of Animals, Tobacco), 189 avoid sexual relations when bitten by snake, 72–73; Myth 12

edible parts, 189; Myth 44

plumed serpent, Myth 60

poisonous weed, "remedy" for snakes, 62–63; Myth 42

shamans (*punakpanes*) immune to snakebites, 250; Myth 60

snakebites, 72–73, 76; Myths 12, 44, 60; Narrations 25, 26

Soto, Beltran (second chief of West Moiety), 38, 46, 51, 62, 75–76

Soto, Doroteo (fourth chief of East Moiety), 4, 5, 42, 50, 55–56

Soto, Julia (mother of Alfonso), 59, 60–62, 65; Narrations 24, 25, 42

Soto, Julio (present chief of West Moiety), 42, 51

Soto, Leónor (third chief of West Moiety), 5, 12, 32, 39–40, 42, 51, 75–76, 94; Narration 29

Soto, Pedro (first chief of West Moiety), 20, 26, 28, 29, 30, 32, 38; Diagrams 1, 2

Soto, Todivia (Alfonso's wife), XIII, 62, 70–75, 80, 89–90

Squirrels, Myth 42; Narration 42

Stars ("Monkeys of the Night," kinkajous) (cf. Myths (resumés)), Myths 26, 59

Starvation(or scarcity) (cf. Tubers), 48, 89; Myth 12

Stones (deer's magic) (cf. Hunting), 173–174

Storage, 44

String magic (cf. "Cat's Cradle," "Proof" of the cords)

Subirana, José Manuel (cf. Missionaries), 17–20, 21, 22, 23, 257; Narration 47

Suicide (cf. Oropang), also Myth 59

Sun (sometimes called *Dios*, God)
(cf. Myths (resumés)), 94; Myths
26, 27, 34, 59; Narrations 9, 10,
47; Q&A 17

Sumus (neighbors of Jicaques),
13–14, 262

T

Tapirs (cf. Hunting, Masters of
Animals, Tsets'em Jamayón), 184,
281; Myths 21, also 42

Tata Dios (cf. Masters of Animals,
Myths (resumés)), 94, 158, 280;
Myths 2, 3, 7, 8, 31, 32, 35, 36,
55; Narrations 1, 11, 47

Tegucigalpa, 1, 4, 28, 31, 37, 50, 52,
54, 81, 83, 87, 90, 91–94;
Narrations 5, 33

Temptations (cf. Devils), 221–222;
Myths 5, 17; Narrations 5, 33,
35, 36, 38, 39, 42

"Tigers" (cf. Majordomos of Animals
(Jaguar, Puma, "Tigre," Tigre
Mortete), also Myths 45, 50,
52, 53

Tobacco (cf. Snakes (snakebites)),
29, 189; Myths 11, 44; Narrations
37, 38

Tolupans (cf. Montaña de la Flor),
passim, defined 13

Tomam, Grandfather, 137–138;
Myth 1

Tomam, the Elder, 94–95, 137–139,
250, 278, 279; Myths 1, 2, 3, 7,
11, 12, 13, 18, 20, 21, 23, 24, 25,
27, 28, 29, 31, 34, 35, 37, 39, 40,
41, 43, 60; Narrations 3, 4, 9, 35,
42, 47, 49; Q&A 1

Tomam, the Younger, 68, 138–139,
250, 278, 279–280; Myths 3, 5,
12, 13, 18, 21, 27, 43, 44, 58;
Narrations 44, 47, 49; Q&As 1, 2,
7, 9, 10, 11, 12, 18

Tortillas (cf. Meals, Women's work),
48–48, Myth 9

Totarapei (cf. Cockroaches, Masters
of Animals), 204, 281; Myths 47,
48

Trade (cf. Barter), 31–32, 46–49, 65,
75, 81–91, 95; Myths 6, 11

Trees (cf. Cedar tree, Guamo), 27,
29; Myths 23, 26; Narrations 7,
16, 38

Trujillo, 15

Tsëncley Jamayón (cf. Masters of
Animals), 168, 179–180,
280–281; Myths 2, 9, 14, 21, 36,
40, 52; Narrations 14, 21, 22

Tsets'em Jamayón (cf. Masters of
Animals), 184, 281; Myths 21, 43;
Narrations 23, 24

Tsitsih-pine (harpy eagle) (cf. Masters
of Animals)

Ts'ipaytsju (bird from Glory) (cf.
Masters of Animals), Myth 4

Ts'iu (the monkey, mother of the first
humans), 183, Myth 1

Tubers (guarantee against starvation),
33, 41, 48; Myths 9, 11, 19;
Narration 35

Tungsus (Master of Rain and
Clouds), 150, 280; Myths 24, 25

Turkeys (cf. Domestic animals;
Masters of Animals), 160, 280

Tusmai (Master of Sickness), 207;
Narration 34

V

Vaho (cf. Fetid vapor)

Velázquez, Julian (cf. *Punakpanes*),
17, 64, 172, 249–250; Narrations
30, 47, 48, 49

W

Wasps (cf. Masters of Animals), 146, 280; Myth 22; Narration 5

Weasels, Myth 42

Wildcat, Narration 12

Wind, 148, 278, 279; Myths 17, 23

Women, 2–4, 6, 7–8, 33–34, 35, 36, 37–38, 59, 66–70, 70–77, 78–79, 79–80, 89–90
ladino women (cf. López family)
Myths in which women play a role: 1, 4, 5, 7, 8, 10, 11, 12, 13, 15, 18, 20, 28, 34, 35, 43, 44, 45, 47, 48, 49, 56, 57, 59
Narrations: 3, 13, 14, 15, 16, 24, 35, 38, 40, 41, 42, 44, 47, 49
Q&As: 12, 13
references to index specifically concerning women: Burial practices, Children, Clusters, Deaf mutes, Dreams, Endogamy, Inbreeding, Labor, Marriage, Master of Plants (Beans), Mother Earth, Moieties, Moon, Sexual relations, Temptations
Tolupan women: Lupita, Soto (Julia), Soto (Todivia)
women's work: 2–4, 33, 34, 35, 48, 73

World (falling down), Myth 17

X

Xicaques (cf. Jicaques), 13–16
defined, 13

Y

Yoro (department), 1, 5, 8, 11, 16, 21–27, 49, 81, 84–86, 249–250, 256–257, 259–260, 284
Jicaque population of Yoro, 11
towns and hamlets of Yoro:
Laguna Seca, 23–24, 26, 256–257
Las Vegas, 257
Luquigue, 15, 22–23, 28
Santa Marta, 21–22, 26, 256–257
Subirana, 24–25, 26, 257
Yoro (town), 18–20, 84–86

Zahorines, (cf. *Punakpanes*), 78; Myths 46, 55; Narration 17
defined, 249

Zamba nation, Narration 47

Zozots Jamayón (Masters of the Snails), 201, 281